D0809027

American Cool

The History of Emotions Series

EDITED BY
PETER N. STEARNS, CARNEGIE-MELLON UNIVERSITY
JAN LEWIS, RUTGERS UNIVERSITY—NEWARK

American Cool

Constructing a Twentieth-Century Emotional Style

Peter N. Stearns

NEW YORK UNIVERSITY PRESS
New York and London

NEW YORK UNIVERSITY PRESS
New York and London

Library of Congress Cataloging-in-Publication Data
Stearns, Peter N.
American cool : constructing a twentieth-century emotional style /
Peter N. Stearns.
p.   cm. — (History of emotions series)
Includes bibliographical references (p.) and index.
ISBN 0-8147-7979-4 (cloth : alk. paper)—ISBN 0-8147-7996-4 (pbk. : alk. paper)
1. United States—Social life and customs—20th century—
Psychological aspects. 2. Middle class—United States—Psychology.
3. Emotions—Social aspects—United States—History—20th century.
I. Title. II. Series.
E169.S786 1994
305.5'5'0973—dc20   93-42152
CIP

New York University Press books are printed on acid-free paper,
and their binding materials are chosen for strength and durability.

Manufactured in the United States of America

10   9   8   7   6   5   4   3   2   1

For my family, some of whom think they're pretty cool.

Contents

Acknowledgments

A number of people have contributed to this study. Research assistants have been invaluable, not only in ferreting out data but also in collaborating on thinking through the results. Steve Tripp, Timothy Haggerty, Amy deCamp, Mark Knapp, Steve Beaudoin, and Barry O'Rorke have carried out important phases of this inquiry. Charles Hachten and Daniel Fiore also contributed directly by generously sharing undergraduate research projects. Scarlett Townsend, Karen Callas, Clio Stearns, and particularly Gail Dickey and Naomi Wahlberg assisted in various phases of manuscript preparation. Barbara Lassonde provided vital editorial help. Niko Pfund and Despina Papazoglou Gimbel, of New York University Press, offered encouragement and a host of additions and corrections. Many colleagues have contributed not only suggestions but essential research ideas as well: John Modell, Jan Lewis, Stephen Lassonde, Deborah Stearns, Steve Gordon, Wendy Wiener, and Linda Rosenzweig head a long list. Both the sociology department of the University of Amsterdam and the International Society for Research on Emotion gave me opportunities to try out key ideas in the final phases of the synthesis. I am particularly grateful to my ISRE colleagues for the regular interdisciplinary stimulus and support they provide. Last but definitely not least, Carol Z. Stearns has contributed suggestions, criticisms, and fundamental ideas all along the way.

I

Introduction

Cool. The concept is distinctly American, and it permeates almost every aspect of contemporary American culture. From Kool cigarettes and the Snoopy cartoon's Joe Cool to *West Side Story* ("Keep cool, boy.") and urban slang ("Be cool. Chill out."), the idea of cool, in its many manifestations, has seized a central place in the American imagination.

By the 1990s, the word has come to mean many things, but it always suggests approval. A university student writes on an examination that Columbus received a hearty welcome on his return to Spain; when asked why he made such an egregious historical mistake, he points to the textbook, which states quite clearly that the explorer had received "a cool reception." This anecdote encapsulates the recent history of the word "cool." The textbook writer had used the word according to its dictionary definition—"restraint"—but the university student under-stands it to mean "good." Thus the positive connotation of "cool," along with its increasing usage, symbolizes our culture's increased striv-ing for restraint. Being a cool character means conveying an air of disengagement, of nonchalance, and using the word is part of the process of creating the right impression. The popularity of the word is accompa-nied by other revealing usages: one can "lose" or "blow" one's cool. Cool has become an emotional mantle, sheltering the whole personality from embarrassing excess.

Where did this preoccupation with dispassion, with "cool," come from? How did it arise and evolve? How was Victorian emotional culture, seemingly so ensconced, replaced with the current emotional status quo? Whence came American cool?

This book addresses these questions by analyzing a major change in American middle-class emotional culture, a change that took place between approximately the end of World War I and midcentury. In the last half of the nineteenth century, a complex emotional culture flourished among the Victorian middle class, exerting a powerful influence on the entire range of social relationships. This influence extended into the twentieth century, but by the 1920s Victorian standards were being irrevocably transformed, preparing the way for a cooler approach to emotional expression. *American Cool* exposes a major break in what have been called "feeling rules"[1]—the recommended norms by which people are supposed to shape their emotional expressions and react to the expressions of others.

American Cool focuses extensively on the transition decades, from the erosion of Victorianism in the 1920s to the solidification of a cool culture in the 1960s. Beyond describing the characteristics of the new directions and the ways in which they altered or amended earlier standards, the book seeks to explain why the change occurred.[2] It then assesses some of the outcomes and longer-range consequences of this change.

Emotional culture is an important topic in its own right, being a component of those deeply held popular beliefs that are sometimes summed up in the word "mentality."[3] Involving preachments and definitions by a variety of popularizers, emotionology[4] addresses emotional goals in family settings, in childrearing, in work relationships, in codes of politeness. It affects the way people describe their own emotional standards and, often, the way they actually evaluate aspects of their emotional experience. Interesting in its own right as a part of cultural identity, emotionological change also affects social interactions and elements of emotional life itself. Both Victorian and twentieth-century emotional culture helped define family law, for example, including the criteria by which couples could seek divorce.[5] Social protest and popular leisure constitute two other areas in which changes in emotionology may combine with other factors to create new patterns of behavior. Sorting out the impact of emotional standards in these areas is not easy, but some strong correlations can be identified. Analysis in each emotionological period, Victorian and twentieth-century, will thus move from widely disseminated emotional norms to evidence of middle-class reception to consequences in public behaviors.

And the analysis will address actual emotions, despite the difficulty of separating them from the surrounding emotional culture. Most emotionologists argue that cultural standards at least partially shape "real" emotional life itself.[6] Emotional culture forms the basis for constructing reactions to one's own emotions, and in some respects the emotions themselves. Emotions researchers loudly debate the balance between "basic," biological or natural emotions[7] and those that derive from social requirements and cultural norms.[8] No definitive resolution of this debate is in sight. The present study certainly assumes that basic emotions are not the whole story—that emotional experience contains a strong cognitive and self-reflective element that is greatly affected by the cultural standards applied to the experience. However, this study also deals with the probability that cultural change must itself be assessed in terms of its success or failure in dealing with some natural impulses.

Certainly the assumption of considerable social construction is essential to the present study's demonstration of significant change. An assumption of basic emotion, in contrast, is not essential.[9] But the issue of basic impulse will reemerge when we chart some of the complex results of change emerging from Americans' pursuit of new outlets for passions and from specific emotions that had been redefined.

For the shifts themselves were considerable, with far-reaching implications. In the 1890s American men were advised, by leading scientific and educational authorities, to use their anger: "If [a man] reacts positively, out of that very stirring may come achievements and performance of a high level." Merely a half-century later, childrearing authorities warned parents against encouraging temper in boys, for an angry man is "possessed of a devil." Motherhood, a sublime emblem of generous, intense love in the late nineteenth century—"she sends forth from her heart . . . the life-giving current"—became by the 1930s an emotional hazard: "Motherlove is a dangerous instrument." On another love front: Victorian men routinely wrote of their transcendent feeling. Theodore Weld intoned, "I don't love you and marry you to promote my happiness. To love you, to marry you is a mighty END in itself. . . . I marry you because my own inmost being mingles with your being and is already married to it, both joined in one by God's own voice." A scant century later, men's tune had changed, as love became essentially sexual: "I snatched her into my arms and held her as in a vise. . . . I was madly infatuated, tingling in every atom of my being." Popular writers and fraternity men alike contended that men should press themselves on women even when the latter begged to stop; the man who could not do this, as writer Charles Malchow put it, had "not progressed very far in 'the art of love.' "[10] Changes in love and anger, signaling also basic shifts in the emotional rules meant to define men and women, marked the replacement of Victorianism with a new framework, not just in the abstract but in the daily acts of raising children or dealing with the opposite sex. Passion itself was redefined, becoming suspect unless it was sexual. *American Cool* traces the nature and process of cultural change, building the specific ingredients into a larger reevaluation of emotional intensity.

This study focuses primarily on the middle class of business people and professional families. Like many studies of the middle class, it is biased toward evidence from Protestants in the North and West, but regional factors will be considered to some extent, particularly as they involve the South. The class limitations constitute the most important point to emphasize. The Victorian middle class used its emotional culture to help differentiate itself from other groups, particularly working-class immigrants. Changing middle-class standards in the twentieth century were less blatantly class specific, and in discussing impacts we will encounter some evidence of spillover into other groups and their behaviors. Emotional culture forms an aspect of middle-class standards that had some hegemonic power, both in its nineteenth-century version and, more extensively though more subtly, in its twentieth-century formulation. And of course, by 1950, some 85 percent of all Americans were claiming to be middle class, which does not mean that they shared the most widely accepted middle-class emotional norms (the claim was above all an incomes claim) but certainly suggests the growing potential resonance of bourgeois emotionology. The middle class did not entirely triumph, however. Therefore, the distinction between my primary emphasis—the middle class—and American society seen as a complex combination of classes, ethnic groups, and subcultures must be constantly recalled. This book analyzes a class culture that had demonstrable influence on national culture, but it is not a full study of the larger and more diverse national experience.[11]

Even with this important limitation, the present enterprise is undeniably ambitious. It claims that a general middle-class emotional style shifted ground, with measurable manifestation in a host of specific emotional areas, within roughly three decades. The subject of overall emotional style is not unprecedented, but it is hardly commonplace. Despite the relative novelty of historical study of emotion, three approaches to the subject have emerged to date. The first involves examining another topic that includes emotional components; emotions history was partially launched by histories of familial relationships in the seventeenth and eighteenth centuries that inevitably extended to claims about emotional change.[12] The second approach more explicitly focuses on emotional standards and their periodization but limits itself to individual emotions like love or anger. This approach has produced the clearest advances to date in the historical understanding of emotion, defining the causes and effects of change and the relationship between cultural construction and natural and invariant emotional impulses. But the third approach, which this study is intended to further, involves an effort at larger synthesis. Still focused explicitly on emotional standards and their results, this approach seeks to determine larger consistencies in emotional norms that relate specific emotional standards to a broader style. The Victorians had such a style, though it has often been erroneously characterized in terms of blanket repression. The middle class in the twentieth-century United States gradually but definitely revisited that style, producing a new amalgam. This book examines this sweeping, partially unwitting process.

The idea of a major twentieth-century emotionological transition follows from, and relates to, several widely accepted findings about American social and cultural experience. This study builds on these findings, though it modifies them while dramatically extending their scope.

It is generally accepted that a significant difference existed between the social patterns that began to emerge in the United States during the 1920s and those that had predominated through the later nineteenth century. Some have indeed dubbed the 1920s "the end of Victorianism." Change is of course both constant and cumulative, which makes any effort to identify particularly crucial transition decades difficult and contestable. Nevertheless, this study is by no means unique in claiming that the 1920s formed a point at which several varied trends converged.

By the 1920s the United States had become predominantly urban, shifting focus away from the classic small town. Classic individual entrepreneurship was also increasingly replaced with corporate management, and consumer values were increasingly glorified. New approaches to sexuality and a growing emphasis on personality over character constitute two other trends identified with the 1920s that are still more closely related to a redefinition of emotional standards. Recent work explaining the 1920s rise of the Ku Klux Klan according to an inchoate realization of how much was changing, of what desperate efforts might be necessary to recapture older values, identifies this transition decade from yet another, but clearly related, vantage point.[13]

My exploration of change in middle-class emotional style did not begin as an attempt to flesh out yet another aspect of the 1920s turn away from Victorianism. Indeed, whereas existing periodization schemas tend to posit a sudden Victorian collapse in the 1920s, this study treats the decade as the beginning of a more extended transition. The significant break in emotional culture coincided with changes in other areas, for this break reflected these changes, thus illustrating the kind of functional causation that social constructionists have characteristically claimed without always providing historically precise illustration. Emotional change, in other words, resulted from new social needs, and it also helped promote change, turning this transition into a still more extensive reevaluation of nineteenth-century conventions that reverberated into subsequent decades.

The idea of a major change in emotional style stems most directly from findings about shifts in specific emotional standards. My own earlier studies, several of them collaborative, of anger, jealousy, and fear all identified the 1920s as the point when Victorian signals were reconsidered, in a process that extended for several decades.[14] In approaching anger, my first venture into emotions history, my coauthor and I had initially expected to see the more decisive changes later in the twentieth century, associated for example with the heralded rise of permissive childrearing. In fact, however, we found that the central new themes began earlier. A subsequent investigation of jealousy uncovered a very similar chronology though with many different specifics. Other emotion or emotion-related histories that had focused largely on the nineteenth century produced similar (if not always fully explored) claims that something different began to take shape by the early twentieth century.[15] This was particularly true of several studies of love, both those directed to heterosexual romantic love and those focused on the decline of the peculiar nineteenth-century fascination with motherlove as a familial emotional icon.

My exploration of the transition in emotional style thus synthesizes a variety of existing findings about explicit emotional change. Owing a great debt to the many historians, sociologists, and social psychologists who have identified the basic ingredients, this study seeks to retain the advantages of the relative precision of these focused inquiries while also ranging more broadly into general threads of change and tying the origins of specific shifts to the origins of a novel overall emotionological framework.

It is important to note that a small number of specific emotions studies devoted to the United States have shunned an overall twentieth-century periodization in favor of much smaller chunks of time that coincide with specific childrearing fads[16] or other short cycles. My study argues that while shorter-term variations can be usefully identified, they should not obscure the larger style shift. Indeed, by identifying part of the nature and much of the timing of the twentieth-century transition in emotional culture, inquiries into shorter-term variations have made the need for a larger synthesis increasingly obvious. This synthesis identifies the general themes previously identified while also extending into other emotional domains less fully explored, such as grief.[17] The challenge of the specific studies is clear: what are the underlying ingredients that appear, along with other, more limited attributes, in redefinitions as varied as a new concern about anger at work and a growing aversion, in middle-class men's culture, to Victorian standards of romantic love?

A number of imaginative researchers have already ventured into the challenging area of overall emotional styles and their alterations from one period to the next. The best-developed case for a sea change in emotional style focuses not on the twentieth century, however, but on the eighteenth. Its analogy to the present effort will help clarify my intent, and its content relates to the Victorian baseline as well.

There are two principal formulas applied to an eighteenth-century emotional transition, both of which connect to more familiar aspects of cultural change in the period. Norbert Elias's civilization-of-manners schema, recently applied to the nineteenth-century United States as an extension of its West European point of origin, emphasizes an increasing discipline of emotions and bodily functions alike. Starting with the upper classes, people learned new and more rigorous forms of impulse control. Applied to emotions, the schema helps explain not only a general set of goals but also more specific and measurable redefinitions, such as disgust as an emotional reaction to "uncivilized" sanitary habits and personal manners; a growing hostility to emotional spontaneity, manifested in disapproval of excesses in traditional popular festivals and religious behaviors; attacks on crude uses of fear in religion and childrearing; and a growing revulsion against emotionally charged vengeance in punishment and unwonted anger in both public and familial settings.[18] Emotional self-control, in sum, underlay and united a number of changes in particular emotional goals, many of which have been explored in their own right.

A second schema, compatible with the idea of emotional control but supplementing and complicating it in important respects, involves a concomitant reevaluation of the emotional functions of the family, which also took shape in Western Europe and North America in the eighteenth century or a bit earlier. The family began to extend into areas beyond economic production and material welfare, and family relationships gained new priority over community ties and other friendships. This was another reason why anger and fear were reevaluated, with particular emphasis on the need for control in parent-child contacts, as part of an effort to create loving bonds and a lessened sense of hierarchy within the family. Jealousy was also redefined to focus on romantic relations rather than more general disputes over honor. Guilt gained ground on shame as a source of emotional discipline because it is possible to instill guilt initially as part of intense emotional contacts within the family and to maintain it through threatened deprivation of those contacts. The importance of love between parents and children and of love as the basis for marital choice increased. Grief over the deaths of family members became more central.[19] Taken in tandem, family reevaluation and civilization of manners provide a framework for, and a causal link among, most of the vital shifts in emotional standards that occurred in Western society toward the end of the early modern period. This framework also illustrates the analytical potential of seeking a big picture in dealing with emotional change, lest basic ingredients get lost amid attention to detail.

Basic cultural frameworks normally have considerable staying power, and when gradual changes do occur, they remain within the existing framework. As we will see, this was the case with Victorian variants on the trends established before the industrial revolution. A genuine framework change, however, did occur in the twentieth century, and several scholars have already theorized about its nature.

Some have described the change as a transformation in basic American character taking shape around the middle of the twentieth century or a bit later. David Riesman has argued that there was a general shift from inner-directedness, strongly oriented toward achievement and attuned to internal motivations and promptings, toward other-directedness, emphasizing attunement to signals from peers and media as the source of appropriate goals and standards. Christopher Lasch played a variant on this theme in his briefly celebrated lament on the decline of American character.[20] For Lasch, the inroads of meddling experts and other changes in American society—including the weakening of the family resulting from women's new work roles—produced a decline in strong individual motivation and an increase in shallow self-indulgence and concern with peer approval. Neither Riesman nor Lasch heavily emphasized the emotional corollaries of their claims, but clearly such corollaries would exist. While the present study does not propose anything quite so sweeping as a modal personality change, and while it certainly eschews Lasch's empirically dubious claims about a shift in psychoanalytic dynamic, it does acknowledge a definite shift in emotional norms from an implicit emphasis on individual drive toward a greater concern with group conformity and attunement to peer reactions. In fleshing out this argument and explaining the causation and results of change, we tread at the edges of a trail blazed by earlier analysis.

Emotions theorists have recently cleared a trail of their own, venturing several overlapping arguments about a twentieth-century emotional style markedly different from its Victorian predecessor. For a time, American sociologists assumed a high level of repression in American emotional culture prior to the twentieth century, which gave way during this century (there was little concern for precisely when) to a radically different emphasis on self-expression and self-actualization. Modernization, in this sense, meant jettisoning "traditional" limits on venting emotion and delighting in a new individual freedom to let everything hang out. This formulation was not entirely wrong, but it was unquestionably oversimple, beginning with its faulty identification of Victorianism with traditionalism and undiluted repression. Interestingly, more recent sociological work on emotion has tended to eschew broader formulas in favor of attention to specific emotions or to a much more modest set of shifts and cycles within the twentieth century itself.[21]

Several Dutch and German sociologists, however, have picked up the theoretical gauntlet with a vengeance, working on the twentieth century within the broader historical perspective provided by Norbert Elias and his model of an earlier transformation toward impulse control. For example, Jürgen Gerhards argues for a "postmodern" emotional culture that escapes the bounds of Elias's framework, though not simply in a release from repression. Cas Wouters develops the idea of "informalization" as the key description of the new emotional culture, in which strict codes of behavior diminish in favor of a more complex, mutually negotiated series of emotional self-restraints. Wouters even posits a correlation between the shift in emotional standards and the dominant mode of emotional analysis: "Just as Freud's 'discovery' of 'animalic' emotions and motives occurred at the peak of their repression and denial, by analogy, the 'sociology of emotions' began to spread when rejection of repression and denial of emotions seemed to reach their height." Abram de Swaan, even before Wouters, referred to growing informality and ad hoc negotiations about emotional display as part of an increasing democracy in social relationships. He, too, distinguished a decline in rigid rules against spontaneity, and like Wouters he argued that more spontaneity could be tolerated because of lessened insistence on hierarchy and growing confidence that most people knew without prodding how to avoid undesirable excess.[22]

This, then, is the recipe for twentieth-century emotional change that has already been prepared. It is plausible and correct in many respects. Why not simply reheat it; why review the ingredients directly? Why, in sum, a whole new cookbook? For the following reasons, all explored in the subsequent chapters:

1. The idea of a twentieth-century movement away from impulse control incorrectly reads Victorian emotions as repressive and nothing more. This is not the case, at least as applied to the nineteenth-century American middle class. It is essential to correct this baseline in order to arrive at a true verdict on the twentieth century.

2. Many of the generalizations emanating from Dutch researchers, and echoed by Jürgen Gerhards in Germany, rest on fairly slender empirical evidence. Important studies are cited, particularly a Dutch attitudinal survey in the 1960s. But generalizations have outraced data, sometimes producing sweeping claims based on remarks by the American novelist Tom Wolfe.[23] Further, important studies demonstrating new forms of twentieth-century repression have not been incorporated in the dominant model. Finally, the "informalization" model assumes a transatlantic equivalence in emotional trends, with scattered American and European evidence used interchangeably. A fuller examination of specific cultures, like that of the American middle class, is imperative.

3. Evaluations of the timing of change are suspect, at least for the United States. The Dutch work focuses on the 1960s as the transition point. *American Cool* will argue that in the United States the more decisive break began to emerge four decades earlier.[24] Only by properly identifying timing can we address causes and consequences.

4. The informalization model, while more right than wrong, simply does not capture the full substance of the emotional culture that emerged from the decline of Victorianism in the United States. Despite its attractive caution and complexity, it overdoes the liberating elements and, still more important, downplays the vital corollary of growing informality itself: the growing aversion to emotional intensity that such informality requires. It is the very un-Victorian suspicion of intense emotional experience, far more than a simple renunciation of Victorian repression, that forms the essence of the transition in American emotional culture. This is what must be explained. Emotional restraint must be seen as itself a causal force that has reshaped various relationships in contemporary social life. Even more than the informalization proponents have realized, fundamental features of the emotional culture that emerged from the ashes of Victorianism are counterintuitive, involving actual emotional constraints of which many middle-class Americans have remained unaware.

Source materials for this book cluster primarily, though not exclusively, in what is generally known as prescriptive literature. Victorian popularizers, and their readers, felt a need for guidance in various aspects of emotional socialization, and the popularity of the numerous manuals directed at parents and youth has been well documented. Then, in the 1920s, a new set of popularizing authorities entered the marketplace. The audience their work achieved forms one index of middle-class Americans' quest for some real innovation in emotional guidelines.

For the Victorian period the manuals referred to above form a vital starting point. Most of them addressed various kinds of emotional standards.[25] Popular short stories—particularly those with a strong moral purpose as featured in *Godey's Ladies Book, Peterson's,* and the *Ladies Home Journal*—etiquette books, and hortative stories for older children and youth add to the prescriptive mix.[26] Many of these genres continued in the transition decades of the twentieth century, although the youth-advice literature began to decline rapidly, and stories aimed at children shifted toward escapism (which itself reveals a new emotional tone).[27] Marital advice manuals and popular magazines for men as well as for women increased in volume and utility, while childrearing advice in various forms remained essential. Also vital for twentieth-century emotionology was the burgeoning prescriptive literature focused on emotional standards at work. The cumulation of this various material, combined with many other studies that provide additional evidence on key points—such as recent interview and questionnaire data and private letters from the Victorian period—yields a fairly full picture of emotional culture and the range of its audience. The same material also provides suggestive evidence about causation, when used in combination with information about larger social and cultural trends available from existing historiography for both the nineteenth and the twentieth centuries and from additional research in areas such as popular health attitudes. Supplemented by a more disparate range of materials, including several key interview studies from the 1930s onward,[28] this body of evidence enables us to venture some conclusions about actual internalization of the recommended standards and about the larger impact of these standards in all areas of life, from leisure to law.

One final point, which no introduction should be without: So what? What is the point of attending to emotional culture at all? Emotional culture is hard to study, yet the game is worth the candle, and not only because the quest is intrinsically challenging. In the first place, the study of emotional culture makes an essential contribution to other kinds of emotions research, aiding scholars who seek to understand what emotions are and what roles they play. Emotions study is on the upswing of late. Cognitive psychologists, even researchers on artificial intelligence, probe links between emotional reactions and other forms of thought;

though typically interested in formulas yielding high generalization, and thus often partisans of the idea of inherent, basic emotions, they are not immune to an interest in cultural change as a variable. Social psychologists, dealing with emotions in a collective context, have contributed directly to historical study and have examined various categories of emotional standards and behaviors that may or may not be open to historical change. A growing group of sociologists, and some anthropologists, includes the most articulate advocates of the idea of social or cultural construction, in which emotional standards and even internal behaviors respond at least in part to evolving functional needs. Yet it remains true that reasonably general, reasonably precise, and reasonably analytical tests of the idea of basic emotional change are not numerous. The present study contributes additional substance to the constructionist venture and links with other kinds of inquiries into the relationship between emotion and variations (including changes) in social context.

Emotions research also adds new and important dimensions to historians' examination of several familiar developments, and it helps connect these developments. Here, an example quite relevant to this study will serve better than a general formulation. The concept of consumerism is a staple in American social and cultural history. We all know that new passions for acquisition had flamed by the 1920s; though it can be argued that basic changes occurred somewhat earlier, important discussions of precise timing need not obscure the basic point that growing numbers of Americans, headed by the middle class, developed a new relationship to goods and the process of obtaining them. We know also, if in fairly general terms, that the rise of consumerism, as distinct from earlier, more subsistence-based forms of acquisition, promoted or reflected broader changes in outlook.[29] But we are far from knowing the full effects of growing commitment to consumerist behavior. A study that explores the emotional corollaries of this trend, which is what this book is in part, thus adds considerably to our grasp of the human meaning of a familiar new social pattern. It is hardly surprising that increased interest in acquiring nonessential goods had emotional consequences, so that other kinds of emotional contacts changed as people put more emotional energy into consumption. But these ramifications have rarely been examined. Catching the connection as it took shape — that is, treating the connection historically — is an essential step in improving understanding. Further, growing consumerism was connected to other developments, familiar in themselves and coincident in time, such as changing religious values. By looking at the larger framework for measurable shifts in emotions culture—by looking beyond a single major factor such as consumerism—emotions history can reveal how concomitant changes were brought home to real people in that substantial segment of their lives pervaded by emotional reactions and evaluations.

Emotions history does not, however, simply measure the results of other changes in human terms. It also adds to the explanation of change. Emotions research, particularly in the constructionist school, tends to downplay this vital facet of emotion, looking mainly at the context for emotional standards and at the ways standards shape individual lives. Emotions are treated either as isolated phenomena or as dependent variables; their own impacts are not assessed. From the historical side, much social history has focused on emphasizing the rationality of various groupings. One of the first claims in social history, for example, was that lower-class rioters were not impelled by blind passion, that they chose targets carefully according to well-defined goals. These goals certainly differed from modern, middle-class goals; there was no disputing the importance of cultural context. But within this context cool rationality prevailed. Only recently have social historians developed any real interest in going beyond rationalism to look at other kinds of reactions and relationships. But their probes remain tentative and characteristically confined to family patterns and other private behaviors. The potential for examining the wider consequences of emotional change—for taking emotions seriously as a source of social behaviors, within families to be sure but also in a variety of other, more public settings—has not been tapped. This kind of emotions history is not, it must quickly be noted, in conflict with rationalist social history. Emotions are not irrational; they relate to the cognitive process in that they involve thinking about one's own impulses and evaluating them as an intrinsic part of the emotional experience itself.[30] When changing emotional standards thus affect social protest, as I will argue occurs in the twentieth century as a consequence of the emotional transition this book explores, the result is not that protest becomes more or less rational. Emotions form part of the motivational package that includes culturally logical goals and careful choice of targets. They do, however, have a causal force of their own, and in this respect, as in numerous other areas, we short-change our power to explain if we leave out the impact of emotional culture. When this culture changes, as it did in the second quarter of this century, other results follow. We will see elaborate results in law, protest, leisure, and other areas—some of which add fundamentally to general understanding of the behaviors involved and the needs that underlay them.

Finally, because emotional standards play a significant role in translating other changes into human routine and in contributing to change, a study that seizes on a recent basic transition inevitably contributes to an understanding of emotional patterns, and some wider behaviors, in the United States today. The transition that began to take definite shape in the 1920s still reverberates in ways that have been partially delineated elsewhere.[31] Without claiming to explore the connection fully where emotions are concerned—this is a study of the transition and not of contemporary emotional patterns—I intend to suggest some probable implications. In the transition that formed a new emotional culture, we find a mirror in which we can see and understand some of our own features and compare them with the emotional faces of our Victorian forebears.

2

The Victorian Style

The image of repression has long haunted Victorian culture. Most reconstructions of twentieth-century Victorianism assume a blanket repressiveness. Partisans of the civilization-of-manners schema developed by Norbert Elias assume that Victorianism simply extended and stiffened already-brewing efforts to constrain impulse and rigidify emotional and physical habits. John Kasson illustrates this connection for the American middle class in the nineteenth century by exploring etiquette standards, recommended audience behavior, and emotional control. Twentieth-century popularizers began a process of labeling Victorian repressiveness early on, attacking, for instance, old-fashioned notions of childrearing. Even before Dr. Spock in the 1940s, traditional insistence on children's docility was criticized, and greater openness to expression and attention to childish needs were urged. Victorian school discipline came under attack in the 1920s, with recommendations for greater flexibility and responsiveness to individual traits. By the 1960s, contrasts between contemporary freedom for self-expression and repressive Victorian gloom became a staple, particularly, of course, in discussions related to sexuality.[1] In scholarship and popular opinion alike, Victorianism and constraint often go hand in hand.

Defining Victorianism as repression is a considerable oversimplification. In some respects, the twentieth-century fascination with labeling and condemning Victorianism owes more to the needs of this century than to the characteristics of the previous one. Blasting Victorian shibboleths is a convenient means of trying to persuade contemporary Americans that they are truly free—and in the process concealing the many constraints that in fact have been introduced in our own time. Victorianism was to some extent invented after the fact, to simplify the twentieth century's own self-satisfaction; with such a repressive past, progress became easy to claim.

The imagery is not all wrong. The Victorian emotional style contained strong repressive elements. So do all emotional styles, but even so, Victorian repressiveness in some respects went unusually far. Children were routinely enjoined to obedience, a recommendation that could cover a host of parental efforts to keep their offspring in line. Many Victorian childrearing manuals seem amazingly undetailed by current standards, largely because the injunction to obedience could cover such a multitude of sins. Sibling spats, for example, were almost never mentioned, and a leading reason for this was that the larger dictate, to obey parents' commands, reduced the need for attention to such petty emotional or behavioral details.[2] Correspondingly, when attention to sibling quarrels began to increase, by 1920, one reason was that the blanket insistence on obedience was now dismissed as outdated and repressive, requiring a new, more nuanced attention to specific problem areas.

In addition to the routine insistence on obedience, Victorian popularizers showed their repressive side in many other ways. Women in particular were to be kept in emotional check, and this standard contributed to many of the symptoms of distress disproportionately present in the nineteenth-century middle class, including the kind of hysterical paralysis suffered by repressed figures like Alice James. Victorian men and women alike frowned on spontaneity; uncontrolled impulse was a mark of poor breeding and a real social and personal threat. To this extent the civilization-of-manners schema fits Victorian goals fairly well. Emotions required monitoring, and children were taught this lesson early on. Generalized injunctions to obedience were combined with serious warnings about the dangers of displaying anger within the family, particularly toward parents. The margin of tolerance was narrow. Even as Victorians moved away from physical punishment—which was a constriction of parental spontaneity widely preached from the early nineteenth century onward—other disciplinary systems, including isolation of children, maintained a severe pattern of will breaking.[3] Finally, Victorian popularizers talked a great deal about the importance of rationality and calculation, which fits a century devoted increasingly to business planning, growing organizational sophistication, and heightened faith in formal education. One of the real differences postulated between men and women involved men's natural superiority in matters of the head and women's corresponding inferiority because of weak-minded sentimentality—and the resultant imagery, along with its gender impact, constrained both men and women to distrust emotional tugs.

There is no convenient reversal for the Victorianism/repression oversimplification. Victorians cannot be seen as emotionally tolerant, certainly not as freewheeling. Accurately characterizing their emotional style requires subtlety and must acknowledge a strong repressive element. Aspects of Victorianism have been invented to bolster twentieth-century self-confidence, but the characterizations are by no means entirely off the mark.

Revisionist views of the Victorian style have already been applied to sexuality, and the close relationship between this area and emotion warrants a brief comparison. Traditional scholarship on Victorian sexuality played the repression chords resoundingly; Victorians, or at least Victorian women, were turned into virtual museum pieces of unimagined repression. Victorian popularizers, like Lord Acton in Britain or some of the American faddists like Kellogg, were trotted out to show how Victorian women were told that all sexual impulse was wrong and, in women, unnatural, dangerous to propriety and physical health alike. For a time, the scholarship on Victorian sexuality could be summed up in the image of the respectable woman told to endure the indignity of the sex act by lying back in a darkened room and "thinking of England." This standard was supplemented, for males and females alike, by instructions not to damage health by contemplating sex more than once a week, to shun sex before age twenty-three, and to avoid masturbation like the plague it was—this last injunction being enforced by bizarre physical constraints on male adolescents and even institutionalization for insanity.[4] Surely Victorianism and repression were identical where sex was concerned. Actual Victorians might evade the repressive standards—male users of the double standard and consumers of prostitution and pornography were most commonly cited—but even they were indirectly constrained, condemned to furtiveness and to the separation of "respectable" male-female contacts from healthy sexuality.

Yet it turns out that this image, amusing or appalling as it might be to twentieth-century eyes, was simply not accurate. Victorian prescriptions did include some extremists, but they were atypical. Popular advice varied, and it generally recognized that a moderate sexual appetite was legitimate. Women were considered less sexual than men, to be sure, but even for women, physical and mental health required some regular sexual expression; occasional procreation was not the only goal. Writers on marriage, though hardly in the Masters and Johnson league, assumed that sexual satisfaction was an important ingredient in marital love. A few revisionist historians have gone so far as to assert a quiet Victorian sexual delight, citing married women who acknowledged not only their reliance on sexuality and their dismay when sex relations had to be curtailed for reasons of birth control but also their frequency of orgasm—a frequency that, if taken literally, actually surpasses contemporary twentieth-century self-reports. Yet extreme revisionism can go too far.[5] Victorian attacks on child and adolescent sexuality were quite real, and they had some impact even in married adulthood, when a less repressive regime was widely advocated. Victorians did respect the validity and importance of sex, but they distrusted overemphasis on it and sought other primary bases for heterosexual relationships. A fully accurate formula for the subtleties of Victorian sexuality has yet to be worked out, but while it would include due notice of some special repressive features (and the needs that underlay them, such as birth control and social and gender hierarchy), it would not simply end with the repressive theme. Just as a twentieth-century flight from sexual repression is a simplistically misleading conception, so the Victorian acknowledgment of sexuality's validity must be included in any characterization.

Students of Victorian emotionality have launched a reevaluation similar to that applied to sexuality. Although some recent work plays up the repressive theme alone, the idea of Victorian emotional repressiveness has been substantially modified. The various modifications need to be drawn together and then integrated into a more accurate vision of the nineteenth-century baseline. Yet the analogy with sexuality must be made with caution. Victorian sexual repressiveness was by no means complete, but it was more pervasive than was repressiveness in the emotional arena. In fact, Victorians hoped to use emotional opportunities to deflect certain kinds of unwanted sexuality, particularly in courtship.[6] Thus the repressive model is farther off the mark where emotions were concerned than where sexuality was involved. This distinction is vital to an understanding not only of Victorianism but also of the changes that followed in the twentieth century.

For Victorian acceptance of emotion was in principle quite whole-hearted. Natural emotions were basically good, though they must be controlled and properly targeted. Even less fortunate emotions, like anger or even fear, whether natural or not, could be put to good use. "No person should be afraid of his finer feelings," wrote one Pittsburgh minister in 1880, capping a long evolution away from early nineteenth-century sermons in which a more traditionally Calvinist gloom about this world and its works had prevailed. Victorianism was born, after all, in an atmosphere shaped by romanticism and its appreciation of emotion, or at least of sentimentality. To be sure, Victorianism was also shaped by the Enlightenment emphasis on the importance of reason. However, the driest kind of rationalism was modified at the level of practicing intellectuals, and it had never caught on widely among the reading public.[7] In contrast to sexuality, then, emotion was not regarded with anxiety and suspicion. Management and appropriate use, not systematic limitation, were the guiding principles.

The Victorian emotional style began to take shape in the 1820s, building on many of the emotionological principles that had developed in the previous century, including a strong emphasis on family emotionality.[8] For about two decades, a new genre of family advice literature, partially secular though heavily informed by Protestantism, suggested a sentimental tone that, beginning in childhood, could maintain family harmony. Prescriptive writers, like Catharine Sedgwick, writing from a Protestant perspective but generally without emphasis on religious goals, emphasized several emotional criteria for an appropriate family life, some of which they explicitly contrasted with more traditional standards.[9] Loving relationships were essential.[10] The 1830s saw the genesis of an unprecedented fascination with motherlove. The Reverend John Todd told the readers of *Mother's Magazine* in 1839 that "God planted this *deep*, this *unquenchable* love for her offspring, in the mother's heart." From this love, in turn, would come the inculcation of appropriate affection in the children themselves, male and female alike. "It is the province of the mother, to cultivate the affections, to form and guard the moral habits of the child, for the first ten years of life, and to all intents and purposes the character of the *man* or *woman* is substantially laid as early as that period of life."[11] The equation of love and morality was virtually a commonplace in prescriptive literature from the 1830s onward, though in fact it was a substantial innovation in a culture that had traditionally doubted that human affection could be compatible with an appropriate focus on things divine.

The emphasis on love spilled over to other family relationships. Portrayals of siblings emphasized their deep affection. A staple of popular middle-class fiction involved sisters so deeply loving that the introduction of an outsider in their midst, in the form of a successful suitor for one of the sisters constituted a great crisis of emotion. Deep affection was also routinely portrayed in discussions of brother and sister, though here qualified by the different strengths each gender could bring to a relationship. The *Rollo* series for boys involves many an episode in which *Rollo* saves his sister from some disaster, demonstrating courage and affection simultaneously.[12]

Love between spouses also received high praise as one of the chief benefits of family life. "Men find so little sincere friendship abroad, so little true sympathy in the selfish world, that they gladly yield themselves to the influence of a gentle spirit at home." Love and serenity were closely linked in this image, providing the essential emotional underpinning for a growing commitment to hearth and family. Emphasis on the special emotional qualities of women was linked to the other durable image being generated at this point—the idea that women had special domestic qualities, including appropriate emotional warmth as wives and mothers.[13]

The focus on loving families prompted other emotional standards as well. Most obviously, emotions that might jeopardize affectionate family life were now discredited, and a good-bad dichotomy based on family impact was developed. Here, too, trends in the prescriptive literature built on the earlier shift in emotional culture toward family centeredness and self-control, but with new fervor deriving from the heightened emphasis on family intensity.

Fear was reassessed. A standard argument from the 1830s onward held that children would have no reason to develop fear "unless it was put into their heads." Fearful adults, or even worse, reprobate adults who used fear as part of discipline, were seen as disrupting children's emotional tranquillity. The obvious solution was to urge adults, particularly mothers, to swallow their own fears lest they induce them in their children, "embittering the whole existence of her offspring." And all adults must be prevented from deliberately scaring their children: "She who can tell a frightful story to her child or allow one to be told, ought to have a guardian appointed over herself." No obedience was worth the poison of fear when affectionate, gentle guidance could win even better results without negative emotional side effects. Even safety was no excuse for inducing fear. A child made afraid of spider bites might get bitten just as easily as a child who had not been terrified, and bites are preferable to a "fear that troubles one all life long." Servants who delighted in scaring children came in for particular criticism, as the middle class and popular culture began to diverge. "It is utterly impossible to calculate the evil" that imposing fears could wreak on sensitive souls. Instances of actual death resulting from children's fears were cited in warnings about a host of traditional disciplinary measures that must be rejected as an "undefined species of horror." Loving motherhood, not corroding terror, provided the emotional lodestar for parents. As the God-fearing qualities of religious virtue began to decline in mainstream American Protestantism, a fearful individual was no longer considered appropriately pious. Rather, he or she was emotionally crippled, incapable of taking the kinds of initiatives or displaying the kinds of confidence desirable in middle-class life. Most obviously, if fear became an emotional link between parent and child, long-term affection would be excluded even if short-term discipline was served. Fear, quite simply, became an emotional abuse of parental authority, a theme that continued through the twentieth century in virtually all the prescriptive literature.[14]

A key facet of the new campaign against fear in childrearing involved the presentation of death. American Calvinists had long emphasized death images as a means of inculcating religious obedience in children. Elements of this theme persisted into the nineteenth century, with authors like James Janeway writing that unrepentant children were "not too little to die," "not too little to go to hell."[15] But middle-class opinion was shifting rapidly, and the idea of sinful children who deserved to be frightened by terrifying images of death became increasingly distasteful. By the 1820s, clergymen who refused to accept the growing, romantic belief in childish innocence were frequently confronted with rebellious congregations, so that many changed their tune or at least sought refuge in silence. Lyman Beecher and others helped steer Protestantism away from emphasis on original sin and its corollaries infant damnation and legitimate fear of death. Avoidance of fear again related to the larger emotional package being developed by the early Victorians. In 1847 Horace Bushnell ventured a synthesis: "A proper nurture could counteract mere 'tendencies' to depravity if nurture began while wickedness was weakest—that is, in infancy. . . . Kindness, love and tender care by a mother who exemplified all the virtues would adequately prepare the child for salvation and a life of moral responsibility." Lydia Child anticipated the sentiment in her *Mother's Book* in 1831: "They [infants] come to us from heaven, with their little souls full of innocence and peace; and, as far as possible, a mother's influence should not interfere with the influence of angels." The lessons obviously applied to the presentation of death. "Great care is required that children do not imbibe terrific and gloomy ideas of death; nor should they *incautiously* be taken to funerals, or allowed to see a corpse. It is desirable to dwell on the joys of the righteous in the presence of their heavenly Father, freed from every pain and sorrow, rather than on the state and burial of the body, a subject, very likely, painful to affect the imagination." Happiness was the key: death was to be presented as a joyous release and an opportunity to achieve the greatest possible serenity. Thus a child might be told, on the death of a playmate: "she would like to live but she was ready to go . . . she had a happy life in this world but felt sure that a still happier one awaited her in the next."[16] Epitaphs, similarly, were altered to displace fear with religious cheer:

> Go peaceful Spirit rest
> Secure from earth's alarms
> Resting on the Saviour's breast
> Encircled by his arms.[17]

The overall message concerning fear was unambiguous: it must not disrupt the positive emotional bonds between parent and child. Fear was an "infirmity" that was "most enslaving to the mind, and destructive of its strength and capability of enjoyment. . . . How cruel, then, *purposely* to excite false terrors in those under our care."[18]

Anger was the second emotion to be excised from family life.[19] At least as much as fear, anger could corrode the affection essential to the family. Fiction in the popular women's magazines around midcentury, and advice literature even earlier, crystallized this belief in an endless series of accounts of the horrors of first quarrels. "Cultivate a spirit of mutual and generous forbearance, carefully abiding anything like angry contention or contradiction. Beware of the first dispute, and deprecate its occurrence." "Quarrels of every sort are exceedingly destructive of human happiness; but no quarrels, save those among brethren in the church, are so bitter as family quarrels; and . . . should be so sedulously avoided." Women particularly received advice about their role in promoting domestic serenity, for it was noted that, unlike their husbands, they were cushioned from the frustrations of business life. Wives' good temper was vital because men needed solace from their harsh workday realities. But men were held to the same domestic standards. William Alcott, in an advice book for husbands, intoned: "The reign of gentleness. . . . is very much needed in this jarring, clashing, warring world." Phrenologist Orson Fowler noted wives' sensitivity, such that a single "tart remark" might make her wretched. Anger, quite simply, was too dangerous to play with, for even a little dispute might so contradict the loving tranquillity of the home, the "soul blending" that a real marriage involved, that irreparable damage might ensue. "Let [the First Quarrel] be avoided, and that hateful demon, discord, will never find a place at the domestic hearth. Let it have its existence, no matter . . . how brief its duration, the demon will feel himself invited and will take his place, an odious, but an abiding guest, at the fireside."[20]

First-quarrel stories drove the point home by describing ensuing disaster. An angry wife makes a husband so ill that he almost dies, though in this case reform saves the marriage. A man's anger leads to his wife's death and also to the ruin of most of his children. A wife, repenting her stubborn anger too late, sees her husband go off to India, where he dies. Another wifely outburst causes a man to seek solace in the woods, where he is almost killed by a falling tree. Another angry wife almost dies herself: her face reddens with rage, every vein swells and stands out, every nerve quivers, foam covers her lips, and finally she falls as blood gushes from her nose and mouth. The theme of possession by rage, and accompanying references to demons, recalls an earlier set of beliefs about the causes and consequences of emotional excess, but the principal focus at this point was family misery. The result was an extremely rigorous standard, in which true love and harmony forbade a single harsh remark between husband and wife, and avoidance, rather than conciliatory strategies, held center stage. Here was Victorian emotional repression at a peak. For not only was anger to be shunned, but the early Victorian formula also held that one party was always to blame in any lapse: anger identified the bad person, which left the good, calm party free from responsibility. Anger showed bad character, pure and simple. And while occasional remarks suggested that men might not be as gentle as women because of men's work responsibilities outside the home, there was no particular emphasis on a wife's obligation to suffer anger in silence. The gender difference with regard to anger lay in the notion that men had to work to live up to standard while truly feminine women had an inherent gentleness that excluded even the need to exercise self-control. Correspondingly, though this was rarely explicitly stated, an angry woman was worse than an angry man.[21]

Anger between parents and children was condemned as thoroughly as that between spouses. Indeed, proper childrearing would so exclude anger as to create the personalities (presumably, particularly in women) that would later allow the marital standards to hold sway. Given growing assumptions about childish innocence, it was thought that if parents controlled their own anger, children would not learn anger themselves. "I say to any father or mother, are you irritable, petulant? If so, begin this moment the work of subjugating your temper." "Fretfulness and Ill temper in the parents are provocations." Fortunately, self-control and, above all, maternal love, calm, and cheer could save the day; few manuals between 1830 and 1860 dwelled on childhood anger as a particular problem. In the event that parental models might fail, prescriptive writers offered uplifting children's stories featuring George Washington's efforts to control his temper and good boys who avoided responding angrily to taunts. But mother was key. "A mother must have great control over her own feelings, a calmness and composure of spirit not easily disturbed." "And can a mother expect to govern her child, when she cannot govern herself?" T. S. Arthur, that ubiquitous advice giver of midcentury, put it more simply still: "As mother is, so will be children." And the goals of avoiding or subjugating anger applied to boys as well as girls. When children were being discussed, emphasis on the bestiality of anger and its inappropriateness in family life took precedence over any effort to delineate gender traits. Anger was bad, and a good family would escape it. Correspondingly, though the connection was not elaborately explored, anger in a husband or wife was frequently blamed on a bad upbringing that left the individual "spoiled" or "capricious."[22]

As with anger and fear, so jealousy came under new scrutiny when early Victorians applied the familial lens to emotional standards. Redefinitions of this emotion had been anticipated in the earlier reevaluation of family emotionality, but because jealousy was not seen as posing the same kind of threat to family harmony as anger or fear, it received less articulate attention. But the implicit shift was considerable even so.[23]

In the first place, when jealousy was mentioned it was now focused primarily on love relationships, particularly among courting couples and married adults. (Children's jealousy came in for little comment at this point.) Earlier ideas about jealousy in defense of honor or jealousy as a spur to righteous action (this last a recollection of the emotion's original etymological link to zeal) simply disappeared amid the new concentration on family emotionality.

In the second place, romantic jealousy, when discussed, was now uniformly condemned. Earlier Western tradition had been ambivalent on this point. Some authorities, like Shakespeare in *Othello,* had attacked jealousy's tendency to possess a person and poison a couple's relationship, while others had praised jealousy's capacity to add spice to love and even to bring about greater commitment in love. Amid early Victorians, ambivalence officially withdrew: when jealousy was formally assessed, it was condemned. For jealousy contradicted the purity of love, adding a selfish and possessive quality that fouled this now-precious emotion. "There is no real love where there is no abandon and complete confidence." Love, whose "truest, purest, highest form is that of strong, unselfish affection blended with desire," "ennobles" the individual; it is "the beautifier, the glorifier, the redeemer." Marriage itself was "complete union of amity and love, of life and fortune, of interests and sympathies, of comfort and support, of desires and inclinations, of usefulness and happiness, of joys and sorrows." Small wonder, then, that popular commentary occasionally reminded middle-class readers of the dangers of jealousy. *Godey's Ladies Book* ran a verse on "The Jealous Lover" in 1841, terming the emotion the "worst inmate of the breast; a fell tormentor thou, a double pest, wounding thy bosom by the self-same blow thy vengeance wreaks on the imputed foe." An occasional story showed how baseless jealousy might ruin a romance while causing great personal agony. Young women's jealousy of sisters or cousins who were being courted occasionally set the theme for a moralizing fictional comment. In one case, a woman is briefly assailed by the "old demon in her breast" but rises above it, rejoicing to God for "awakening her to a nobler life and higher aims than that of mere self-gratification." Because real love so obviously made jealousy unnecessary by the mutual devotion and selflessness it entailed, jealousy was seen as requiring far less attention than anger. But the evils of jealousy, which could spoil love and prevent proper self-control, were quite similar. "We may even blight and blacken our happiness by jealousy, which is really an admission of our own inferiority, of our own cowardice and conceit."[24]

Finally, early Victorian emotionology began a process by which jealousy came to be viewed as a disproportionately female problem. To the extent that romantic jealousy had long been seen as a sign of weakness, this attribution had some precedent. Other traditional uses of jealousy, however, as in the pursuit of honor, had been disproportionately masculine. No more. Women's family focus and their own sentimental, loving nature made them particularly susceptible. "As in matters of the heart in general, females are more susceptible to the passion than men." By the same token, some popularizers argued that women should exercise particularly repressive vigilance: "Jealousy is, on several counts, more inexcusable in a woman than in a man." Because women's principal emotional contribution was selfless love, and because as a practical matter jealousy might drive a suitor or spouse away, women needed to keep their possessiveness under wraps. Other stories, while implicitly confirming jealousy as a female issue, suggested a bit more leniency. A housewife's manual in 1858 described a woman's growing jealousy of her husband's preoccupation with work. She is ashamed of her feelings but grows increasingly distracted by them. Finally the husband becomes aware and includes her in his work (in appropriately simple terms). Jealousy in this case is not good, but it can be handled by a compassionate male response with the result that a marriage is recemented.[25] When jealousy was considered female and therefore somewhat understandable, and when it might quietly enforce a couple's unity, it was open to constructive adjustment. Here was another reason why, though officially reproved and considerably redefined, jealousy drew less concerted fire from Victorians, early and late, than did anger or fear. Again, the litmus was the impact on family ties, which in this case, in practice, proved modest.

Overall, the early Victorian emotional style was disarmingly simple, though potentially demanding. Building on the earlier focus on family ties, it also incorporated an initial reaction to the growing separation of work from home. However, although emotional life outside the family was evoked in references to life's storms and the pressures on men as agents in this murky world, standards for nonfamilial emotions were not set. Real emotion meant family, and family meant solace and calm.[26] Emotions that supported this, various forms of love being atop the list, were good and were praised without reservation. Emotions that threatened it were bad and were condemned. Adults were urged to restrain themselves and spare their children in this ominous second category.

The result could be oppressive. Women especially were urged into a single, exiguous emotional mold: they must love, but they had no other legitimate emotional outlet. Anger, in particular, was denied them, and even fear had to be tightly controlled. At the same time, they encountered some criticism for disproportionate emotionality, a vague claim that nonetheless served as an additional constraint. But men had severe emotional chores as well, even though their emotional nature was not so narrowly defined. For both genders, difficult emotions were degraded as bestial or animal-like, and loss of control harked back to demonic possession.

Whether this culture's prescriptions were thoroughly repressive might be debated, for the early Victorian style certainly did not seek to limit all emotion, nor are we certain about readers' actual acceptance of prescriptive advice. Yet, while the standards added up in principle to a tidy package, from childish innocence to marital and parental harmony, their very idealism invited dismay over sordid realities. These standards led to criticism of emotional reactions by other family members and, even more, to criticism of one's own impulses, with repressive consequences. Quite apart from the obvious attack on "bad" emotions, the sanctity of harmony and the drumbeat emphasis on serenity offered emotional rewards of a sort, but also a deadening uniformity—and they put a serious damper on any emotional flare.

Important elements of the initial Victorian formula persisted into later nineteenth-century emotionology, including some of its gender implications and the real tensions between emotionality and a longed-for calm. But the early Victorian statement was not the final word. From the later 1840s onward, new ingredients were blended in. The mature Victorian emotional style, which would in most respects persist into the early twentieth century, inserted previous emotional standards into a much more complex amalgam. Family no longer ruled so completely, though its special domain was acknowledged, and the primacy of tranquillity yielded to a growing delight in appropriately targeted emotional intensity. The Victorians became increasingly, though selectively, passionate.

Mature Victorianism: The Uses of Dangerous Emotions

One general index of mature Victorianism emerged about midcentury, when standard setters displayed a growing interest in putting dangerous emotions to good use. The bad-good dichotomy remained, still defined mainly by compatibility with family solidarity, but the later Victorians became more interested in emotional challenge and emotional motivation, and this caused them to reevaluate desirable emotional range.

The emergence of a more nuanced approach to anger was a key component in this change. Even in the early period, a few advice writers, while hewing to the party line on anger as a family scourge, suggested that complete absence of anger was undesirable in men. William Alcott wrote, "I should not envy those, who were so indifferent—so wanting in sensibility—as never to have a single feeling of displeasure"; and he criticized those who felt that the best temper was one "incapable" of being moved. A story in *Peterson's* drove home a similar point, as a young wife mused that "Tom was spirited and quick-tempered—great, loving hearted men always are."[27]

From the late 1840s—T. S. Arthur's 1848 manuals for young men and women signaled some of the change—these themes were more explicitly picked up, as Victorian culture developed a new ambiguity where anger was concerned. The basic message was simple, though its ramifications were potentially complex: anger was a bad emotion at home, but it was a vital emotion in the world of work and politics. Women should remain anger free, in keeping with their domestic roles, but men were set the challenging task of curbing their anger within the family while utilizing its potential to spur actions necessary to competition or social justice. At the same time, invocations of childish innocence began to decline as popularizers saw a real and vital natural anger that, at least in men, must be tamed without being excised. Darwinian findings played a role in this redefinition of childhood from the 1860s onward, as popular literature began to acknowledge a "natural" anger that must be confronted, not simply preached away.[28]

Some early Victorian advice persisted, notably in the constant concern that parents curb their anger in dealing with children. Emotional control remained essential, and it was up to parents to initiate this control by regulating their reactions.

Anger could still be excoriated, though the demonic imagery tended to fade. And while family harmony remained a crucial reason for anger control, the justifications now broadened to a wider social realm. Anger was now a public problem as well, a shift that would be extended further after 1920. Thus childish anger necessitates serious "counsel and punishment, an atmosphere of grief and disapproval," for it can lead to "wars, rapine and misery." "Anger is not lovely," and children's rages create such ugly physical symptoms that the person seems "a child no longer, but a creature under demoniacal possession." Children must not be permitted to gain anything by showing anger, for they must learn to solve problems by other means. Motherlove was still invoked, but childrearing manuals began to pay more attention to practical advice on how to avoid irritations and insufficient sleep. Etiquette books, in contrast to family advice manuals, continued to stress the importance of temper control, particularly avoiding arguments and monitoring conversational style.[29]

The crucial revision, however, involved the notion of anger's usefulness. Even the etiquette books distinguished between polite conversation ("general society") and other social settings, such as earnest discussions with friends. Other literature, however, suggested the crucial norms more clearly. Horatio Alger's books on work and mobility urged the importance of aggressive, competitive behavior, in which serenity had little place. Darwinians like G. Stanley Hall simultaneously condemned anger's destructive potential, even its threat to physical health, while also urging that "a certain choleric vein gives zest and force to all acts." In the same vein, early in the twentieth century the American Institute of Child Life warned against anger in a pamphlet directed toward the parental role in temper control, while simultaneously venturing that the emotion should be "a great and diffuse power in life, making it strenuous, giving zest to the struggle for power and rising to righteous indignation." Boys' stories and children's advice literature pushed the same theme: "the strenuous soul must fight or grow stagnant or flabby"; "better even an occasional nose dented by a fist . . . than stagnation, general cynicism and censoriousness, bodily and psychic cowardice." A child-study manual in 1903 took up a similar view toward anger and fighting; a boy with no tendency to fight would be unnatural, a "nonentity": for, in the long run, "competition is a form of fighting that is very permanent all their life." Pushing more toward social justice, the National Congress of Mothers urged girls to maintain good cheer and prepare a tranquil home but wanted mothers to school their sons in "righteous indignation"; for with such training, even a violent temper can be a "splendid force" providing "royal service."[30]

The key was proper control and direction, which gained pride of place over the earlier blanket cautions. Parents were urged to react strictly to defiant childish anger but to avoid breaking their sons' spirits. Stories showed boys angrily attacking bullies and other legitimate targets, while sports such as boxing were specifically recommended as an ideal means of preserving anger while channeling it into healthy activity. The goal was to teach controlled use, so that properly socialized adults would be masters of a fund of anger, with the experience to target it appropriately. In the mid-1890s G. Stanley Hall approvingly cited a teacher who argued for more anger in schools, in precisely this spirit: "There is a point where patience ceases to be a moral or pedagogical virtue but becomes mere flabbiness." Into the 1920s childrearing manuals combined sincere condemnations of anger's role in crime and violence, which should be prevented by proper discipline and large doses of maternal affection, with praise for anger's role in motivating and energizing. Here, the emotion had value for individual and society alike: "If he is stirred, if he reacts powerfully, out of that very stirring may come achievements and performance of a high level."[31]

Along with the reassessment of anger, fear was also reevaluated from the late 1840s onward. The early Victorian admonitions against using fear to discipline persisted, but they were now supplemented by active praise for the fearless child. In 1847 Horace Bushnell urged that children must not be taught to fear parent or God, but he added a new and explicit note on the "natural state of courage" that children could utilize in their familial and religious lives. Not merely absence of terror, but active courage now served as the goal, and while parental caution played a role in developing this more active emotional stance, it must be supplemented by children's own encounter with, and triumph over, the power of fear. Family writers rarely expounded on this theme at great length. T. S. Arthur's uplifting but curt appeal, "Train up your children to be virtuous and fearless. Moral courage is one of the surest safeguards of virtue,"[32] was a characteristic sample. Yet the idea of active engagement with fear as a source and test of emotional bravery became an increasingly common staple.

The same theme resounded in popular boys' fiction through the last two-thirds of the nineteenth century. Oliver Optic, one of the most widely sold writers in the boyhood genre, offered a representative story: a lad stops a plunging horse, shrieking lady atop, without considering his own danger. He has had neither time nor wish for deliberation, but he has emerged with a new kind of emotional confidence. "He was a boy who would not fight even in self-defense, but he had the courage to do a deed which might have made the stoutest heart tremble with terror." Harry Castlemon's boy in the pilot house exhibits similar bravery: "We have seen that he felt fear. Had it been otherwise he must have possessed nerves of steel, or have been utterly destitute of the power of reasoning; but that fear did not so completely overpower him as it had but a short time before. . . . On the contrary, it nerved him to make the greatest exertions." Courage involved control over emotion amid great intensity. Fear became an essential experience in the inculcation and testing of bravery.[33]

In the aftermath of the Civil War, military settings routinely drove the message home in boys' stories. An injured lad was urged to "keep up a good heart. . . . A little pluck does more for a wound than a good many bandages." Invocations of mother and prayer provided the basis for courage in this and other cases. In another instance, a boy faces a mad dog, "cool and courageous in the moment of danger," then in a later trembling reaction realizes that a kindly God had sustained him.[34]

Fear differed from anger, of course, in that its role in character development was more indirect. Whereas anger could be usefully channeled, fear had no direct utility. Its role was more subtle, providing the test that allowed males to learn their own moral and emotional courage. The links between fear and anger were nevertheless real. Both emotions provided moments of great intensity vital to effective living. Both could be used for motivation and moral development, if properly mastered.

The spirited Victorian boy was one who did not avoid fear, but faced it and triumphed over it, while using anger as a spur to action.[35] The connection between fear and anger showed clearly in the evolution of the word "sissy," which by 1900 had clearly come to mean an effeminate boy who was too cowardly or unaggressive or both. The word had been coined in the 1840s as an affectionate term for "sister," but in the 1880s it began to become a derisive term for spineless boys and men, almost exclusively in the United States.[36]

As the role of fear evolved in the Victorian emotional lexicon, it was seen as less problematic. While parents were still reminded not to frighten infants unnecessarily, no elaborate discussions were considered necessary. Most late Victorian prescriptive writers, like Felix Adler (the last popular childrearing manualist who wrote in an almost purely Victorian mold), assumed that older children could learn essential goals through literary example and appropriate parental advice. The goal was moral courage, an emotional resource that could overcome physical cowardice and so conquer the "paralyzing" effect of fear "by a powerful effort of the will." Character training, derived from good reading and good teachers, would do the trick.[37]

The Victorian reversals on fear and anger were not matched by a revised outlook on jealousy. Because this emotion was more feminine and more fully attached to love, earlier warnings largely prevailed, tempered by some practical advice on the need to help a partner overcome jealousy by reassurance. Even with jealousy, however, the later Victorians evinced a strange, almost anachronistic fascination with emotional power that, without establishing a really new emotionology, was linked to the larger preoccupation with intensity.

Typically, the setting was a murder trial in which a man had killed the lover of his wife or fiancée. The period between 1859 (the Daniel Sickles trial) and about 1900 saw a series of such courtroom dramas, widely publicized and greeted by general popular acclaim, in which well and expensively defended men argued that jealousy had overcome them to the extent that they could no longer control their actions. While the specific defense rested on loss of control and technical insanity, the larger argument suggested that here was another emotion whose power could lead to just and vigorous action. "For jealousy is the rage of a man; therefore he will not spare in the day of vengeance. . . . Those who dishonor husbands are here warned of their doom. . . . Jealousy, which defies and bears down all restraint, whether it be what we technically call insanity or not, is akin to it. It enslaves the injured husband, and vents itself in one result, which seems to be inevitable and unavoidable." So argued the successful attorney for Daniel McFarland, whose acquittal in 1870 won warm approval from hundreds of well-wishers. Daniel Sickles's lawyer, while duly noting how jealousy took possession of his client like a "consuming fire," similarly pointed to the justness of jealousy: "He would have been false to the instincts of humanity if that rage of jealousy had not taken possession of him." Here, too, the jury accepted the plea.[38]

The mature Victorian emotional style accepted and admired the power of passion, for this emotional arsenal underlay the strong wills and vigorous actions that identified good and successful male character and that yielded positive economic and political results. Untrammeled passion that mastered a person's reason was not acceptable; in this regard the use of jealousy defenses, rare in any event, was genuinely exceptional—though this exception may be explained by the role of jealousy in protecting home and family. But where emotions brought fire to the person who controlled them, and where they entailed no disruption to a calm and loving family, they were positively courted. Management, not repression, was the key, so that dangerous emotions were kept in their proper place—largely away from the hearth—and used to achieve rationally chosen ends.

Love

Later Victorianism also built growing fervor into the vision of love, particularly romantic love. This was another area in which intensity won active support, here involving women equally with men. The early Victorian definition of romantic passion was not fully revised, as were those of anger and fear. But there was change, as calm sentimentality was supplemented by a transcendent emotional charge.

Continued emphasis on motherlove formed part of the framework for the growing attention to emotional goals between the sexes. Its potent impact on boys as well as girls established a link between motherlove and children's ability to form deep affective ties. In fulfilling her varied special tasks—"it is the province of the mother, to cultivate the affections"—mother set standards for all her offspring. As Catharine

Beecher put it, "the mother holds, as it were, the hearts of her children in her hand." And while mothers offered a host of qualities, including serenity and morality, the central ingredient was "disinterested love, . . . ready to sacrifice everything at the altar of affection." Not only family but also the community and the wider world would be transformed by this deep, redeeming passion. As *Mother's Magazine* gushed, "Love— flowing from the hidden spring in a mother's heart . . . [flows] deeper and wider as it goes, till neighborhood, friends, and country are refreshed by its living waters." Instructing by example, the mother "teaches our hearts the first lesson of love . . . around [her] our affections twine and closely and surely, as the young vine clasps itself about the branch that supports it: our love for [her] becomes so thoroughly a part and portion of ourselves, that it bids defiance to time and decay." Children of a loving mother would come to "revere her as the earthly type of perfect love . . . they cannot but desire to conform themselves to such models."[39]

Motherlove was intense; it knew no bounds. It was "untiring," "imperishable," "unquenchable," and "irrepressible." Its very intensity imprinted the mother indelibly on her offspring: "Yes! You will live in your children." "Working like nature . . . she . . . sends forth from [her] heart, in pure and temperate flow, the life-giving current . . . her warm affections and irrepressible sympathies." The religiouslike qualities of this love were no accident; they were deliberately signaled by many advice writers, evangelical and secular alike.

As with other intense emotions, motherlove required self-control. While expressions of love itself could be fervent, a more generalized emotionality was not recommended; mothers must be calm, avoid anger, shun displays of fear. Here, too, at least in the domestic realm, motherlove showed its relationship to the broader Victorian emotional style: "We must bring our own feelings and our own actions under a rigid system of discipline, or it will be in vain for us to hope to curb the passions and restrain the conduct of those who are looking to us for instruction and example." The resulting tension between praise for women's natural, perfervid emotional endowment and suspicion of women's potentially excessive emotionality was never fully resolved. Maternal self-control was essential in conveying the good qualities of motherlove to the child without the complications of idiosyncratic emotionality or disconcerting emotional expressions. Intensity should underlie, not dominate. Here, too, the relationship with the general Victorian style was apparent in the recommendation that natural impulse combine with focus and control.[40]

Along with the growing emphasis on men's ability to utilize anger and fear, masculine emotion was increasingly connected to motherlove in middle-class popular culture in the later nineteenth century. (Girls required less attention because they presumably shared their mothers' natural emotional endowment and easily followed the maternal model.) A standard popular story, common in boys' fiction and adult fiction alike, involved men who strayed from home in youth or young adulthood, sometimes causing their mothers great pain in the process, but who retained the fervent image of motherlove throughout their wanderings, only to find how it sustained them and ultimately brought them to redemption. Love, here, was salvation. Even at his most reprobate, the young man retained his mother's love as "the only humanized portion of my heart. . . . I shall never be an infidel while I can remember my mother." Many men wrote to women's magazines precisely in this vein, carrying fiction into fact: S., for example, recalled how his mother's love and prayers brought about his religious conversion, bringing salvation quite literally. In a lower key, the same message was transmitted in boys' stories that referred to mother and prayer in the same breath, as sustainers in the face of fear.[41]

The sublimity of mother's love was echoed in the growing literature on love between man and woman. In all the advice literature in the later nineteenth century, motherlove contrasted with, although it did not necessarily preclude, sexual attraction. As Eliza Duffey claimed in *The Relation of the Sexes,* while granting the importance of sexuality, "Is it not possible that there may be a love strong enough and abiding enough, untinged by [sexual] passion, to hold a husband and wife firm and fast in its bonds, and leave them little to desire? I believe it; I know it." "I believe in marriage all through—the soul, the mind, the heart, and the body, and I would make the last the weakest and least indispensable tie." And the popular medical adviser Henry Chavesse added: "But while we thus speak of pure and passionate love, we may refer to the animal passion, which in no way is akin to love." The phrenologist Orson Fowler tried his hand at the same topic, distinguishing love from mere physical attraction. "True love . . . appertains mainly to . . . this cohabitation of soul with a soul. . . . It is this spiritual affinity of the mental masculine and feminine for each other."[42] Religiouslike intensity was love's hallmark, though proper incorporation of physical expression was allowable. Popularizers disagreed about how openly to acknowledge sex in the equation, but they united in distinguishing love from sex and in highlighting the soulful fervor of love.

Writers addressing women sometimes presented the goals of love with a special gender twist. Because of their sacrificing, maternal propensities, women could more readily live up to the love ideals than men, whose greater carnality was a constant distraction. Again, Eliza Duffey: "Women are not like men in sensual matters. They . . . do not love lust for lust's sake. Passion must be accompanied . . . with the tender graces of kindness and . . . self-denial or they are quickly disgusted." "Women . . . have more of the motherly nature than the conjugal about them."[43] But beneath the agreed-upon focus on a transcendent, essentially spiritual, certainly selfless love, there was disagreement over women's sexuality among the Victorian popularizers. Stories in the women's magazines frequently addressed the ennobling power of love, but they did not necessarily distinguish men from women in this emotional area, and they were widely read by both genders. Furthermore, advice literature directed to middle-class men picked up the same focus on fervent, spiritual love. A religious tract noted: "Love is the secret element or power in universal life," with spiritual love serving as "the bond of wedded souls in heaven." A few popularizers commented not only on men's distracting sensuality, which caused men to spoil love by failing to discipline lust, but also on their tendency to lapse from the most fervent devotion after marriage or their failure to show deep feeling in contrast to women's greater frankness. "Men who feel deeply, show little of their deepest feelings." But this motif had been common even in the early Victorian decades, and after about 1850, the male control/female fervor theme became too simple. T. S. Arthur noted that men and women loved different objects because of their different natures but claimed that the love itself was equally deep. Love is "the richest treasure of our nature, the most human, and yet the most divine, of our aspirations." As Frederick Saunders put it, pure and refined love is "unequaled by any other emotion." "When there is great love, and it is shared by two . . . every difficulty is cleared away, and concord ends by hoisting its banner over a man's house"; "love is the strength of strengths." Arthur himself noted how love perfected both genders through the "mystical and holy" union it provided.[44]

Love was, for mature Victorian culture, a universal emotional solvent. Properly spiritual, it knew no bounds. It united the otherwise different emotional natures of men and women in deep communion. It constituted one of life's greatest goals. Here, as Karen Lystra has pointed out, is decisive evidence of the central role of open, intense emotion in Victorian culture. In discussions of love the Victorians built on an eighteenth-century definition as they castigated not only selfishness but also restraint. The pleasure of love lay in openness, revelation, and, ultimately, the emotional transcendence involved in union with the other. More even than motherlove, this definition of romantic love (and some Victorians disputed the term "romantic" as too prosaic) required no limits. Even publications by previously dour religious groups, like the Pittsburgh Presbyterians, carried love's banner with poems about couples in a swirling mountaintop fog, "their pale cheeks joined."[45] Love became a panacea.

Grief

Victorian engagement with emotional intensity showed clearly in the embrace of grief. Grief was, in the first place, a vital component in the cultural arsenal. It was frequently discussed, a staple not only of story but also of song. Grief was heartrending, as Paul Rosenblatt has demonstrated.[46] The depth of grief followed directly, in fact, from the emphasis on great love, for Victorian convention held that even the temporary absence of a loved one was a real sorrow. As Nathaniel Hawthorne put it in a letter to Sarah Peabody in 1840: "Where thou art not, there it is a sort of death." Death itself, correspondingly, would move one to the core. Despite its pain, the essence of grief was a vital part of Victorian emotional life. Children were prepared for it by frequent references, while adults developed various conventions to permit its open expression. In its intensity and its link to love, grief indeed could have a bittersweet quality: immensely sad, but almost a welcome part of a full emotional experience. It could express and enrich the very love Victorian culture sought. As a Protestant minister put it in a family advice manual of 1882: "It may truly be said that no home ever reaches its highest blessedness and sweetness of love and its richest fullness of joy till sorrow enters its life in some way."[47]

Efforts to present grief and death to children in a benign though sorrowful context continued through the later nineteenth century.[48] In McGuffy's *Fourth Eclectic Reader* (1866), sixteen of twenty-nine "poetical lessons" dealt with death, including one entitled "What Is Death?":

> Child. Mother, how still the baby lies.
> I cannot hear his breath;
> I cannot see his laughing eyes;
> They tell me this is death.
> They say that he again will rise,
> More beautiful than now;
> That God will bless him in the skies;
> O mother, tell me how.

In this case, the mother responds with the image of a butterfly emerging from a lifeless chrysalis. In other poems, again in school readers, the dominant theme was the reunion of loved ones after death in heaven.

> Oh. we pray to meet our darling
> For a long, long, sweet embrace.
> Where the little feet are waiting—
> And we meet her face to face.

Tragic death scenes remained commonplace in stories for children, as they were asked to live through the sorrows of illness and passing while being assured that an outpouring of emotion was valid and ultimately healthy: "Elsie's grief was deep and lasting. She sorrowed as she might have done for the loss of a very dear brother, . . . a half remorseful feeling which reason could not control or entirely relieve; and it was long ere she was quite her own bright, gladsome sunny self again." Louisa May Alcott wrote of a sister's "bitter cry of an unsubmissive sorrow," of "sacred moments, when heart talked to heart in the silence of the night, turning affliction to a blessing, which chastened grief and strengthened love."[49] Mother's assurances, repeated references to protecting angels, and the increasing theme of familial reunion in heaven all linked the power of grief to hope and love; but the power was not evaded. Stories of death were now disengaged from fear and from moral admonitions about life's transiency to become part of the characteristic Victorian emotional style, in which intense emotions served as a desirable part of life and, ultimately, an enhancement of human ties. The starkness of death disappeared under sentimental overlays in these portrayals, but the inescapability, even the benefit, of a period of deep grief was generally confirmed.

The same themes pervaded popular parlor songs in the Victorian decades. The 1839 song "Near the Lake Where Droop'd the Willow" became an immense success in American concerts and inspired several decades of imitations. The song focused on a girl loved in youth, who had died long ago:

> Mingled were our hearts forever, long time ago;
> Can I now forget her? Never. No, lost one, no.
> To her grave these tears are given, ever to flow,
> She's the star I missed from heaven, long time ago.[50]

In contrast to eighteenth-century songs about death, which were set in the artificial pastoral world of shepherds and written in the third person, Victorian grief songs were personal and immediate. Death and its aftermath became a field for emotional exploration. Minstrel shows dealt with the emotions of death, often without much reference to plot or character. Deathbed scenes, the emotional ties between dead and living, and the idea of ultimate reunion in heaven all figured prominently. Literally hundreds of songs about dying girls were published, particularly in the 1860s, when they obviously served as a combination of focus for and distraction from the terrors of the Civil War: "Wait for me at heaven's gate, Sweet Belle Mahone"; "Though we may meet no more on earth, Thou shalt be mine above"; "Angels guard her with your wings. . . . Bid her dream love-dreams of me—Till I come, sleep, Eulalie." But along with the sentimentalized heaven came real sorrow on earth, with frequent emotion-laden visits to the cemetery: "I'm kneeling by thy grave, Katy Darling; This world is all a bleak place to me"; "All night I sat upon her grave, And sorely I did cry."[51]

> Oh, a huge great grief I'm bearing,
> Though I scarce can heave a sigh,
> And I'll ever be dreaming, Katy Darling,
> Of thy love ev'ry day till I die.[52]

The pervasive themes of grief and pathos formed an important part of Victorian culture, making the sorrow of bereavement seem natural, even desirable, though also to some degree consolable. Grief could soar, as love did. At the risk of trivializing grief (and certainly Christian doctrines concerning the afterlife), Victorian emotional culture embraced this sorrow openly, returning to it with almost endless fascination at least until the final decades of the nineteenth century.

Victorian Intensity

No single work, either expert or popular, conveniently summed up Victorian emotional culture. In examining the real though complex consistency of the amalgam that emerged after 1850, we are piecing together a wholeness that the Victorians themselves did not explicitly encounter. One result of the patchwork approach to popular presentations of Victorian emotional style was, inevitably, a host of inconsistencies. For example, men as well as women were urged to have intense emotions, and yet Victorian statements could imply that male superiority rested directly in the ability to control and suppress emotions. This inconsistency doubtless reflected some genuine ambiguity about how to defend gender goals in the emotional arena. Anachronistic standards also continued to intrude, including an occasional epitaph or story designed to discipline children through fear of untimely demise.

Nevertheless, once the transition away from the simpler emotional view of the early Victorians was complete, advice literature, mainstream Protestant sermons, and moralistic popular fiction presented a fairly uniform picture about anger, fear, jealousy, grief, and love. There were no clear dissenting voices in the most widely read directives. An evangelical segment, to be sure, maintained a somewhat more traditional view of discipline through fear as part of their religious stance. Utopian communities also dissented, though less directly. In arguing for cooperativeness instead of competition, they did not adopt the mature Victorian idea of channeled anger. Nor did they countenance intense love as a means of joining a couple (and therefore emotionally isolating it from the community). On the other hand, they actually intensified the new view of jealousy in arguing against possessiveness, including sexual possessiveness.[53] These subcultures, both of which related to the mainstream middle class, must not be forgotten.

Nor, of course, should the class base of the dominant Victorian emotional style be lost from sight. Popularizers intended their wares for all readers, but there is no question that their emphasis was class based.

As we will see in the following chapter, evidence suggests that many Victorians translated their emotional culture into assumptions that lower classes and immigrants were incapable of the finer feelings it embodied. Victorian emotional style became part of a cultural arsenal that allowed middle-class publicists both to preach at the lower classes, confident of the superiority of their emotional standards, and also to condemn them for failing to live up to the necessary control or to express the ethereal qualities of true love. While the Victorian style did not address alternative norms, which testifies both to substantial middle-class agreement on goals and to the dominant cultural position of the middle class, there is no reason to assume that it displaced various working-class and ethnic alternatives or that the Victorians really expected it to do so. The history of ethnic and lower-class emotionologies, immensely desirable, has yet to be written, though some material on expressions of parental and romantic love warns us not to expect total differentiation.[54]

At any rate, a surprisingly coherent emotional culture was purveyed to the middle class during the second half or two-thirds of the nineteenth century. The culture had two main foci: the need for control, for directing emotional fervor to appropriate ends; but also the need for intensity, for the spark necessary to a full life and to the functions essential in modern society. Emotional excess was obviously condemned, but so was emotional flaccidity. The Victorians sought, as basic ingredients of good character, the capacity for deep feeling along with the capacity to direct that feeling to appropriate targets.

Regional and Gender Variants

Agreement on the goal of controlled intensity allowed major features of the Victorian emotional style to transcend, though not to obliterate, two key cultural divisions within the nineteenth-century middle class: region and gender. It is not yet possible to offer definitive statements about these segmenting factors, particularly where region is concerned; but it is possible to suggest how emotionology relates to the larger cultural debates involved.

Recent work on gender and family has revived the question of the distinctiveness of southern culture, particularly around the middle of the nineteenth century. Regionalists appropriately insist that too many

"American" studies, even when carefully confined to the middle class, have relied disproportionately on materials from the Northeast. It is unquestionably true that most of the advice literature and popular magazines privileged authors from New England, the Midwest, and the Middle Atlantic states. But several important studies on middle-class values in the South have argued that families in this group read much of this material and shared many similar goals.[55] The principal features of Victorian emotional culture also suggest that there were more shared standards, stemming in part from shared reading, than images of hot-blooded Rhett Butlers and calculating New England moneychangers might suggest. While further research explicitly focused on the South is essential, it is clear that regional factors affected but did not hopelessly entangle the Victorian style.

Southern distinctiveness did shine through in emotional criteria that related to honor. While Americans generally could still resonate to jealous intensity in defense of honor (at least when the intensity involved men disputing the sexual activities of "their" women), southern standards were more single-minded than was true in the rest of the nation. Thus southerners preserved habits of dueling or at least fighting in order to vent their jealous reactions against the claims or slights of others. Men sought to redress wives' infidelity through private, emotionally charged action, as southern law castigated any "degrading" behavior on women's part. Courtship rivalries were common. The law in southern states articulated the idea that jealousy could legitimately excuse violence, well past the point at which northern states began to rein in this particular emotional approach to justifiable homicide and crimes of passion.[56]

Some historians have argued that southern culture supported passionateness in general, not just passion related to gender and honor. Michael Barton, for example, in an impressive analysis of letters by Civil War soldiers, concludes that the upper class in the South displayed an emotional articulateness and vivacity that markedly contrast with the careful, almost disembodied control that ran through letters by Union soldiers from virtually all social groups. He concludes, not surprisingly, that emotional style constituted one additional arena in which, whether they knew it or not, southerners and northerners disagreed.[57] Again, the existing state of research does not permit decisive dismissal of Barton's approach,[58] though most available evidence points in the other direction.

Southern Victorians wanted control along with their passion—this was one of the changes in upper-class culture in Virginia by the early nineteenth century, as Rhys Isaacs has shown. And, as I have insisted, northerners wanted passion along with their control. It is probable, in fact, that differences in emotional culture were greater in the colonial period than in the nineteenth century, precisely because many southerners came to accept the idea of targeting emotionality more carefully while northerners rediscovered the usefulness of channeled anger and insisted on the delights of soaring love.[59]

Southern families, in the middle and upper classes, certainly shared with their northern counterparts an interest in respect and obedience from children, which logically led to some emotional constraint. But they did not seek abject docility, and fathers seem generally to have aimed at a rapport in which sons could discern the legitimacy of appropriate emotion, including affection. Dickson Bruce, while emphasizing some distinctive southern features, notes an ambivalence toward passion in the South—a desire to promote strong emotional attachment to family and a belief in the legitimacy of a passionate nature combined with a real concern lest emotion overwhelm reason. The same ambivalence, defined as an attempt to juggle control and intensity, effectively describes the emotional style of the Victorian North. Middle-class families in both regions generated a related ambivalence toward male violence. After the greater pacifism of early Victorianism, northern child-rearing manuals (often read in southern cities as well) stressed the necessity of encouraging the emotional impulses that would lead boys to fight when the goals were just. Southern culture similarly taught its boys that, while sheer hot-headedness represented a fatal loss of control, violence was often inescapable.[60]

It is wrong to assume either a southern nonchalance about restraint or a northern emotional turgidity, or both. Northerners were a bit more wary of jealousy than southerners seem to have been, though there was some inconsistency even in the North. Both regions valued targeted anger, though northerners might speak more about its uses in competition than in defense of honor. Both regions claimed adherence to ideals of love, and both showed some acceptance of its concomitant, intense grief. Soldiers from both regions displayed intense and unembarrassed family affection. While northern Civil War soldiers tended to conceal emotions experienced in battle from their wives and mothers, they wrote more freely of their fear and their efforts at courage to their fathers, so that even here the idea of uniform emotional control is off the mark. Thus Charles Francis Adams, in the best boys' story fashion, wrote proudly of his first response to combat, when he displayed "a vigor and power which, under the circumstances, I had never hoped [I] possessed."[61] Such articulations of the concept of facing and mastering fear were also common in southerners' accounts.

The Victorian emotional style crossed regional boundaries in the nineteenth century. Later developments, in which southern culture proved more durably wed to Victorian standards than was true in the North, reopened gaps between the regions for a time, and these later differences help explain contemporary scholarly confusion about regional differences in the nineteenth century itself.

If Victorian popularizers dwelt little on regional factors, they were profuse in identifying emotional differences between the genders— again, particularly after the somewhat androgynous early Victorian interlude. No summary of emotional style can ignore the profound contrast between the standards assigned to men and those applied to women. In fact, Victorian emotional standards depended explicitly on gender differences. Women were supposed to supply an emotional charge that men lacked while accepting men's greater rational sense as a constraint; and at the same time men needed women to help them achieve certain kinds of control that they might naturally lack. Only through the very different contributions of both genders could the twin goals of passion and restraint be met. Yet despite these contrasts, the underlying goal of emotional intensity under control did apply to men and women alike.

Unquestionably, the passion/control dualism in the mature Victorian emotional style applied most literally to men. While women were clearly regarded as "more emotional," both in popularized literature and in scientific renderings such as those of psychologist G. Stanley Hall, actual discussions of emotional force concentrated on men. Anger was regarded as unfeminine in women, but men were supposed to be able to use anger. Children's stories, such as the *Uncle Wiggily* books popular during the early decades of the twentieth century, routinely assumed the sweetness of little girls (whether in human or in personified animal form) while often noting temper problems of boys. The result was a clear image of girls as emotionally preferable; but, translated to adulthood, the same imagery held that men had far more drive. Correspondingly, the boy or man lacking the emotional spur was shockingly feminine, a sissy. Similarly, within marriage, while popular literature occasionally cited the justified wrath of a much-abused wife and certainly commended patient husbands, the dominant tone urged particular care on the female side. Within the sacred confines of family, men were supposed to keep their temper, but it was acknowledged that their nature and their cares at work might expose some rough edges. Women were much better suited to the kind of self-control necessary to keep the home a tranquil place. "If there isn't one person in the house who simply shoulders more than his share and goes on quietly saying nothing about it, there are going to be friction and unhappiness"—and that one person was characteristically the wife, particularly in depictions after 1850. More simply put, "the average American girl believes that womanly, domestic methods are most effective." And more directly still, from an early Victorian address to young ladies, "An enraged woman [is] one of the most disgusting sights in nature"—a theme that etiquette books repeated through the century.[62] Whether this devotion to calm followed from women's real lack of anger or simply from their greater effort at self-control was not always clear, but the message came through regardless: women had no legitimate need for anger. All the devices developed to ritualize channeling that were urged on middle-class families, particularly aggressive sports like boxing, were concentrated on boys; girls remained confined to the anger-free models developed early in the Victorian period.

The passionate encounter with fear was another male preserve. Nineteenth-century popularizations did not mention courage as a female attribute; this was true even in the early scouting movements, extended past 1900. Boys were routinely told to face fear and conquer it. Girls were simply not discussed, or at most were advised not to be more fearful than necessary. Advice to mothers, to hide fears from children, assumed that women could manage some control but had not undergone the transforming emotional experience that would really make them brave. Thus T. S. Arthur, urging adult women to conceal fear, clearly implied that they would suffer from it. In his twin manuals directed respectively to girls and to boys, only his boys' book includes the characteristically long section on moral courage; the girls' pamphlet is mute on this subject.[63] Boys' stories, like the *Rollo* series, liked to show girls paralyzed by fear while their brothers dealt with danger. Courage was nice, but courage in front of trembling females was even nicer. Again, the word "sissy" clearly showed the distinctions between gender standards where the encounter with fear was concerned.[64]

The basis for the gender-specific rules on handling the dangerous emotions lay, obviously, in assigned roles. Women, being domestic creatures, did not need and, regarding anger, could not afford the emotional range men required because of their work in the world. Public-private emotional divisions were crucial to Victorian culture, and these provided gender markers as well. The home was a haven in which disruptive emotions had no place. Women should therefore be emotionally gentle. The burden on men was in some ways greater, as they had to develop two emotional faces, one domestic and the other economic and political. But this same dualism gave them a far greater range for emotional intensity.

The distinction is interestingly revealed in the recurrent popular comments on jealousy. Men and women were held to differ here as well, as jealousy became feminized. With regard to female jealousy, a certain ambiguity developed that was not granted to men in Victorian culture: a bit of jealousy might be expected from dependent, emotional women, and a loving man might respond by changing behaviors even though the emotion was petty and potentially disruptive. Men were more constrained with respect to low-level jealousy; there was no acceptance of a jealous male in routine commentary. But when jealousy rose to heights of passion, motivating vengeance, men alone held the keys. Women could not, in law, use the claim of jealous rage to excuse attacks on their spouses' lovers. The few who attempted this defense were uniformly convicted. Even where defense of family was concerned, intensity, again, was male.[65]

Thus women were seen as emotional but not passionate. The intensity that would lead to dramatic, effective action was a masculine preserve. As part of the larger imagery of female passivity, women's emotions were often seen as soft and desirably gentle. Men were not only more highly sexed but were also possessed of more driving emotions, which served both for economic competitiveness and as a foundation for broad social action. Women, as befit their domestic sphere, had no such range. Songs of grief persisted in using examples of women's deaths, which served to emphasize a male role in grief but also reminded the audience of female frailty. Beliefs about female hysteria, though not commonly discussed in the popular prescriptive literature, may have added to the sense of women's emotional boundaries.

Even motherlove, that deep wellspring that women alone possessed by nature, was a sacrificing, subterranean emotion more than a driving force. As Jan Lewis has demonstrated, motherlove lived in the children, but it must not overwhelm them. Mothers "must beware of disclosing [their] feelings, or at least, let there not be an apparent *attempt* to exhibit them. . . . This would be most ruinous. Rather let [the child] feel that there exists in your bosom a well spring of feeling and anxiety, which others know nothing of, and which even he cannot fathom." Women's maternal intensity, in sum, must be self-effacing; it did not motivate powerful action. A woman endowed with "warm feelings" and "quick apprehension" must exercise "self-control" so that she might display only a "calm good sense." Emotion was not an unqualified good, and to the extent that women were particularly emotional, they could complicate their own maternal tasks. As John Abbott insisted, in discussing "The Mother's Difficulties," "We must bring our own feelings and our own actions under a rigid system of discipline, or it will be in vain for us to hope to curb the passions and restrain the conduct of those who are looking to us for instruction and example."[66]

Unquestionably, male and female emotions were held to differ, as were the functions of their emotions. The same rules that defined a combination of passion and control also clearly specified areas where women could not tread. Criticisms of women's excessive, debilitating emotionality surfaced recurrently.

Yet a full differentiation was not attempted, and even the male passion/female sentiment distinction should not be pressed too far. Men, too, could fail through emotional excess, as when they displayed ungovernable temper. They, like female hysterics, could be subject to medical controls. Women, for their part, though disbarred from channeled anger or the passions of courage, had intensities of their own. The fact that mothers must monitor their display did not automatically differentiate them from men, who were also required to be watchful. Though manipulated for the child's good, deep emotional expression could be part of maternalism: "Another outlet for thy womanly heart: a mirror in which thy smiles and tears shall be reflected back; a fair page on which thou, God-commissioned, mayst write what thou wilt; a heart that will throb back to thine, love for love."[67] Here was some female equivalence for the male joys of channeling anger toward a justified target or conquering the pangs of fear through courage triumphant.

The point is that pronounced gender separation and a passion/control combination coalesced in Victorian emotional culture. Control for women was more severe, as it enforced domesticity and was constantly associated with the insistence on sweetness and calm. But a version of the characteristic tension applied to both genders.

In romantic love, finally, men and women shared the field. Love was the intense emotion meant to unite two different characters, but in this case with equal fervor. While some Victorian advice suggested a slight concern that men might not love as well as women (because they were too reserved or distracted by other things and of course because their lusts might get the better of them), the injunction for men to love deeply was a standard fixture in the emotional culture. Women's capacity to love was seldom doubted, though an interesting subgroup, in men's advice literature after 1870, began to worry about women's "other" interests, including incipient feminism, as a distraction from love: "Why do not women marry?" The idea of love, however, burned brightly still, for the same author who fretted about rising divorce and distracted women praised a pure love that was "unequaled by any other emotion." No restraint was necessary. Men and women could and should love with equal, unbounded intensity. It was this very fervor, indeed, that could bridge the gaps between the genders and reconcile different emotional natures with the equal necessity of a tight marital bond. With the same intensity, in effect, men and women would love different things. As T. S. Arthur put it, a woman would fall deeply in love with the "moral wisdom of her husband," while men would fall just as deeply in love with the affectionate nature of good women.[68]

The passion/control combinations ascribed to emotionally correct men and women differed greatly. They unquestionably privileged men in a host of ways. Yet the formulas suggested for each gender were nonetheless somewhat comparable. Each had needs and outlets for intensity, each must of course learn important management controls. And the whole package was assembled by the one kind of intensity that could be sincerely enjoined on men and women alike: the intensity of a deeply spiritual, faithful, consuming love.

Guilt

Victorian emotional culture capped its central themes by developing a growing reliance on guilt as the central enforcement mechanism for proper behavior, including suitable expressions of feeling. John Demos has outlined the process by which middle-class Americans shifted from primary reliance on shame to primary reliance on guilt between the mideighteenth and the midnineteenth centuries.[69] While the change entailed a host of ramifications, reflecting declining reliance on community cohesion in the northern states and the need to provide more family-based and ultimately internalized emotional discipline, the relationship to the larger evolution of emotional style was vivid. Guilt may be seen as a reaction to the possible loss of cherished relationships, with expression of guilt helping to restore those relationships. The intensity of family emotional ties in Victorian culture created precisely the environment in which the intensity of guilt could itself receive new emphasis.

The enforcement of shame in colonial New England went beyond the fabled stocks, pillories, and badges that exposed offenders to public ridicule. Even whipping, though producing physical pain, was carefully scheduled in public to inflict scorn as well. Thus on one occasion a female offender who was spared the whip because of infirmity was ordered to stand at the whipping post "that she may in some measure bear the shame of her sin."[70] Concern about shame is revealed in many lawsuits designed to avenge wounded honor, for the culture urged one to measure up to external standards, and hence vigorously to redress false assertions that one had failed to do so. The orientation to shame began in childhood, as wrongdoers were abundantly exposed to the mockery of siblings and peers, and continued in the insults that pervaded neighborhood life.

This orientation shifted by 1850. Even a bit before this, Catharine Sedgwick had offered a paradigmatic tale of family punishment.[71] A boy attacks a family pet with boiling water. The father sternly orders the boy to go to his room—by this time, a form of punishment greatly preferred over physical discipline. Aside from the act of removal, there is no attempt to encourage shame even within the family. Indeed, after initial horror over the scalded cat, the family expresses sympathy, "grief," and support. The point is for the boy to look within himself, to punish himself, during a period (in this story, two full weeks) of removal from the family, and then to disclose his internal process by a sincere apology. Internal emotional turmoil, not externally applied scorn, becomes the central disciplinary theme.

The reform movements that proliferated during the nineteenth century hung heavy with the themes of guilt. Temperance literature emphasized personal degradation and material and moral damage to family. Realization of guilt was intended to motivate sincere commitment to change—"conscience-stricken" was a favorite term used to convey the passage through guilt. It was the harm done to others, particularly those whom the drunkard loved most, rather than the scorn emanating from others that gave substance to the message of guilt. New movements in penology, particularly the idea of isolating criminals in prisons, and sometimes within prisons through solitary confinement, similarly moved from shame to guilt. One advocate of the solitary confinement system wrote that "each individual [convict] will necessarily be made the instrument of his own punishment; his conscience will be the avenger of society."[72]

Guilt did not, of course, fully replace shame, and an element of shame continued to inhere in both family reprimands and public chastisements. Guilt and shame are not entirely discrete in emotional terms, in any event, nor need it be argued that shame is necessarily less intense emotionally than guilt. It can be superficial, laughed off, as was not infrequently the case in colonial New England; but it can be deeply anguishing as well. The inculcation of guilt, however, was intended to make intense emotional and moral wrestling part of the fundamental experience of recognizing one's own wrongs; and the wrestling was internal, part of an emotional arsenal that was teaching people to acknowledge, manage, and, finally, utilize the intense passions of which they were capable. Indeed, inculcation of guilt could simply add to the depths of shame. Victorian etiquette books, as John Kasson has demonstrated, multiplied rules of dress and bodily control, thereby increasing the number of occasions on which private shame might be felt in public. When these occasions were magnified by a conjoint feeling of guilt at the omission, the overall emotional intensity, and its designed deterrent effect, could be greatly heightened.[73] Finally, inculcation of guilt, particularly at the familial level, depended on the larger loving environment that Victorian emotionology preached. Isolation from family plus consciousness of damage to loved ones was now experienced as a separation from a deeply positive emotional environment. Guilt, as an experience of self-hate, flourished readily in this context, and again it differed from the reactions that simple scorn from the outside world could generate.

Guilt, then, must be added to the other intense emotional attributes encouraged by Victorian culture. The person who could not react profoundly to his or her own shortcomings—the person who might depend simply on regulation from the outside—was emotionally inadequate. Just as a man of good character had the anger necessary to spur achievement, the courage to face fear, and the capacity to love, so he must, as needs be, have the ability to feel guilt. The woman of good character needed the capacity to love in several forms, and she also needed to be capable of feeling guilty when other emotional norms like serenity of temper escaped her. The harsh bath of guilt did not mean being overwhelmed—for like other intense emotions, guilt must finally be mastered through action, apology, and correction; it should not paralyze. Again we see real consistency in Victorian emotional culture, in which capacity for guilt related readily to other emotional goals.

Conclusion

Victorians approved of passion, and they used the word frequently. They wanted men to have the passion to impel them to great deeds, and they wanted women to share with men a certain spiritual passion in love. The blander word "emotion," which has gained currency in the twentieth century, appeared rarely in Victorian discussion, where certain kinds of quiet, moral impulses were described as sentiments and the equally important, more vigorous surges came under the heading of passion. Word use is tricky, of course, and Victorians used the word "passion" more generally than we do. But they also used it openly, without an inevitably accompanying caution and without confining it to the sexual realm. In this respect, their vocabulary corresponded to the real values culturally ascribed to targeted anger, courage, love, and grief.

Contrary to some bloodless stereotypes of the nineteenth century, the Victorians even associated passion with civilization. They saw what they termed more primitive societies (by which they meant every society but their own) as calmer and more restrained. They granted that tight-knit, sedate communities avoided certain problems, like frequency of suicide, but they found the stimulus of modern urban life—where "all human passions are exercised with more fourfold constancy and intensity"—both inevitable and desirable on balance.[74]

Victorian emotionality surely included more standards than those applied to the dangerous emotions, to love, to grief, and to guilt. It certainly emphasized disgust, when moral disgrace, uncleanliness, or odor was encountered. It could include, particularly in early Victorianism and later among women, a proclivity to tearful sadness that deserves exploration in light of the larger emotional culture. The emotional charge behind the rise of humanitarian sentiment, which ultimately became part of the Victorian emotional style broadly construed, also needs further assessment, for its promptings of intense empathy with distant peoples readily connected to other features of the emotionology. We know that humanitarian urges were novel, arising in part from changes in philosophical beliefs and economic systems. Their fit with the new emotional culture needs more attention, for humanitarianism served as an additional outlet for vigorous feeling. The full range of Victorian emotional criteria has yet to be probed, and there may be some further surprises. The main point is clear, however. Underlying the extensive discussions of various kinds of emotional goals was a desire to prevent untoward expression or excess combined with equal insistence on the importance of appropriate emotional vigor. Northerners, men, middle-class Victorians in general were told to expect to experience passions, beginning in childhood, that they must learn to direct, use, and savor. Victorian relish in intense, if focused, emotionality related to a host of other interests—in strong wills, in romantic idylls, in evocative cemeteries, in tales of heroism, and of course in true, loving womanhood. The Victorian era began with the recognition of emotion's central role—such that a leading Unitarian could seek to dispel charges of dry rationalism with appeals to a "heart-stirring energy"—and the same theme picked up momentum in subsequent decades.[75]

The emotional culture was purveyed in a variety of forms. Advice to parents was intended to launch appropriate socialization, for after the early period, in which childish innocence seemed only to require parental restraint, Victorian prescribers judged that parents had more positive lessons to impart, providing models of love and guidance in handling the essential but risky emotions. The emotional culture did not, however, assume that early childhood ended the process of emotional development. This is why children's stories assumed such a hortatory aspect, offering models for courage and warnings against both loss of control and emotional vapidity. A related genre of youth advice manuals, some authored by the same people who wrote children's fiction, drove the same lessons home and added pointers on love. Adult fiction, as found in the women's magazines that were popular among men as well, and marital advice completed the picture.[76]

Variations existed, to be sure. Advice manuals differed considerably in the amount of space they gave to particular emotional issues. Jealousy, for example, might be passed over completely in youth advice materials, or it might receive a few cautionary paragraphs. But mainstream middle-class literature did not vary much in content, and when variations did occur, they seemed to involve an author's judgment about whether or not her audience needed to be reminded of the basic rules. There were no widely circulated dissenting views on the necessity of properly directed emotional spark.

Not surprisingly, Victorian emotional culture interacted extensively with formal scientific comment on emotion, as it began to emerge under the aegis of Darwinian theory by the 1870s and 1880s. The chronological relationship was clear: popularized Victorian culture came first. Psychologists like James and Hall added a formal evolutionary twist in looking for species functions for particular emotions, but they did not create the underlying tone. Rather, knowingly or not, they echoed established wisdom, and of course gave it added authority in the process. James commented scientifically on the link between emotions and the body, but then lapsed into standard advice about mastering emotions through diligent practice without destroying passion.[77] Hall, as we have seen, precisely delineated the dangers but also the necessity of anger in men. Like the larger culture around him, he equivocated somewhat on jealousy, seeing in it female pettiness but also some motivation for action and for family solidarity. Divisions in emotional characteristics between men and women were faithfully replicated, though the Darwinian experts discussed gender distinctions somewhat more formally than the more popular materials did, dwelling more extensively on female frailty. But Hall could praise women's affectionate warmth as well as their docility, if in somewhat less rigorous scientific terms than those he applied to the emotions behind masculine achievement. Overall, however, what had begun as a moralistic, half-Christian, half-secular advice literature informed a generation of scientific research on emotion as well.

In the first formal study of emotion after the decline of comprehensive philosophies that had, through the seventeenth century, worked on elaborate emotional definition, scientists sponsored direct research on emotion, and they generated findings that would actually help undermine the Victorian synthesis later on. But the established wisdom on the importance of emotional vigor, qualified by differing gender traits, was if anything amplified by the initial new scientific pronouncements.

Thus a characteristic Victorian advice giver of 1870 and a modern purveyor of science around 1900 agreed in their emotional recommendations. Jacob Abbott, author of twenty-eight *Rollo* books and several advice manuals, was a Congregational minister bent on practical interpretations of Christianity, combining moral lessons with various kinds of factual information. He was big on courage tested by fear, on controlled anger, and on redeeming love. Alice Birney, writing in the early 1900s, was a consumer of the new psychology, having trained with Hall. She participated in various organizations designed to provide mothers with the latest expertise. Explicit moralisms and applied Christianity were not for her. But the emotional content of her work was scarcely different from that of Abbott. She too wanted loving mothers, sweet daughters, morally indignant sons, and courageous boys (though as we will later see she did complicate this last goal slightly).[78]

The relationship between Victorian emotionology and other aspects of Victorian culture was complex, which is one reason why it has frequently been misconstrued. As Victorians sought to preserve emotional depth while inculcating appropriate targeting and control, they were also involved in a progressive attack on poor bodily discipline. Their etiquette books, another expanding cultural genre that arose with the other kinds of advice literature and attempted to meet similar needs in guiding middle-class families amid strangers and in unfamiliar urban settings, pressed for increasing civilization. Spitting, lack of cleanliness, sloppy posture, brazen stares, drumming of fingers—all were brought, in principle at least, under growing control. Not only etiquette books but also costume itself added to bodily discipline, providing tight collars for men and tight bodices for women along with a host of rules about proper accoutrements from head to toe. Far more space was devoted to proper bodily control when walking and to proper clothing and manners—"If there is any man whom you wish to conciliate, take off your hat to him as often as you meet him"—than to comments on emotion.

Concerning the body and its etiquette, a theme of increasing discipline and repression prevailed without significant qualification—except insofar as middle-class people might modify or ignore the rules in actual practice.[79] Where emotion had physical manifestations, the standards were again severe, as in the disapproval of public laughter and other conversational excess in the nineteenth-century manners books.

Emotions themselves, however, were different. The etiquette books preached control of anger and other impulses, to be sure, though we will see that even they allowed exceptions for issues like politics that followed the more general emotionology. But the control theme overall was combined with the positive emphasis on passion—which means that the standards applied to emotional life were, quite simply, different from those addressed to the body. Severe physical discipline might in fact have prevailed precisely because emotional life offered so many opportunities for compensatory fervor that purely corporal regulation seemed rather trivial by comparison. Many a tightly dressed, respectable young man or woman could pour out his or her passion with no sense of contradiction—indeed, their physical rigors could be endured precisely because the emotional outlets seemed so much more important. Twentieth-century observers, looking back on Victorian dress and manners, might readily assume that emotional cramping was just as severe, particularly on discovering that there were indeed some strict emotional rules of real importance. But the equation would be wrong; indeed, as we will later see, such an assumption reveals a characteristic twentieth-century confusion about what constraint means.

As noted, sexuality rested somewhere between constraint of bodily habits and emphasis on appropriate emotional fervor. Sexuality had its place, according to most Victorian advice, though it was potentially even more dangerous than the riskiest emotions and even more hemmed in by age and frequency restrictions. As emotional prescriptions themselves made clear, however, sexuality should supplement, never rival, emotional intensity. Again, the power of true love could make the merely physical limits that were part of the Victorian concept of respectability seem readily endurable. Here too, twentieth-century views about the centrality of sexual standards should not lead to confusion about the Victorians; repression in one area did not mean repression across the board. In fact, sexual "repression" actually could facilitate the emotional sparks the Victorians cherished; keeping sex in check, though not to the point of complete neglect of its pleasures, aided love and vice versa. Correspondingly, while sexual constraints produced clear attempts to establish compensatory outlets—in pornography, for example—no such catharsis was needed in the area of emotion, where intensity was allowable.[80] Despite their undeniable concern for respectable behavior and their attacks on rudeness, the Victorians did not see the body, sexuality, and emotions as cut from the same cloth. They approached each with varying degrees of rigor and in the end heightened their reliance on emotional intensity precisely because their goals in managing body and sexuality were so demanding.

The mature Victorian emotional culture served advice literature and uplifting fiction from its emergence in the 1840s until well past 1900. The culture was complex, asking men and women to relate to each other emotionally but also to differ, insisting on emotional intensity amid injunctions of strict etiquette and family discipline, informing men that emotions absolutely essential in the public sphere needed to be suppressed at home. Yet, clearly, it was also serviceable. It met Victorian cultural needs. Its very complexity promoted its durability: themes of control could be emphasized against uncivilized behaviors, while themes of passion could drive home the sanctity of family or the joy of action (this last lest the middle class become too stuffy). While we will shortly turn to the demise of this culture, it will be no surprise that elements of the Victorian amalgam persisted in the new synthesis. Ideals of motherlove, intense romance, or anger-propelled social crusaders continued to inspire, complicating the process of change. Before addressing this process, however, I must complete my presentation of the Victorian baseline by discussing the causes and effects of this rich emotional culture. After all, claims of relative consistency and persistence—the themes of this chapter—mean little if the emotional culture is only loosely related to the driving forces of middle-class life, or if it did not connect to real beliefs and behaviors. To be taken seriously, emotional culture must be caused, and it must cause; the Victorian version met both tests.

3

Evaluating the Victorian Emotional Style: Causes and Consequences

Major features of Victorian emotional culture have been well described in recent years. Despite persistent and erroneous oversimplifications about blanket repressiveness and hostility to spontaneity, in fact the picture painted in the previous chapter blends a host of familiar portraits.[1] Victorian interest in emotional intensity combined with greater strictures concerning sexuality and bodily control, with emotion actually offering some relief from the more rigorous standards applied to other areas.

The causes of the Victorian style are, however, less well known, partly because the emotional culture has not previously been addressed in its entirety. Furthermore, although we will see that some of the specific consequences have been traced, analysis of effects can be improved by looking at the impact of the whole culture rather than individual parts such as love or gender norms.

Cause-effect evaluation of the Victorian style is essential, for without it, the purely descriptive summary provided in the previous chapter may prove deceptive. Despite widespread and substantial concordance in the cultural prescriptions to the middle class, emotional standards must be considered mere window dressing if they did not respond to real needs in Victorian society; pinpointing causation is vital. Even more obviously, if the emotional norms had no demonstrable consequences aside from filling up advice literature and moralistic fiction, they could well be dismissed as meaningless. In fact, however, despite incomplete evidence on private beliefs and behaviors, it is possible to trace a number of results that issued from the widely preached culture and to conclude that, like the culture itself, these results were persistent. Finally, cause-effect evaluation is essential in preparing for analysis of subsequent change; for change could occur only as causation shifted, and the impact of causal shifts had to be formulated in contest with previous cultural impacts.

Causation

Basic causes of emotional standards have been discussed less often than the standards themselves, both in historical work and to a substantial extent in sociology. Anthropologists, who deal extensively with emotional culture, pay even less attention to causation since, with rare exceptions, they pick up well-established patterns (or assume that they do) and do not emphasize change. For them, prior culture causes present culture, with other causes stretching back in the mists of time. Yet causal analysis is vital in dealing with emotions as social or cultural constructs, for we need to know what factors prompted particular patterns to emerge. Constructionist theory has emphasized the importance of changing social functions in reshaping emotional life, an approach that invites exactly the kind of causation assessment historians seek; but practicing constructionists have spent more time discussing their propositions in the abstract than providing concrete case studies.[2] Their approach has been brought to bear on twentieth-century change, and I will turn to it in due course, but middle-level generalizations, based on more than recent developments, are hard to come by. As a result, important debate among constructionists, about what kind of functionalism underlies emotional standards, has remained largely implicit. Constructionists would generally agree that emotions serve particularly to maintain the moral order and the social status quo, but this may beg the more precise question of which particular moral and social factors are involved. James Averill defines these factors as social and cultural, but practicing constructionists like Arlie Hochschild construe functionalism more narrowly, emphasizing primarily economic and organizational factors.[3] Yet the anthropologists who have contributed to constructionist theory emphasize cultural functions as well. There are important issues here, which I will address in applying functionalist explanations both to Victorianism and to subsequent twentieth-century change; but there are no precise models to guide our inquiry.

Causation is a tricky concept in historical discussion, particularly in dealing with an already-slippery descriptive category like emotional culture. Explaining Victorian culture is a far more challenging task than assigning causes for the War of Jenkin's Ear. Historians have no laboratory basis for testing replicability. They cannot present causation findings in the same manner as scientists, who do have this capacity. Yet, granting the imprecision and openness to further debate, historical change can be identified and it can be subjected to probabilistic evaluation, yielding a fair sense of the major factors involved.

One further issue requires some preliminary comment: the relationship between the causes of standards applied to individual emotions and the causes that generate a larger emotional style involves overlap but not complete identity. For example, the Victorian emphasis on parental love for children built on cultural trends that had been taking shape for some time, but there were also more specific reasons for it. The American middle class was busily cutting its birth rate from the late eighteenth century onward. Smaller family size often encourages a more intense relationship between parents and children and also, when it is first developing, a rather anxious concern to justify novel demographic behavior. Arguing in terms of great love and extensive maternal obligations helped Victorian parents ease their minds about having fewer children, on average, than their own parents had expected. While emphasis on love for children also fit, of course, in the larger Victorian style and indeed played a major role in some of its other ramifications, its specific origins must be acknowledged. It is also important to recognize that events may carry impact on some emotional standards without particularly altering others. For example, the Civil War obviously helped heighten earlier emphasis on channeled anger and courageous encounters with fear,[4] but it had little impact on standards of love. Again, particular factors can be identified without contradicting the larger causal analysis, but they do add complexity. Explaining the Victorian style itself constitutes the most important analytical task, but it does not exhaust the process of evaluating factors relevant to more specific ingredients.

Two other illustrations highlight specific contexts applicable to individual emotions. Victorian grief, which served a central position in the larger culture, stemmed in part from the continuing high child mortality rates (all the more keenly felt with the birth rate steadily declining) in a culture that now saw children as more precious, child mortality as less inevitable. This specific formula for intense grief bore little relationship to channeled anger or several of the other Victorian staples.

Finally, Victorian romantic love ideals stemmed in part—possibly in large part—from the tension-filled combination middle-class couples attempted between extensive emotional exchange and pronounced restrictions on premarital sexuality. Courting couples were given considerable freedom for mutual contact in the United States—far more than outdated Victorian imagery had suggested. They were encouraged to think about love, and of course their culture had already prepared them, well before courtship, to expect some decisive emotional charge. Young men, for example, thought about women and love long before their economic circumstances permitted them to go courting.[5] But they were not supposed to have sexual intercourse even as they built an intense relationship, and while a few couples crossed this barrier, most did not. It is hardly fanciful to see the emphasis on overwhelming but ethereal passion as in part a compensation for sexual limitations and an aid in enforcing restraint among couples who firmly believed that premature sex would sully their true love. Sexual constraint may indeed have informed other facets of the Victorian emotional style, providing a physical basis for the need to find channels for emotional intensity, but it applied most directly to the love connection. It is obvious that larger emotional cultures like the Victorian style result in part from the accumulation of smaller changes that relate to more specific parts of the emotional spectrum.

Accumulation, however, is not the only explanatory approach. Just as individual factors involved in particular emotional reactions informed the Victorian style as a whole, so the style had roots of its own that helped shape particular emotional reactions. Interestingly, despite the recent flurry of attention to Victorian emotionality, we have only incomplete glimpses of the larger causation. Just as the style itself has not previously been synthesized, so the causes of the style have not been directly addressed.

Victorian emotional culture contrasted with eighteenth-century styles in several key respects, particularly in the decades of maturity after the

1840s. Indulgence of grief was novel, for while individuals grieved in the eighteenth century, the public interest in this emotion was limited.[6] The mature Victorian definition of romantic love, while it built on prior trends, went well beyond eighteenth-century precedents. The idea of channeled anger meshed neither with traditional indulgence in certain kinds of anger—in defense of hierarchy or religious orthodoxy, for example—nor with growing eighteenth-century concern about keeping anger in bounds. Attacks on disciplinary uses of fear emerged specifically in the early nineteenth century, and in this case were quite consciously directed against prior standards. The same holds true for some of the new uses of guilt. The Victorian emotional style was not, then, simply a carryover from prior standards or even from some of the newer cultural trends, though it involved the latter. Thus it is necessary to isolate the causes of the Victorian emotional style, for such analysis will in turn facilitate exploration of the reasons for yet another, more profound, post-Victorian set of shifts.

The simplest basic explanation of overall Victorian culture would focus on combining an understanding of emotionological trends that had been part of the transformation of mentalities throughout Western society from the late seventeenth century onward with attention to the impact of industrialization and urbanization in the nineteenth-century United States. According to such a reading, the Victorian emotional style was not a fundamental departure from eighteenth-century trends, themselves rather new. We have already seen that in highlighting explicit concern about anger, in attacking traditional disciplinary uses of fear, and in emphasizing various kinds of love, Victorianism amplified currents already present in American culture a century before. Victorianism thus built upon the reorientation of family functions toward greater emotionality and the attempt to introduce greater restraint in manners; it had no need to create. But while not fundamentally innovative, it did introduce its own flavor—the idea of motherlove, for example, while an outgrowth of the familial emphasis, was a distinctive Victorian product[7]—and this is where the new functional demands imposed by the growth of industry and the city made their mark.

The origins of the preindustrial cultural transformation are themselves not entirely clear. Several historians have cited the role of growing commercialization in prompting new concern about family emotional rewards as public life, in many communities, became increasingly competitive. Protestantism, as it transmuted into a wider belief system in the seventeenth century, unquestionably encouraged greater focus on family ties, emotional ties included. English writers pushed this theme hard and had obvious impact on attitudes across the Atlantic as well. Sources for the increasingly rigorous definition of civilized manners are not as easily pinned down. European upper classes grew increasingly suspicious of popular crudeness under the impact of Renaissance styles, which provided them a clear alternative to the prevailing version of mass culture. Growing prosperity brought a taste for refinement of habits. Capitalism also exacerbated divisions between propertied and unpropertied classes, which in turn generated an interest in habits of emotional restraint that would allow the former to distinguish themselves while conveniently blaming the latter for their own miseries. None of this bore fruit as quickly in the American colonies as in Europe, but, with the added effect of European cultural imitation, it began to have an impact by the later eighteenth century.[8] Thus, well in advance of Victorianism per se, American emotional norms had been shifting, and these changes prepared the response to the challenges of a new economy.

By the 1830s the impact of an increasingly commercial economy was becoming clear. Victorian emotionology reacted, as we have seen, by seeking to enhance the special emotional role of the family; here was part of the functional charge behind the redefinition of motherlove. In the slightly longer term, the increasing absence of husbands and fathers, as work separated from the home, added fuel to the fire, and emotional standards had to be intensified simply to protect the established value of family life. Concern about the taints of commerce, present even among people who embraced commercial opportunities,[9] provided yet another function for family-enhancing intensity and an emotional style that would clearly separate private from public activity.

But this was only an initial functional reaction in emotional culture. By the late 1840s, people began to realize that the same industrial world that required the family as emotional haven also required new emotional motivations for competitive work. (The lag behind actual economic change was interesting, as it meshed with other delayed reactions, for example, in schooling styles;[10] but it was not acute.) The resultant response explains why Victorianism introduced its most distinctive emotional emphases in arguing for channeled anger and courageous encounters with fear. Military interests played a role, but the vision of emotions necessary to succeed in new entrepreneurial and professional roles was preeminent. Family values were preserved—and the virtual sanctification of motherlove preserved this goal even as other purposes were embraced—but the emotional range expanded as understanding of functional necessity broadened. Victorian emotional standards were meant to enshrine family while also providing the spur to achievement in public life.

Early industrialization and growing cities generated other functional concerns as well, which further shaped the Victorian style. Boundaries of social class became more vivid, even if American democratic values muted some of the conflicts that developed in the European version of industrialization. A recent article has shown how increased concern for cleanliness—a form of bodily discipline potentially related to emotional constraints—was in part a response to the need to formalize class divisions. Just as the middle class separated itself through the use of soap, so it prided itself on emotional restraints and subtleties whose absence marked other social groups as inferior.[11] Channeled anger thus differed from the emotional propensity to brawl and certainly from real or imagined lower-class anger released within the family. Comments on fear routinely distinguished between what middle-class folks could aspire to and the baser emotions of the hoi polloi. Thus Dick, in an Oliver Optic story, spews out class pride when he contrasts his sort of courage with the actions of a host of deserters:

I can pity without blaming them, for it was a fearful ordeal for men such as you describe. As I heard my father say . . . , it requires a moral force behind the physical to enable a soldier to stand up before the enemy, facing death and mangling wounds, without flinching. We have always found that the most ignorant and ruffianly men make the most unreliable soldiers. As father said, it is the soul, rather than the body that makes the true soldier.[12]

Similarly, intense, properly spiritual love could serve as a differentiator. When late-nineteenth-century divorce law came to enshrine this quality through the concept of mental cruelty, provable through the absence of appropriate affection as well as blatant nastiness, the middle class was correspondingly privileged. Divorcing working-class couples could not point to absence of love as an excuse, for their natures precluded the finer sentiments in the first place. Mental cruelty grounds of this sort were denied them until after 1900.[13]

Emotional culture had begun to take on qualities of class identification even earlier, at least in the minds of middle- and upper-class proponents, as in late-eighteenth-century Virginia.[14] It became part of a larger dispute over respectability throughout much of the nineteenth century. And while respectability claims focused in part on workers' and immigrants' lack of civilized restraints, they also highlighted some subtle intensities that were open only to people of refinement.

Class boundaries aside, urban and commercial life required rules that would assist in the identification of strangers. As familiar community monitoring proved increasingly inadequate, Victorian culture responded to the need to provide cues that would help people distinguish the trustworthy from the unreliable.[15] Identification of correct responses was a result of this need.

Finally, and even more obviously, Victorian culture served gender purposes, and new functional demands also impacted this arena. Emotional arguments helped justify confinement of women to the home, which was seen by men and many women as a functional necessity given changes in the location of work. Beliefs about motherlove as well as female lack of motivating anger did not cause gender division, but they certainly helped support it. Men welcomed special emotional badges, like their aptitude for channeled anger and courage, not only because they put women in their place but also because they bolstered male qualities at a time when certain aspects of industrialization created masculine insecurities. With property ownership and traditional skills now threatened, with family role complicated by new work demands, it was comforting, perhaps truly functional, to have an explicit, if demanding, emotional identity.[16] Emotional masculinity in this sense complemented increasing reliance on men's role as economic provider, which replaced a more traditional and less anxious gender definition. Here, too, function was served.

Growing industrialization, in sum, created new needs for family enhancement, for personal motivation, for justifications for class boundaries, and for gender roles. The Victorian emotional style responded faithfully, particularly in its fuller version after the 1840s.

Yet the functionalist approach should not be pressed too far, for the emotional adjustments to industrialization were based on cultural preparation. For example, the value of intense family ties had to be established before they could be further emphasized. Functional logic, here at least, was prepared by beliefs, which is one reason why Victorianism did not fully break away from emotional patterns set up the century before.

Furthermore, three kinds of cultural shifts during the nineteenth century itself added to the imperatives of industrial work and urban social stratification in promoting the full-blown Victorian emotional style. The first involves implications from emotionological change itself: until interrupted by other factors, shifts in emotional culture tend to cause additional modifications in the same direction. Thus an emphasis on motherlove contributed directly to the heightened intensity attributed to romantic love. Hypertrophied maternal love increased the need for strong adult passion to aid products of emotionally intense upbringing in freeing themselves from maternal ties; love of a new sort must counter the love into which both boys and girls had, at least according to Victorian standards, been socialized. This aid in emotional weaning, particularly important for girls, was functional in a broad sense, helping to form the emotional underpinnings for new families, but it would have been far less necessary with a cooler familial background. Not surprisingly, Victorian fiction picked up elements of this motif in stressing the emotional anguish that young women might encounter in breaking, through ardent courtship, the bonds that had tied them to parents and to siblings.[17]

New emotional rules that urged more intense love, along with those that proscribed anger and fear in the discipline of children, obviously expanded the realm of guilt. While the culture urged socialization toward guilt as part of childrearing, adults readily expanded the connection—which heightened their own emotional response to guilt and further legitimated efforts to instill guilt in their offspring. By the later nineteenth century many parents reported guilt when they inadvertently shouted at or frightened their children. The sense of being morally monitored against spontaneous impulse both contributed to and complicated the task of living up to some of the Victorian norms.

A second strand of cultural causation stemmed from a source outside emotionology: changing conceptions of the body made emotions far more separate from somatic function than they had been in traditional conceptions or would be again in the twentieth century. Prior to the nineteenth century, dominant beliefs, medical and popular alike, attached anger, joy, and sadness to bodily functions. Hearts, for example, could shake, tremble, expand, grow cold. Because emotions were embodied, they had clear somatic qualities: people were gripped by rage (which could, it was held, stop menstruation), hot blood was the essence of anger, fear had cold sweats. Emotions, in other words, had physical stuff. But during the eighteenth century, historians increasingly realize, the humoral conception of the body, in which fluids and emotions alike could pulse, gave way to a more mechanistic picture.[18] And in the body-machine, emotions were harder to pin down, the symptoms harder to convey. Of course physical symptoms could still be invoked, but now only metaphorically. And although women's emotional makeup was tied to the body in medical literature through discussions of how uterine development weakened the nervous system (and the brain) and so enforced a domestic emotional role, in popularized advice women's emotions, like men's, were discussed largely as independent entities. Popular stories could refer to the impact of emotion in causing blushing or sudden paleness, and in some stories, dire illness could follow from emotional experiences like love or anger, but in the United States, accident rather than illness seems more commonly to have befallen certain kinds of emotional victims in fiction.

Despite some evidence to the contrary, it is safe to say that a traditional and automatic connection between emotional experience and physical sensation was challenged by the new, mechanistic idea of the body. Cultural adjustments resulted. Emotions in a sense became more abstract, and we are only now coming to grips with the consequences of this basic change in outlook. Victorians were unaware of their involvement, but they reflected it. Their recurrent tendency to see certain emotions as animal-like reflected a desire to achieve distance from the physical. Certainly their delight in ethereal emotional encounters—such as true spiritual love or the moral courage that could face down fear—reflected a desire to find a new basis for emotional intensity outside the corporal shell. Changing ideas of the body did not clearly cause basic adjustments in emotionology, but they contributed to the desire for regulation and to the particular Victorian version of soulful (not bodily) intensity. This same adaptation helps explain why Victorians, bent on disciplining the body through demanding clothing, posture requirements, and sexual constraints, did not see the relationship between these structures and their fascination with emotional fervor. Emotions came now from the spirit; they need not be constrained just because the body was regulated. Similarly, twentieth-century observers tend not to perceive the Victorian distinction between emotion and the body because they are accustomed to a more complete relationship between the two (though not, one hastens to add, a traditional, humoral relationship).[19]

Finally, and in relation to the spiritualizing of key emotions, Victorian emotional style depended heavily on rapid changes in religious culture and in turn contributed to these changes. Here we see most clearly the inadequacy of defining functional requirements only in terms of economic structure and urbanization. A richer mixture of factors prevailed.

Religious change intertwined with the Victorian version of emotional culture in two ways. First, several changes in mainstream Protestantism supported Victorian optimism about the consequences of vigorous emotion and were in turn supported by this optimism. The concept of a benign God stood behind motherlove, helping to explain the common association between the maternal image and prayer. The idea that God is benign also affected presentations of anger, further reducing any claim that wrath could be used to enforce hierarchy though not, ultimately, undercutting the notion of righteous anger against evil. God's benignity also reduced the credit given to fear, for a more rosy-hued religion no longer saw an association between this emotion and true piety. Terrorized children, indeed, would not be able to discern God's sweet mercy. One of the key arguments in early-nineteenth-century Protestantism focused on precisely this point, with the partisans of religion as an emotionally positive experience triumphing clearly, even in such previous bastions of dour Calvinism as Presbyterian Pittsburgh.[20] Solace for intense grief related to the declining attention paid to hellfire and the unprecedented notion of heaven as a divinely organized reunion of loved ones.

In general, as several historians of middle-class religion have pointed out, American Protestantism shifted increasingly toward providing a positive emotional experience as its commitment to rigorous theology declined. The resulting assumptions undergirded common beliefs about the viability of courage in the face of fear and the bittersweet experience of grief while also encouraging restraint on some traditional uses of emotion such as fear in childrearing, now regarded as dangerous. Variant religious strands dissented from the norm, particularly in the case of the Evangelicals, who maintained a more traditional approach to anger and fear, seeking a more anxious piety and generating unacknowledged anger.[21] Mainstream Protestantism, however, shared the directions of emotional culture, supporting the combination of control and intensity.

Emotional intensity derived also, however, from the very process of weaning from traditional Protestant doctrine. Many middle-class Americans questioned their own religious commitment, aware that the theology of their forebears was being watered down; some, no doubt, simply became less religiously active given the growing hold of science and the bustle of the urban, industrial world. Thus emotional intensity could be sought as an equivalent to a religious experience that many Americans realized was slipping away. Motherlove, as Jan Lewis has pointed out, took on Christlike overtones: it was consuming, it expressed itself in self-sacrifice, it served as a beacon through life even when mother herself had passed from the scene. Indeed, many popular stories about male redemption featured an errant son, rescued from wicked ways by the inspiration of his mother's love, returning to find his mother dead and vowing to devote his recovered purity to her memory; only the crucifix was missing. Ideals of romantic love picked up the same theme: in intense, spiritualized passion, couples hoped to find some of the same balm to the soul that religion had once, as they dimly perceived, provided. A few worried that their love contradicted the primacy of faith in God, but more concluded that true love was itself a religious experience. Byron Caldwell Smith put it this way in letters to his Katherine in the mid-1870s: "I feel somehow that the Holy power which sustains and moves the ancient universe . . . reveals itself to me as love. . . . To love you . . . and to sink my life in the Divine life through you, seem to me the supreme end of my existence. . . . Love is a cult and our love shall be our religion. . . . To each other we shall reveal only the divine attributes of tenderness and patience." Karen Lystra has plausibly suggested that many young men, apathetic toward conventional religion, imbibed the commitment to intense love as a direct surrogate during the second half of the nineteenth century. And the words they used in love letters, soaring beyond the more cautious romantic spirituality of the advice manuals, point precisely in this direction. But men were not alone in this regard, despite women's greater religiosity. Angelina Grimke worried about love and religion in her letters to Theodore Weld: "Am I putting *thee* in the place of Jesus? I am alarmed and confounded by my feelings. . . . I feel at times as if I cannot live without thee. . . . Am I sinning or would the Lord our Father have it so?" She answered in the affirmative, arguing that "our Father has enjoined us together, he has given us to each other" as both she and Theodore convinced themselves that their love was effectively a religious duty. Angelina again: "True love . . . is the seeking of the spirit after spiritual communion, . . . the union of *heart* and *mind* and *soul*."[22]

Victorian emotional culture stemmed in part, then, from an unusual moment in middle-class religion, when effective doctrinal changes created an environment in which God could be seen as supporting positive emotions but also in which many individuals came to regard intense, earthly love as a spiritual experience in itself as they made a transition away from more conventional religious commitments. Other cultural currents, notably social Darwinism, also supported the dominant emotionology after it had been established, providing it some new vocabulary and a scientific aura; but the link with religious adjustments remained more crucial.

The causes of Victorian emotional style were thus varied, which is no surprise. Despite the temptation to seek a single main ingredient in a functionalist interpretation of emotionological change, historical reality suggests that a larger emotional culture requires a number of overlapping factors for its genesis and dissemination. The Victorian style built clearly on prior cultural change, combining a host of specific factors, such as the new need for greater sexual abstinence in the interest of birth control, that impelled particular emotional formulations as part of the larger framework. It adapted emotional trends to the apparent needs of an industrial work environment and the tensions of social class relations in the growing cities. But it also incorporated important cultural shifts, including a new and puzzling distance between emotion and the body and two kinds of religious imperative that reflected a distinctive combination of confidence and concern. No one of these ingredients suffices to explain the Victorian mixture. Correspondingly, as we will see, when this skein began to unravel, the process responded to changes in most of the supporting elements as both social and cultural functions shifted ground.

Impacts: The Public Sphere

Describing an emotional culture offers the challenge of identifying common elements in discussions of particular emotions and in varied kinds of popular media. Explaining how this culture arose and what needs it seems to have filled forms the next step in analysis, challenging in its own right. These first two steps are meaningless, however, unless a third can be completed as well: indicating that the emotional culture had genuine resonance, affecting the way people believed and behaved.

Victorian emotionology had impact. This is certain despite the impossibility of ever demonstrating with full precision exactly how many people merely mouthed certain beliefs or exactly how they carried belief into action. More middle-class parents continued deliberately to use fear in childrearing than Victorian standards recommended, but a growing number accepted these standards at least in part, either changing disciplinary behavior or regretting anachronistic impulses or both; but how many fell into which camp cannot be determined. We do not know how many young, middle-class men actually experienced the transcendence of Victorian love or how many sustained the passion after marriage (when even the prescriptive literature suggested some lapse from perfection).[23] Yet without claiming exactitude, it is possible to demonstrate impact. Victorian emotional culture, distinctive in itself, helped shape a distinctive emotional reality.

The best means of sorting through the impact of an emotional culture is to proceed through three layers, the first of which is, frankly, the easiest. If an emotional culture does not affect public arrangements, then it is scarcely worth talking about. People responsible for translating emotional standards into laws and organized activities inevitably reflect the values preached around them, whether they internalize these values in their own emotional lives or not. The fact that this first impact is obvious—public culture and organizational behavior inevitably coincide to a degree—should not obscure its importance. Victorian experience was shaped in significant ways by changes that responded to or reflected the new emotional values. Even if no private echoes of these values could be found—which is not the case—the salience of Victorian emotionology for "real life" would be amply demonstrated—along with, admittedly, a strong dose of hypocrisy. As will be shown, the first layer of cultural impact, at the level of institutional response, displays clearly the Victorian impulse not simply toward repression of undesirable emotional impulses but also toward the promotion of essential intensity.

In 1904 Andrew Carnegie set up a trust for the Carnegie Hero Fund to provide moneys for people who had been injured performing heroic acts, or for survivors of people killed in such acts:

We live in a heroic age. Not seldom are we thrilled by deeds of heroism where men or women are injured or lose their lives in attempting to preserve or rescue their fellows; such the heroes of civilization. The heroes of barbarism maimed or killed theirs.[24]

Carnegie's fund followed on a common newspaper genre that had developed by the 1890s, featuring stories of ordinary people who, as one journalist put it, "were suddenly confronted with the question of whether or not they would risk death to save the lives of others" and describing "the manner in which they met, without preparation or forethought, that supreme moment." Feature stories and the special fund for heroes obviously institutionalized Victorian concepts of facing and conquering fear. They institutionalized the stuff of boys' stories, emphasizing the ability to experience intense emotion and channel it toward socially useful ends. They highlighted the importance of spontaneity and impulse against any Victorian temptation to stodgy caution. The purity of the emotional experience was primary.[25]

The Carnegie Fund was not a transformative organization in America, though thanks to the wonders of capitalist investment it survives to this day. But along with the public expressions of belief in courageous mastery of fear written into boy scout literature, newspaper stories, and other genres, the fund did concretely express the extent to which Victorian emotional values could be translated into action. Some Victorians, clearly, were willing to put money where their emotional commitments lay.

Victorian emotionology translated abundantly into sports. There are all sorts of reasons for the rise of sports in the nineteenth-century United States, but among them, and particularly important in the distinctively American enthusiasm for introducing sports into school programs and other sites of youth socialization, was the profound belief that sports helped translate emotional goals into the character-building process. Sports like football or boxing in particular gave young men an opportunity to retain the spark of anger but direct it to particular, appropriate targets; and the same sports offered opportunities for the conquest of fear. The prescriptive literature of the late nineteenth century made abundant connections between sports interests and proper training in handling the dangerous emotions, and sports advocates did the same in touting boxing lessons for middle-class boys or high school football teams. While sports were meant to civilize working-class boys, whose aggressiveness needed restraint, they were no less important in preventing middle-class feminization. Women's sports, correspondingly, were recommended more ambivalently and for more exclusively physical benefits—the relevant emotional lessons were missing.[26]

Changes in the law explicitly echoed the Victorian shifts in emotional culture. The incorporation of jealous rage into a crime-of-passion defense in selected murder trials has already been noted. By the 1890s, however, most states were rejecting the idea of passion-induced insanity, denouncing it, as in the case of the North Carolina Supreme Court, as an encouragement to lawlessness and bloodshed. However, juries, particularly in the South, maintained the tradition, and some states like Texas passed justifiable homicide statutes confirming the right to kill for jealousy when a husband discovered the act of adultery, "provided the killing takes place before the parties to the act have separated."[27] (The assumption of accuracy in shooting, so that the wife might be spared, was a tribute to the Texan spirit.) Southern culture, then, refused to resolve this tension between restraint and passion.[28]

Penology reflected the growing hostility to anger-based vengeance in a number of respects. The decline of corporal punishment and its confinement to private rather than public places mirrored growing embarrassment at vengeful motives. The rise of the prison movement and experiments with presumably guilt-inducing isolation provided an emotional basis for treating criminals. Obviously, a host of other motives went into the shift in punishment, and the hopes pinned to incarceration were soon muddied by the realities of prison life and the impurity of social motives. But an emotional shift against shame and tainted anger and toward the role of guilt in rehabilitation continued to find some expression. Later nineteenth-century movements that acknowledged appropriate anger against criminals, as in vigilante movements, reflected the complexities of the middle-class outlook, which had never entirely converted to early Victorian promptings about human innocence, but they also reflected the new acceptance of the idea of channeling anger toward the service of justice.[29]

Love also met the law, contributing to the evolution of divorce provisions and breach-of-promise suits. From the mid—nineteenth century onward, American law increasingly acknowledged a version of torts targeted at alienation of affections.[30] Such a suit could be directed against an individual who purposefully alienated the affections of another's spouse. The suits obviously expressed proprietary attitudes toward marriage (male and female alike), but they also emphasized the mental anguish caused by loss of a spouse's or a fiancé's love. There was no particular reference to material inconvenience, unlike earlier suits against enticement; the focus was on love and the pain of its disappearance. (Interestingly, this kind of action, common in American courts until the 1930s, did not develop in England despite the many similarities in other legal precedents.) Breach-of-promise actions, though less distinctively American, also increased in the later nineteenth century, based again on the enormity of love, even in courtship, and the bitter loss entailed in its disruption.

Divorce law recognized love through the back door of mental cruelty provisions.[31] Allowances for divorce in cases of physical cruelty developed only haltingly in various American states in the early nineteenth century; even proof of substantial bodily harm did not always suffice. Further, several courts ordered juries to ignore the question of whether a marriage had "that tenderness and affection which should characterize the matrimonial relation."[32] But the increasing emphasis on positive emotional bonds in marriage, along with beliefs in women's frailty such that even words could sting, gradually widened the mental cruelty concept from a landmark Pennsylvania decision in 1849 onward. Insults could cause as much suffering as bodily pain, for, as the Massachusetts Supreme Court put it in 1867, a "deeply wounded sensibility and wretchedness of mind can hardly fail to affect the health."[33] Even the need to claim damage to physical health gradually loosened, so that wounding the "mental feelings" of the other spouse might suffice, as in a path-breaking Kansas Supreme Court decision of 1883. This court connected this trend clearly to the new emotional ideals, noting that "the tendency of modern thought is to elevate the marriage relation and place it upon a higher plane, and to consider it as a mental and spiritual relation, as well as a physical relation."[34] A California court repeated this sentiment in 1890, adding that marriage must now be seen "as a union affecting the mental and spiritual life of the parties to it," exhibiting "mutual sentiments of love and respect."[35] Once launched, of course, the mental cruelty clause outstripped all competitors as grounds for divorce in states that allowed it, but its popularity testifies to its vagueness rather than to mass adhesion to Victorian love ideals. The point is the thinking that underlay the nineteenth-century court decisions: a good marriage now carried such positive emotional valence that cruelty could be found in mere withholding of affection.

Love of other sorts found institutional expressions that reveal what middle-class people actually thought, not just what public agencies decreed. The monetary value of children soared at the end of the nineteenth century, as expressed in the cost of insurance policies and adoption alike. Just as their economic utility was disappearing, belief in the emotional significance of children inflated their market worth.

Psychohistorians pointed out a decade ago that one obvious expression of Victorian emphasis on intense love, and delight in appropriate manifestations of deep feeling, was the introduction of the honeymoon as a ritual following middle-class marriage. The honeymoon was designed to allow a couple to explore mutual feelings as well as sexual interests, and ideally helped translate the emotional intensity of courtship into more permanent bonds. Here was a significant change in the de facto institution of marriage, fully in keeping with, and presumably supportive of, the Victorian valuation of love.[36]

Grief, finally, had its outlets as well. Death had rituals, inherited from the past, involving family and community participation in the act of dying whenever possible. Rituals after death more clearly changed in the nineteenth century to accommodate heightened emotion. Victorian funeral procedures, unlike those before or since, were intended both to remove the fear of death and to allow open expression of grief through ritual. Increasing use of cosmetics on corpses, and ultimately the rise of professional undertakers and embalmers who took over the handling of death from bereaved families, expressed mainly the desire to allay fear and to direct emotions away from decaying flesh to the bittersweet grief at a loved one's loss. The practice of wearing mourning clothing spread. Funerals became more elaborate, cemeteries and tombstones more ornate and evocative. Scholars have legitimately argued over whether the paraphernalia of middle-class Victorian funerals expressed simply growing wealth and status rivalry, or real grief, and the sensible conclusion has been that both were involved.[37] Families really did need rituals that would allow them to show their grief. Where child death was involved, funeral monuments of unprecedented size combined with haunting epitaphs to convey the sorrow and love that sent the child to heaven. Gravestone euphemisms about death as sleep, or as going home, expressed the grief-induced need to see death as something less than final.[38]

Love, anger, grief, fear, jealousy, and, somewhat ambivalently, guilt— all had repercussions in public arrangements designed to express intensity as well as regulate its targets. Law and leisure, not to mention burial arrangements or penology, were significantly altered as a result of emotional values, as jurists, school authorities, and other officials faithfully acted under the guidelines of Victorian emotionology. Public expression of the new emotional culture peaked between about 1870 and 1910, suggesting a not surprising lag between the first expression of the culture and its capacity a generation later to affect major institutions.

Private Beliefs and Emotional Experience

That Victorian leaders liked to claim adherence to new emotional standards is no surprise. The new policies that resulted were significant, but they beg basic questions about the extent of real belief. Did Victorians internalize the new standards—not uniformly or completely, to be sure, but sufficiently to make a difference in their own emotional lives?

The answer is yes, though again there can be no claim of precise measurement. Many Victorians clearly enjoyed the possibility of analyzing their emotional state, though there is evidence as well that the demanding rules of the culture made this process more than a bit bewildering. Henry Adams described a woman's process in his 1880 novel, *Democracy:*

Madeleine dissected her own feelings and was always wondering whether they were real or not; she had a habit of taking off her mental clothing, as she might take off a dress, and looking at it as though it belonged to someone else, and as though sensations were manufactured like clothes.[39]

While women were most vocal about their emotional inventories, men too, as we will see, frequently offered comments, particularly in the throes of love or highly charged friendship. The evaluation process reflected the importance of the emotional culture in many private lives.

Several historians have already developed a convincing case concerning the internalization of restrictions on anger on the part of some middle-class women. Barred from expressing their real emotions, or even admitting unladylike sentiments to themselves, some women converted anger into psychosomatic illness, with such manifestations as hysterical paralysis. Intense familial love could have its pathological side as well. Smothered by parental affection that they could neither deny nor fail to reciprocate, some girls began to develop anorexia nervosa as a means out of the emotional trap. Here, Victorian standards showed their repressive edge and their reality, however distorted, in the experience of a minority of middle-class women.[40]

Certainly there is widespread evidence of women's concern about living up to the emotional ideal by working sedulously against impulses of anger or jealousy. Lucilla McCorkle, a southern minister's wife, urged the following duties on herself in her private journal: "Self-denial—in food & clothing & keeping the *tongue.* early [sic] rising—industry—economy system—cheerfulness & sobriety—keeping down & quelling the spirit of malevolence, fault finding—covetousness or rather jealousy," adding that she feared she suffered from "that *disease.*" Many women recalled specific attempts to keep anger under control when they were girls: "As I grew up I learned to keep intact a second self . . . who walked in tranquil beauty . . . [who] maintained her place unruffled when the other self was annoyed, dismayed." Elizabeth Parsons Channing noted in a diary entry in 1874: "Irritable. Ashamed of myself when I am so alive to the desirableness of a sweet temper." Or Lydia Sigourney, anxious about feeling unpleasant the day before: "I'll try to carry a sunbeam in my heart today." Many women claimed in private diaries to feel no anger against their spouses, though some would single out a particular issue—such as policies toward slaves—that allowed some indignation to be expressed. Many reported both the goal of repressing anger and the real difficulties encountered en route, including the complication of guilt when anger was discerned, even privately. As Charlotte Gilman put it: "The task of self-government was not easy. To repress a harsh answer, to confess a fault, and to stop (right or wrong) in the midst of self-defence, in gentle submission, sometimes requires a struggle like life and death." Many women reported, in sum, a temperament hardly as magically anger free as some advice writers ascribed to femininity, but a very definite effort in that direction. A few even reported gleeful triumphs in which errant husbands were cast down through their own unjustified rage while the wife stood calmly by. As Mrs. Abigail Bailey put it in her memoirs, "I felt obligated to bear my faithful testimony to him against his wickedness; which I repeatedly did." Here of course was the suggestion of very real anger, but carefully manipulated both to fit the Victorian norms and to use those very norms to confound the offending spouse.[41]

Women continued to work toward appropriate anger control throughout the nineteenth century. Winifred Babcock, admitting fury when her boyfriend dumped her, quickly returned to the party line in her memoirs: "But rage! What has it ever done to heal even the slightest hurt or wound. Oh I could tramp up and down . . . and wring my hands . . . but alas! would that bring me any comfort?" Adults, particularly men, increasingly applied teasing to anger in young girls, who registered the idea that they were being laughed at. While this suggests a slight loosening of the strictest rules concerning girls and anger consistent with a generally more permissive approach in end-of-the-century childrearing, girls nonetheless learned that grownup dignity and displays of temper were incompatible. A middle-class Pittsburgh girl's memoir notes admiration at an oath by a peer—"Oh, the dickens"—while quickly adding that "since even the mildest oaths were discouraged at home, I never dared to use such a vigorous expletive." And there were mothers who managed to provide role models of apparently complete mastery over temper. Whatever the realities of the case, their daughters could discern no chink in mother's emotional perfection, and under her tutelage they also learned not to quarrel with any frequency or bitterness. Mother was simply never angry.[42]

Whether blessed with sunny dispositions or not, Victorian women showed other signs of contact with the goals of controlling the dangerous emotions. Vocal concern about dealings with servants was a staple of nineteenth-century domestic life. Among other things, these concerns expressed a very real anxiety that it was impossible in practice to preserve the calm demeanor that the emotional culture required. Many servants were simply too trying, too willing to resort to anger in confrontations with their mistresses. The domestic side of Victorian emotionology urged "equable and cheerful temper and tones in the housekeeper" as part of the larger atmosphere that should inform family life. Servants were vital to this atmosphere but were often criticized for improper emotional signals to the children in their charge. In fact, many housewives found it difficult to "refrain from angry tones" in dealing with servants, and their resultant guilt often worsened the atmosphere still further. Inability to live up to stated goals contributed to the tension in the mistress-servant relationship throughout the century, and to the decline of live-in service toward the century's end.[43]

Finally, girls imbibed the messages about restraint of anger well into the early twentieth century. Even if they displayed a temper later as adults, they concealed it in childhood, in contrast to boys, whose adult personality was in this regard much easier to discern.[44]

On the repressive side, in sum, many women were deeply affected by the Victorian norms, fighting for control when the standards proved difficult, often conveying considerable success, sometimes suffering psychosomatic ailments because of the strain involved.

In actuality as in culture, however, repression was not the whole story. Men and women alike expressed deep commitment to the ideals of intensity in love and grief. They spoke about their fervor, wrote of it in letters, and gave it a prominent place in many diaries.

Expressions of love could start early. A child's letter from 1899:

My dearest Mother,
Words cannot express how I miss you.
[then some chitchat]
(I love you with all my heart with all my soul and all my body.)
[more chitchat]
Your most devoted daughter,
    Sweetest Mother,

And from a recollection years later: "We all loved Mother with all our hearts, with all our souls and with all our bodies, and when she went away we missed her more than tongue could tell. In later years, she said that she was afraid she had let us love her too much, that she sometimes thought we had put her in place of God. If we did, we might easily have had a less worthy idea of God."[45]

Mothers could respond in kind. Although women's magazines late in the nineteenth century began trumpeting a crisis between mothers and daughters, in which the former could no longer approve of the lifestyle changes of youth and/or the latter had lost the affectionate respect due their elders, actual middle-class mothers and daughters shared a deep emotional bond, with apparently few exceptions. When their daughters left for work or college, their mothers wrote them with ardent support, visited often, and in some instances actually stayed with them for a time. Disputes occurred, to be sure, but they were usually surrounded with reassuring love. As one wrote, "Your life must not be stunted by us [the parents]. . . . Our love can make any leaps of time and distance."[46] Reciprocating, even the "new" young women who were building careers referred to their mothers as "the anchor" of their lives. Both the depth of this feeling and the willingness to express it in ardent terms reflected real correspondence with the emotional culture of child- and mother-love, even at a time when middle-class women's lives were changing noticeably.

The love theme pervaded courtship, again leading to expressions, from men as well as women, fully in keeping with the most soaring versions of Victorian culture. Byron Caldwell Smith, pressing Katherine Stephens in letters between 1874 and 1876, urged, "Oh write, write I am perishing to see on paper the words—I love you." Describing the "great passion that fills me," his "great life-passion," he distinguished his love from mere romance, assuring her of "true" love and constancy. "It [true love] is to love with all one's soul what is pure, what is high, what is eternal." "A tender true heart that loves unselfishly, and seeks and understands a love which is not the mere surprise of the senses . . . but why should I go on to describe what I love to her I love." And of course the religious connection was ever present: "I feel somehow that the Holy power which sustains and moves the ancient universe . . . reveals itself to me as love." "To love you . . . and to sink my life in the Divine life through you, seem to me the supreme end of my existence." Women could respond in kind, as Angelina Grimke did to Theodore Weld: "Yes my heart continuously *cleaves* to you, deep of my nature is moved to meet the reaching agonies of your soul after me." "Why does not the love of my own dear sister . . . satisfy. . . . Why do I feel in my inmost soul that you, you only, can fill up the deep void that is there?" And Theodore answered flight with flight: "How many times have I felt my heart . . . reaching out in every agony after you and *cleaving* to you, feeling that we are no more twain but one flesh."[47]

From at least the 1830s until 1900 thousands of middle-class couples, during their courtship years and sometimes afterward when separation necessitated letter writing, tried to describe the deep, spiritual love that filled them. The themes were almost commonplace. Granting of course that the letters still available today may not be fully representative of courtship sentiments, studies of middle-class youth reveal a virtually unquestioned assumption that intense, spiritual love would be the basis for engagement and marriage. Autobiographies and other commentaries echo these sentiments, while the Mosher survey, addressing upper-middle-class women at the end of the century, reveals similar, if somewhat less ethereal, beliefs in the centrality of abiding love in marriage.[48] A central tenet of Victorian emotional culture, in sum, corresponded to the real emotional aspirations of much of the middle class and to the felt experience of a sizeable number within it. Childhood experience (including deep love for siblings as well as for mothers), encounters with the standards of love through fiction and advice books, and the promptings of religious feeling and sexual deferment all combined to create this relationship between belief and reality.

Furthermore, the quest for deep emotional fulfillment in love also spilled over into friendship and many lifelong relations among sisters. The searing language used in letters between women friends has been frequently noted as a Victorian characteristic; it obviously transferred into friendship much of the intensity with which the culture surrounded love in general. "Dear darling Sarah! How I love you and how happy I have been! You are the joy of my life. . . . I cannot tell you how much happiness you gave me, nor how constantly it is all in my thoughts. . . . My darling how I long for the time when I shall see you." Marriage did not necessarily interrupt these outpourings, in some cases, no doubt, because the emotional expectations brought to wedlock were not fulfilled. References to kissing, eternal love, and devotion pepper the letters of women to each other. "I wanted so to put my arms round my girl of all the girls in the world and tell her . . . I love her as wives do love their husbands, as *friends* who have taken each other for life—and I believe in her as I believe in my God." Religiouslike qualities helped women identify their emotions, as Mary Grew wrote: "Love is spiritual, only passion is sexual."[49]

Young men developed similar passions in the period of life during their early twenties when they had separated from parents but were not yet positioned to launch courtship. In letters and journals they described themselves as "fervent lovers" and wrote of their "deep and burning affection." Like the women, they commented on their physical contacts with each other and dreamed of a life of mutual intimacy. When the time came to separate, usually when one friend married, the emotionality of friendship came to the surface again: "[O]ur hearts were full of that true friendship which could not find utterance by words, we laid our heads upon each other's bosom and wept, it may be unmanly to weep, but I care not, the spirit was touched."[50]

Male intimacy almost always ended with marriage, and most men, even in their passionate youth, knew that this would be so. Women, in contrast, might preserve the passion or might use it to generate intense resentment against the marital threat. Thus in a letter of congratulation to a newly wed couple, one friend addressed the husband: "Do you know sir, that until you came along I believe that she loved me almost as girls love their lovers. *I know I loved her so.* Don't you wonder that I can stand the sight of you?" Here, real experience not only gave substance to the fervent love preached by Victorian culture but also to the common theme of separation emotions that sustained so many short stories dealing with sisters or friends adjusting to the marriage of one of their number.[51]

As with love in its principal forms, so, logically enough, with grief: the Victorians who expressed themselves in letters, diaries, and often in ritual commonly expected, articulated, and felt the sharpness that grief was supposed to generate.[52] The intensity resulted above all from the attachments of love, but it was heightened by emotionological approval of grief itself, such that its presence was expected, its absence a potential occasion for guilt. Grief applied most poignantly to death but also to departures and other separations. Nellie Wetherbee recorded in her diary as she left her family to head west, "I only cried as the steamer sailed away—bitter, bitter tears." The death of children produced almost overwhelming emotion, as an 1897 diary reported: "Jacob is dead. Tears blind my eyes as I write . . . now he is at rest, my little darling Jacob. Hope to meet you in heaven. God help me to bear my sorrow." Here, clearly, not only the pain of grief but also the conscious handling of grief with references to reunion and divine support reflect the currency of the larger Victorian culture. Men as well as women expressed their sorrow. A Civil War soldier leaves his family in 1863, crying for days before the final departure, then musing in his diary both on his great love and on the "cruelty" of the separation. A minister, coincidentally in the same year, asks Jesus to "support me under this crushing blow"—his brother's death. Another man, recording in 1845 the death of a brother-in-law, ended his entry: "Oh! What sorrow burst in upon us at the melancholy news of his death. . . . All is sorrow and weeping." Even nostalgic recollection brought grief, as when Sarah Huntington recalled a loss of two years earlier: "Reading these letters revived all the exclusiveness and intenseness of my love for him I once called husband."[53]

Some facets of grief varied, to be sure. Different personalities responded differently to death. Death could still call up diary entries dwelling on the transience of life and the uncertainties of God's judgment. Some diaries report that intense grief followed death for a month or so, then tapered off; others record a fresh renewal of grief well over a year after a death or separation. In the main, however, the obligation to record grief and the felt intensity of grief as a direct reaction to love rather than to fears of death reflected real-life experiences of the culture's emotional standards. Deep loss, hopes for reunion in the afterlife, bittersweet recollections of the ongoing love—all were commonplace in the private reportage.

Of course grief intensities also varied with the level of acquaintance and the kind of death. Deaths that were lingering, providing the chance to prepare, sometimes caused less grief than sudden departures; the concept of a "good death" may have cushioned grief in the former instances. Where sheer pain dominated, as in the unexpected death of a child, the bittersweet theme might be absent entirely. But efforts to see beauty in death, to emphasize the sharing of grief by friends as well as the consolation of a better life in heaven, expressed some of the qualities urged in the more general commentary on this emotion. Christian resignation entered into the formula, along with frequent references to the "happier world" beyond and the beauty of the dead body (a clearly Victorian theme expressed for example in death kits for children's dolls), but so did hopes for reunion—a child "spends this Sunday in Heaven with all her departed relatives," wrote a Schenectady Protestant—and a sense of propriety in the love shared, through grief, in the family circle and beyond.[54]

Prescriptions against unacceptable expressions of dangerous emotions, particularly by women, were thus matched by even more open references to fervent love and grief. The final ingredient of the Victorian amalgam, successful channeling of fear and anger, received less frequent comment, but here too there was real experience.

Courage and controlled anger showed most openly in what Anthony Rotundo has called Victorian middle-class boy culture. Groups of boys, fiercely independent of their mothers, developed a host of games to test aggressiveness and courage. They teamed up to throw stones at each other. They developed hazing rituals to test their ability to withstand fear—a habit that was institutionalized by the 1830s in male fraternities and lodges, where hazing challenges were extended into young adulthood.[55] These activities and the emotional values that underlay them contrasted magnificently with the maternally dominated domestic sphere, which was precisely their purpose. Yet they also corresponded, in tenor if not in cruel specifics, to the advice being offered about male ability to use and channel dangerous emotions. A game of "soak-about" involved boys hitting one of their number in a vulnerable spot with a hard ball—a test of the ability to endure fear and pain. "Dares" were endemic—"the deeper the water, the thinner the ice, the longer the run, the hotter the blaze, the more certain [was] the challenge." Again, Victorian courage found a daily puerile expression. The taunts of "crybaby" and "sissy" awaited any who could not pass the tests. Anger was tested as well, as boys preferred to settle "a personal grievance at once, even if the explanation is made with fists." And while cultural pundits clucked about boys' wildness, they, too, approved of hearty play that would assure, as "Mrs. Manners" put it, that no male child turned into a "girl-boy."[56] This boy culture began to be curtailed somewhat by the 1880s, as length of schooling extended and new, adult-run institutions like scouting introduced more supervision and regulation into boys' lives. But even these institutions, as we have seen, maintained an emotionology that valued and tested courage in the face of fear and the ability to summon up channeled anger. The culture had real impact on the ways Victorian boys lived.

Adult men manifested their adherence to the dominant emotionology as well. Men may have been fearful in the face of business innovations and intense competition, as one author has recently argued, but the commitment to express courageous joy in facing down the odds was high. This was one reason why many businessmen and professional people were open to the doctrines of social Darwinism, which provided a scientific basis for the values of male conquest of fear or of anger-fueled rivalry. Middle-class soldiers in the Civil War, like Oliver Wendell Holmes, delighted, as we have seen, in writing about their reactions to battle in terms of heroic boys' stories, expressing wonder at their coolness under fire. Adherence to the ideal of channeled anger showed in at least two settings. Male politicians and reformers routinely used angry invective and anger-inspired moral fervor in debate, with no sense of inappropriateness or need for subsequent apology. They, like the larger culture, shared the view that anger in a just cause was useful; calm, rational presentations would not alone suffice. Businessmen showed their anger too. A foreman angrily replied to complaining workers in Chicago, "Quit if you want to. You are welcome to quit." Worker protest brought anger into the open, with employers frequently "raging like tigers," as one employee put it around 1900.[57]

Documentation of male commitment to utilizing the dangerous emotions is hardly voluminous, and of course, quite apart from the question of individuals' adherence to cultural standards, personalities varied. References to fear and justifiable anger were frequent, however, suggesting genuine correspondence between the dominant emotionology and the ways in which many men perceived their own emotional responses. Not surprisingly, the same atmosphere produced frequent real-life conflicts between emotional standards at work and those desired at home. Many a man, like the harassed coal company manager described in a Pittsburgh memoir, came home irritable, repairing to his library (and its bottles) in silence—not living up fully to the domestic ideals so much as carving out a certain solitude in their midst. Precisely because the dangerous emotions were tried at work, the cultural tension applied to manhood in principle could prove difficult in the daily experience.[58]

Emotional reality is a complex entity, and its historical documentation is maddeningly elusive. In contrast to the institutional expressions of emotional culture, personal experience admits of tentative generalizations at best. Available diaries and letters provide strong evidence that the standards for intense love and grief were internalized, but obviously most people's emotions, even within the middle class, went unrecorded. Whether the experience of love, guilt, or grief (or, for men, anger or courage) differed from experiences in the past cannot be decisively determined. Individuals' descriptions of experience did change, but emotions are more than verbal reports. They also involve behaviors and physiological changes, and the latter, in particular, do not permit historical measurement.[59] Furthermore, individual variation around norms is impossible to track. We know, in contemporary society, that some individuals are more anger prone than others, and experiments show that anger-prone people respond differently to the same stimuli. Such personality variation surely occurred in the past as well. Nevertheless, cultural norms may affect the available range of personality types, as well as the way individuals present their personalities. Norms clearly affect the verbal presentation and self-evaluation aspects of emotional experience, even if other reaches remain unclear.

Thus, Victorian emotional culture did shape real emotional life, though it did not describe it perfectly or completely. The way people loved or grieved or encountered fear was defined in part by what they were taught; and to an extent, both emotional experience and emotionology were shaped by the same functional and broader cultural factors. Exactly how much the distinctiveness of the culture is reflected in a similar experiential distinctiveness is not clear. Basic physiology, personality variations, or even the time lag between the generation of new standards and widespread assimilation may have limited the cultural hold on emotional reality. A tension between lived emotional experience and beliefs is a common aspect of emotional life, which means that the beliefs are important but not always determinant; and this was surely as true in relation to the demanding standards of the Victorian decades as it is in a rather different emotional culture today. Nevertheless, from illnesses encouraged by emotional constraints to expectations formed in search of love, the Victorian encounter with intensity expanded beyond the covers of the advice books and popular romances. Many people lived the culture in substantial measure.

Emotional Interactions

A third area in which reality and perception intertwined also reflected Victorian emotionology. In addition to its impact on public institutions and individual experience, emotional culture also colored the way middle-class people reacted to the emotions of others. This final realm is just being opened up in sociology and social psychology, as researchers turn from a preoccupation with the emotional impulses of individuals to an inquiry into broader emotional functions. In this new view, emotions are primarily designed to affect relationships, and thus they must be tested not only in terms of the signals an individual sends or wishes to send but also in terms of the likely responses. Grief, for example, though perhaps initially designed as a way of restoring the lost loved one, ultimately serves the function of encouraging emotional support from others to ease the griever through the loss; it builds compensatory relationships. Yet this purpose is served only if the relevant others accept the grief signal. For Victorian emotionology this raises a question: Were people ready to accept the intensities of others, even as they wrote certain intensities into sports programs or sought to describe their own emotional lives in culturally appropriate terms?

Here, too, the answer is affirmative, though a host of research opportunities remain. Victorians clearly expected to deal with intense emotional expressions from other people so long as the settings were appropriate—just as they expected suitable restraint, as part of proper etiquette, in other settings. Public reactions to the crime-of-passion trials, for example, suggested a widespread belief by both genders that extreme jealousy was a valid emotional response in certain equally extreme instances, even when accompanied by violence. The defendants who won their pleas received considerable outpourings of popular support at the close of trials and in subsequent letters. On a more ordinary basis, despite cultural disapproval of jealousy, many Victorians seem to have accepted jealous responses from a suitor or partner and to have been willing to adjust behavior accordingly. Thus husbands were urged not, in their wives' presence, to "enthusiastically praise the sterling qualities of other women," while wives should not "invidiously eulogize the seemingly incomparable character of other men." Men often concealed behavior that might cause jealousy—which was an indirect recognition of its potential intensity—while wives were urged to do the same. Love letters, while sometimes attempting to assure that possessiveness did not taint the spiritual qualities desired, sometimes also admitted jealousy at least circuitously. "Do not think I assume the right to control your actions; but I love you too fondly to share our smiles with another."[60] And the appropriate reaction from a lover was adjustment, with promises not to give reason for jealousy in the future. Response here was complex, for jealousy was not to be accorded too much status. Yet there was little attempt in practice to deny the emotion's validity (except by some of the experimenters in utopian communities). While jealousy could be acknowledged, this was not an emotion to be flaunted.

Responses to emotion changed demonstrably in certain instances. During the eighteenth century upper-class southern men had professed considerable indifference to women's anxieties about childbirth. After 1800, however, they changed their tune, admitting real validity to women's fears, sharing some of their anxieties, and even cooperating in reducing conceptions in order to limit the risks. There were many reasons for this behavior, including of course the increasing belief in female frailty, which made admission of fear and weakness seem more appropriate. But enhanced emotional attachment and even anticipated grief joined in as men empathized more fully with women in this area in part because of their own awareness of potential emotional loss. Emotional reaction to expressions of concern thus changed far more than did the women's fears that evoked it.[61]

Expectations toward guilt also changed. As we have seen, the standard use of guilt in childrearing involved isolating the offender from the family network until guilt had done its work and could be suitably expressed in sincere apology. Then the incident could be officially forgotten and relationships restored. Parents taught, then, that indications of guilt were vital cues in preserving or recovering social contacts, and these lessons were carried into later life. Functional guilt surely operated in the eighteenth century as well, but a greater reliance on shame produced different expectations, as community disapproval might be meted out in any event. Again, responses to intense expression shifted.[62]

Intense expressions of love were obviously regarded as acceptable by many of their recipients. This process may well have begun in childhood as boys and girls learned the normalcy of fervent maternal affection. Certainly love letters suggest scant hesitation to express soulful depths. The only apparent concerns about expression of love were the fears that passion might not be reciprocated or that it might somehow complicate appropriate religious duties. No evidence suggests that lovers attempted to defuse the intensities of their partners, and even rejections of affection treated the emotion itself, if not its particular target, as appropriately fervent.

Nor did most same-sex friends hesitate to receive expressions of passion from their partners. Most exchanges seem to have involved mutual expressions of deep emotion with no warnings against excess. Expressions of friendly love were naturally more muted when there was uncertainty about whether the love was reciprocated, or in the rare case when parties worried that their fervor might be misconstrued as sexual. A breakup of a friendship might also occasion disparities between the continued passion of one friend and the new indifference of the other, as on the occasion of a marriage. But even in these cases the appropriateness of passion itself was not questioned; it was simply less welcome due to altered circumstances. Because most male friendships dissolved on marriage, men rarely questioned expressions of intensity: these were fine while the friendship thrived, and they stopped when it was over. Only in the case of some women friends, particularly when one partner married, was there any significant implication that the suitability of emotional fervor was at all in doubt. Thus, Mary Hallock Foote wrote her friend: "Imagine yourself kissed a dozen times my darling. Perhaps it is well for you that we are far apart. You might find my thanks so expressed rather overpowering." And later: "You know dear Helena, I really was in love with you. It was a passion such as I had never known until I saw you. I don't think it was the noblest way to love you."[63] Some of these hesitations may have related to sexual desires or manifestations, complications that cropped up in expressions of heterosexual love as well; but some may have captured an otherwise unusual doubt about intensity itself, as it would be perceived by the other or might be judged by outsiders.

Many other settings, besides those involving love, showed acceptance of deep emotion. Boys obviously expected channeled anger from others and expected to see others react to, and conquer, fear. Their derision was reserved for those who shunned intensity, not for those who revealed it.

Grief was also accepted. Its function of building supporting relationships to cushion loss seem normally to have worked. Many adults drew close on the death of a child as they accepted each other's grief and the terms in which it could be consoled. Grieving diarists commented on the "sympathy of friends" and the importance of shared ritual. Etiquette books emphasized appropriate rituals for expressing grief and channeling reactions to it, but they too acknowledged the validity of the emotion and the need of supportive friends and relatives to respond to it. Writers on manners deplored any disruptive potential in conversation, to be sure. A few, in this vein, urged that signs of mourning be ignored in dealings with mere acquaintances. This advice, particularly common in the first half of the century, recognized emotional intensity—"any allusion to the subject of his grief [is] very painful to him"—but recommended an aloof reaction. More common was the recommendation that good manners obliged people of good breeding to call on a bereaved family and then to take the cue from the family's own tone. If the family was attempting to put up a brave front, one should keep the conversation distracting; but "if they speak of their misfortune," one should "join them" by speaking well of the dead and showing active, saddened sympathy. Almost all manners authors felt compelled to address grief as a significant part of public interactions.

Of course, as in previous centuries, grief might go on too long in certain individual cases and require assistance from doctor or minister. But emphasis was placed on the enhancement to spiritual love that might be derived from emotional sharing, not on the dangers of excess. It is possible indeed that Victorian culture encouraged acknowledgment of grief over an unusually long span, as in the case of the father who noted long after the death of a child, "There are some wounds which are never healed—which break out afresh and trouble the afflicted heart. . . . I find but little abatement of that yearning and longing for his dear face."

References to grief in letters and diaries are notable for their open expressions of the intensity of grief, but they are equally as notable for their uniform assumption of emotional harmony as families and friends grouped to help each other articulate and cope with grief. Mourners frequently recorded the importance of family and community support. A father, grieving for a dead son, recalled the "substantial and visible tokens of sympathy from our numerous friends and neighbors." Along with religion, this support made grief endurable. "The sympathy of friends is valuable but vain is all that man can do if the love of God be wanting. . . . We feel confident that it is well with our dear boy and that our loss is his gain." The growing cultural response to grief, as well as individual acceptance of cultural norms, underlay what Philippe Ariès has termed a nineteenth-century transition from fear of death of self to fear of death of others.[64]

Sadness, in contrast, became perhaps more problematic than it had been before. A distaste for sadness had increased in the eighteenth century, at least as suggested in diaries, and by the nineteenth century this was enhanced by a masculine aversion to tears. The passive qualities of sadness, its lack of motivational intensity, may account for the decreased willingness to respond to this emotion. Against life's minor tribulations, a cheerful countenance and a willingness to take effective remedial action won the readiest response. Sadness, if it must exist, should be private and undemanding of others.[65]

The most elusive of the culturally sanctioned emotional intensities involved anger. Victorians hedged intense anger with cautions in any event: it should not apply to women, and even in men it should be directed only at justifiable targets. Quite apart from such complexities, the fact that expressions of anger normally arouse anger in response (except where pronounced social inferiority compels concealment) prevents any facile statements about response. Victorians by no means enjoyed being the targets of others' anger, even when they believed in principle that intense anger could serve good purposes. Thus factory owners, confronted with angry workers, could refer to "troublemakers" and "big mouths" as if the emotion behind protest formed part of the problem. Even here, however, there was no elaborate effort to argue that workers' anger showed bad character or personality deficiency. The arguments referred more to violation of hierarchy than to a rejection of anger. In settings of greater equality, angry exchanges might be perversely enjoyable. Japanese visitors to the U.S. Congress commented on the emotional ferocity of political attacks and their odd compatibility with subsequent cooperation. Even adult women, after 1860, might win public approval for expressions of angry outrage in a morally sanctioned cause like temperance.[66]

Revealingly, etiquette codes, which were far more inclined toward restraint than other prescriptive materials, themselves waffled on the issue of anger. The manners books stressed the importance of restraint and decorum as part of good breeding. No wanton anger could be indulged. At times this preoccupation with restraint went so far as to suggest that no occasion warranted a quarrel, that tranquillity made flight preferable to loss of control. Thus *The Mentor* warned, "To get angry with an inferior is degrading; with an equal, dangerous; with a superior, ridiculous." But most etiquette advice for men actually suggested that in certain circumstances anger might be displayed and therefore socially accepted. Thus inferiors should be treated calmly, but if they must be disciplined, anger might be added "sufficiently far to make the reprimand more severe." An angry attack from an inferior should be ignored, and if it came from one decidedly inferior, or from a woman, it should be handled by calling the police. But if anger stemmed from a near equal, or if it involved violence, or "when it places you in an awkward position in presence of equals," it could appropriately be acknowledged and answered in kind.[67] Anger remained dangerous. But if it issued from a social superior it might have to be swallowed. And if it occurred in a situation of some social equality, among men, it might legitimately open an angry exchange. Anger, in sum, did not automatically disqualify; it could be accepted by others either through submissiveness (the lot, the manners books implied, of many gentle women) or by inducing a quarrel, sometimes even a violent quarrel. In this latter case intensity could beget intensity in a process that both parties might find legitimate and (though this must be glimpsed between the lines of the manners books) perhaps even enjoyable—an emotional recollection of boyhood tests.

Victorians, in sum, were frequently willing not simply to express emotional fervor on their own but to receive it from others as well. In some respects their reactions differed from those of the eighteenth century, just as the emotional norms themselves had altered. Intense love was no problem so long as both parties shared the attraction. Grief, with its bittersweet pain, was meant to evoke sympathetic response, as of course were sincere signs of guilt. Only the milder, more cloying emotions, like sadness, may have evoked increasingly annoyed responses in nineteenth-century relationships. The dangerous emotions, like jealousy and, particularly, anger, though sometimes producing rejections or evasions, could themselves elicit active response; they did not automatically place the emoter on the defensive. Evidence about emotional response is, to be sure, sketchy, particularly when one moves beyond the emotions most involved in family relationships—love, grief, even jealousy. Yet there are indications that Victorians accepted the implications of their culture not only in their perceptions and expressions of their own emotions but also in many of their reactions to intensity in others.

Conclusion

Victorian emotionology was distinctive in many respects, and it produced behaviors that were distinctive as well. The tenor of address to lovers and friends, dotted with "My Beloveds" and "My Adoreds," rings odd to the modern ear. So does the idea of responding to anger with anger as part of proper etiquette (albeit severely hedged). Emotional paragons who could express deep love and persuade their children that they were never angry seem almost too good to be true—yet in the nineteenth century, some of these were thought to exist. Culture by no means perfectly described real emotional experience or responses to others, but some correspondence with professed values clearly existed. The causes of the culture itself affected actual emotional perceptions, and the culture, widely disseminated from childhood onward and essentially undisputed within the mainstream middle class, also helped mold these real emotional reactions. The same holds true for public institutions.

Thus the major themes of the culture—the effort to combine selective restraint with insistence on real intensity—threaded through emotional life itself. Friendships, love, uses and expectations of guilt, responses to anger, and responses to bereavement all showed the distinctive marks, even though our ability to gauge all the ingredients is limited. The intensity component of the culture affected self-perceptions and the responses anticipated from others, which is why it translated into lived experience.

Intensity is itself elusive. Because its mark on Victorian life was so important and because its hold was soon to be challenged, it deserves definition as well as repeated reference. Interestingly, contemporary emotions researchers have just begun attempts to define and measure emotional intensity. In one taxonomy of emotional fervor, several evaluation criteria have been proposed, including speed of emotional arousal, level of peak emotional experience, and duration. These criteria do not necessarily move in the same direction. Levels of intensity vary according to certain factors that, if stated very generally, apply to all imaginable societies and time periods, to wit: proximity of the individual or event that triggers emotion; nature and immediacy of the trigger; and social similarity of the individuals emotionally interacting, with greater perceived similarity heightening arousal, peak, and/or duration.[68]

Victorian culture and aspects of Victorian experience conduced to unusual emotional intensity as defined by several of these criteria, though of course Victorians did not address the subject in explicit fashion. The word "intenseness" does crop up, as we have seen, but with no scientific rigor attached. Emotional rules certainly encouraged high peaks and considerable duration where love or grief was concerned, early arousal and high peaks in cases of deserved guilt. Encounters with fear could involve arousal and peak intensities as well. Early arousal to anger was not recommended in this more complex of the Victorian intensities, but when the target warranted, peak and duration could both be extensive. Emphasis on the importance of family members and friends urged recognition of immediacy and proximity and of course generated a sense of social similarity even across gender lines, at least where love or grief was involved. There are, in sum, reasons to believe that a general map of emotional intensity highlights the ways in which Victorians promoted and accepted fervor. The special commitment to intensity is also explained by the causes underlying Victorian emotionology, including not only the need to cement family bonds in an uncertain environment but also the effort to find an equivalent for religious emotion and motivation.

Intensity, and resulting appraisals of one's own and others' emotional reactions, is a historical variable. All societies, of course, produce emotional experiences of varied intensity and personalities susceptible to varying emotional loads. Thus, although Victorian culture and many of its institutional and private manifestations facilitated emotional engagement, it did not make all middle-class people alike and indeed, it deliberately separated the genders according to the types of intensity available to each. It did not prompt uniformly intense reactions and explicitly discouraged certain kinds of emotions while recommending a number of careful controls. But even as Victorians accepted constraints in many aspects of life, they welcomed, even depended upon, emotional depth. From boyhood challenge to adult grief, they assumed strong passions.

4

From Vigor to Ventilation:
A New Approach to Negative Emotions

Beginning clearly in the 1920s, with hints a bit earlier, middle-class advice literature began to move away from the Victorian standards. Writers seemed sometimes aware of their innovation, sometimes oblivious, yet even in the latter case the change in tone became quite clear.

We deliberately move in this section to a synthesis of the major changes in American emotional standards, as they took shape from about 1920 to the 1950s, before turning to the essential task of explaining why the changes occurred—the theme of chapter 7. Obviously both types of analysis interrelate, but the nature of change must be identified before its causation can be assessed.

The basic direction of change will hardly come as a surprise, except insofar as we have come to think of twentieth-century Americans according to simplistic labels of emotional liberation. Amid a host of specific shifts and undoubted complexities, twentieth-century emotional culture moved away from approval of emotional intensity, even as standards in other areas, like costume and personal manners and sexuality, quite clearly loosened. Just as Victorians had, everything considered, been most tolerant of emotional fervor, so twentieth-century American culture became most repressive precisely in this area, relaxing greatly, by contrast, the standards for many forms of bodily expression.

This shift in emotional direction means that emotions already admitted as potentially dangerous in the Victorian lexicon now became completely unacceptable. Fear and anger had no positive function in the new schema; rather than being directed, they were to be avoided as fully as possible. The same shift meant that emotions previously regarded as good, like love, were now surrounded by new warnings and restrictions and on the whole downplayed, though not attacked in all possible manifestations. The shift meant, finally, that certain emotions the Victorians had cherished, like grief, were now regarded more negatively, almost as negatively as anger and fear. The twentieth century, in sum, preserved an emotional dichotomy but now defined it in terms of good versus bad rather than good versus dangerous-but-useful. The new culture shifted specific emotions into what was effectively the bad category, defined in terms of personal discomfort and demands on response from others. Most surprisingly, even with emotions still regarded as good, Victorian flights of fancy were now curbed amid an increasingly uniform sense that no emotional tug should pull too hard.

The changing winds concerning the "bad" emotions are easiest to discern, as not only anger and fear but also jealousy came in for new disapproval and new strategic management in the 1920s. Here then is an appropriate starting point for tracing the replacement of Victorianism, though again it is only that—other emotions were also involved. The increasing tendency to designate emotions as bad, or negative—a tendency that has continued in the social science literature as well as in most popularizations to this day—itself marks an innovation. Victorian pundits had regarded emotions like anger as bad in certain circumstances—when manifested by women, for example, or when expressed by men in ways that threatened the peace of the family. But the bad-good distinction was too simplistic for the Victorians. Almost any emotion could be made useful, and the extent to which it caused discomfort was not the central criterion. Indeed, appropriate use of emotion often allowed the individual to rise above discomfort, most obviously where fear was concerned. Twentieth-century negative labels applied most readily to emotions that the Victorians would have granted were dangerous—a connection between the two emotionologies is undeniable—but considerable shifting occurred, constructing a new kind of pleasure-pain index. This shifting was itself part of the new caution where emotions were concerned.

Hints of Change

While most advice literature maintained a Victorian emotionology into the 1920s, some fissures began to emerge late in the nineteenth century. Between 1900 and 1920 the advice-literature genre shrank somewhat, as measured by the sheer volume of new titles. With the exception of one interesting summary attempt by William Forbush in 1919,[1] which largely recapitulated Victorian formulas but with a few apparently un-self-conscious hesitations, no widely popular titles relevant to emotional standards appeared between 1906 and the 1920s, either in the marital or in the childrearing categories. In the 1920s, however, a new surge occurred, including the establishment of *Parents' Magazine* as well as a host of popularized manuals in which a strongly innovative tone emerged.

Apparently, then, Victorianism remained sufficiently widely accepted to obviate the need for any flood of popular prescriptions in the years before 1920. In the popularized literature that did appear, growing concern about children's physical health tended to displace emotional standards as a dominant topic, as in the government's best-selling manual, *Infant Care*. Only a few scattered sources suggested that Victorianism was being reconsidered. The hints are worth noting not because they established a new emotional culture but because they suggested themes that, disseminated and intensified, would dominate the new rush of advice in the 1920s.

Fear was the most obvious area for some implicit revisionism. Boys' stories in the 1890s began to acknowledge that fear in battle might be understandable—though still primarily for the untutored lower classes. Felix Adler's 1901 revision of his 1893 manual maintained an essentially Victorian stance—his childrearing manual was in fact the last widely sold, barely diluted Victorian statement in this genre—but spent a bit more time than usual warning against needless early childhood anxieties such as frightening fairy stories. Adler urged "moral courage" on older children, granting that it could not prevent fear but could overcome physical cowardice. In 1904 Mrs. Theodore Birney resolutely repeated Victorian formulas about channeling anger as part of building boys' character, but she sounded a different note concerning fear.[2] Devoting considerably more space to early childhood fears than Victorian-style manual writers had done, Birney detailed the unaccountable fears present in early childhood. In this rendering infants could be terrified by darkness or animals even if their parents had generated no tensions at all. Fear now seemed to originate within a child—gone was an aspect of emotional innocence. The result, equally clearly, was a new and vital task for parents. They must not dismiss childish fears, and to punish them was particularly dangerous, being likely to "harden" fears into a durable emotional flaw. Birney did not fully follow up on her new approach, for later in the discussion she reverted to stories of brave deeds that would instill courage, but there was no question that she had begun to break with the Victorian pattern.

William Forbush's 1919 manual offered the same amalgam of old and new, expressing great concern about the fears of children between two and six. Correspondingly, parents now were told that it was not enough to avoid scaring children; they must also conceal any fears of their own lest they be subtly communicated. Fear was on the way to becoming a new kind of emotional issue. Again, full innovation lay in the future, for Forbush, like Birney, reverted to Victorian type, urging activities like camping or boxing to toughen up a fearful child. "We can strengthen a child who is . . . afraid of a fight etc. by experiences . . . that will prepare him imaginatively to face other perils, even though their exact character may be unknown." Along with this Victorian advice, however, Forbush cautioned against outright confrontation with the frightening object; parents should help a child afraid of water or fireworks avoid these perils. Avoidance of emotional trauma was beginning to overcome courage as the primary childrearing goal, even for that staple of Victorian heroism, the boy.[3]

Jealousy was also beginning to draw novel attention, though in this instance, because the emotion had already been disapproved, the change involved increased concern, not basic reevaluation. Here Felix Adler pointed the way in his first, 1893 edition (the most widely read childrearing pamphlet to appear for two decades). Adler talked about inequalities among brothers and sisters that would result in "ugly feelings in the hearts of the less fortunate" if parents were not carefully evenhanded. No longer, as in previous manuals, could basic childish goodness and brotherly or sisterly affection be relied upon. Adler displayed a Victorian fondness for preachments, urging children to "be more eager to secure the rights of your brother than your own," but children could not really be relied upon in this area. Thus parents had another new task: they must get to the root of children's quarrels, for neglect could promote an "incipient hatred" among siblings, despite the fact that love should infuse family life.[4] Adler's treatment of what would soon be known as sibling rivalry was brief and somewhat offhand, for he continued to emphasize childish innocence and offered no elaborate tactical recommendations for besieged parents. But he was the first to point to yet another redefinition of children's nature, to yet another dangerous potential.

Early symptoms of a transition from nineteenth-century emotionology to a more cautious approach to childhood emotions flowed from several factors. Psychological research—even some of it conducted by staunch Victorians like G. Stanley Hall—provided new information about childish emotions. Hall's long study of fear, for example, provided graphic evidence of how many children were afflicted with night terrors.[5] Formal sibling research still lay in the future, but a new sense of children's emotional vulnerability stemmed from widely publicized scientific findings. At the same time, popularizers began to rely less on the authority of moral common sense and more on that of science. Thus, for example, whereas Adler was a partisan of arguments derived from morality and intrinsic good character, Hall's student Alice Birney referred to research findings, albeit in passing, in staking out her new claims concerning fear. New scientific claims and novel invocations of science in the emotional realm would solidify only in the 1920s, by which point other factors increased adult receptivity to innovative emotionology, but the straws in the wind before this juncture were hardly random.

Beyond the specifics, which applied particularly to childhood and a tentative new breed of childrearing expert, a wider shift in cultural mood was beginning to develop. As specific Victorian formulas began to change, the larger balance between physical/sexual restraint and permissible emotional intensity came under new scrutiny. Not long after 1920 Judge Ben Lindsay, a self-styled marriage pioneer, offered an early statement of the upcoming major effort to restrict emotions that Victorians had either found selectively useful or unpleasant but petty: "Anger, hatred, jealousy and the like are far more destructive of human happiness than any amount of sexual irregularity." Lindsay then focused on jealousy, which he argued was changing but not fast enough; a "capital crime against marriage," jealousy constituted a custom that, in giving "two free persons the ownership of each other is a device of the devil."

Briefly, Lindsay evoked what would be an even larger twentieth-century truth: that not only jealousy but also other powerful emotions like anger had lost all utility and could be linked with more clear-cut faults like malice with no apparent distinction. American emotionology was beginning to generate a new list of targets, simpler but more pressing than the Victorian combination of risk and relish.[6]

Fear

As popularizers like Birney had already suggested, fear was one of the first problematic Victorian emotions to undergo reevaluation. Childrearing manuals from the 1920s onward generated standard formulas about avoidance and control that built on but expanded Victorian values. Nineteenth-century emotionology had already attacked traditional uses of fear in childrearing, and the new breed of experts also condemned deliberate attempts to frighten children and urged similar revisions of conventional fairy stories that might produce undesirable emotional strain. Yet the new warnings against fear ranged far more broadly. The nature of the problem expanded, and a host of new strategies developed in response. Most notably the goal of courage, though never explicitly renounced, tended to disappear from view.

Standard childrearing manuals of the 1920s and 1930s displayed heightened, generalized anxieties about fear in several ways. Attacks on parents for conveying their own fears mounted steadily. "What help is there for this little boy [a child terrified of water]? As long as his mother cannot overcome her own fear, there is little hope of her doing anything for James. It would be like trying to prevent malaria while leaving the house full of the wrong kind of mosquitoes."[7] This concern obviously added greatly to the emotional tasks of parenthood. It also introduced important tensions between the standards urged for children and those applicable to adults. Children were to be shielded from fear, including their parents' fears, but adults must mask their own. Presumably, with improved parenting the tensions would be reduced in subsequent generations, for properly raised children would not have the terrors that afflicted some of their parents (mothers being particularly singled out, as we will see). For the time being, however, adults must feign composure. Revealingly, they were not directly asked to be courageous. Concealment, not moral conquest, seemed to be the prescribed goal. To this extent, the innovations being urged in the treatment of children promoted a new approach to adult fear as well.

A second innovation involved greatly increased detail about the nature of fear, which now commanded a full section in most childrearing manuals, plus article after article in the new *Parents' Magazine* (established in 1927). "Fear is essentially an unpleasant and sometimes even painful emotion marked by the threat of some vague or imminent danger." While this new, scientifically precise vocabulary granted some "protective value" to fear in keeping children from danger, the emphasis rested squarely on how disagreeable it was to be afraid. Here was another indication of how focus was shifting away from the potential usefulness of risky emotions toward the discomfort they arouse. Physical sensations were delineated. "During fears, the mouth becomes dry, due to the fact that the glands in the mouth stop secreting; digestion stops as does the movement of the intestines. A substance is discharged into the blood which increases muscular energy and does away with effects of fatigue"—all this is a chapter on "children's fears" in a book on young children. While some physical components of fear were acknowledged as galvanizing, emphasis rested on the unpleasantness of fear. Above all, as a *Parents' Magazine* article emphasized, fear inhibited thought. Here was the key point. Children should be taught to think things through, and fear prevented this process, so fear was bad. "Strong emotion interferes with the functioning of reasoning power; it is impossible—especially for a young child—to recognize the absence of danger when his intelligence is inactive because of fear." "Too intense fear, like too intense anger, interferes with biologically adequate behavior."[8] Fear as an instinct became oddly counterproductive in this formulation (a far cry from the evolutionists' recognition of fear's utility in the nineteenth century), while moral courage became irrelevant as well. Avoidance, not conquest, must be the chief aim.

The third innovation involved a focus on very young children and a new emphasis on the durability of emotional styles formed early on. Aside from the strict injunctions against using scare tactics, Victorian emotionology had downplayed the importance of early socialization for fear; childish innocence was secure enough to obviate any need for detail. Victorian comment focused on later childhood and youth, when, for boys at least, courage could come into play in meeting, challenging, and resolving fear and emerging all the better for the process. Twentieth-century popularizers, on the other hand, felt that only the first years were crucial; from the 1920s onward parental literature on adolescents simply omitted significant comment on fear. The new wisdom stressed the early formation of fear "in response to loss of support, sudden pain, or a sudden loud noise." More important still, it typically also stressed the lasting results of these early reactions. While properly raised children could learn to avoid fear ("to forestall future occasions for it"), fear could also "become a habit of the person, preventing his accomplishments." Even the severe but purely physical sensations of fear might last "for some time after," but it was the emotional scarring that went deep. John B. Watson put the case starkly in his chapter on children's fears:

At three years of age the child's whole emotional life plan has been laid down, his emotional disposition set. At that age the parents have already determined for him whether he is to grow into a happy person, wholesome and good-natured, whether he is to be a whining, complaining neurotic, an anger driven, vindictive, over-bearing slave driver, or one whose every move in life is definitely controlled by fear.

While most popularizers were not strict Watsonians, granting some importance, for example, to heredity as well as environment, the Watsonian emphasis on infancy seems to have struck a particularly important chord concerning the new perceptions of fear, as evidenced by the currency of Watsonian thoughts on this subject in *Parents' Magazine* through the later 1930s. Even before Watson, William Forbush had articulated the new wisdom: inadequate management of childhood anxieties could permanently distort a personality, leading to lifelong unhappiness and behavioral problems, including delinquency and crime, when wayward souls used violence to mask their inner terror. "An untold dread may become a veritable poison in the mind, bringing its evil to fullness years later."[9]

Thus there were three basic changes in the presentation of fear: a new urgency for parents, an increasing stress on discomfort and loss of control, and a singling out of infancy. Together these ingredients produced the fourth major shift in the popular childrearing advice: a new insistence on avoidance and support. Whereas Victorians had assumed that restrictions on deliberate scare tactics sufficed in dealings with younger children, twentieth-century emotional culture required far more elaborate strategies. Manipulation became crucial, for "children do not appear to 'get used to' things which they fear." Fear increases with contact, which meant that the whole apparatus of courageous encounter became not just irrelevant but downright counterproductive. "In fact, it [forced encounter] may cause the fear to spread to other situations similar to the one in which the first [fear] occurred." "The important thing in dealing with a child's fear is not to force sudden contact with the dreaded object or situation. Instead, grownups should at first shield the baby from whatever frightens him and be casual about the matter. The shielding must be inconspicuous, with no comment whatsoever." [10]

From Forbush onward, popular manuals devoted considerable attention to the new strategic requirements. Parental calm remained central; parents must set the example of reason triumphing over emotional intensity. They should help children evade their fears. Words like "mastery" and even "courage" were still used, but the emphasis lay elsewhere. Talk became important, as parents should patiently listen to children's admissions of fear. Concession was essential: whenever a child evinced fear, it was time to retreat, to allow avoidance of confrontation. Remediation would come (and then only gradually) not through noble, heroic stories or stiff-upper-lip injunctions, but through guile. The child who feared the dark should be elaborately reassured, given a night light, or lured with candy into a darkened room. Parents were advised to place candy near the door the first night, a bit farther in the next time around, and so on until appetite and experience combined to submerge the initial dread. By the 1920s, as emotional prescriptions began to be combined with purely medical advice, popular manuals, including those issued by the Children's Bureau, repeated details of these stratagems in virtually every edition. [11]

The popularizers recognized that the new advice required substantial adult reeducation. Adults still needed to be told not to frighten children with threats and bogeymen, but now they also needed to learn not to display their own fears (especially mothers, a clear concession to nineteenth-century claims about female emotional frailty), and they must be taught to renounce the impulse to exhort fearful children, an impulse particularly rooted in Victorian emotionology. Given children's newfound and extraordinary sensitivity, there was no moral challenge left in fear—only emotional risk and pain. As a leading 1920s manualist, D. H. Thom, argued, for even seemingly neutral new experiences parents should be prepared for potential fear rather than rely on assumptions of courage.[12]

Presumably the long-term result of careful parental strategies would be a personality capable of coping with fear. In this very broad sense, the new emotionology shared goals with the nineteenth century. But whereas capability once meant courage, now it might mean sedulous avoidance or anxious discussions with others. In this transformation fear became even more awesome than it had been. The new discussions of children ignored gradations of fear in favor of emphasis on the extreme, incapacitating terror. At the same time, however, fear lost its moral stigma. It became a potentially overwhelming emotional problem the resolution of which, however, brought no particular credit. Admission of fear was no longer a moral weakness, which meant that its management, rather than a triumphant emotional conquest, became relatively trivial as well.

The rising concern about children's fears and the risks they entailed continued through the 1930s in leading manuals written by popular authorities like Winnifred de Kok and Sidonie Gruenberg. The authors emphasized the importance of reconsidering an array of traditional parental approaches beyond the lazy and damaging use of fear in discipline. Children's fears should be coddled and heeded rather than scorned or ridiculed, for as attacks on fear became ever more straightforward, the strategic responses increased in complexity. The nineteenth-century practice of urging fearful boys to buck up—as in T. S. Arthur's injunction—was now completely rejected. "When a child evinces fear, the one danger to avoid is repression. As long as the fear is brought into the open and discussed, little harm can be done." Parents were advised to talk it out and to attach pleasant experience to the object of fear, leading young children to replace fear with anticipation. Fear became one of a string of "bad" emotions that must be ventilated to be defused, lest repressive dismissal or misguided efforts to overcome through moral intensity drive the feeling deeper, to fester and corrupt. Revealingly, examples of frightened children disproportionately emphasized boys. No one claimed that boys were particularly afraid. Rather, the new conventional wisdom stood in such opposition to Victorian assumptions that it was particularly effective to use the Victorian candidates for courage as object lessons in the need for parental coddling and sanctioned ventilation. Always, warnings against insistence on courage underscored the distance from the nineteenth century. As Gruenberg, an indefatigable manual and encyclopedia writer, urged, "There is always the danger that the fear resulting from such methods will reach the 'overwhelming' stage and leave its mark for a long time." [13]

Two successive theoretical approaches to fear operated within the new cultural context. Neither created the context, which developed more amorphously in the advice literature of the early 1900s, but both extended this context and offered firmer explanations for fear than the average manualist could muster, as well as a clearer rationale for the resultant strategies.

Watsonian behaviorism, as we have seen, provided a presumably scientific method for approaching children's fears that fit the growing concern of childrearing experts and many expertise-consuming parents during the late 1920s and the 1930s—chronologically after, it must be noted, the concern itself began to be manifested and the basic new strategies devised. According to Watson, interestingly echoing Victorian assumptions, by nature children had virtually no fears at all. Watson claimed that a series of experiments had revealed no instinctive fears of the dark, of fire, or of snakes; only noise and falling produced innate reactions of fear. All other fears, such as fear of animals, derived from associations with one of the two innate fears. This discovery led to a series of admonitions to parents, who must limit loud noise, close windows during storms, and buy houses set well back from the (now increasing) sounds of the road. It also reinforced the idea of reeducating children who were afraid by associating the feared object with pleasurable sensations to produce behavioral modification. This was a difficult, demanding, and time-consuming task, but it involved no moral grappling with powerful elemental emotions. Watson was interested in producing not a courageous personality, but rather a personality that knew how to avoid and manage, with successful adult management including finding material compensation in adult equivalents of candy in the darkened room or treats offered in the presence of an intimidating stranger. [14]

Watson's vision stressed the complexity of the child's environment while also providing parents with the Victorian reassurance that no problems were innate. This combination helped move parents through a transition in which worry about fear could be combined with real hopes for successful manipulation. The fact that courageous character and confrontation with intense emotion now gave way to clever tactics seemed to pass unnoticed. Watson was himself interviewed on controlling children's fears in an early issue of *Parents' Magazine,* and Watsonian protégés continued to hold forth through the 1930s. The message also remained consistent: "The main job of the parent should be to prevent fears, since some fears are extremely difficult to cure." Caution, here, had supplanted courage as the alternative to fear. Courage was dismissed not only because confrontation increased children's fears but also because it might promote foolhardy antics that simply added to fear's effects of "making it impossible for one to think clearly." Passionless good sense and a controlled environment were the new preconditions of sound behavior and a properly restrained emotional life.[15]

By the 1940s, as fear gained new attention in association with World War II, Watsonianism yielded to a selective kind of Freudianism in American childrearing literature. This approach maintained earlier arguments about strategically minimizing fear and manipulating its treatment, but it undermined the blithe Watsonian assumptions about lack of natural fear. Now, fears lay deep in the psyche, and no amount of parental caution could prevent their emergence in some form. Avoidance should still be stressed wherever possible, but the premium placed on letting children articulate their fears went up. Adult support and affectionate reassurance became even more important than before.

The first full articulation of this second-phase, mid-twentieth-century approach to dealing with fear came in Dr. Benjamin Spock's initial manual of 1945. As in turn-of-the-century comment by people like Hall and Birney, before the Watsonian deviation, children's fears were presented as unpredictable and varied. Now, however, they required careful adult response. Parents must sit up with the sleepless child in whom fear had taken root. "Don't be in a hurry to sneak away before he is asleep. . . . This campaign may take weeks, but it should work in the end." Parents were advised to delay travel plans when children around two years of age seem anxious; to be very careful about going off to work; not to push toilet training to the point of causing fear; and to assure an anxious child that their love would withstand any number of soiled diapers. Adult calm became all the more precious, even with older children who evinced fear, because "the child is scared enough of his own mental creations." Lavishing affection was essential. "This is the time for extra hugs and comforting reminders that you love him very much and will always protect him." Crude strategies like candy bribes were downplayed as the fear sources became more diffuse, though play-acting was recommended.[16]

The selectively Freudian revisions of Watsonian simplicities spread widely in the 1950s, appearing in the most common childrearing manuals and the relevant segments of *Parents' Magazine*. The range of this emotion was now vast: "The fact is that a child can get to be afraid of almost anything." Adult assistance was absolutely essential, for children had no emotional resources to deal with fear unaided: "Unless some grown-up helps them, each frightening experience leaves them weakened for the next assault." While early infancy remained crucial, parental support now extended into later years, as in accompanying a frightened first grader to school for weeks or even months. Security against emotional threat was crucial. Children would still be afraid, but the occasions would be "reduced to a minimum." The replacement of mere strategy with abundant reassurance did not, however, reawaken an interest in courage. The goal remained use of parental presence to deflect emotional intensity. Adult stage managing, replacing the Victorian delight in a virile confrontation with fear, extended still farther. Spock, to be sure, used the word "courage," but he meant by it a process of carefully guided adjustment and dilution, not a moral challenge.[17]

Amid the important, though limited, gyrations of expertise, parental interest in popularized advice on fear management gained ground steadily from the 1920s onward. Worried parents began to refer fearful children to therapists or to the increasingly available resource of guidance clinics, both of which recourses are noted in early issues of *Parents' Magazine*. An inquiry during the 1940s into the problems parents perceived with children, though not as precise as one might wish in retrospect, uncovered great concern about childhood fears. Fears loomed large in the overall category of emotional problems, which category in turn loomed large among all issues treated in the study. Problems were rated highest among younger children and focused on reactions to darkness, water, animals, germs, and death, as well as generalized fearfulness. Parents did not point to any particularly admirable instances of courage among children, and the concept was almost never cited. Parental perceptions, in other words, particularly among the suburban middle class, paralleled the kinds of signals that had been provided in the larger emotional culture for over two decades.[18]

Parents also had their own comments to make, suggesting that popularizations not only created new emotional values but also reflected them. Letters to *Parents' Magazine* appeared regularly from the late 1920s into the 1950s, detailing concerns about children's fears and successful (initially, largely behaviorist) strategies for coping. In 1929 the magazine posed a problem to its readers based on a five-year-old's night fears. A bevy of mothers responded, dutifully warning against maids who told bogeyman stories, fearsome images of a punitive God, and, on the positive side, recommending carefully planted benign images and the after-all-small-enough expense of a night light. The respondents admitted the temptation to impose discipline but sedulously warned against yielding to it. The contest, of course, was a sponsored event, and its demonstration of parental response may be limited. More interesting, though still self-selected, was the spate of spontaneous submissions from parents from the late 1930s through the subsequent decade in which children's fears of dogs, darkness, and other threats were detailed and compensatory strategies based on explaining the source of fear and distracting with treats were recounted. The goal was always removal of a particular fear, not (overtly at least) development of a courageous personality or a desire to introduce moral challenge. By the 1940s, if not before, middle-class parents had widely assimilated the idea that childhood fear was a substantial problem and were eager to offer tactics that would allow their children to cope without requiring direct, courageous confrontation.[19]

A similar tone emerged in responses of older children to survey questionnaires about fear, although again the interests of the eliciting researchers may well have influenced the result. The 1956 assessment by Arnold Gesell and his colleagues yielded no preteens dreaming of facing stampeding horses or calculating the bravery needed to turn aside an enemy attack. Rather, they described a group of older children eager to demonstrate that they had surmounted the characteristic fears of earlier years. The narrowed equation of fear with childish terror had clearly triumphed over the earlier, Victorian use of fear in stimulating heroic response to danger. Fear and childishness were more likely pairings than fear and moral challenge, which meant that avoidance rather than ongoing mastery held center stage. Thus ten-year-olds pointed proudly to the waning of a previous fear of dogs or darkness. A few imaginative children admitted potential fears about spending a night in an old castle alone or encountering a lion, which evoked Victorianlike calls on courage. By age eleven, however, even these occasional fancies had passed, and children preferred not to discuss fear at all or to redefine it in such a way as to apply the term to anxieties about being liked by peers. Claims of courageous intensity did not crop up. By age fifteen, fear had become entirely a matter of reminiscence about childhood frights or initial sports anxieties. Maturity meant claiming to do without fear, not claiming emotional resources necessary to grapple with it directly.[20]

Thus, within two decades of the inception of a new approach toward fear in the prescriptive literature, both teenagers and parents seem to have adjusted their own perceptions. This does not prove that the experience of fear itself changed, or that courage declined, but it does suggest a real shift in emotional self-presentation, particularly on the part of boys and parents dealing with boys.

Growing emphasis on the avoidance of fear affected two other cultural manifestations, one as early as the 1920s, the other more clearly during World War II. By the 1920s children's fiction had lost most of the moralistic qualities of its Victorian counterpart, a development that had begun a few decades earlier. Entertainment, even escapism, triumphed over idealized middle-class virtue. Yet it was revealing that, while some themes of courage persisted as part of fictional excitement— creeping into girls' stories now with nurse and detective heroines—a new kind of hero increasingly predominated. Stories and radio shows, like "Jack Armstrong, All-American Boy," presented one dangerous setting after another, and an imaginative audience might well project fear and wonder how it could be handled. Yet the heroes themselves, in marked contrast to their Victorian analogues, usually claimed no process of encountering and mastering fear. They were not so much courageous as emotionless, building on the tough-guy models that had begun to enter boys' stories, adult dime novels, and Westerns in the nineteenth century.[21] Rather than grappling with fear, or even considering fear in retrospect, the new breed of Tarzans and, later, Supermen, had no emotions to deal with one way or another. Their coolness was as remarkable as their ability to fly or withstand bullets or communicate with apes. Adventure and courage were dissociated as excitement was divorced from the larger process of considering fear. It was almost as if the superheroes, the new models of masculinity, had been reared in an ideal Watsonian setting in which the emotions had been entirely inhibited. The increasing popularity of youth science fiction extended the trend of depicting incredible adventure minus emotional load. Fantasy life, in sum, shifted from idealizing the control of fear to celebrating its absence.[22] Even real-boy heroes, like Frank Dixon's Hardy boys, participated in this new trend. Called upon to fly a blimp with no prior experience, Frank and Joe are briefly "tense with excitement," but that is it. After being shot at, they might remark "I thought we were dead ducks" without talking about how they had surprised themselves with their emotional bravery. Lesser colleagues, like chubby Chet, might admit fear, but such acknowledgments were made only in passing, with none of the savor of Victorian evaluations of emotional experience. Boy heroes themselves accomplished far greater wonders than ever before, but they were not described as courageous because they had no complicating emotions to surmount.[23]

Again, children's fiction continued to present some older imagery, and stories for young children were increasingly purged of scary references of any sort, as in Disney reformulations of classic fairy tales. The audience most explicitly affected by the rise of the new supraemotional Superman, however, was precisely the group that had been most exposed to the distinctive emotional challenges of Victorian fare: older boys. Though parents and experts railed against much of the new reading, particularly the comic books, because of its horrific context, in fact the fare meshed with the new emotionology in its presentation—or rather, its omission—of fear itself.

The second cultural manifestation of the new standards for fear involved the American military and the advice, even the vocabulary, it offered to soldiers and the general public concerning fear. Through World War I, military authorities had emphasized physical trauma in explaining the psychological hardships of war. Military heroism was of course widely praised, and soldiers who had not measured up were either condemned as cowards or excused on grounds of "shell shock" or concussion. During World War II, however, there was an increasing use of terms like "war neurosis" or "battle fatigue," which covered a constitutional inability to cope with fear as a darker side of the military experience. Manuals for soldiers, correspondingly, moved away from injunctions of heroism. An infantry pamphlet for the Fifth Army in Italy thus noted: "Don't be too scared. Everybody is afraid, but you can learn to control your fear. . . . Being too scared is harmful to you." The gap between this pragmatism, which suggests an adaptation of parental advice to manage emotion while admitting its unpleasant existence, and the more courage-filled presentations of Civil War soldiers is obvious. Military rhetoric did not change entirely, and stories of individual heroism remained staples of public relations campaigns, but it did shift toward downplaying transcendent courage and allowing open admissions of fear in one of the adult settings where the emotion simply could not be avoided. Civilian personnel authorities also moved away from deliberate uses of fear in interviews on the grounds that it incapacitated interviewees rather than revealing strength of character.[24]

As the military example suggests, the twentieth-century effort to avoid or manage fear had to become more complex as attention moved from childhood to other areas. Earlier emphases on courage continued to affect not only military life but also sports values, where qualities of emotional toughness and intensity built on Victorian premises. Such complexity will return in even greater force when we assess the consequences of twentieth-century attitudes toward fear. However, despite complicating continuities with Victorianism, it is still the case that the culture changed with respect to fear and that new popularized formulas fanned out from childrearing into other perceptions and other institutional statements. Both fear and the appropriate approaches to it were redefined, yielding a new and more open level of distaste and a search for methods of management to replace courageous emotional encounter. In the process, Victorian scenarios, and even words like "courage" and "sissy," began to assume a certain quaintness, as if our ancestors could not really have known what the whole emotional experience was about.

Jealousy

As with fear, a major new attack on jealousy among children developed in the 1920s and extended into the 1950s. The specifics of this cultural shift differed considerably from those regarding fear. First, whereas concern about children's fear followed in part from new scientific data, the furor about sibling jealousy preceded scientific studies—though such studies emerged to confirm the new common wisdom during the late 1920s and the 1930s in a series of sibling experiments that demonstrated how much most children suffered from jealous pangs.[25] Second, no large theory like Watsonianism ever captured the jealousy campaign, though behaviorism and (to a very modest degree) popularized Freudianism had some bearing; instead, the movement against jealousy was more fully defined by vigorous but unsystematic popularizers. Finally, the initial focus on young children—also apparent in the new approach to boys' fear—yielded more fully in the case of jealousy to a followup among adults. By the 1950s and for the ensuing two decades, explicit advice on adult jealousy dominated the relevant popular outlets, building on but greatly extending the early-socialization campaign.[26] The shift in fear culture also affected adult culture, as we have seen, but more diffusely.

Jealousy had been officially reproved in Victorian culture; there had been no special, approved encounter with jealousy as there had been for male courage in the face of fear. Thus, whereas the twentieth-century reevaluation of fear had involved some formal redefinition along with expanded treatment, the new anxiety about jealousy involved few official new rules, only a greatly heightened attention level. The new culture involved a great deal more talk and breast beating about jealousy than in the Victorian decades because more rigorous treatment forced more frequent personal evaluations. And whereas with fear twentieth-century culture led to more open admissions of emotional distress, most admissions of jealousy were quickly followed by disclaimer or apology.

Despite these variations, the campaigns to modify fear and to prevent jealousy shared a host of ingredients, besides the initial focus on early childhood and the use of apparently scientific findings. In both cases expansion of concern amounted to a virtual invention of new problems not dealt with explicitly in Victorian culture. The explosion of attention to "siblingitis," as children's jealousy came to be termed, thus rivaled dramatic new discoveries of fears about animals or darkness. In both instances, childhood suddenly became emotionally far more complicated than before, requiring new strategic guidance from adults. Tactics overlapped, particularly in recommendations of reassurance, tolerance for verbal venting of emotion, and distractions through candy or toys—a children's consumerism. The resulting attention also increasingly muted Victorian gender rules. Just as fear increasingly became a problem for children, not an occasion for boys to demonstrate emotional resources girls did not have, so jealousy, though still disproportionately attributed to girls into the 1930s, increasingly became genderless as well: males and females shared the task of ridding themselves of jealousy and neither had a natural disadvantage in measuring up.[27]

Above all, jealousy, like fear, came to be seen as a deep emotional threat, capable of overwhelming reason and good taste alike. Its cancerous potential had to be identified early and specifically combated. Here was a second negative emotion now viewed in terms of its great power to fester and consume a personality to the point of complete adult dysfunction. The remedy involved sedulous training in avoidance or trivial ventilation. Emotional maturity, for fear and jealousy alike, meant an ability to disclaim and sidestep. While the official Victorian verdict on jealousy was confirmed, implicit Victorian leniency toward this emotion was lost in this process, and the central importance of avoiding the contagion of emotional intensity was driven home far more explicitly than before.

Victorian culture had not only avoided extensive discussions of jealousy; it had also assumed that adults could convert the intensity of jealousy into the development of character—and that while the process might be painful, they could accomplish this on their own. (The exception, murderous jealous rage, was clearly an anomaly in this pattern.) The most common fictional jealousy theme involved a woman jealous of a sister, cousin, or (more rarely) friend who was in love, sometimes with a man the woman herself secretly loved. Jealousy and guilt wrestled for a time, but in the end good character won out. Quite frequently, the woman became better friends with the envied sister or cousin as a result. While this process did not have the explicit gilding attached to courageous triumphs over fear, there was some similarity; in both instances, intensity was converted to self-improvement and a net gain.

In the decades after 1920 this scenario disappeared. Jealousy was simply misery—a deep, grinding distortion that the individual might well be unable to control. Dorothy Baruch, in recommending that jealous children be allowed to tear dolls apart, talked of "getting the poison out." Many advice writers, dealing with child and adult jealousy alike, referred to the imminent loss of control. John Montgomery, describing jealousy as a "strong and disturbing emotion," went on to insist that parental assistance was essential for children: "If he does not have the right kind of help, his personality may be damaged. Unfriendly, disagreeable, selfish, self-conscious adults often show these traits because of unsolved jealousy problems in their childhood." Dr. Spock, a bit more mellowly, confirmed this reaction: "Jealousy is a strong emotion, even in grownups, but it is particularly disturbing to the young child"—and again, an unpleasant adult personality "can often be traced back to the habits created in the small child by the arrival of a baby brother or sister." Hence the advice to parents: "To prevent it or to minimize it is worth a lot of effort." As for adults themselves: "Jealousy has an insatiable appetite and will possess you if you don't come to grips with it." "Jealousy . . . is a continual compulsion." "The emotion of jealousy limits our freedom, time, energy and attention from our daily tasks. It deprives one of a sense of control and autonomy in our lives." "Obsessive" and "primitive" were two other adjectives frequently used in describing the emotion's dire effects.[28] By the same token, management of jealousy was essential simply to permit decent interactions. The process of management involved damage prevention, not the ennobling experience imagined in Victorian stories. The depth of jealousy's potential harm, beginning in early childhood, the management needed to avoid or escape its intense snares, and the preoccupation with permanent personality flaws and loss of control—these were the themes that transformed jealousy from an emotion that could produce some passing difficulty to a major instance in which control must be imposed over potentially consuming intensity.

One of the first salvos in the new war on children's jealousy—the first stage of what turned out to be a two-pronged campaign—came in a government publication on childrearing by D. H. Thom published in 1925: "Few emotions are experienced by man which from a social point of view are more important than jealousy. . . . The jealous person becomes an object of dislike. Often he develops the idea that he is unjustly treated or persecuted, and all too frequently this idea causes uncontrolled resentment and disastrous results." Therefore parents must attend carefully to jealousy in their children. In 1926 a Child Study Association of America pamphlet similarly identified the inevitability and the evil of jealousy, noting that the emotion is "so intense that little but harm can come from rousing it. . . . Even in its higher form of rivalry and emulation great caution must be used." A child who was too competitive probably suffered from a dangerous level of jealousy: "there is no limit to the depths to which he may sink." This kind of warning was soon followed by a full set of relevant tactics. Under the heading "Nobody likes a jealous person. A jealous person is never happy," the Children's Bureau in 1930 offered a full set of instructions on how to cushion the arrival of a new baby—the most likely trigger for onset of the vile emotion. "Tony was happy again. Now he loves his baby brother. He is not jealous anymore." With these thoughts, a veritable flood of standardized advice began to dominate major sections of popularized childrearing literature. Only briefly did a countercurrent surface in the prescriptive advice, arguing that children's jealousy might serve a useful purpose in encouraging competition and emulation.[29]

Children's jealousy was now held to be inevitable, as popularizers interpreted the series of sibling studies revealing that a majority of children overtly expressed significant jealousy and, through quarrels and possessiveness, behaved accordingly. In a catch-22 argument, popularizers argued that those who did not show it were probably suffering from it particularly severely: "A child whose jealousy is not easy to recognize . . . has greater need for help." The evils of sibling jealousy were twofold. First, jealousy posed a real danger to other children; behind a three-year-old's resentment of a newborn lurked a potentially murderous impulse. For the safety of infants, and obviously for family harmony and decent relationships among siblings growing up, children's emotional nature must be corrected. In the second place, jealousy unchecked would generate an adult personality that simply could not function properly, not only in family relationships but also in business, where habits of cooperation were essential. Childish jealousy "indelibly stamps personality and distorts character"; "we have only to read the daily paper to see the results of ungoverned jealousy in adult life."[30]

The new wisdom insisted that children could not handle the jealousy problem by themselves, though it offered the hope that parental tactics could reassure children and teach them that love could be shared without personal loss or harm. As de Kok noted in 1939, "If we succeed in getting him to accept the situation happily, we have done much towards making him grow into an adult who looks upon all love as a sharing with others, not as a possession which must be calculated and selfishly held against all comers."[31] Yet the recommended strategies were more complex and various than the blissful goals implied.

Ventilation was of course central. Children should be taught to identify and label jealousy and freely to express it as a means of relieving the inner tension without damaging themselves in the short term or others in the long term. No guilt should be attached, for this might make matters worse by adding one emotional intensity to another. Children should make no direct gains through expressing jealousy, but they should receive lots of parental coddling. "I know how you feel, dear.

Come on over and I'll give you a hug and we'll see if that doesn't help."
Through admission and subsequent reassurance, jealousy could be de-
fanged, rendered passive and thus incapable of motivating undesirable
behavior.[32]

Other tactics stressed avoidance, particularly as popularizers warmed
to their task after some initial vagueness in the 1920s. The litany became
increasingly standardized: Tell children that a baby is coming so the way
is prepared. Don't force children to share rooms if at all possible. Give
each child separate furnishings, toys, and clothing; this is money well
spent. Tell grandparents and other intruders to make a greater fuss over
the older child than over a new baby who wouldn't know the difference
anyway. Conceal breast feeding and other provocative acts involving the
baby. In sum, parents were advised to anticipate jealousy by reinforcing
individualism and providing privately owned material distractions.[33]

As with the simultaneous campaign against outdated approaches to
childish fear, the war against sibling jealousy raged before an apprecia-
tive audience. Parents in the interwar decades, whose own parents had
somehow suffered through their own childhoods with no elaborate advice or up-to-date terms like "sibling rivalry," clearly shared the discovery of immense emotional problems with the experts. Guidance authorities reported widespread parental concern over jealousy in their young
children. Letters from parents to family magazines showed the same
patterns from the late 1920s into the 1950s. As one woman noted in
1955, jealousy was "by far the most troublesome, the gravest issue I've
met so far in my career as mother." In a mid-1940s poll of 544 families,
53 percent reported significant problems of jealousy among siblings,
rating this the third most important issue in dealing with children and
the most serious of all concerns about children's personality and temperament. Among suburban parents, sibling problems stood second in the
overall list, compared to an eighth-place ranking for the urban poor and
fourteenth place for urban blacks. Parents also increasingly reported
adoption of the recommended strategies of reassurance and distracting
purchases, and some of them put a good bit of time and money into
their efforts. In another indication of the cultural success of the new
standards, teenagers increasingly identified jealousy with immaturity and
liked to downplay their jealousies, particularly where siblings were concerned.[34]

Some of the missionary fervor began to drop from the childrearing literature by the 1960s. Reversions to older formulas remained possible, as in a 1977 manual's claims that "nothing so greedily consumes a child's inner emotional reserves than feelings of jealousy," but in general experts reduced their dire warnings about permanent character damage and began to admit that the problem varied significantly from one set of siblings to another. Recommended tactics for dealing with jealousy also persisted beyond the 1960s; indeed, one of the reasons why the urgency notched down in the prescriptive literature was that most parents now knew the strategies by heart, having been raised on them. Thus, while the decades between about 1925 and 1960 constituted the high point in the juvenile division of the antijealousy campaign, basic goals and concerns persisted even beyond.[35]

Furthermore, by the 1950s the attack on jealous intensity in children extended to adults. This effort was based on the assumptions that had been developed about jealousy in childhood, and it had been anticipated by widely publicized statements originating in the 1920s. Antijealousy arguments for adults in the 1920s issued primarily from avant-garde marriage reformers in Britain and the United States. Judge Ben Lindsay publicized the doctrines most widely, summoning up his experience as a divorce court judge. Jealousy was a contradiction of true love, which should be selfless and unpossessive. It led to compulsive behaviors and even crimes, while forming an unhealthy basis for marriage itself. "Any custom that gives two free persons the ownership of each other is a device of the devil," Lindsay argued, claiming that 90 percent of divorces stemmed from strains caused by jealousy.[36] This line of argument was more open than nineteenth-century discussion, particularly in its frank attack on sexual possessiveness, and it was more widely publicized. But it maintained some essential Victorian thinking, particularly in its reliance on arguments about the ideal nature of true love.

The 1920s burst of frankness led to important attacks on jealousy by some feminists and, relatedly, new analysis by various social scientists. Social psychologists began to attack jealousy as harmful to the personality and counterproductive in relationships. Margaret Mead, in the 1930s, opined that jealousy is "undesirable, a festering spot in every personality so affected." Kingsley Davis, in 1936, offered a more extensive anthropological view, showing how jealous mistrust poisoned "the harmony of perfect intimacy."[37]

In the 1930s these strains against jealousy began to enter popularized marriage advice literature as well as the now-dwindling genre of advice to teenagers. Readers were told that jealousy was a blemish and a cause of disruption—that it was "irrational and completely unwarranted." Further, accusations of immaturity were now added to the mix; an inability to control the emotion, or a need to display it openly, was a sign of improper childhood experience. Now that parental guidelines were so well established, the jealous surge could be dismissed as a sign that, somehow, one's childhood had not been correctly managed. Not just love ideals but also the demands of appropriate adulthood compelled redress and shamed the jealous individual. As a 1945 booklet aimed at high school girls argued, in what had become by then the standard message: "Jealousy is probably the most common of all the unhelpful attitudes. . . . Why do we act this way? The reason is that we haven't outgrown the selfishness of early childhood. . . . We must grow up."[38]

The insistence on immaturity was a striking theme that tended to preclude other kinds of thinking about jealousy. Legitimate reasons or purposes for jealousy were hard to come by when readers were constantly told that their impulses were childish. Even the intensity concern was held at a remove, for the infantilism argument trivialized the darker passions jealousy might involve. Attacks on jealousy in adults did not need to address these passions, or any other issues aside from childishness. They could rely on assumptions developed in the discussions of the previous decades that had thoroughly explored the power of jealousy in childhood and beyond, so that the accusation of childishness was now an adequate deterrent. "The jealous lover is a child hugging his toy so closely that no one else can see it. Jealousy is almost always a mark of immaturity and insecurity. As we grow confident of love and of our loved one, we are not jealous . . . we need not cling in desperation."[39]

As the antijealousy campaign became a standard ingredient in marriage manuals, themselves a rapidly growing medium for popularized expertise between the 1930s and the 1950s, damage to love was conjoined with blasts against immaturity. "Jealousy kills love. It is a symptom of weakness and of selfishness. Wanting a suitor, or a wife, or a husband to pay exclusive attention to one has nothing in common with real devotion." Sentiments of this sort, which held that jealousy conduced toward absolute monopoly of a partner's interests, assumed that jealousy had an all-or-nothing quality. Thus the antijealousy campaign indirectly picked up the anti-intensity theme. The idea of a moderate jealousy or an acceptance of intense jealousy devoted to basic fidelity rather than exclusiveness had dropped from view. One famous advice writer, Paul Popenoe, moved against the tide in arguing that jealousy was a vital support for monogamy (so long as it was expressed "on an adult level"—Popenoe admitted that jealousy could easily transgress proper bounds, becoming "a childish and destructive habit"). With this interesting exception, the marriage literature united in condemnation: "Jealousy is a terrible emotion, one of the extreme forms of psychological cruelty." While jealousy indicated problems in a relationship, it pointed even more clearly to deficiencies—insecurities or even a hidden desire for infidelity—on the part of the jealous individual. Advice writers mastered the put-down on immaturity, stating that even infidelity should be manageable: "We are upset to varying degrees, but usually not so deeply as we think."[40] Intensity, once more, need not apply.

The attacks on jealousy fed into the culture of the 1960s as both feminists and advocates of open marriages and other experiments continued the salvos against emotional possessiveness. Some partisans of these movements shifted ground slightly by arguing that jealousy was itself unnatural, a learned emotion, and that a proper person should be jealousy-free. Others, however, acknowledged the problems of deficient childrearing and the need for rigorous adult self-control as sexual experimentation became increasingly common and overt. One open-marriage manual instructed a spouse on what to say when a partner called to report that he was spending the night away: "Fine, I'm glad things are going so well. Enjoy yourself and I look forward to hearing about it tomorrow." In the 1970s a jealousy workshop movement briefly flourished in some American cities, run by practitioners like Larry Constantine and Robert and Margaret Blood; the idea was to train people to get used to their partners' sexual involvements with others. Designed for those "who are strongly motivated to outgrow jealousy," the workshops defined success as acceptance of full marital freedom. Jealousy would not be concealed or denied; it simply would not exist as partners would learn to praise the advantages of their mutual excursions. In the words of one exemplar: "I really appreciate the fact that after you've been with Ann you seem more accepting of me and the children."[41]

The language of the movement against adult jealousy was widely accepted within the middle class. During the 1960s and 1970s many partners reported their ardent efforts to live up to jealousy-free standards and their embarrassment when the emotion refused to disappear. "I think it comes from possessiveness and I'm trying to grow away from that." Or, if individuals were unable to deny some pain when a partner was unfaithful, they tried to minimize their emotion. Thus the muted remarks by people who found a mate in bed with someone else: "Somewhat disconcerting"; "It was kind of rough"; "I was sort of put down." The sloppily qualifying language in these remarks—"kind of," "sort of"—related to broader language changes that, as we will see in a later chapter, reflected the more general turn away from admission of emotional intensity. Even before the sexual revolution decades, American men professed widespread disapproval of jealousy and complained loudly about their wives' anachronistic jealous nagging. Thus a survey of California husbands in the 1930s listed jealousy-induced nagging as their eighteenth most pressing grievance against wives (far ahead of worries about wifely infidelity, which placed forty-fifth). While women were more ambivalent about jealousy than men professed to be (and even many men admitted jealous responses in certain situations, particularly during dating), agreement about the evil of jealousy increased steadily. By the 1960s a major social psychology study demonstrated that the vast majority of middle-class Americans believed that jealousy was a sign not of love, but rather of immaturity and dangerous insecurity.[42] Decades of cultural conditioning had paid off in a new and impressively uniform set of criteria by which jealousy could be described and condemned.

Anger

The final transformation concerning negative emotions involved anger, where the complex Victorian emphasis on combining control and focused intensity was rejected outright in favor of an effort to manage and avoid. The phases of the redefinitions of anger differed noticeably from those concerning fear and jealousy. The first efforts concentrated on adults in the workplace, and only gradually did the implications spread to new standards for family life, particularly for childrearing. Yet despite distinctive features, both the basic timing and the underlying criteria of the campaign against anger overlapped with the attacks against the other unpleasant emotions. Growing anxiety about anger involved the same revulsion against disagreeable intensities and potential loss of control that had motivated the concerns about fear and jealousy. With anger, however, the Victorian formula had taken such deep roots in American culture that the need for wholesale transformation emerged somewhat gradually, with changes in one sector not initially resonating in others. By the 1950s, however, a systematic culture was in place that meshed smoothly with the simultaneous campaigns against jealousy and avoidable confrontations with fear.

Novel attention to anger in the workplace began to surface in the 1920s. It had precedent, to be sure. Employers in the nineteenth century had tried to identify "troublemakers" among their labor force as part of an attempt to prevent or crush protest. They could make it abundantly clear that they did not appreciate open anger directed against management. Nineteenth-century work rules, however, concentrated on behavior, not mood, and there was no explicit discussion of anger as a labor issue or of methods to improve emotional restraint. Hotheads, if identified, might be fired, but they were not told to seek counseling. Only in domestic service, where family rules about anger applied, was explicit attention paid to anger in an employment relationship. Here, family manuals routinely insisted on the importance of temper control in the interests of integrating servants into the proper emotional mood of the household. Here also, uniquely, employers—in the form of middle-class housewives—talked about their own battles with anger as part of their ruminations on dealings with staff.[43]

Elements of the household standard began to shift into work outside the home in the 1920s as the indirect approach to anger on the job began to yield to a host of specific recommendations. To be sure, the Victorian idea of channeling still emerged. As late as 1919, an industrial engineer, claiming that scientific management allowed anger to be constructively directed against things rather than colleagues or supervisors, argued: "Pugnacity is a great driving force. It is a wonderful thing that under Scientific Management this force is aroused not against one's fellow workers but against one's work." On balance, however, it was the scientific management movement, maintained not only by engineers but also by the new breed of industrial psychologists, that first reconsidered the role of anger as part of an effort to make workers more machinelike and the workplace itself a smoothly running engine. Frederick Taylor, for example, thrust onto the factory floor from a conventional middle-class background, talked about his shock at the choleric surliness of many factory workers; this became one of his targets when he talked about inducing a "mental revolution" on the job.[44] Still more significant were the reactions of Elton Mayo and his associates in the famous General Electric Hawthorne plant experiments launched in the 1920s. Mayo's initial goals involved better use of time and avoidance of fatigue, but he was soon drawn into a concern about anger as he discovered a level of "irritability" among workers that he could not ignore. Raised like Taylor in a middle-class home, Mayo was purely and simply disturbed by the angry atmosphere, and he translated his disturbance into a sense that production must suffer from workers' irritability. From this, an emphasis on morale, defined as producing better cheer and less workplace anger, became a major focus of personnel initiatives not only at Hawthorne but also in the growing field of personnel psychology around the nation. Mayo's beliefs that, as he put it, angry outbursts on the job were equivalents of nervous breakdowns in individuals generated a host of experiments to curb anger when expressed and, even better, to prevent it in the first place.[45]

Two other currents joined with industrial engineering in producing the new campaign. Even before Mayo, the growing presence of women workers produced a separate strand of comments about the inappropriateness of workplace anger. Women, after all, were not supposed to be angry or to serve as emotional targets, and the finding that women might cry when exposed to supervisory ire led to new appeals for restraint. It is also probable that encounters with angry working women shocked middle-class observers accustomed to a more docile femininity; no personnel manual stated this directly, but the frequency by the 1930s of female examples in case studies on misplaced anger suggests a potential connection. At the same time a growing literature on salesmanship, capped late in the 1920s by the emergence of Dale Carnegie as the personification of appropriate guidance, created yet another anti-anger strand. Salesmen, as Carnegie and others pointedly argued, should not get angry because this would inhibit sales. Cheerfulness, turning the other cheek, became part of a new-style work personality designed to subordinate personal reactions in the interests of moving goods. No matter how unreasonable the customer, Carnegie argued, the salesman must keep a smile on his face. Describing a confrontation with an insulting customer, Carnegie writes: "By apologizing and sympathizing with her point of view ... I had the satisfaction of controlling my temper, the satisfaction of returning kindness for an insult. I got infinitely more real fun out of making her like me than I ever could have gotten out of letting her go and take a jump."[46]

The message was clear, in offices, stores, and factories alike: anger at work was ugly, counterproductive, and unnecessary: "The angry man may himself be the chief victim of his emotion. It incapacitates him from dealing with his problems in a corrective way." Industrial psychologists, bent on pleasing employers interested in fuller control over their labor force and uneasy about the tide of protest that had briefly surged after World War I, argued that work did not really cause anger but merely suffered from it. A standard line in the late 1920s and 1930s held that angry workers were merely "projecting their own maladjustments upon a conjured monster, the capitalists." "It is known that complaints, very often, have nothing to do with the matter complained about." This notion translated older but more generalized beliefs about workers as a badly bred subspecies into a new excuse for devising strategies to manipulate emotional response. Since workers had rotten home lives that generated an anger to which civilized middle-class folks were superior, the main effort was to get rid of the anger without cost to the work process. The central finding was that anger could be readily talked away. "Sometimes a worker just bursting with rage at the 'unfairness' of her foreman is able to proceed normally with her work after expressing her feeling ... and receiving a few words of sympathy or explanation." This ventilation took a bit of time and patience, but it cost little; no substantive response was required. Sometimes the supervisor barely had to sympathize, for if a worker could be asked to repeat the grievance two or three times, he or she would usually become sheepish and embarrassed, and the emotion would recede; often the worker would even apologize for having come on so strong.

However, in the eyes of the new personnel gurus, it was also important for management to mend its emotional ways. Along with advice about how to defuse workers' wrath, handbooks began to instruct foremen, middle managers, and office personnel about the importance of keeping their own tempers and avoiding provoking a needless confrontation by waspishness. "Bullying begets bullying" was the new cry as a growing amount of attention turned to the anger habits of the middle and lower-middle class itself.[47]

Secretaries were told to keep their emotions in check. Whereas nineteenth-century secretarial manuals had focused on trustworthiness and responsibility, from the 1920s onward advice turned to temper control. The good clerk would smilingly confront an angry boss, and anyone with a quick temper was "faced with the problem of remedying these defects." "The secretary should never forget that in order to please people, he needs to exert himself." [48]

Foremen received growing attention. Their role in production decisions was curtailed by the rise of industrial engineers, but their responsibilities for preventing worker anger increased apace. Instead of snapping at workers, foremen must learn to listen to complaints "even when they are silly." They must recognize that "the day of the 'bully' and 'slave-driver' had gone, and the day of the 'gentleman' and 'leader' had arrived." The foreman's checklist: "Do I correct the mistakes of my workers considerately, and in a manner to indicate that I am more interested in helping them to avoid future mistakes than I am in the opportunity merely to 'bawl them out'?" The key to the kingdom was self-restraint, for the foreman who let emotion show would simply be asking for trouble from below: "Control your emotions—control your remarks—control your behavior." Shouting and ridicule were passé. The new standard involved tact and rationality—what by the 1950s was being called, by human relations experts, "consideration." [49]

In the new wisdom, anger had no place at work. The emotion was a sign of some personality flaw—"some disturbance in the equilibrium of the individual"—or of some irrelevant distraction, particularly in home life. This meant that control was all the more essential lest the work flow be needlessly interrupted. While workers must be manipulated, the chief responsibility for placing reason firmly in command of emotion lay with those who should know better than to be angry in the first place—the growing white-collar and middle-management groups. Maturity was crucial here, as with jealousy. Personnel counselors felt free to tell an angry employee, "You look silly having a temper tantrum at your age." The key to the new emotional style, for counselors and managers alike, was to be "impersonal, but friendly." [50]

Attacks on anger, particularly in middle management, readily suggested wider concerns about emotions in the workplace. Rationality became central in the new personnel litany: "Effectiveness decreases as emotionality increases." Grievances, particularly, must be approached in low-key fashion, "with as little heat as possible." And the word "cool" began to creep in as a talisman of desirable emotional control: "It is of the utmost importance that the foreman remain cool," as a 1943 personnel relations article put it.[51]

The work-based campaign against anger quickly transcended rhetoric, for in this case the means were at hand to put money where the mouth was. The spread of industrial relations departments in American business during the 1930s, when 31 percent of all companies maintained such services, and then the further surge during World War II under the sponsorship of the War Industries Board provided an increasing number of experts eager to undertake the task of defusing workplace anger. New personnel journals and a host of textbooks preached the standard messages widely, along with popularized manuals directed toward secretaries and salespeople. Counseling services grew apace, expressly designed to provide emotionally neutral experts who could intervene in angry disputes. A woman janitorial employee in Chicago, caught sleeping on the job, so abused her supervisor that he became afraid to take action. The solution was counseling. The worker poured out her dislike for the job as the counselor listened patiently, waiting for the anger component to subside. Calmed, the custodian agreed that things weren't so bad, and when the counselor also recommended that the foreman show more tact, the issue was closed, with no substantive changes required to remove the emotional component. Not only as intermediaries but also as role models, willing to listen while manifesting no emotion save plastic cheer, counselors helped change the anger standards on the job.[52]

From personnel expertise and counseling came other changes designed to minimize emotional tension. Counselors often participated in job interviews to estimate (among other things) the candidate's ability to control temper. Interviews themselves shifted. Instead of deliberately provoking anxiety as a means of probing character, they now established superficial bonhomie so that emotion would not distract from the task at hand. Exit interviews were designed not only to find out why an employee quit a job but also to defuse any residual anger associated with grievance. Personnel testing programs were extended from the 1930s onward, not only to evaluate aptitude but also to identify undesirable emotional characteristics. Indeed, Doncaster Humm, author of one of the most widely used screening tests, argued in the early 1940s that such tests were more useful for assessing workers' emotions than for evaluating their abilities. According to Humm 80 percent of all problem workers had testable deficiencies in temperament while only 20 percent were assigned to jobs inappropriate for their aptitudes. Similar authorities warned that untested workers might demonstrate "explosive temper and readiness to take offense." [53]

The second major implementation area, along with counseling and testing, involved explicit retraining programs directed particularly at foremen, which burgeoned between the late 1930s and the 1950s. Foremen were schooled not to press workers too hard, to aid them with problems, and to allow them to air their feelings before any serious anger could become entrenched. Examples from the bad old days, involving shouting and callousness, were contrasted with the new, correct styles of courtesy and tact. Role playing allowed foremen to try out cool responses to angry workers. Told that their main task was now not technical expertise but human relations, foremen were given the message that while workers might get angry (wrongly, but inevitably), they should not. The ideal foreman is now "sensitive to the feelings of others and exercises restraint in expressing his own." [54] New personality tests for foremen sometimes combined with retraining, as foremen were asked such questions as "is a disappointment more likely to make you angry than sad?" with sadness clearly preferred. [55] Retraining programs multiplied to embrace literally hundreds of separate operations, reaching tens of thousands of supervisors in manufacturing, insurance, and other areas. A 1944 survey claimed that 80 percent of all foremen either received or sought new human relations training.

While formal retraining subsided after the 1950s, on the assumption that old hands had learned new ways and recruits would know them in the first place if properly screened, subsequent fads reinforced the anger control message. For example, sensitivity training groups, or T-groups in the 1960s, gave higher-level executives more expensive exercises in emotion control and compromise. In their attacks on authoritarian management styles slogans like "the rationality of feelings and attitudes is as crucial as that of the mind" indicated that the purpose of workplace anger control still burned bright. Many campaigns were doubtless superficial, and the whole movement against anger invited a certain amount of public relations window dressing. Nevertheless, not only the professed goals but the sheer range of institutional initiatives revealed a genuine sense of mission in remaking the emotional context of the modern job.[56]

For about fifteen years, from the late 1920s when Mayo and his colleagues began to articulate their emotional concerns to the early 1940s, the work-based movement against anger seemed isolated from other areas of emotional culture. Notably, family advice concerning anger did not significantly change. There were three reasons for the odd disjuncture. In the first place, family advice had long warned against domestic anger, so no full revision of standards was necessary in pre- scriptions directed toward the middle class. Second, because industrial psychology is such a separate field from social work and child develop- ment programs, the concerns of the former were not communicated to the latter and thus did not quickly translate into popularized advice directed to the middle class. Third and most important, however, the Victorian interest in channeled anger had lodged so deeply in middle- class culture that it could be rethought only with difficulty. Even as work norms explicitly moved away from the idea of directing anger toward competitiveness, more diffuse middle-class values continued to embrace the belief that a proper boy should be able to direct anger at appropriate targets. As late as 1962 Lloyd Warner claimed that internal contradic- tions in the anger standards conveyed to American boys constituted, along with sexuality, one of the two leading areas of confusion in American socialization. Here Warner accurately noted how persistent the Victorian approach to anger had been.[57]

Childrearing advice thus continued to repeat the Victorian anger formulas, even as they revised the discussion of fear and jealousy. Thus in 1931 Ada Hart Arlitt wrote that anger should not be trained out of a child, for "it serves an excellent purpose if it is not carried to the point of temper tantrums." Anger motivates hard work and political reform, so parents, while preventing needless conflicts within the family, should teach children to use anger to achieve righteous purposes. Thus the good parent should tell a child that "big boys do not get angry about that," but should also be ready to say that "every big boy should be angry when smaller children are frightened by bigger ones." Emily Post, writ- ing in 1940, urged cautious use of anger—"Anger is a force which, like a savings account, should be drawn upon prudently"—but went on to repeat the common assumption that anger well used could motivate great deeds and promote acts of chivalry. In 1933 John Anderson urged, in behaviorist fashion, that anger need not be a big problem—"a child can learn either to throw tantrums or not"—while noting that anger could be valuable in "socially useful" channels as an antidote to passivity, which was a far greater threat.[58]

This line of argument was clearly at odds with the new work advice, which was pointing directly at home tensions and improper socialization as the sources of the most damaging emotional outbursts at work. As early as 1933 Elton Mayo had pointed to the home problems that led workers to import their resentments to the job and had urged counseling to resolve such issues when the family itself could not cope. By 1945 personnel authorities themselves were blaming bad parenting for anger that might be directed at the counselors, whose skillful emotional disarmament efforts might not be able to overcome past abuse. The tension between the newly demanding standards applied to anger at work and the Victorian standards carried over to discussions of the family was increasingly hard to sustain.[59]

By the 1940s the new approach to anger control began to spread into the childrearing literature. As early as 1939, in fact, child development psychologists began a revealing substitution of the word "aggression" for "anger" in discussing this emotional area, and by the 1950s "aggression" carried more page references than "anger" in the indexes of popular manuals. "Aggression," with its connotations of violent behavior and imposition on others, obviously suggested meanings rather different from those embraced by "anger." It would be hard to imagine a childrearing manual insisting that children's aggressive impulses be carefully preserved. Even so, the move away from Victorian formulas was hesitant at first. The initial 1945 edition of Dr. Spock's manual repeated Victorian ideas about channeling anger into useful work in the world, as Spock (already very concerned about jealousy and fear) advised nonchalance in the face of temper tantrums. Some new commentary stressed the depth of anger in children—"Angry emotions are deeply ingrained in human nature"—which suggested new dimensions to the problem but no very clear guidelines. Other innovators attacked older ideas piecemeal. A 1951 manual, for example, demolished the notion that children should be encouraged to control anger by boxing or other exercises that might allow them to pretend they were punishing their enemies, for these approaches exacerbated rather than drained the emotion. Here, in fact, was a renunciation of much of the Victorian approach, though the author seemed unaware of his innovation: draining, not channeling, had become the key goal, and with it a new set of conventional strategies for dealing with anger in childhood. The same author, Harold Bernard, went on to note that anger almost never led to the solution of problems and that even righteous indignation, though occasionally a boon, required strong rational control; the message was that anger should be avoided. Even pouting was condemned as allowing a child to store anger. Still, however, Victorian throwbacks could emerge as late as 1958, as in Schwartz and Ruggieri's manual, which contended that the "nondestructive" expression of legitimate anger, as when children stuck up for their rights, was healthy. In such situations parents should be willing to admit they were wrong, and they should in fact worry about children so repressed that they never showed anger at all.[60]

Nevertheless, the mood was clearly shifting. Schwartz and Ruggieri's advice was already somewhat anachronistic, for an implicit, meandering debate about anger in socialization had been occurring for almost two decades, with the balance of power steadily shifting toward innovation. Even Schwartz and Ruggieri, despite the Victorian passage cited above (modernized to include the parental obligation to respect children's rights), hedged anger with a host of new caveats. Angry people had been bottled up from childhood, "only dimly aware of their underlying passion"; incapable of self-control, "they are possessed of a devil."[61] Childhood authorities were in fact widely admitting what personnel experts had long contended: that anger had roots in personality disorders themselves derived from childhood. This was the same message that popularizers had been spreading about fear and jealousy for some time.

Full statements of the new approach emerged as early as 1941. Ruth Fedder then began to apply the unassailable idea of emotional maturity to anger and aggression, arguing that, as with jealousy, maturity meant control. The adult must accept frustration without blaming others; he or she should assume that all problems can be rationally solved. Anger was simply infantile, a sign of insecurity. "For anyone to pout, sulk, rage or indulge in other displays of violent emotion is to confess frustration and inability to face the actual problem." Aggressiveness simply bred anger in response. Only when rage might lead to effective action, as in fighting social wrongs like slavery (a revealingly extreme and anachronistic example), might the older Victorian ideas retain any validity; it was socially useful, for example, that Abraham Lincoln had been morally angry. Within a few years Dorothy Baruch and a host of other childrearing experts joined the hue and cry against anger, though a fully consistent stance was not achieved until a decade later (as in Dr. Spock's subsequent editions, where he treated anger more anxiously). Teenage advice books chimed in as well, condemning excessive competitiveness and urging the importance of controlling anger for the sake of popularity ("Do you try to prevent outbursts of anger and thoughtless remarks?").[62]

Anger had become bad, not complex or potentially useful. "Anger shows a definite attempt on the part of the angry person to dominate another. Anger does not lead to growth, learning, or harmony. Anger is rigid, inflexible, unyielding; it expresses not the slightest desire or intent to reach a better understanding. It produces either submission or further disharmony and greater antagonism." As the definition of maturity became less nuanced and good personal relations took precedence over interest in raising children to be champions of justice or productive competitors, the references to channeling anger, rather than controlling it completely, dropped from sight.[63] At the same time, discussions of anger and aggression became increasingly extreme, dotted with references to "explosions" and to deviant children "choking with rage."

The new approach recognized that some anger was unavoidable. Like fear and jealousy, anger became an emotional cross parents had to help children bear. The central aim was to convert potentially horrifying anger to bland and harmless expression. Further, it was now taboo to punish or moralize about angry expressions: both would simply make the child more angry and/or drive the emotion deeper, another potential cause for festering. Parents should also of course avoid the Victorian impulse to approve displays of childish temper as demonstrations of "spirit": anger was a serious problem, even in infants. The goal was to provide an understanding, supportive response to children's anger, designed to "prevent emotional sores from bursting." A child who learned to handle anger at home would not develop the kind of truculent character that would blow up at work or in marriage: "The more [the child] releases the anger, the less of it will remain, *provided* it has been handled in an acceptant way that doesn't make new anger take the place of what has drained off."[64]

The positive strategy involved in all this combined the same elements recommended in fear and jealousy socialization—avoidance and ventilation. Parents should be careful to remove as many sources of anger as possible by promoting good sleep, allocating material possessions fairly, and of course avoiding anger themselves. Children should be taught to identify their own anger—being able to label emotions early on received growing emphasis—and they should learn, though with no overt disapproval attached, that feeling angry was unpleasant. Further, they should be encouraged to talk their anger through, to learn that verbal expression would make the nasty emotion go away and that no physical actions—even diversionary ones like hitting the floor—and no positive results were associated with the experience. At most, some role playing might aid the process if talk alone did not suffice. Children's angry impulses must be diverted, replaced with other feelings "more socially useful and personally comfortable." "Feelings *can* be changed, with changed behavior intelligently following." [65]

In the familiar pattern, adult anger was now seen as resulting from childhood mishandling and repression. Angry adults were immature, though no less dangerous for their childishness: "they are possessed of a devil," becoming tyrants in office and home alike. In his later editions Dr. Spock, moving away from his initial, inadvertent Victorianism, specifically associated temper control with maturity. Properly adult behavior meant solving problems without anger, and American society, in the good doctor's mature judgment, needed more of this kind of control. Other authorities had moved to this position by the 1940s, emphasizing the negative results of aggression. Earlier ideas that anger might be useful in righting social wrongs were jettisoned (with a partial exception in a childrearing manual directed toward blacks): children should see authority as just and problems as resolvable through calm compromise. Rules encountered in both childhood and adulthood might not always be right, "but we cannot break them or have temper tantrums because they do not suit us personally." [66]

The new approach to draining anger was born at a time when childrearing advice was largely permissive, directed against real or imagined traditions of repression. Early recommendations thus stressed the effort to provide an understanding and supportive response, though the goal of reducing anger and preventing its formation in character was firmly maintained. This approach easily passed into the somewhat stricter mood of the 1960s and 1970s, when the goals of compromise and conformity could be more explicitly identified. Just as the attack on sibling rivalry survived the transition from behaviorism to neo-Freudianism, so the overriding interest in defusing childish anger superseded more superficial fads in expertise.

Ventilationist strategy assumed that the family must play an important role in listening to expressions of anger, and this provided a certain verbal leeway that contrasted with the greater Victorian desire for harmony at all costs. Children might need to do more than verbalize or purge their anger; they might need to tell their parents that they were angry at them. This seemingly permissive concession, however, was immediately hedged with restrictions, for anger must be released without damage or even hostility: "You don't want to worry or irritate anyone else when you use your Rage Release." Any admission of anger must quickly yield to kisses and hugs, and the emphasis on calm statements— "do you know that makes me mad?"—suggested that the goal was to impose rational control even before the emotion was vented. Highly regulated, passionless discussion, not emotional conflict, was the goal when a family dispute emerged. Marital advice literature followed essentially the same approach, as a "fair-fighting" fad emerged in the 1960s. Angry spouses were urged to shout into closets to "vent hostility." While marital disagreements were inevitable, quarrels should be postponed until the couple could be "calm" and under "control." [67]

The twentieth-century approach to anger decisively rejected some of the tensions inherent in the Victorian style. Popularizers disdained the public-private dichotomy, nor did they try to teach people to control their anger in all sorts of situations while saving the essential passion as motivation. But in place of these complexities, a new anomaly was introduced: because anger was inevitable and could not safely be repressed, some open manifestations had to be allowed; yet because anger was thoroughly unproductive and unpleasant, these manifestations must be as circumscribed as possible. Apparent tolerance, in this situation, barely masked a whole set of control mechanisms.

For angry family members were, like angry people generally, simply immature. There was no just cause for anger. Here, family advice joined the earlier workplace wisdom. Marital conflicts were thought to result from displaced anger in childhood, and ideally, this knowledge should cushion a spouse's response. As the increasingly popular "Can This Marriage Be Saved" column in the *Ladies Home Journal* argued from the 1950s onward, "Try not to take personally everything a spouse says in anger. His anger is often based on his own insecurity." Marriage counselors chimed in, repeatedly associating anger with immaturity. While the new tolerance allowed that marriage could survive an occasional quarrel, it was still the case that "most bickering in marriages would stop if husbands and wives would just be polite and 'behave like adults.'" Authorities like Robert Blood distinguished between arguing and quarreling: the former, quite compatible with a good marriage, occurred "as long as two people are able to cope with their problems objectively.... as long as emotions are still under control." As for real anger in marriage, images of warfare and "nuclear explosion" bedecked discussions of it. Communication, which might include calm, purely verbal expressions of anger, was touted as the healing alternative to angry exchange, for there was no grievance that could not be emotionally controlled by free and frank talk. Anger was either avoided in mid-twentieth-century marital advice or, its inevitability reluctantly conceded, it was trivialized, dismissed as superficial rather than deeply felt. As with jealousy, accusations were turned against the accuser: is your spouse unreasonably angry or is it you?[68] Victorians, at least as concerned about the results of quarreling in the family context, conveyed a sense of deep passions under stern control—and, of course, available for deployment elsewhere. The new-style family advice sought to dismiss anger with a laugh and a reminder about immaturity; intensity gave way to cuddles and bemused questions about what the fuss had been about in the first place. Ideally, deeper passion had disappeared by adulthood, for if it survived it would denote an antisocial, aggressive personality; and there was no useful function for anger, in the home or outside it.

Conclusion: The Larger Campaign

The trajectories of the new attacks on negative emotions were not identical, partly of course because the emotions themselves vary. Fear roused concern because of its damage to the individual; jealousy and anger also harmed the individual, but these emotions were condemned primarily because they interfered with constructive dealings with others. Moderate differences in timing combined with significant distinctions in the audiences addressed: discussions of fear began in the childrearing manuals and only gradually spread to the cultural expressions of adult institutions like the military, whereas the revisions of Victorian anger standards moved in almost literally the reverse order.

Nevertheless, the overriding similarities were striking. The concept of bad emotions united fear, jealousy, and anger around an emphasis on unpleasantness and destructive consequence. This categorization built on Victorian disapprovals, particularly of jealousy and anger, but it went well beyond Victorianism in denying the usefulness and emphasizing the extreme inner discomfort of the negative emotions.

New cultural standards began to emerge in all three cases in the 1920s, and their full statement required about three decades to develop. By the later 1950s mature and multifaceted expressions of the reasons behind hostility to these emotions and the strategies designed to curb them were readily available, and middle-class audiences were, if letters to magazines and questionnaire data can be believed, routinely consuming them.

Hostility to fear, jealousy, and anger displaced the gender distinctions that had been so prominent in Victorian culture. Remnants of the Victorian connection between jealousy and femininity survived, to be sure, but popularizers made it clear that boys as well as girls could be threatened by the monster. Moving in the opposite direction, the campaign against anger deprived men of disproportionate access to the emotion, at least in principle. Childrearing authorities no longer distinguished between girlish sweetness and desirable boyish pugnacity, and the standards at work quite explicitly urged control on both genders. Fear, finally, became a problem for people in general, not a sign of feminine weakness and an occasion for masculine challenge. Men and women did not necessarily respond to the new culture in the same ways, but there is no question that, in all areas, Victorian assumptions about distinctive characteristics and distinctive functions declined rapidly. Negative emotions were now too devastating to form part of either masculine or feminine identity.[69]

One of the symptoms of the decline of gender emphasis was the uniformity of concern about young children. The new wisdom saw dangerous potential in the nature of infants; Victorian innocence was a thing of the past. Unattended, children were quite likely to develop bad emotional character as they were victimized by fear, jealousy, or anger. Popular articles stressed, however, that while emotional problems were to some degree inherent, they could be contained and shaped. The underlying consistency in twentieth-century approaches to the negative emotions lay in this insistent focus on early childhood, in two respects. First, proper socialization laid the groundwork for adult ability to avoid or largely control the emotions that had been so menacing in infancy. There was real, if nervous, faith in the results of parental watchfulness, and real dependence on these same results to produce anger-, jealousy-, and fear-free adult capacities at work and in the home. Second, the dominance of childhood experience allowed adult deviance to be condemned and dismissed as immaturity. Significant expression of one of the negative emotions—as opposed to mere ventilation—now became the symptom of individual fault, demanding no particular response except (should the onlooker be so inclined) a patronizing tolerance. Twentieth-century popularizers took the task of emotional socialization extremely seriously: "Anger and fear are behind most behavior problems. Help your child to the security and self-reliance which insure self-control," read a *Parents' Magazine* heading of 1932, expressing the urgency of the whole childrearing issue precisely because of its adult implications.[70]

The emotional gap between childhood and adulthood widened in this process. Whereas the Victorians tended to see a continuum between relatively early childhood and subsequent experience, with character-building learning occurring at all major points, the new wisdom stressed the importance of granting children support that mature adults should not require. Thus children could vent, require compensations, command diversions, but adults, as products of this careful childhood, should need less care. They might maintain earlier habits, arranging distractions for themselves, but they should have passed the point of expecting peers to rally around to help out.

The somber new emotional demands of adulthood were masked by recurrent references to greater openness and tolerance in childrearing. Manifestations of negative emotion by children were to be greeted with great caution; punishment and even overt disapproval were to be avoided, and popularizers made considerable show of their distaste for "traditional" harsh reactions. In all three cases, however, supportive reactions were designed to dampen fervor, and they were accompanied by clear, if implicit, messages designed to teach the young to be embarrassed by their childish displays. In adulthood, constraint was more obvious still, for knowledge of what constituted immaturity served as a vivid reminder of which emotions had to be avoided or concealed. Verbal venting might be permitted to a degree, amid congratulations about triumphing over Victorian "repression"; but the margins of expression narrowed as a systematic rational suppression Victorians had never claimed moved to center stage and negative emotions lost any motivational role. The fact that the new standards for negative emotions arose concurrently with liberalization in other areas, such as sexual behavior, posture, and clothing, indicates at best a superficial relationship between the two phenomena. Though some scholarly observers have claimed a coherent pattern of "informalization,"[71] the claim is off the mark. Casual clothing, more open sexuality, or a lounging gait were signs of a more flexible personal identity and defiance of rigid standards; the trajectory of these developments was quite different from that of the new norms of emotional maturity, though the new informalities might make the new emotional standards more tolerable.

As the standards applied to negative emotions coalesced, so did appropriate strategies. To prevent inevitable surges of jealousy, fear, or anger, Americans were told to stay away from provocative situations; avoidance was the first rule of wisdom, prepared by parental manipulation and ideally maintained in independent adulthood. Distraction was a second weapon, though more clearly for fear and jealousy than for anger; material inducements might modify fear or dilute resentment of a sibling. Finally, a third recourse was for a child to announce an emotion, properly labeled, in expectation of parental reassurance or its equivalent—though whether this strategy was sustainable beyond childhood was open to question. The new emotional culture waffled on the issue of whether the desired strategies would produce a mature personality immune to jealousy or significant anger or simply a personality capable of controlling and concealing these emotions.

Management of the negative emotions most obviously focused on sustaining personal relationships, whether in the family or on the job. Along with inner unpleasantness (whether experienced or taught), potential damage to the ability to get along with others justified the "negative" label in the first place. But the negative emotions were also attacked because of their potential intensity, their capacity to escape control. Twentieth-century popularizers dealing with jealousy, fear, or anger advised against any expression, save the carefully verbal, lest it run wild. Here lay a crucial departure from the Victorian confidence that dangerous emotions might be successfully used. In the new view, emotions became all-or-nothing propositions, a set of impulses that could run a person into the ground. This is why childhood, in the twentieth-century view, became such an emotional mine field, filled with traps for the unwary or untutored. Emotions like jealousy were condemned not simply because they were negative but also because they were strong. Words like "devastating" were routinely applied.[72] For all three negative emotions the image of festering, or explosive potential, permeated the popularized literature, particularly on childrearing. Emotion here became a powder keg, whose charge increased with each mismanagement. Frequent menacing imagery appeared in discussions of all three negative emotions, which were replete with references to juvenile delinquency, Nazism, and a variety of social ills—all the more frightening in that the emotions involved were now seen as to some degree inevitable, at least early in life. Beyond the repercussions of specific judgments on individual emotions or even the new management strategies, the redefinition of emotion to emphasize the inherence and threat of vigor raises some of the most important questions about the meaning and impact of the post-Victorian style.

Soon after the new emotional culture began to take shape, psychiatric redefinitions of insanity began to include a "borderline" category that, though always vague, embraced a number of instances of "emotional immaturity," including chronic anger, impulsiveness, and fearful anxiety. Building on efforts since the 1880s to devise a category that would include excessive manifestation of normal responses without extreme behavioral symptoms—to provide a label for diffuse personality disorders, in sum—the borderline concept provoked dispute from its introduction in the late 1930s. Its diagnostic use increased steadily, however, particularly by the 1970s, and it was formally included in the standard psychiatry manual in 1980. Borderline definitions offer important tools in diagnosing mental illness, but they also suggest the importance of new and increasingly defined standards of emotional normalcy, making what nineteenth-century observers would have termed "character disorders" into outright maladies. This development, to be sure, was distant from the more mundane popularizations of new standards of adulthood, but it potentially reinforced some of the same points.[73]

As the mainstream middle-class emotional culture emerged progressively from the 1920s onward, its contrast with Victorian norms gained a growing range of expressions. While a few messages remained constant—don't get angry at the kids or scare them deliberately as part of discipline—most of the lessons and accompanying strategies were new, as childhood became more emotionally vulnerable, adulthood ideally more rational. Victorians had worried about fear, jealousy, and anger, but they thought they could put these emotions to use. Twentieth-century popularizers worried massively about the same emotions, and they urged Americans to avoid or conceal them.

5

Dampening the Passions: Guilt, Grief, and Love

Growing hostility to the emotions labeled as negative was an important development, involving rejection of several basic emotional reactions that Victorians had regarded as functional and motivational if properly handled. To be sure, twentieth-century emotional culture did not create the newly negative verdict from thin air. Victorians and their predecessors had already warned about aspects of anger and jealousy and even about their potential for racing out of control, and they had raised new cautions about fear as well. To some extent, then, twentieth-century developments involved highlighting and extending these precedents in light of new contexts. For example, while the campaign against jealousy was new, given greater Victorian confidence in positive affection between siblings or lovers, it followed in part from increased social interaction between men and women, which raised the possibility of sexual jealousy considerably. The change was significant, but it was not entirely startling.

Through the heightened attention to negative emotions, Americans became increasingly conscious of the gap between pleasant and unpleasant emotional experience. By the later twentieth century several studies revealed the great capacity of Americans (as compared to other cultures) for distinguishing between unpleasant and pleasant emotions and, of course, markedly preferring the latter. While other cultures, such as the Chinese, manifested a sense that certain emotions were difficult or even unpleasant, they might also believe that these emotions served important functions, as a result maintaining a less simple pleasure/pain dichotomy in their emotionology. Comparative studies also revealed how unusually eager Americans were to deny experience of negative emotions or to conceal this experience. Thus, for example, by the 1990s Americans were far more likely to disapprove of jealousy than were the Chinese, but they differed even more in their professed eagerness to hide the emotion. The same held true for anger, in comparison with Chinese, West Indians, and Greeks. Pride in self-control also applied particularly to the negative emotions. A major opinion survey in the early 1970s listed ability to keep one's temper as one of the five most commonly desired character strengths: "When I get into an argument with someone, I know how to calm things down quickly."[1] Americans, in sum, clearly picked up the cultural signals about negative emotions and liked to believe they lived up to the standards, at least when they talked about values to pollsters and similar academic intruders. These qualities replaced Victorian-style claims to courage or moral passion, granting of course that comparable questionnaires did not exist in the nineteenth century. Aversion to unpleasant, presumably antisocial emotions formed a major part of the transition from Victorian to twentieth-century culture as the multifaceted preachments, reaching the middle class from home and workplace alike, struck an increasingly responsive chord.

The growth of systematic hostility to the negative emotions was not the only shift in emotional norms, however. Also taking shape from the 1920s onward was a substantial redefinition of several emotions that Victorian culture had not warned against at all. Guilt, viewed as unpleasant but essential in the nineteenth century, now took on dangerous overtones, verging on inclusion in the negative-emotions category. Grief, which no one could argue was explicitly antisocial, also earned new warnings and constraints. Finally, love, while still very positively valued, was also redefined as Americans learned that intensity even in a good emotion could be risky. Explicit attacks on Victorian love ideals emerged in several quarters, and a more restrained vocabulary was urged in a variety of personal encounters.

These developments, as much as the attack on the negative emotions, changed the dominant emotionology, redefining which emotions could be publicly expressed or urged and reducing the level of intensity that could be regarded as healthy or normal. These changes were linked to the more straightforward attacks on fear or anger by a common aversion to undue intensity and potential loss of control or vulnerability to frustration. Love, unlike anger, was still good, but like concentrated anger, too much love might lead to distortions, generating maladjustment and bad decisions. The most impressive feature of the new, underlying attempt to replace intensity with a blander emotional regime involved the spreading impulse to keep not only unpleasant experiences but even agreeable emotions under careful wraps. Playing it cool meant not being carried away in any direction, even one that in moderate proportions could be approved.

Guilt

The reassessment of guilt followed logically from the growing emphasis on distinguishing between emotions as acceptable because pleasant and unacceptable because painful. Attacks on guilt had been part of the growing warnings in the childrearing literature about anger, jealousy, and fear. One of the new taboos in dealing with childish manifestations of these emotions involved making things worse by adding guilt. For example, it was thought that the angry child would become more angry (whether overtly or not) if guilt were applied. Guilt became a source of frustration that might in turn exacerbate durable emotional malfunction. Up-to-date advisers were quite aware of their innovations in this area; guilt became part of a repressive Victorian past that had to be exorcised.[2]

In addition to reflecting concern about the impact of unpleasant emotions, the growing warnings about guilt fit amid the shifts in emotional culture in other ways as well. Guilt's potential power was recognized and addressed in essentially the same fashion as anger or jealousy: it should be ventilated so that it would not take hold. Children were increasingly trained to recognize guilty feelings and express them in hopes of adult sympathy. "I am feeling guilty" became a plea for reassurance that in turn should quickly replace any intense inner experience.

Then, too, the lack of vivid emotional replacements for guilt confirmed the twentieth-century tendency to seek nonemotional substitutes for profound emotion. Guilt in this sense was attacked not only because it was unpleasant but also because it could run too deep. Whereas the increasing distaste for undue shame in the early nineteenth century involved an immediate if implicit quest for a substitute form of emotional enforcement, the attack on guilt was not matched by any clear replacement. In terms of recommended norms, the danger of severe emotional sanctions tended to preclude any systematic effort to develop alternatives for guilt. Revealingly, in the later twentieth century, characteristic punishments for children emphasized temporary deprivation of material comforts and leisure activities, not emotional sanction beyond a certain embarrassment in front of one's peers. Whereas Victorians had adopted a clear, emotionally symbolic punishment to replace prior shaming—the idea of going to one's room, being separated from normal family affection, and thus developing guilt to the point of being able to apologize on the strength of the emotion—twentieth-century parents moved increasingly to the more emotionally neutral practice of "grounding"—interrupting a child's normal enjoyment of toys, television, or excursions with friends. Grounding was punishment, and it carried emotional overtones of mutual annoyance, but its thrust was not primarily emotional. Thus it fit precisely the notion that explicitly emotional sanctions had become too risky.

Ruth Benedict correctly noted a move away from traditional shame and guilt in a 1946 essay: "Shame is an increasingly heavy burden . . . and guilt is less extremely felt than in earlier generations. In the United States this is interpreted as a relaxation of morals, because we do not expect shame to do the heavy work of morality. We do not harness the acute personal chagrin which accompanies shame to our fundamental system of morality."[3]

This judgment can be readily confirmed and partially explained by an examination of characteristic childrearing literature and related child psychology from at least the early 1930s onward. Writing for the Child Study Association of America in 1932, for example, indomitable popularizers Dorothy Canfield Fisher and Sidonie Gruenberg wrote that it was "undesirable for a child to develop a deep sense of guilt and of failure" (the equation is of course revealing in itself). The authors admitted that children should learn to be concerned about wrong behavior, but their attempt to distinguish between such learning and the emotion of guilt was rather inchoate. A popular manual in 1934 clarified, though only in passing, that guilt had become undesirable: "Practice in controlling adverse emotions is often necessary." Authors Carl and Mildred Renz urged parents to control their own emotions in the interest of avoiding guilt in their children. In dealing with childish sexual interest or toilet training, for example, a child should be "protected from an impression that there is anything shameful or disgusting about his misbehavior."[4]

Treatment of this sort made it clear, in fact, that guilt was being linked to other negative emotions in several senses. First, it was not constructive, being likely to cause either harmful distress or outright misbehavior in a child. Dr. Spock, for example, while not discoursing on guilt directly, warned against harsh discipline in such areas as toilet training, where punishment could damage a personality by making it durably hostile or inducing such generalized guilt that the child would suffer from pervasive "worrisomeness." Guilt feelings could be blamed for aggressive and even criminal behavior, or it could undermine confidence in much the same way that fear could do. The role of guilt in anxiety was frequently noted as part of the reason why the emotion could not be viewed as positive, and the "repressed energies" resulting from guilt could induce all sorts of mischief.[5]

Second, like the more obviously negative emotions guilt had the capacity to fester, building up in children to the extent that adult functioning would be hampered. Thus a child made to feel guilty will suffer "a harmful effect upon his mental health as long as he lives." Guilt about sexuality received particular attention, with the related topic of toilet training being a close second. Sexual guilt laid on a child might "unfit the individual for adult conjugal relations." Far more than the campaigns against fear or anger, concern about guilt generated a direct attack on childrearing practices of the past, when parents had used the emotion to discipline children and had created damaging inhibitions in the process; as Fischer and Gruenberg noted, "traditions of guilt and sin" needed to be rigorously overthrown.[6]

Third, as with the negative emotions, avoidance of guilt also involved new duties for parents. Parents should help children bypass behaviors and situations that would arouse great guilt. They should keep their own impatience in check by not expecting too much too soon (in toilet training, for instance), and they must avoid humiliating a child. Precisely because many parents had been raised amid guilt, they needed to take careful emotional stock before they dealt with disciplinary issues. "Unless he [the parent] can keep his own emotions under control . . . he will not be able to train his child properly."[7] Parents must come to terms with their own repressions lest they pass them on to their offspring. From this initial parental injunction, the notion developed that an individual who induced guilt in another was in many ways the greater offender than the person whose behavior caused the confrontation in the first place. Ironically, instillers of guilt now had much to feel guilty about, for causing emotional distress was more reprehensible than many bad actions.

Finally, and above all, guilt became a negative emotion not only because it was unpleasant (its association with anxiety conveyed this link) but also because its intensity might so easily incapacitate. Popularizers and research psychologists alike talked of "floods" of guilt or of people "laden with their feelings of guilt." They lamented the way guilt could induce a "merciless kind of self-condemnation" and a host of related irrationalities. Guilt could paralyze thought and so prevent proper self-direction and control. Adults who had been made to feel guilty as children could be infected with feelings that they could not easily recognize and therefore could not govern.[8]

In the childrearing manuals guilt did not command the systematic attention that fear, anger, or jealousy did. The emotion was somewhat more abstract, and some observers wavered between the new wisdom that guilt was bad and the earlier recognition that it served some undeniable functions. Thus a 1959 text offered the usual condemnation of guilt as a cause of frustration and anxiety but also noted in a separate section, with no attempt to reconcile the contradiction, that the emotion was essential for society in serving as a "silent policeman." The main reason for such scattered treatments of guilt, however, lay in the fact that commentary on guilt was diffused among more specific commentaries on sexuality, toilet training, and general disciplinary approach. Brief comments on guilt's harmfulness and deleterious intensity undergirded more specific efforts to teach parents to be patient, to "take it easy" in order to avoid making children feel guilty about perfectly natural functions and interests. Another reason why elaborate comment on the emotion itself was not judged necessary was that guilt, unlike fear or anger, was avoidable. If parents broke through the customs of the past, they could raise children free from this particular emotional distraction. Thus strategies for avoiding guilt were downplayed in favor of urging parents to gain command of their own "repressed neuroses" in the interests of raising emotionally healthier personalities in the next generation.[9]

Increasingly, the new attitude toward guilt blended with attacks on anger and jealousy as part of the effort to reverse Victorian cultural emphases and produce an emotionology systematically purged of dangerous intensities. But the new approach concerning guilt required more than warning labels and parental strategies. It also demanded some attention to alternatives. For despite their eagerness to escape Victorian repressiveness and blind insistence on childish obedience, the new breed of popularizers clearly recognized the need for self-restraint. Therefore, if they advised that guilt was no longer an appropriate enforcer, then they obviously needed to indicate what would take its place. The classic negative emotions did not require this next step: anger, jealousy, or fear could be branded as bad, strategies developed for avoidance or control, and that was that. Guilt, in this sense, was more complex, which was one reason why many popularizers groped for some distinction between guilt and a healthy (presumably less emotion-laden) conscience.

Three alternatives to the Victorian emphasis on guilt developed, two of which were explicitly discussed in childrearing manuals. First, parents were urged to help children avoid guilt, not only by restraining their own emotions in discipline but also by monitoring behavior so that potentially guilt-inducing situations became unlikely. Here, behavioral attention could make emotionally based self-criticism less necessary in the early years of childhood.

Second, parents should help children understand appropriate behaviors rationally. The reason for patience in toilet training, for example, was that at a certain point, after age two or three, children could be talked to about proper cleanliness. They might even, as Dr. Spock suggested, want to control their bodily processes on their own. Discipline of all sorts should make children think. Emotion should be avoided precisely because it beclouded reason. Calm parents could talk to their children, who would, equally calmly, come to agree on goals—if parents did not press the goals prematurely. Ideally, then, a combination of behavior strategy designed to avoid distressing situations and rational control would generate the good behavior families and society had a right to expect. Guilt need not enter in, and indeed, in some formulations, no emotions of any sort were necessary to achieve propriety in word and deed.

But the larger campaign to control other negative emotions and some of the language in the comments on guilt itself suggested a third, implicit but probably most important attack on guilt. According to this approach, people would learn through their upbringing that inappropriate emotional expression could be condemned as immature. The warnings to parents to keep the results of their own misguided upbringings under control not only credited the possibility of rational dominance—parents could learn to behave before they distorted their own kids—but also reminded parents that mistakes reflected an essential childishness that should embarrass any mature adult.

As in the Victorian period, explicit emphasis on shame in childrearing remained fairly subdued. Children were not to be taunted or exposed to the scorn of their siblings. Indeed, twentieth-century parents, and even the schools, moved farther from reliance on shame than the Victorians had done, reducing public humiliations in the classroom, for example. With shame still downplayed and guilt now attacked as well, emphasis in childrearing, at least as conceived in the mainstream middle-class culture, shifted to rational explanation and persuasion as the proper reactions to bad behavior, supplemented by an emotionally neutral denial of privileges if necessary. Unpleasant emotions were neither to be scorned nor attacked through guilt but rather ventilated, enabling children to defuse the emotional experience through labeling and talking out. Because it dissociated emotion from action, this tactic minimized the need for formal adult response. Ventilation was the alternative to adult riposte (with its potential for harmful guilt) and to the dreaded festering that might convert a passing negative experience into a personality trait. Reliance on ventilation formed the new first stage in the complex task of disciplining oneself without rousing intense emotional impulses either as motivations for good behavior or as side effects. This strategy was supplemented, of course, by parental tactics designed to constrain opportunities for bad behavior or negative emotional experience. Revealingly, school honor codes, a classic way to express reliance on a regime of guilt, ossified after the mid-twentieth century, with only two American universities (Air Force Academy and Dartmouth College) launching a new honor code program after 1945.[10] Here, too, efforts to help avoid both temptation and potential guilt pangs forced new kinds of adult supervision or manipulation.

The childhood phase did not, however, directly carry through to adulthood. Whereas in Victorian days guilt instilled in childhood was meant to serve as a lifelong guide, in the twentieth century the relationship between the two life stages became more complicated. The same prescriptive literature that urged anxious attention to children's experiences of anger, jealousy, or fear—and avoidance of guilt—cold-shouldered the same negative emotions expressed by adults, blanketing them with the label "immature." Immature emotions expressed by adults, in turn, should be corrected by embarrassment, which involved a different type of ventilation technique. Most obviously, the strategy of allowing people to repeat angry grievances was designed to make them see their own childishness until, sheepishly, they would realize their folly and bring their emotionality under control. Well-bred people would need to experience this technique rarely, for their rational controls would normally operate. But where breeding failed, embarrassment provided the technique that would allow reason to replace emotion, without setting in motion defensive emotional intensities that could weaken control still further. Both guilt and shame were involved in the new reliance on embarrassment, but in typically muted fashion. Embarrassment was less profoundly internalized than guilt in that it required outside stimulus and was not intended to cut too deep. At the same time it was less public and more subtle than shame, involving individual recognition of childishness, not overt derision from the outside. Evisceration of intensity, not passionate judgment either by self or others, was now the goal as twentieth-century American culture sought to combine emotional control with avoidance of excess even in defense of proper standards.[11]

The effort to replace guilt with embarrassment in regulating negative emotions and other unacceptable behaviors not only worked against intensity but also assumed an audience. New sensitivities to peers and immediate superiors were essential to the successful operation of embarrassment. Revealingly, advice to adults about anger frequently included the otherwise bizarre recommendation that anger might be expressed completely in isolation if necessary—shrieking in the closet—because this outlet would produce no audience response, and hence no embarrassment. Thus concealment also flourished in this atmosphere, since people could avoid the new methods of reproof by hiding their emotional reactions.

The overall effectiveness of the new system of regulation and suppression must await subsequent comment. Its intended superficiality did not preclude impact. At present it is most important to note that the increasing aversion to guilt fit in with the overall shift in emotional style, becoming a part of a new emotional regulatory system that not only required a host of novel tactics, beginning with parental treatment of young children, but also deliberately avoided emotional depth. In this system, sensitivity to others' reactions would allow individuals to correct their courses without intense internal responses—a strategy that would effectively overcome the threat to rational control posed by guilt.

Grief

The transformation of twentieth-century grief has yet to be explicitly studied. Commentary on twentieth-century reactions to death from historians like Philippe Ariès and psychologists like Elisabeth Kubler-Ross indicates an increasing distaste for death; a desire to isolate it in alienating hospital environments; and (though more rapidly in Europe than the United States) an increasing preference for cremation as a replacement for traditional memorials and rituals. Lack of adequate outlets for mourning resulting from the decline of formal periods and markings of grief has also been noted. But the actual historical process by which a rich Victorian grief culture yielded to the colder reactions of the twentieth century has not been examined.[12]

Unlike guilt, grief did not exactly become a negative emotion. However, the experience of grief was regarded as unpleasant, lacking the saving graces that Victorian culture had provided for it. Even more important, its potentially consuming qualities inevitably drew growing disapproval. Precisely the feature of grief that had seemed most suitable to nineteenth-century observers—its capacity to take a person out of normal reality in reaction to loss—now became menacing. Thus, while grief was not blackened quite as thoroughly as were the negative emotions, it began to encounter a combination of concern and neglect that marked a pronounced shift from nineteenth-century standards.

The initial reconsideration of the Victorian valuation of grief began in the 1890s, mainly through the medium of opinion articles in middle-class magazines. Although preliminary to a full emotionological change, this reconsideration entered into the process of reshaping basic standards as magazines like *Outlook,* the *North American Review,* and others offered an array of articles on death and its emotional overtones from the 1890s through World War I.

Two factors, at least, accounted for the early start on a revisionist approach. First, death rates began to drop rapidly in the United States from the 1880s to the 1920s, particularly among children.[13] It was almost inevitable that such a dramatic development would have cultural repercussions. Second, and perhaps even more important to the editorials about death, discussions of Victorian ideas about mortality followed from the "warfare between science and theology" generated by the debates over evolution.[14] Death proved to be one of the areas where enlightened modern opinion found it easy to attack old religious beliefs, Victorian among others, and while this focus was not directly emotional, it had emotional implications that were gradually taken up. For these reasons the chronology of the attack on grief was somewhat different from that of the other attacks on Victorian emotionology. However, as the early results fed into a more explicit review of grief from the 1920s onward, when editorial debate declined but explicit socialization advice increased, the concordance between attacks on Victorian grief and reconsiderations of jealousy, fear, and guilt clearly emerged.

One side of the debate in the 1890s and 1900s featured careful restatements of Victorian values. *Outlook,* as a Christian periodical, particularly defended the importance of grief. Editors urged readers to experience the vitality as well as the inevitability of sorrow "by bearing its full impact with patience, sweetness and faith." In 1906 Lyman Abbott reminded readers that suffering educates and ennobles and extolled the strengthening effects of grief: "We are perfected in character in the school of suffering." "Who would live in a world of sorrow and never know sorrow? Blessed are they that mourn, because in their sorrow they can, if they will, strengthen those that sorrow, sharing their grief and bearing their burden for them." A 1902 article echoed the Victorian belief in the union of loved ones in heaven as a hope that could undergird grief: "It is in the pain of separation that the deepest joy of reunion is born; it is in the anguish of loss that the bliss of final recovery is prepared." The link between love and grief remained: "To be conscious that others grieve and not to grieve with them would be not to love."[15] But this Victorian continuity now had a defensive cast to it, for other arguments were more widely disseminated.

One subtle source of attack on Victorian grief really involved a Panglossian extension of Victorianism itself: If death involved quick union with God and only brief separation from loved ones on earth, why bother to grieve at all, and why dread death? "Why should it not be to all of us the Great Adventure? Why should we not look forward to it with anticipation, not with apprehension?" In this upbeat Christian rendering, joy, not grief, should predominate, and the bittersweet ambivalence of Victorian culture was muscled aside in favor of assertions of perpetual happiness. In 1907 Jane Belfield wrote on death for *Lippincott's Magazine*, stressing the folly of great pain. After all, not only death but also reunion with family is certain, so death need not involve intense feelings at all but rather "emotions and aspirations hushed." Another tack, slightly different from Christian optimism, increasingly emphasized the debilities of old age, such that death could and should be calmly greeted if, as was increasingly the case, it had the courtesy to wait until people had passed through normal adulthood. *Outlook* also took up this theme, stressing death as a pleasant release from decrepitude: "The stains of travel were gone, the signs of age had vanished; once more young, but with a wisdom beyond youth, she started with buoyant step and with a rising hope in her heart; for through the soft mist beautiful forms seemed to be moving, and faint and far she heard voices that seemed to come out of her childhood, fresh with the freshness of the morning, and her spirit grew faint for joy at the sound of them." Clearly, in this picture, neither fear for one's own death nor grief at the passing of an older relative made much sense.[16]

Popularized science attacked grief and fear of death from another interesting angle. A steady, surprising series of articles countered the traditional belief that death involved pain. Many modern spirits argued that this belief was one of the sources of Christianity's hold on the masses, who used religion to counter anticipated suffering, but that it was empirically incorrect. This was not, of course, a direct attack on Victorian emotional culture, which had also downplayed the physical side of death in favor of a vaguely religious spirituality, but it had implications concerning grief. Science, so the modernists repeatedly argued, suggested that most deaths were actually rather pleasant. A *New Englander and Yale Review* article launched a seemingly bizarre debate in 1891, attacking the "popular belief" that "the moment of death is to be anticipated as one of bodily pain and mental discomfort." Granting that there is a natural dread of death in anticipation, the article contended that most deaths involved a "pleasurable sensation." Death in old age, most notably, resembled going to sleep; it was "a slumberous condition, not unlike that at the end of a toilsome day." Even sudden death or convulsions, however, did not indicate pain. People under anesthesia, after all, reported "delightful sensations" and "beatific visions." Whatever pain might be involved was largely unfelt, according to the best medical evidence.[17]

This line of argument continued to receive considerable attention for over two decades. In 1901 a *North American Review* piece noted that morality would improve if death were no longer used as a threat, for its pain is in fact illusory. The *Fortnightly Review* contended more generally that with medical improvements, plus the new understanding that death need not be feared as painful, "death is disappearing from our thoughts." "Perhaps the most distinctive note of the modern spirit is the practical disappearance of the thought of death as an influence directly bearing upon practical life." Because death was losing its terrors—being now "regarded rather as a welcome friend than a grisly visitant"—and because beliefs in personal immortality were fading, the death of another "frequently causes more relief than grief to those who remain." The article claimed that a host of new developments, including the tensions involved in medically prolonged life and the growing popularity of cremation, evidenced major changes in reactions toward death, particularly a decline in fear and sorrow. In 1909 *Current Literature* returned to the medical view, which reduced death's terrors and emphasized gradual, rather peaceful decay. "We do not die suddenly; our existence perishes gradually with the weakening of the organs." So, by implication, why a great fuss when the final stage occurred? By 1914 *Living Age* could refer in passing to virtual unanimity in the claim that "the 'death agony' is an unscientific conception," which in turn meant that the whole atmosphere of death needed review. *Current Literature* attacked the idea that death or loss of consciousness should provoke fear; people should get used to the "hard facts of science" and stop emoting so much about what was in fact not only inevitable but also rather tranquil. Churches needed some other argument (if they could find one) to attract reasonable people back to attendance; death and grief were outdated religious motivations.[18]

These arguments about science reflected a desire to expose death to the cold light of reason and also to pick up on medical advances, including the growing emphasis on organic deterioration as the leading killer rather than epidemic or disease. The scientific approach included a number of idiosyncratic byways. Some commentators explained increases in suicide as evidence that attitudes toward death were losing emotional charge. Others argued that euthanasia followed logically from the new understanding of death's painlessness. Popularizations of Elie Metchnikoff's arguments that death-causing microphages could be defeated, thus allowing massive prolongation of life, constituted another means of arguing against conventional attitudes toward death. The main point here is the steady current of attention given to the necessity of challenging traditional responses in the name of science and progress. As death became a scientific topic and older attitudes were presumably exposed as fallacious, the emotional overtones of death, including not only fear but also anger, lost justification, and thus the need for pronounced grief was obviated.

Other commentary on emotions associated with death flowed from a series of articles on foreign death practices, which could be used to highlight American gains in objectivity. Another popular theme involved critiques of expensive funeral practices and the increase of professional morticians. A *North American Review* article of 1907 distinguished between appropriate recognition of the gravity of death and the exploitative ceremonies that played on grief. "Nobody goes to see a man born, but the entire community turns out to see him buried." Funerals had become perverse. "We could never understand why old women should, as they unquestionably do, love to attend funerals, or how anybody could be induced, except as a matter of duty, to make a business or profession of the handling of corpses." The only undertaker worth his salt was the progressive practitioner interested in helping a family save money and curtail needless agonizing, though the author granted that traditional grief should not be assailed too frontally. A *Harper's Weekly* piece echoed these sentiments, with emphasis on minimization and low cost: a cheap funeral should be entirely adequate "to satisfy any one except those who want really unnecessary display." *The Survey,* for its part, condemned grasping undertakers. "Nothing less than ghoulish are some of the stories of the pressure put upon grief-distracted people to honor their dead at excessive expense." Emphasis, of course, rested on economic good sense, but a corollary implication was that sensible people would not let themselves be so overcome by emotion as to fall prey to the greedy.[19]

Finally, a trickle of articles played up a somewhat different theme of modern life, noting the rise of death-defying behavior in auto racing and flying. Thrill seeking here transcended caution, and death receded to the background. And just as the new moderns defied the fear of death, so should those confronted with the sudden death of an acquaintance handle the situation coolly. "The best psychology of life is equally the best psychology of death": be glad to live and gladly die. Even religious authors had to agree that nineteenth-century death attitudes had been rather "vulgar and morbid," resulting in funeral practices that were often "in bad taste"; they also castigated the "old idea" of grief as heart-break.[20]

While death itself received more explicit attention than emotional reactions to it, up-to-date authors did comment on grief as well. As the *Independent* noted in 1908, "Probably nothing is sadder in life than the thought of all the hours that are spent in grieving over what is past and irretrievable." Time wasted was only part of the problem; loss of control was the other: "It is only man [of all the species] that allows his sorrow so to overcome him that he spends hours calling up the pictures of past happiness which cannot be brought back." People know this, but their grief overwhelms their reason, with the result that they nurse sorrow rather than looking for happy distraction. Here was a direct attack on Victorian emotionology: grief has no function, its effort to maintain contact with the departed being foolish at best, unhealthy at worst. Modern "psycho-therapeutics" must be invoked to help people escape conventional grief, and medical attention was necessary to combat any physical causes of "melancholic feelings." A bit of grief might be tolerable, but weeks of tears suggested "something morbid, either mental or physical." Women of course were the worst offenders: "When a woman cannot rouse herself . . . from her grief there is need of the care of the physician." The *Independent* editorial acknowledged that grief used to seem consoling, when a young spouse, for example, mourned the death of a partner, but went on to say that a great deal of unscientific nonsense used to be written about pining away from grief when often the cause was "the transmission of the bacillus tuberculosis." "This may seem a very crude and heartless way to look at such a subject, but it is eminently practical and above all has the merit of being satisfactorily therapeutic. Nothing is more calculated to arouse people from the poignancy of their grief than the realization of a necessity to care for their health." Thus, although grief might always be with us to a degree, Victorian wallowing had become ridiculous. Modern medicine suggested that mental and physical healing often make grief entirely unnecessary. Even religion might be legitimately used, if all else fails, to pull people out of their misery. Whatever the remedy, grief "in excess" must be attacked. As the editorial concluded, in an orgy of scientism, grief is a "contradiction in the universe, an attempt on the part of a drop in the sea to prevent the tidal progress of the ocean of life of which it is so small a part, yet every atom of which is meant to serve a wise purpose in all its events."[21]

The new view of death and grief was both confirmed and enhanced by recommended reactions to the massive slaughter of World War I. This event, which might have prompted a return to older notions of the comfort and bonding qualities of grief (and doubtless it did, in individual cases), in fact served in most public commentary as yet another sign of grief's misplaced, even offensive qualities. The dominant theme emphasized the need to put grief aside—as a British article put it, "to efface as far as possible the signs of woe." While this approach called upon a Victorian sense of mastering fear, it added the explicit component of downplaying grief in the interests of carrying on, even providing cheerful encouragement. The idea of death as routine and unemotional gained ground in this approach: "we are beginning to hold [death] in contempt." *Current Opinion* summed up the dominant thought in an essay on "the abolition of death," specifically noting the new revulsion in both England and America against Victorian habits, including elaborate, mournful funerals. The *Literary Digest* built on this theme in 1917: "Death is so familiar a companion in war-time that a revision of our modes of dealing with its immediate presence is pertinent to the relief of human anguish." The old Christian bugaboo, fear of death, must be put aside, as even Christian outlets admitted. Funerals should be joyful so that they do not distract from the ongoing purposes of life. People who still wanted "an old-fashioned chamber of horrors show"—the tearful funeral—must be brought into line. Referring to some neighbors who were resistant to the new approach to grief, the *Literary Digest* article explained, "Some of them protested at first . . . but before it was over they all took off their hats . . . and let civilization have the right of way." Another journal wanted to use the war to effect permanent improvement in the area of emotion, "evolving greater wisdom and good sense in our mourning usages." Grief should, in this revealing argument, become embarrassing: "To strive to be as natural as possible at such a time is surely the healthy attitude." Self-control, not excessive sorrow, should predominate, and formal mourning practices, which merely encourage grief, must yield accordingly. "Let us have more sweetness—and light— in our commemorating of our dear ones." As another author put it, "When you squeeze the pusillanimous eloquence and sentimentality out of the most elegant funeral discourse, I doubt if what remains is a [fitting] tribute to the essential qualities of a brave man's character."[22]

After the war's end, American middle-class periodicals continued to discuss grief and death for a few years. The theme of the "unexpected pleasantness of death according to modern science" briefly recurred. Fallen mountain climbers, for example, were cited as reporting that agony had not been involved. One essayist ventured, without however offering personal testimony, that "even in cases of death from being torn to pieces by wild beasts, physical pain is surprisingly [sic] absent." Doctors continued to attest that fear and pain disappeared when death itself approached. A few religious writers returned, as in an *Atlantic* essay of 1922, to a defense of traditional grief and bereavement, arguing that modernist dissenters had simply not gone through the experiences necessary to be credentialed. Grief, in this view, must not be tampered with, for it was essential to ultimate recovery. But the *Atlantic* also published a more characteristic article in 1923 that reflected the fruits of what was by now a long transition period from the heyday of Victorianism. Without going into scientific detail, without touting medical evidence or the possibility of psychic contacts with the afterlife (a theme that had surfaced in the discussions around 1900), Sarah Cleghorn discussed her own evolution with regard to grief. Describing her grief experiences in childhood, Cleghorn made it clear that the emotion was something she had largely outgrown in adulthood as death became more familiar, its prospect even pleasurable. Her comment included an attack on her upbringing, which was "Victorian in some of the worst sense of that word." She concluded that the emphasis must be on the positive, including personal efforts to gain ascendancy over "fruitless recollection." Vigor and the full feeling of life depended on this ability to deal with death unencumbered by grief.[23]

With this brief postwar flurry, the long debate over how to end Victorian approaches to grief and death came to a close. Middle-class magazines turned to other topics as the issue of death and its emotional environment faded from view. Transitional themes like the attack on death as painful largely shut down. Beleaguered defenses of Victorianism also ceased in the mainstream magazines. Even the interest in criticizing gouging funeral directors seemed to disappear. Yet the attack on Victorian concepts of grief had three ongoing results that incorporated the new hostility to the emotion more fully in middle-class emotionology. First, while discussions of death and grief became far less common, the occasional comment reminded the middle-class audience of the accepted emotional rules; second, the agreement reached about seeking to reduce grief translated into dominant therapeutic emphases; and third, advice to parents sought to develop appropriate socialization strategies to remove intense grief from childhood.

The first result was the growing silence itself. Into the later 1950s discussions of death and emotional reactions to it seemed out of bounds, either not worth pen and ink or too risky to evoke. After this period, by the 1960s, observers of American (and European) death culture after this began to talk of death as a modern taboo.[24] They exaggerated slightly, as we will see, but the contrast between the 1890s–World War I decades, when active discussion was almost an essayist's staple, and the subsequent cessation of comment was genuinely striking. Either editors assumed that their audience had come to terms with appropriate attitudes or judged that elaborately evoking the topic was risky precisely because the new, upbeat standards were too shakily established to warrant exposure. Whatever the reasons for it, grief now generated widespread avoidance—and in this respect, though to an unusual extent, it joined the other emotional intensities.

An occasional article renewed the death-as-painless theme along lines of scientific refutation of misleading myths. "Medical men assure us that the struggle with which life quits the body is not . . . painful to the dying, however distressing is may be to the watcher." The corollary, of course, was that grief was not, as it had once been held to be, a reverberation of sympathy with the suffering of an expiring person. A 1927 article added psychic evidence, noting that communications from beyond the grave never stressed pain. A 1950s effort in this genre stressed science more strictly, ending with the plea: "Look death in the face. His countenance isn't so terrifying as we are led to believe." Potshots at the ritualistic gobbledygook of traditional funerals still received comment, emphasizing among other things the needless emotional pain that these events caused the "already anguished family." "Why is it that we are able to cast off conventions pertaining to every event in modern existence except the burial of the dead?" The author proposed simpler, more rational as well as less expensive ceremonies designed to ease emotion rather than play on it.[25] Even *Christian Century* urged more "natural and happy" funeral occasions. The same journal did publish a few laments about the inadequacies of modern emotional styles, urging the importance of grief in leading to appropriate spirituality. Modernism, in this rendering, could be dangerously dry, while modern life offered too little preparation for death. "There is safety in grief's greatness." Even these comments, however, did not replicate the Victorian fullness of grief, for they recognized that they were going against the predominant culture, and they also sought a quick end to grief through religion.[26] They were distinctive in insisting that grief must occur and in their emphasis on spiritual solace, but the Christian popularizers seemed to agree that in itself grief was simply painful, to be escaped as quickly as possible. Whether modernist or more traditional, however, articles on this subject were few and far between. Apparently the topic was generally considered best avoided.

Whether this relative silence reflected a desire to make death taboo, however, is debatable. It may instead have followed from a sense among the popularizing pundits that the relevant issues were closed, that by now everyone knew the new rules. The largest number of articles during the late 1920s and the 1930s—and they too were infrequent—suggested an assurance that modern Americans were rapidly moving toward appropriate enlightenment about death and grief. Beatrice Blankenship, writing of many family deaths, noted how rarely death intruded on the routines of modern life. She criticized ritual remnants such as irrational fear of death or disturbing funerals. Death, even a child's death, while it might elicit some grief, should be treated rationally and calmly, even as modern people were losing the false certainty of an afterlife. More bombastically, Mabel Ulrich wrote in 1934 of the decline of religious beliefs and their replacement by scientific curiosity and self-control. Only a few backsliders remained: "Is it too far-fetched a hope that to these when they have forsaken their wavering misty image of heaven there may come a consciousness. . . . of the amazing relevance of life?" "Modern knowledge . . . offers to the intelligent person to-day a conception of living which is a positive answer to old death fears." The *American Mercury* proudly boasted that in contrast to emotion-sodden Europe, "America Conquers Death." "Death, which dominates the

European's thought, has been put in its proper place on this side of the water." This article praises modern Americans for triumphing over their cultural past, when death once hovered much closer to home. In 1940 *Scholastic* acknowledged real grief but urged the possibility of allowing life to go on equably even after a death in the immediate family. Distorting grief, the author argued, usually resulted from some "unpleasant and mystifying experience" in connection with death during one's childhood—another indication that appropriately low levels of grief, like other issues in emotion management, depended on up-to-date child training.[27]

Even World War II produced little general reconsideration of death and grief. A few articles during and after the war suggested that conquered grief could be a goad to constructive action—a new twist that did however evoke a more Victorian treatment of emotion. More commonly, magazine articles stressed that death could be faced bravely: "So we would have to carry on. He would want us to. There was still work to be done in a needy world." Bitterness and moping ran counter to constructive behavior. To be sure, grief must be faced when a loved one dies in war, and some Christian commentators used the occasion to remind their readers about spiritual solace and even the comfort of formal mourning. In general, however, World War II produced less comment on appropriate emotional reaction than had World War I—another sign that death was being avoided more fully and also that cultural rules about constraining grief had circulated more widely. War stories and films, for their part, tried to mute the subject by carefully arranging to have only peripheral figures die; protagonists might see death around them, but they survived to the happy ending. Again, grief need not apply. A surprisingly sparse set of popular articles directed at war widows or other bereaved women confirmed the stiff-upper-lip tone: emotion should not be indulged, and women should plunge into war work or volunteerism to keep their minds off their troubles. "Don't wear mourning too long. It expresses no real respect for the dead, and it is depressing to the person who wears it and to friends and family who see it."[28]

The second result of the reconsideration of Victorian grief involved the dominant therapeutic approach. By the 1920s, partly as a result of Freudian influence but partly, as we can now appreciate, because of shifts in more general middle-class prescriptions, most therapists dealing with grief moved toward what has been called a "modernist" approach. Freud had valued grief as a means of freeing individuals from ties with the deceased, but he had made it clear that detachment was the ultimate goal and had warned against the stunting that could result if grief were not transcended fairly quickly. Later modernists downplayed grief even further, viewing it as a form of separation anxiety, an inappropriate or dysfunctional attempt to restore proximity. In most instances, of course, grief played itself out as mourners gradually abandoned hope that the lost person would return; but from the therapeutic perspective there was constant danger that a more durable imbalance might form. The therapeutic goal, whether outside help was needed or not, was severance of bonds with the deceased or departed. Therapy or counseling should work toward this process of withdrawal, and those who retained grief symptoms must be regarded as maladjusted. By the 1970s even counseling with older widows encouraged the development of new identities and interests and promoted the cessation of grief and its ties to the past.[29] "Grief work" meant work against grief and an implicit attack on Victorian savoring of this emotional state. Appropriate terms were developed for excessive grief—two from the 1960s were "mummification" and "despair." "Chronic grief syndrome" applied to a situation of clinging dependency, most common among women, when a parent or spouse died. The idea that grief followed from love was also attacked; psychologists argued that in cases of spouse death, grief developed particularly strongly when a love-hate tension had existed, grief then picking up on a sense of guilt for the hate rather than a nostalgia for the love. Mental health meant breaking bonds and avoiding dependency. Grief, contradicting both goals, became a target for attack.[30]

Related to the therapeutic approach was the emotional context developed by other health professionals for dealing with death. Because of the desire to avoid grief and emotional entanglement, doctors and nurses, particularly between 1920 and the 1950s, sought to avoid attention to imminent death. Nursing handbooks provided short, matter-of-fact paragraphs on how to recognize impending death and how to lay out a corpse. Both doctors and nurses emphasized concealment of probable death from patients lest unacceptable emotions develop (and in order to protect medical personnel from emotions of their own). Again, grief must be bypassed.[31]

The third area in which the new antigrief regime manifested itself from the 1920s onward lay in a more familiar realm—advice to parents on how to socialize children. Here, the general aversion to Victorian grief was compounded by two factors: the rapid decline in child mortality, which made it progressively easier to dissociate childhood from traditional concern with death; and the rising anxiety about children's fears. From D. H. Thom in the mid-1920s onward, discussions of children's fears frequently embraced the subject of death as popularizers tried to help parents deal with irrational worries about such fanciful prospects as being buried alive. The same new breed of experts warned against the common assumption that children developed attention to death only after their initial years, and they also cautioned that conventional Victorian euphemisms, such as the equation between death and sleep, actually might increase childish fear. As Sidonie Gruenberg noted, "'They go to sleep' is one example of a convenient but dangerous evasion which could make a child approach bedtime with alarm."[32] This new approach to death in the childrearing advice was facilitated by the removal of death from the family context, not only because of rapidly dropping child mortality rates but also because of removal of sick adults to hospitals, grandparents to separate residences, and the dead themselves to funeral homes. Further, the decline in adult mourning that followed from the attack on Victorian ceremony also made it easier to separate children from active comment on death, as did the distancing of cemeteries.

In the new context children's fears of death provoked complex reactions among the popularizers. On the one hand, general instructions about fear urged frankness, talking things out. On the other hand, adults themselves were being urged to keep death at an emotional distance, which made it difficult to follow the general line where this particular fear was concerned. A clearer conclusion was that traditional Victorian approaches would not work. Children should not be widely exposed to death ceremonies, and they should not be filled with stories of angels and heavenly reunions. *Parents' Magazine* cautioned against "conjuring up a heaven of angels and harp playing," for "inevitably the small girl or boy will discover that mother and father are not certain about the after life. Such a discovery augments the fear of death." One handbook urged parents to emphasize death's humorous side, while carefully avoiding ridicule—a clear effort to desensitize. Other authors suggested carefully evasive phrasing so that the child would receive no images that he could easily apply to himself. Referring to a grandparent's death as "all through" might thus be a good idea. "Fear of death arises when the child imagines not mother or grandmother, or the bird, but himself being covered up with dirt. That much the child can imagine; that much is within the child's observable experience. But if the child gets the idea that a dead person is 'all through,' the identification of himself with the dead person or animal is more difficult." [33] Parents apparently obliged, eager to avoid the necessity of dealing with children's griefs or fears. Thus, a 1943 letter to a child described the death of a family member in these words: "That door which opens and swings only one way, was thrown open for Dr. Tuttle." [34] It is doubtful that this imagery would make children stay away from doors or grieve heavily. The entire argumentation assumed that the Victorians were wrong in thinking that children would not be severely touched by grief or might be instructed by it. It also assumed that family unity in grief had somehow become irrelevant, for reactions to death were now gauged purely in terms of their (usually harmful) impact on individual psyches. The whole Victorian grief context had disappeared as grief became simply another problem, though a potentially difficult one, in the emotional raising of children.

Experts urged parents to tell children that most death resulted from old age. "If such an explanation is grossly inappropriate," added Alan Fromme, "reference may be made to a most unusual illness which none of us is likely to get." This approach clearly enabled avoidance. To be sure, when the subject of death could not be avoided and grief did emerge, advice givers urged parents to reassure their children—though this theme received greatest emphasis before 1920. "To childish grief we should give the same loving sympathy that we should give to real grief in any other phase of life. It is a mistake to repress tears or sobs which arise from such a cause; it is far better to let the child 'cry it out' unless the current of his thoughts can be turned in another direction." But parents should avoid showing emotion on their own. One of the reasons for abandoning mourning and its colors was to help children ignore death to the greatest extent possible. When information had to be conveyed, "let us give the facts to the child with as little emotion as possible." For older children, factual, scientific information would help separate death from powerful emotion—here was a child-socialization variant on the medical modernization approach in adult contexts. Parents were advised to tell children about other cultures' ideas about death, and to talk to them about medical data when their understanding permitted, but to keep the whole subject dispassionate. Some authorities also urged not only dry facts but maximum avoidance. Fromme, for example, advising that children be kept away from funerals, wanted to prevent any glimpse of intense adult mourning. Death itself should be acknowledged quickly, lest children suspect dark secrets, but ceremonies as well as emotions might best be removed.[35]

Grief rules were clearly amalgamating with the new emotional norms applied to fear, anger, and jealousy in childhood. Children were seen as far more vulnerable than had been the case in the nineteenth century. Parents were placed under much greater emotional constraint in dealing with children, a particularly novel development where grief was concerned. Efforts at avoidance ran strong, with ventilation coming in a poor second in the overall attempt to shield children from the power and pain that grief entailed. Great emphasis was placed on chasing away fear and also on appealing to reason. One *Parents' Magazine* author acknowledged that the power of grief makes it difficult for parents to maintain rational control but went on to say that this was precisely why the emotion's power must be combated, for it is necessary to "maintain some equilibrium to carry on." Children need not be "bowed down" with grief as are some misguided adults. All fears should be dispelled — and this, rather than grief, drew the greatest attention of childrearing popularizers during World War II. Again, if parents could keep control of themselves and give children cold facts (about the reasons for war, for instance), incapacitatingly intense emotions should be avoidable. "If we try to bear a certain matter-of-factness in our discussion, . . . the child . . . will meet many minor death experiences as just one more interesting phenomenon."[36]

Death scenes also began to decline in children's stories. Killing and, particularly in boys' stories, discoveries of dead bodies occurred more frequently than before, but without emotional context. Lingering illness, the tragedy of a life plucked too soon — these Victorian staples declined. The emotionlessness developed to replace encounters with fear extended also to death. Killings were mechanical, discovery of corpses titillating but not grief stricken. Jack London's Buck in *The Call of the Wild,* to take a fairly representative early-twentieth-century example, is unmoved when he finds an arrow-ridden body and a dog thrashing about in death agony: "Buck passed around him without stopping."[37]

As we have seen, adult grief issues were increasingly minimized, shrouded in silence, or at most addressed through therapeutic approaches directed toward recovery from the emotion as if from a disease. The approach recommended for children—keeping them away from death or, in fiction, from any emotional overtones associated with death—rounded out a consistent picture. After several decades of diverse kinds of attacks on Victorian grief assumptions, middle-class culture resolutely worked around grief. The emotion became unpleasant, potentially overwhelming, lacking in any positive function. Correspondingly, the approach to grief increasingly resembled the approach to the negative emotions.

A final sign of the new grief culture emerged, though somewhat belatedly, in the etiquette books offered up to a still-eager middle-class audience. Emily Post, the leading authority in the interwar period, painted an essentially Victorian picture even in 1934, when she repeated the wording of a long section on funerals that she had initially written in 1922. She urged a variety of mourning symbols and ceremonies, including "hanging the bell" outside a home, and stressed the importance of punctiliousness precisely because emotional reactions to death ran so high. Her main advice was that readers should acknowledge the intensity of grief and respect its varied courses, expressing active sympathy when the afflicted sought company but also respecting their privacy. Grief had no sweetness in this portrayal, but its vigor was viewed as inevitable. Constraint applied only to those dealing with the mourners, who needed to put selfish interests behind them in the interest of providing comfort and calm. "All over-emotional people . . . should be banned absolutely" from grief situations. Emily Post attacked overelaborate funerals— though allowing that they were appropriate for those who found solace in them—but she noted that while formal mourning was in partial decline, it could actually serve as a protection against real sorrow. Etiquette, in sum, lagged behind other areas of emotional culture when it came to reactions to death, in part because recommendations were less frequently reworded, in part because advisers assumed that polite form and continuity with past practices were intertwined.[38]

But even in this area change did occur, and it confirmed the earlier shifts apparent in popular magazines and childrearing literature. By 1952, when Amy Vanderbilt issued her etiquette book, the major signals were quite different, although, etiquette being etiquette, there were still forms to observe. Business matters now received as much attention as ceremonies, for the first job of the bereaved was to check on wills, bank accounts, and medical formalities. Not only funerals but also mourning had become far more simple—Vanderbilt praised the decline of mourning costumes—and these trends were good because they so lightened the emotional mood. Some bereaved individuals could even express happiness, and this was a positive sign. Friends of the bereaved should still express sympathy, of course, but they should be far more careful than before not to encourage grief itself. "It is better to avoid the words 'died,' 'death,' and 'killed' in such [condolence] letters. It is quite possible to write the kind of letter that will give a moment of courage and a strong feeling of sympathy without mentioning death or sadness at all." Most revealing was the advice to the afflicted themselves, who now had an obligation to control themselves. Whereas Emily Post had readily allowed the emotion to overcome all rational or altruistic capacity for a time, not so Amy Vanderbilt and her peers in the 1950s. Grief simply must not be intense. "We are developing a more positive social attitude toward others, who might find it difficult to function well in the constant company of an outwardly mourning person."[39] Whatever went on inside should be kept firmly under wraps. Vanderbilt went on to note, in recognition of the more general culture, that wartime had taught people to restrain their grief because it damaged morale and gave comfort to the enemy. With this, the focus of etiquette shifted largely from appropriate sorrow and condolence to emphasis on restraint and an upbeat mood. Substantial grief had lost its validity in this most conventional and change-resistant of popular advice sectors.

Love

The most striking sign of change in emotional culture involved the new cautions applied to love, the key positive emotional virtue in the Victorian pantheon. Unlike grief or guilt, love was not rejected, and therefore analysis of its reconsideration must acknowledge considerable subtlety and some continuity. It did not become a negative emotion, but new constraints and redefinitions revised Victorian standards considerably, with decline in intensity being the central ingredient in the overall shift.

Love remained decidedly positive, one of the really helpful and pleasant emotions if properly managed. Caution applied to exaggeration and excess, not to affection itself, and lack of affection was unquestionably at least as dangerous as overabundance. Amid considerable debate, however, love lost its Victorian qualities. Its centrality was disputed, its automatic beneficence was questioned, and new dangers were associated with it. Its soaring qualities yielded to prosaic emotional adjustments and compatibilities. Even when love was urged and praised, then, the Victorian aura had vanished.

Motherlove. Victorian motherlove died in American emotionology during the 1920s and 1930s. Given that maternal affection had served as an emotional wellspring in the nineteenth century, the shift away from reliance on motherlove clearly indicated that emotional culture was changing dramatically.

Preparation for reassessments of motherlove surfaced around 1900. Middle-class women's magazines began running a series of articles on the new tensions between mothers and daughters that were arising as young women were exposed (or so wrote the editors) to opportunities that their mothers simply could not appreciate. "The mothers of these modern girls are very much like hens that have hatched out ducks." In this new context essays and editorials began lamenting the serious problems that inevitably developed in mother-daughter relationships and usually blamed mothers for not understanding their daughters' new needs. In this new genre mothers were assumed to be unsympathetic to modern aspirations and, as a result, overly critical, driving away their daughters' confidence by nagging and carping. At the same time, somewhat ironically, mothers were castigated for being overpermissive, failing to instill necessary discipline.

None of these articles directly addressed the issue of emotion, but they strongly implied that whatever the qualities of maternal affection might be, it was no longer adequate to the task. Conflict, not love, seemed to pervade this basic family link, and the primary fault lay with mothers. "The unnatural burden of filial obligations and scruples imposed by some mothers is the prime factor of the secret antagonism existing between them," claimed one magazine in 1901. Advice manuals began counseling mothers to adopt specific strategies to keep their daughters' confidence, again suggesting that love itself was insufficient. While the mother-daughter bond should be the tightest of all, wrote Gabrielle Jackson in 1905, it could misfire—and if it did, "it is . . . mother's fault." A basic need was for mothers not only to keep pace with their daughters' interests but also to relax control and emotional demands in order to grant independence. Again, love was not directly addressed in this discussion, but its potential excesses lurked in the background.[40]

Feminists added a second note to the new questioning of maternal adequacy. Charlotte Perkins Gilman sounded characteristic warnings in 1903. "The mother-love concept suffers . . . from its limitations," she wrote. It restricted women to an unduly narrow field of action, and while maternal nurturance could serve society, in Gilman's view it was misplaced in the home itself. According to Gilman (herself alienated from her daughter), trained professionals could take care of children better. "That the care and education of children have developed at all," she argued, "is due to the intelligent efforts of doctors, nurses, teachers, and such few parents as choose to exercise their human brains instead of brute instincts." The very fact that many mothers manifested fear of competing caregivers revealed the flimsiness of their emotional base: "The terror of the mother lest her child should love some other person better than herself shows that she is afraid of comparison."[41]

Nonetheless, great praise for motherlove did persist. Conservative writers urged the intensity of motherlove for parent and child alike. Aline Hoffman argued that "our lot, our principal office is, then, maternity . . . motherhood is the paramount duty of woman." James Fernald added that unless they were poor, daughters should stay at home until marriage in order to solidify the emotional bond "and help the dear mother who cared so tenderly for [them] in the weary loving years gone by." Scientists added their mite. G. Stanley Hall, criticizing what he saw as a growing career emphasis, insisted on the primacy of maternal affection for adult and child alike. As in other areas, Hall built Victorian emotional assumptions into his purportedly empirical psychology. The woman who did not concentrate on motherlove was the "very apotheosis of selfishness from the standpoint of every biological ethic," losing among other things her "mammary functions" and leaving "love of the child itself defective and maimed." The resultant lack of full affection in turn appeared "in the abnormal or especially incomplete development of her offspring," even more in adolescence than in childhood itself. As late as 1925, Dr. S. Josephine Baker argued for the fundamental importance of maternal love in formulating the character of the child.[42]

This implicit debate about motherlove between advocates of Victorianism and the new feminists and self-styled modernists turned into a more systematic rejection of Victorian assumptions during the 1920s. Disagreement continued as popularizers sought to find a proper definition of affection, but virtually none remained to argue for the Victorian definition of boundlessly good, sacrificial maternal love itself.

Fiction for boys now omitted mother. The theme of mother as a virtually religious talisman, a beacon guiding boys back to morality and domestic bliss, had vanished by the 1920s. Mothers might be heroic, as in the *Matchlock Gun* of 1925, or they might be nagging nuisances, or they might be virtually absent, as in the Hardy boys mystery series, where father Fenton Hardy played a bit part because he at least had an interesting job but where mother was rarely referred to at all. Mothers might play a number of roles, but they were no longer emotional lighthouses.[43]

Building on earlier feminism, a new group of experts attacked maternal emotionalism as a basis for women's work or social service. Scientific training, not motherlove, should guide social workers and nurses in a new, genderless professionalism. In 1921 a woman social worker wrote of dealing with problems of unwed mothers: "Success is achieved in inverse ratio to the degree of emotion involved."[44] Objective science, not maternal love, must serve as the guide. "It is high time that we seriously consider facts, not fictitious heart throbs."[45] Social work must be removed from the field of emotional action; "sentimental or perhaps even morbid motives" must be banned. Not only in social work but also in medicine the idea that women brought special qualities to bear through their actual or potential fund of motherlove declined in the face of this science-based professionalism. The prestige of motherlove, its role as emotional anchor, declined in the process. The terms "maudlin sentimentality" and "philanthropic hysteria" were now used—by professional women—to describe maternalism in the public sphere. Not only lack of a "thorough-going scientific effort" but also love's "super-heated" qualities called it into question.[46]

Most important, motherlove was rendered newly problematic within the family itself in advice literature and other commentary on childrearing. A series of authors hammered home the point that mothers frequently made mistakes; their love did not necessarily guide them accurately. This was not an entirely novel claim, for nineteenth-century authors, while often honoring maternal emotion, had cheerfully pointed out the need for external advice in the physical care of children. Now, however, this need also applied to emotional and moral guidance. In 1927 Dr. Smiley Blanton cited case after case in which mothers had disciplined their children improperly. Children's natural impulses, indeed, were likely to be more constructive than those of many mothers, whose reactions Blanton frequently castigated as "unjustifiable." Blanton took fathers to task as well, but he more commonly noted parental combinations in which both parties were at fault, and he applied the worst strictures to mothers themselves. "There are many women who . . . have the inborn knack of managing children, who seem to understand them, and have a feeling for them. . . . There are other women, often very fond of children, who are conspicuously lacking in this power." The average mother, between the extremes, needed training and expert advice, for whatever her emotional disposition, love alone would simply not suffice.[47]

Motherlove, finally, could easily run "out of control." A growing body of childrearing literature in the 1920s and 1930s argued that mothers were too prone to overreaction, with the consequences of their unrestrained passions harming boys and girls alike. O'Shea put the problem this way in 1920: "While nature has thus widely endowed the mother with all-embracing love for her children, it would have been better if nature had equipped the mother so that she could control her affection by her reason when her children need social training."[48] Or as Gilbreth put it eight years later: "It is too bad that freedom of expression, so admirable, perhaps, for one member of the family, may at the same time be so disastrous in its effects on another. Motherlove, for example. Some sort of control is indicated, unless the technique of sublimation has been well developed." Most notoriously, Watson directly attacked mothers' cloying affections in his chapter on "The Dangers of Too Much Mother Love." Mother became too dependent on her children's affection, wrote Watson, particularly in the modern world with husbands away at work. "Her heart is full of love which she must express in some way. She expresses it by showering love and kisses" upon hapless children, threatening their independence and mental health in the process, transforming a healthy child into a whining, dependent "Mother's boy." "Mother love is a dangerous instrument," for overcoddled children would be particularly incapacitated in marriage because of the sexually inspired love they had received from their mothers. The ideal child, in turn, was emotionally autonomous almost from birth— "relatively independent of the family situation"—and sexually well adjusted. Few popularizers went to Watsonian extremes, particularly in arguing against physical contact with the child, but many joined the master in warning against maternal excess. "There is a whole class of gushy, emotional parents who are always protesting their love by words and embraces and by excessive fussiness about health and safety. . . . Their egotism, their fears and anxieties, and their own lack of self-control are also apparent in a thousand ways."[49]

In these formulations motherlove verged toward becoming a negative emotion outright. It shared with those emotions the qualities of harming others, of befouling them through excess, and it required the same kind of self-control. To be sure, Victorians had urged mothers to keep their love under partial wraps and to emphasize self-sacrifice, but they had assumed an abundance of passion. In the new culture rationality might be preferable to even the most positive maternal emotions.

Love remained essential, however, and childrearing advice did not become entirely consistent on this subject. Guidance to parents in dealing with children's jealousy or fear stressed the importance of emotional reassurance and abiding love. Some authorities attempted to reconcile motherlove and maternal self-control by distinguishing among stages of childhood. Ernest and Gladys Groves, for example, argued that with babies "unstinted personal affection" is vital: "The little baby cannot be loved too much." In the first few months parents were to let the emotions show fully—to "make the most of their opportunity to fill the little life with love." While essential, however, this was a brief phase; thereafter, love became at least as much a danger as a blessing. After infancy "the parents have to guard against smothering the child's developing tendencies in a too vehement love, and thus preventing his ever attaining independence."[50] Further, the Groves' approach, though retaining an element of motherlove, treated intense love in a manner similar to that in which many other twentieth-century emotions were treated, as an emblem of immaturity. Untrammeled love was fine for babies but should be grown out of. These guidelines had the potential to make not only passionate motherlove but also undue intensity in love of all sorts an embarrassing reminder of infancy.

During the 1930s researchers developed the basis for a somewhat more positive approach to mothers. The British psychoanalyst Winnicott, for example, argued for a concept of "good enough mothering," assuring women that most of them could summon up enough affection to get their job done. The concept affirmed the importance of maternal competency and acknowledged an emotional component, but it hardly revived Victorian awe at the powers of motherlove; indeed, it seemed consciously to admit the loss of this culture and to compensate by accepting a much more moderate, even prosaic emotional base as adequate.[51]

From this make-do approach, in turn, beginning with Dr. Spock in 1945, childrearing manuals became a bit more consistently supportive of parental love, urging mothers in particular to have confidence in their emotions. The message reflected the pervasive concern about excess but confirmed babies' need for "gentle and loving" treatment. "Children need to have family affection, loyalty, and love behind them in order that they may grow into self-sustaining, self-respecting persons." While acknowledging love, this new tone reflected the distance from real Victorianism. Fathers were included with mothers with regard to parental emotion; there was nothing very special about maternalism. "Affection" increasingly replaced "love" as the principal noun, and references to affection were frequently combined with injunctions about common sense, harmony, and other virtues—the emotion itself was not singled out, nor was it considered transcendent. As an adoption book noted, "A confident, serene love is what he [the adoptive child] needs and what you will give him. Not suffocating love, not blind, sacrificial love that wipes out your own identity."[52]

Thus, despite a bit more support for motherlove after the 1940s, the cautions persisted in full force—though now they could be mentioned only in passing because the basic standards seemed so well established. Thus the mother and child relationship was "often too intense and precarious," according to a 1952 manual. Or according to a 1970 book, echoing Watson, "Mothers, particularly, rely heavily on their children to give them satisfactions and pleasures that more appropriately should come from the marriage relationship."[53] Under "Emotional Growing

Pains" Sidonie Gruenberg reminded parents of the need for increasing emotional independence, which in turn involved separation from parental love: "Our small isolated family units are likely to get overcharged emotionally, and we do have to bring outside interests and other friends into our lives to help balance things." A dependent child would be incapacitated, going through life seeking only gratification of appetite: "We need no amplification of this point to see how seriously handicapped in life such a child is. Another child may grow to regard the hothouse atmosphere of too much love as stifling to his urges toward independence," and might grow up to feel that "any evidence of love is dangerous to individual freedom."[54]

The basic message persisted, from the interwar decades onward. Love was necessary to a point, but it could be abused. Intensity must be avoided. "We must recognize in this connection a fundamental principle in child care: Excessive stimulation of any emotion in childhood should be avoided, whether the emotion be one of fear, anger, grief, exhilaration, or love."[55] Placidity must conquer fervor, even when the emotion was seemingly pleasant.

Romantic Love. The death of Victorian-style motherlove in some senses encouraged new emphasis on spousal love. Many advice writers, including Watson, urged healthy parents to express their love for each other, thus automatically curbing the risk of emotionally overwhelming their child. From this it could be argued that marital love was unique, permitting no real excess. Letters were cited in marriage manuals that, while not exactly Victorian-type outpourings, suggested boundless enthusiasm. "Dearest of my heart: Lover I do love you so very much. Honey dear I just love, love, love you more and more all the time. Bless your heart you are just too dear for words to utter. Darling 'Daddy' I do love you more and more every second of the day. I'll sure kiss you to death sweetie when you do come [home]." Advice manuals in the 1930s offered formulas for advancing spousal love. One argued that both spouses should not only actively but also publicly express love, should "figuratively—sing it, dance it, look it, and live it."[56] In no sense, then, did love die, and there was undeniable continuity with Victorian love standards. Nevertheless, the Victorian version of romantic love was redefined in three related senses. First, the centrality of spirituality was replaced by the superordinate centrality of sex. Second, the emotion's threat to rational calculation received new emphasis. And third, the very importance of intense love was directly disputed. Even more than with motherlove, some positive valuation persisted. Almost everyone agreed that spousal love of some sort was good, but what kind of love, and under what restraints became basic questions in a variety of popular outlets as Victorian agreement on a soaring, ethereal passion disappeared.

Signs of the new culture began to emerge, though tentatively, in the 1920s. Early symptoms of it were attached to the same kind of self-conscious "modernism" that had attacked conventions of grief and jealousy, and like other branches of modernism, the new view of love emerged on both sides of the Atlantic. The British Mrs. Havelock Ellis wrote in 1921, for example: "If monogamy is to be the relationship of the future, it will have to widen its doors, subjugate its jealousies, and accept many modern devices for spiritualizing physical passion." While the last reference had a Victorian ring, along with more than a little obscurity, Ellis's work on the whole argued for a love that would be decidedly nonexclusive, permitting a variety of relationships, and that would focus fairly frankly on sexual compatibility. Her work, and that of American pamphleteers on modern marriage like Judge Ben Lindsay, bypassed an array of Victorian conventions, most notably the references to ethereal spirituality. Again, unacknowledged links to Victorianism persisted: Lindsay thus wrote of "that free and spontaneous intensity so necessary to love." But the effort to equate love with religious heights was obviously anathema to the new modernists, as was any attempt to speak of love as the spiritual merger of two souls into one—hence the attacks on jealous exclusiveness.[57]

Modernist views on love won some currency in middle-class magazines, if only because of their shock value. The initial books themselves, particularly those by intellectuals like Mrs. Ellis, had a more limited audience. Nevertheless, an audience open to new kinds of advice about love and marriage was developing, and as we will see in a later chapter, behavior changes during the 1920s suggest that standards were changing in directions not totally dissimilar from those recommended by the modernists. Without question, growing emphasis on the validity and importance of sexual satisfaction increasingly entered middle-class public culture during this decade, when various kinds of sexual advice columns became available. Judge Lindsay confidently wrote, "I believe that I have enough evidence to justify the conclusion not that this change in our sexual mores [toward greater expressiveness and openness] is going to take place at some time in the future, but that it has already taken place and is developing and crystallizing into a tacitly recognized and increasingly tolerated code." Marital advice books began to make sex the centerpiece of marriage, finding sexual maladjustments basic to virtually every imaginable tension between spouses. While the new emphasis on sexual compatibility did not directly attack earlier ideals of love—Margaret Sanger, for instance, cautiously stressed a "true union" of souls as part of any sexual contact—it inevitably displaced spiritual concerns in favor of physical expression.[58] Femininity, correspondingly, was increasingly redefined in terms of sexuality. Here was a key factor in the reduction of attention to motherlove: women were now judged by different contributions to family, and motherlove was itself seen as potentially inimical to sexual adjustment. But while sexuality brought new importance to the relationship between spouses, it worked also to redefine love and to downplay the spiritualized passion that love had once, in principle, embodied. The sexual emphasis also tended, if only implicitly, to highlight the rewards an individual should get from a relationship rather than the higher unity of the relationship itself.

Elements of the evolution in the fundamental meaning of love appeared in language. In the nineteenth century the word "lover" embraced some ambiguity in that it could refer to sexual liaison, but the predominant definition was a man who had a special sentiment for a woman. "One who loves; one who has a tender affection, particularly for a female," was Noah Webster's phrasing. This meaning did not vanish, but by the 1880s the word began to take on more specific courtship connotations, as with the rise in lovers'-lane references. And between the 1920s and the 1950s the full about-face occurred, as the word came to connote sexual content and little else. "Lover" came to signify what nineteenth-century dictionaries had more coyly referred to as "paramour," and two lovers, whatever their emotional ties with one another, were physically linked first and foremost.[59]

By the end of the 1920s, shifts in attitudes toward love yielded two specific directions, both of them in open conflict with Victorian delight in spiritual intensity. The first direction involved the emergence of a new male culture bent on freeing its charges from the shackles of emotional involvement in favor of more diverse material interests, sexuality included. The second direction, applicable to both genders, yielded from 1927 onward a new, "scientific" current of marriage advice that was eager to supplant the vagaries of love with more concrete, less emotional calculations of long-term compatibility.

An explicit definition of masculinity that was at once snobbishly middle-class and vigorously anti-Victorian surrounded the establishment of *Esquire* magazine in 1933. The magazine's founder, Arnold Gingrich, combined claims to innovation with appeals to a male audience in explaining *Esquire*'s purpose: "It is our belief, in offering *Esquire* to the American male, that we are only getting around at last to a job that should have been done a long time ago—that of giving the masculine reader a break. The general magazines, in the mad scramble to increase the woman readership that seems to be highly prized by national advertisers, have bent over backwards in catering to the special interests and tastes of the feminine audience."[60] *Esquire* quickly won a substantial readership, boasting 180,000 subscribers within half a year, a quarter-million by 1935, and 750,000 by 1941. Counting newsstand purchases, a 1936 survey estimated over 4.5 million readers, extending from the initial upper-middle-class audience to a more general middle-class audience and including some women as well as men. The 1936 survey revealed a solidly middle-class readership, featuring people who had at least attended college and were eager to keep up with the latest styles and standards.

Esquire paid a great deal of attention to love motifs during its initial years of publication. During 1934, for example, twenty-seven short stories involved love topics, with such titles as "Forgive Me, Irene," "On the Rebound," "All My Love," and "Have a Rosebud." The pace slackened a bit in 1935 with eighteen stories and articles on love, but this rate was sustained through the bulk of the decade.

In virtually all its presentations on love *Esquire* emphasized revisionism. Editorial policy, attacking Victorian love ideals for men, stated that "this is a man's magazine, it isn't edited for the junior miss. It isn't dedicated to the dissemination of sweetness and light." *Esquire* trumpeted the idea of a "New Love," picking up on the more general themes of the previous decade and explicitly countering the etherealized and spiritual definition of love that had been urged on Victorian men.[61]

Esquire placed its attacks on love traditions in a venomously misogynist context, which is itself a fascinating shift away from official Victorian sanctification of women in discussions of love. Articles during the 1930s blasted women's lack of creativity—women were "created to be helpers"—and their emphasis on instinct over reason. "Feelings, not principles, regulate the typical woman's life." This chauvinism was all the more alarming given women's steady march into men's domains— one of the clearest nightmares for *Esquire*'s writers. "After taking over the bars and the barbershops, women elbow into the sports pages." "It may be, indeed, that a gradual and complete shifting of the recognized fields of the sexes is taking place. If this is so, and much current evidence points to it, I am glad that I am an old, bitter man, with not much time remaining." Pushy, oversexed, and irrational, women had become the enemy.[62]

It was not surprising, in this context, that love required reconsideration, which is why the early years of the magazine featured such prolonged attention to the topic. In this first phase, marked by the explicit campaign against Victorianism, the contours of the new love were most directly delineated in articles by marriage experts, though similar notions found in the magazine's many relevant short stories may have sunk deeper roots. The popularizing experts and most of the fiction writers spoke with a consistent voice, extending the pioneering notions of the 1920s while also translating them into an aggressive masculine voice.

In 1934 Henry Morton Robinson launched *Esquire*'s new emotional foray with an article on the "Brave New Love." Robinson, a former Columbia University professor and board member for *Reader's Digest*, saw himself in the front line of a new "rebellion" "in the lives of those persons who most easily and naturally reflect the genius of the time, a brilliant experimental use of the new love." Robinson castigated older love ideals, with their assumptions that "a pair of passion-oozing souls could merge into a mystical unity" as "a dream conceived in fallacy and proposed by childish desires"—an interesting echo of the more general campaign to infantilize strong emotion. The new love had no illusions, being "an adult emotion without that annoying fuzz of pubic hair on its handsome cleft chin." Women might seek the old romance still, but men needed an alternative to the "childish myth" that would weaken them in the face of voracious females while causing needless emotional suffering.[63]

A more positive definition of the new love emerged in a 1936 article. Its author repeated the denunciations of older romantic ideals and emphasized rational, cooperative arrangements between men and women. Soaring ideals and spirituality were largely absent, but so were the earlier put-downs of women. "Love" became a summary word for practical accommodations that could allow a couple to live together harmoniously, sharing various interests, including sexuality. Companionship, not emotional intensity, was the goal.[64]

Esquire's short stories, with their frequent treatment of love themes, drove home the same points, with rare exceptions. A 1936 story implicitly captured the transition in standards. "Sleepless Night" depicted a husband in bed with his slumbering wife:

She rested motionless and it seemed to the young man that her light breath, the faint perfume rising from her hair, the dimly illuminated outline of her slim body, entered into the design; the harmony of this night was its essence, refined and alive. He felt a renewed surge of love and softly bent to kiss the white forehead.

However, as the night wears on, the circulation in his arm is cut off, and he grows uncomfortable with his wife's position. His resentment also grows:

Women, with their ill-timed joys and superficial sadness, never kept the promises given by their eyes. Even the capture they yielded was transitory; after a while, it had a taste of corruption and death.

When morning comes, the husband keeps silent about his thoughts, eager to avoid trouble. Clearly, deep love has been evoked and rejected as the man's emotional outlook has matured during the night. Accommodation, not misleading passion, is the only realistic hope.[65]

Other stories demonstrated the futility or irrelevance of romantic commitment. Plots featured in 1934 and 1935 dealt with partners who differed greatly in their approach to romance. In one, a woman urges her man to be more romantic rather than seeking conquest without love. The man responds, "one must be hard. In love, he who does not devour, is devoured. All the same, it must be a relief, now and then, to give in, to be the weak one, to seek one's happiness in someone else's happiness." In fact, the man does try a more tender approach, only to have the woman leave him because she prefers "a man who compels one to make sacrifices." "Second Honeymoon" involved another unromantic husband who tries to manifest more sentiment under his wife's prompting—but she too leaves, in this case because he is not in step with the New Love that everyone is urging.[66]

Finally, a number of stories treated sexual prowess as a mature alternative to love. A 1938 plot focused on men in college who are initially naive but gain in sophistication as their emotional vulnerability yields to sexual confidence. Another story featured a husband who takes a mistress with his wife's approval—though in this case the man suffers from the mistress's desire for no-strings sex.[67]

Esquire treated love as a prominent theme during the 1930s, arguing against emotional intensity for mature men and offering graphic examples of how often emotional risks backfire. There were no happy endings in which transcendent love is confirmed. The frequency of the motif suggested real audience interest as a complicated cultural transition was underway.

With World War II, however, the inkwell dried up, never, in *Esquire*'s pages, to be refilled. Tacitly, the magazine seems to have decided both that other issues had become more pressing for men and that the new culture was sufficiently understood that it need not be belabored further. *Esquire* turned to war reportage, and its stories dealt with adventure, mystery, sports, and western themes. The love interest, which had already begun to decline in the later 1930s, vanished entirely. Aside from war reporting, feature sections emphasized travel and leisure. Extensive pictorial essays highlighted Hollywood starlets and "Varga" girls, often with captions suggesting that these women sought sex without romance. The same theme of emotionally neutral sex surfaced in coverage of trips by entertainers for troops overseas. *Esquire* was turning, in effect, to the approach toward women and sexuality that would be more extensively taken up late in the 1950s by *Playboy:* emotional love need not apply.

After the war's end, *Esquire*'s new tone persisted. In 1950 the magazine announced a new philosophy, pledging firmer devotion to men's real interests. These included travel, automobiles, and fashion, with little attention to women and none to love. Sex, cars, vacations, and jazz held center stage as consumerism and adventure fantasies displaced romance of any sort. In a rare exception, a 1952 article by a woman cited men's complaints that women had become too career minded and sexually explicit; the author noted that these changes were the results of male prodding, saying that if women had become less domestic, more "sophisticated, undraped and immodest," men had only themselves to blame.

Amid these trends, to move on to a discussion of love might have seemed downright banal.[68]

As *Esquire* and then *Playboy* moved ever further away from romantic themes, mainstream marriage advice, disseminated to middle-class American women as well as men, took its own aim at Victorian standards of love. Less bombastic than *Esquire*'s masculinists, the growing ranks of up-to-date popular authorities were just as critical of intense love and sought alternate bases for durable mating. The 1927 formation of the marriage education movement, begun at the University of North Carolina, suggested a new union between presumably scientific experts in the field, who were eager to apply objective knowledge to the myths of the past, and a growing audience of middle-class youth, who sought appropriate modern standards in a relationship that had become less certain than in the past. Over the next twenty-five years hundreds of thousands of students were exposed to marriage education courses, and an even larger number of readers were exposed to popular articles by experts like Ernest Groves and Paul Popenoe in the pages of leading outlets like the *Ladies Home Journal*. A 1937 *American Magazine* article on marriage education drew thousands of letters in response, while a 1955 poll found that the majority of American women believed that a marriage course and/or serious reading were the best bases for a successful marriage. Pamphlets by authorities like Popenoe, with such titles as "How Do You Know It's Love" and "How to Get Him to Propose," supplemented the courses and the magazine fare. Clearly, advice on love-related issues during these decades reached an exceptionally eager middle-class audience.[69]

The basis for the new wisdom rested on a combination of science and functionalism. As in so many aspects of emotional culture during the interwar decades, science was deliberately contrasted with sentiment. Couples planning marriage should consult scientifically determined criteria of compatibility, which would allow decisions to be made with "less emotion, strain, and regret than would otherwise be the case" because the people involved would be guided by "Science."[70] The functionalist goal emphasized the necessity of day-to-day adjustments, so that people, having chosen mates according to the best knowledge about such factors as religious preference, sexuality, and personality style, could cohabit durably and pleasantly. Soaring flights of passion were not part of this game plan.

The importance of love was granted. One authority, Ernest Burgess, scrawled in hand on the back of one of his marriage prediction charts, otherwise filled with scientific calculation of compatibility, "Once they are in love."[71] But the love envisioned was a companionable affection, not an intense experience. Further, in order to preserve this distinction, love must also be surrounded by cautions. Excessive expectations were at least as dangerous as lack of attraction. As early as 1926, Burgess argued that new trends, particularly women's growing independence, were beginning to destroy old romantic ideals and that this was a good thing because romance provided a poor basis for marriage. Burgess then introduced the companionship motif that was to become a staple of marriage advice literature during the 1930s and 1940s. The aim of the compatibility tests was to determine shared interests and values, not transcendent love or a merger of souls. A well-matched couple would agree about standards of childrearing and would share a number of leisure interests. They should be affectionate, but more transcendent feelings of love were irrelevant. In fact, youth must be warned to place head over heart in making decisions about marriage. Emotional and sexual attractions might overcome sensible, functional decisions and lead to grotesque mistakes—as the growing divorce rate seemed abundantly to testify. Here, as in other emotional fields, sensible, rational restraint would keep emotion in bounds, allowing it to support choices made largely on nonemotional grounds. Real love, indeed, involved building on shared interests and distinguishing compatibility from the misleading snares of transient passion.[72]

After marriage, emotion continued to play only a supporting role in the judgment of the new breed of experts. Few discordant couples were seen as suffering from lack of appropriate love. Rather, they were almost certain to be experiencing sexual problems, for sex became the touchstone of marital success. Sex before marriage involved anticipation but not participation, for the experts remained resolutely conventional in this area. But once marriage was launched, sex became the key to the kingdom. No amount of love could overcome sexual maladjustment, and, correspondingly, successful sex had almost nothing to do with emotional concomitants. The barriers to successful sex involved false information and inhibitions—including, of course, problems inherited from childhood such as the remnants of excessive motherlove. The cures, correspondingly, must emphasize accurate information and mechanical arrangements. Love was no longer centrally involved. Pamphlet after pamphlet drummed home the primacy of sex in determining the fate of a marriage, and love as a separate emotional entity virtually disappeared from view. The theme was launched clearly in the advice literature of the 1920s: love was by nature sexual, and where problems arose, the physical aspect predominated. "Sex is the foundation of marriage. Yet most married people do not know the ABC of sex." "Sex is . . . the most perfect way of showing love." "When sex deserts the bed, love flies out the window. With the breakdown of the sexual relationships comes a corresponding breakdown in every other aspect of love."[73] Developing and maintaining sexual excitement was seen as so fundamental to love that any independent definition of the emotion became irrelevant.

Overall, then, the advice that surged forward between the late 1920s and the early 1960s warned against certain kinds of love, dismissed Victorian standards, replaced love with sex as the linchpin of marital adjustment, and defined the love that should remain largely in terms of an emotional predisposition to share interests and negotiate disagreements. In this modern, functionalist view, love became little more than a collection of routine skills. An avid advice reader could easily have assumed that marriage should be contracted on the basis of carefully calculated shared habits and then cemented through sex. Advice writers who stated quite openly "first comes sex, then comes love" seem to have had exactly this arrangement in mind.[74]

Even as the marriage education movement declined in the 1960s, it was not replaced by any clear reemphasis on intense love. Rather, it gave way to expanding interests in sexuality, particularly premarital sexuality, and to further emphasis on the idea that relationships should be calculated with a careful sense of individual benefit in mind, being exchange arrangements in which sensible partners would make sure that no great self-sacrifice was involved. Innovativeness shifted away from the somewhat conventional modernism of the interwar period to the more radical open marriage concept—which further emphasized the importance of sexual expression and the need to uncouple couples from any constraining sentimentality or emotional unity.[75]

Middle-class emotional culture thus moved from avant-garde challenges to Victorian concepts of love early in the 1920s to two central, overlapping alternatives developed in the 1930s and 1940s. The first, a hedonistic male culture, deliberately attacked intense, romantic love in favor of more pragmatic arrangements with women, including sexual arrangements, and a wide variety of leisure interests. The second, friendlier to the idea of mutual affection, also attacked intensity in love and urged attention to shared interests and sexuality in its stead.

Other definitions of love persisted as well. As with grief, the modernist position did not completely triumph, even at the cultural level. The new popularity of soap operas and Gothic and Harlequin romances among women during these same decades demonstrated a cultural commitment to love themes that men seemed to be decisively abandoning. Soap operas, for example, stressed the importance of love in marriage, defining other motives as invalid. Love could triumph over all sorts of apparent impediments, including the prosaic compatibility criteria of the experts. Love begat complications, of course, which gave soap operas most of their countless plots, including the theme of winning back an errant lover. Romance novels stressed love—either love moving toward horror, or initial fear yielding to love; the emotional mixture was complex, but it was undeniably intense. They also highlighted substantial female passivity in the grip of emotion. Women's magazines, more clearly middle-class in outlook, also maintained a strong interest in love themes, often alternating explorations of how to win men's love with expert articles on compatibility that touted science over affection. Further, the love articles that did persist not only maintained the love motif but often defined it in terms reminiscent of Victorian self-sacrifice.[76]

Yet the very presence of these disagreements over the nature of love within mainstream culture indicated how far the American middle class had moved from the heyday of Victorianism when, except in the writings of utopian dissidents, no real alternative to the standards of spiritualized love was even presented. And while a new ambivalence about modernism did develop in the materials directed toward middle-class women, women, too, participated in the search for appropriate innovations that would guide them toward greater sexual interest and sought measurements of courtship and marriage more practical than Victorian preachments had seemed to encourage. The religion of intense love still maintained some isolated chapels, but the body of the faithful had moved on.[77]

Conclusion

Attacks on Victorian standards of guilt, grief, and love involved several complexities not present in the movement against the negative emotions. The effort to unseat guilt was most straightforward; guilt was seen as unpleasant and therefore simply negative. Grief, on the other hand, gained some negative connotations, but it was not renounced quite as simply; countercurrents persisted in advocating the necessity of grief while the more dominant interest in restraining grief generated considerable vagueness as to how this was to be accomplished. Portraits of grief-free people alternated with scenes in which grief existed but was recognized as unfortunate and therefore erased as quickly as possible. Love was more complicated still, for change here involved massive redefinition and downgrading, but not frontal attack. The result was inconsistency, as the same cultural outlets both praised and warned against love. The further result was considerable lack of clarity as to how adequate love was to be generated and measured—for example, by mothers with their children—and how it was to be combined with the restraint essential to guard against irrationality and excess. Nothing so simple as ventilation was urged in the love field, for real love of some sort remained desirable.

However, while redefinitions of "good" emotions were inherently less straightforward than the attacks on bad emotions, several common themes did shine through. One of these was the idea that infants had emotional needs different from adults and that one of the key tasks of child-rearing was to develop appropriate emotional maturity in which all emotions could be held in check, with embarrassment acting as the guardian of restraint. Another theme was that men and women were not as emotionally different as Victorians had assumed and that neither gender had special license to indulge in a particular kind of emotional intensity. A new set of gender quarrels was implicit in twentieth-century emotional culture, as *Esquire*'s authors seem to have realized, but it did not involve selective freedoms from emotional restraint. Above all, emotional intensity became a consistent danger, whether the emotions involved were negative or potentially positive. Strong emotion served no greater purpose in love than it did in anger. Here was a set of emotional values, clearly distinct from Victorian preferences, that requires brief summary before we turn to the challenging task of analyzing sources and impacts.

6

Reprise: The New Principles of Emotional Management

The articles, pamphlets, advice materials, and stories that articulated the emerging twentieth-century emotional culture redefined Victorian standards in virtually every area. Specific approaches varied with the emotion, and even individual emotions like grief or motherlove were approached differently at different times. Despite this complexity, however, the advocacy of a new emotionology did rest on several shared assumptions. Maddeningly, these assumptions were rarely spelled out in any general way. No one, certainly at the level of popularization, spoke systematically about problems of intensity. Even more limited innovations, like the new approach to fear or sibling jealousy, sometimes seemed almost unacknowledged, the innovators failing to recognize how much their advice differed from that of their Victorian predecessors. Eager embrace of science and modernism created some awareness of the process of change, as in the attacks on older standards of love or grief, but the most fundamental thrusts remained largely implicit.

Acknowledged or not, however, the emotion-by-emotion innovations were propelled by shared assumptions. This is clearly indicated by the timing of change. While suggestions of new directions began to emerge shortly before 1900, the larger emotionology began to be staked out during the 1920s, with a period of eager advocacy extending from that point into the 1950s. Shared timing does not prove shared purpose, but it suggests that the rethinking applied to specific emotions rested on shifts in assumptions regarding emotions in general, which in turn did not gain full coherence until the second quarter of the century.

The new emotional culture called for new abilities in emotion management. Victorian standards had also urged management, as in controlling the use of fear and anger, but they had also recognized certain emotional areas in which regulation was not necessary, either because individuals were not considered to have certain emotions (as in the case of women and anger) or because restraint was not appropriate (as in spiritualized love). Twentieth-century culture, on the other hand, called for management across the board; no emotion should gain control over one's thought processes.

The culture also suggested a clear socialization pattern applicable to the acquisition of emotional maturity regardless of setting. Children, in the new view, were no longer innocent; rather, they were characterized by a frightening emotional vulnerability. They had all sorts of irrational passions that needed careful handling, and at the same time they could be exposed to parental excess not only in the form of misuse of anger or fear in discipline but also in the form of misguided love. Infancy, in this new culture, became a crucial developmental stage, with the later stages of childhood considered less open to revision and guidance (except perhaps through professional therapy). Through parental reassurance, techniques of ventilation, and appropriate doses of affection, children might begin to climb the ladder of emotional control. Whether they would lose certain dangerous impulses—as was sometimes suggested for jealousy—or merely learn how to keep the impulses in check, they would ideally move toward an adulthood that placed reason over emotion and moderated emotional expression in virtually every imaginable encounter. Parenthood itself became a test for managed emotion. Not only anger and fear but even love itself must now be carefully weighed, its expression never allowed to become excessive. Advocates of unbounded love for infants assumed that the parent could turn off the taps when, at age three or four, the child needed to gain greater emotional independence. Emotional control was now as uniform a principle within the family circle as it was in wider spheres, including the workplace, where Victorian emotionology had not carried over at all clearly.

As the demands of emotional maturity increased in many respects, the childish terrain came to seem rockier. Victorians had been able, in principle, to assume an early period of considerable innocence when the main effort was simply to avoid unnecessary problems, followed by later stages in which children were open to appeal through a combination of guilt and character building. The new culture invited a great deal more manipulation precisely because infancy was at once so crucial and so difficult. To wean children away from emotional impulsiveness and to prepare the way for guidance through embarrassment, signs of childishness were now transformed into sources of personal shame. Even excessive love, because of its taint of infancy, might provoke embarrassment in a mature adult accustomed to managed restraint.

Emphasis on emotional management reduced the salience of the public-private divisions that had underwritten Victorian emotional culture. Family guidance was vital to the maturation of young children, to be sure, but the rules they were to learn applied to work settings and intimate settings alike. Anger was no longer of greater use in public than in private life; the result was that a bit more anger might be acceptable in the family, but much less anger was permissible on the job than in the Victorian heyday. Reductions in the acceptability of grief limited one kind of familial emotional bond, and the redefinitions of love, while preserving an emotional space near the hearth, limited the special quality of this domestic emotion. Parents, courting couples, coworkers, and spouses all needed to manage and control their emotional expressions, keeping reason in charge and pulling back in embarrassment when the bounds were overstepped. Home became less sacredly separate.

The emergence of a new emotional culture in the 1920s coincided with growing efforts to homogenize national culture as a whole. The cessation of immigration combined with various kinds of Americanization programs, in companies as well as the public schools, to give a wider portion of the population access to essentially middle-class standards. During the decades in which the new emotionology was being forged, growing agreement emerged among Americans, at least in principle, about the goals of childhood socialization. A recent literacy study emphasizes the standard-setting homogenization of the leading American media precisely in the 1920–1950s period, when the emotional redefinitions were debated and presented. In the emotions area, then, a dual process was occurring in which middle-class Americans revised previous norms while maintaining their confident assumptions of cultural leadership, while other groups gained new access to these same changing norms. The middle class was itself changing, with new divisions being created between the service-sector population and older entrepreneurial and professional groups, as well as between suburban and urban styles. It was the service-sector and suburban contingents that, as we will see, proved most open to change, using new emotional standards to help shore up their self-identity as modern and up to date. Homogenization thus warred with important new divisions in American society, but the uniformity of the mainstream emotional culture, as now redefined, remained striking.[1]

Social class and ethnicity remained important variables in emotional culture. It was revealing that efforts to curtail anger at work, initially directed at blue-collar workers on the factory floor, shifted focus toward the middle and lower-middle class, which was expected not simply to respond to anger-control strategies but also to internalize the necessary restraints. Here was implicit recognition of some continued social gaps in emotional standards. Nevertheless, the middle class itself was growing rapidly in size with the expansion of the service and management sectors and of exposure to secondary and college education. Popularizations like Dr. Spock's childrearing manuals reached all strata of the middle class. A sense of social cohesion with respect to basic emotional values probably increased, and with it the expectations applied to social and ethnic groups outside the middle class itself.

Regional differences persisted. We will see that the South, for example, retained traces of earlier distinctions concerning jealousy and grief, preserving a greater interest in intensity than was publicly acknowledged in the North. Here too, however, the region seems to have integrated its standards with those of the rest of the country. Southern laws that gave special consideration to jealousy changed, though belatedly by national standards, moving closer to the general assumption that jealousy could and should be suppressed. As with class, regional distinctions must be treated, but particularly with respect to the impact of emotional culture, no fully alternative regional culture was sketched.

Traditional Protestantism, increasingly visible in the 1920s because of its contrast to mainstream religious trends, did provide a haven for several older cultural impulses—a fact that warns against any overly facile assumption of growing uniformity in emotionology. Fundamentalists and other articulate Christians tried to go against the general grain in their view of grief, and they could also harbor older, sometimes even pre-Victorian standards concerning emotions such as anger or fear.[2]

Gender counted for far less than it had in the nineteenth century, at least on the cultural surface. This was one of the clear themes of the new emotionology. Almost all the advice literature downplayed gender as a major factor in emotional standards—or even, indeed, in etiquette.[3] This shift emerged in the new emphasis on self-conscious management. The Victorian assumption that women's special nature provided them with spontaneous emotional guidelines faded, and women became subjected to even more stringent formal management requirements than men, given their need to monitor motherlove. Men's special rights or requirements with respect to anger were swept aside; both men and women had to keep their tempers at work. Experiments on jealousy reflected the Victorian assumption that women were more susceptible to it than men, but the standards were more insistently the same for both genders than in the nineteenth century. Fathers had an easier time than mothers when it came to managing love, and their more easygoing style might win praise (though some advisers also cautioned about men's tendency to distance themselves unduly from familial emotional involvement).[4] Again, however, the standards of undemanding, carefully controlled affection were identical for fathers and mothers alike. The decline of a special status for motherlove, in fact, was revealed in advice writers' tendency to talk of parental, rather than specifically maternal, affection. This trend appeared well before the 1980s, when paternal emotional competence was more actively called forth. Marriage advice literature, for its part, addressed men and women similarly, urging rational assessment of compatibility for both sexes. And, of course, placing bedroom adjustment at the marital center reduced the Victorian gap between men and women in the area of sexuality. Again, men might be cautioned against too little affection, and women's initiatives in sexuality were downplayed in favor of men's, but by nineteenth-century standards the differentiation had shrunk dramatically. Finally, the decline of a special male calling to courage matched the attacks on motherlove in eroding key Victorian symbols of gendered emotionality.

Beneath the surface another cultural reality took shape. Even as official declarations of differences between male and female emotional nature declined, both in science and in popularizations, new gaps emerged. The early efforts of *Esquire* to attack pushy, careerist women suggest that new distinctions advanced almost because the old ones were disappearing. *Esquire*, as we have seen, urged men to free themselves from women's manipulation of Victorian love while also arguing that women were irrationally emotional in any event. Here, growing insistence on emotional management provided a framework for accusations that one gender was not living up to the norms. Whether simply traditional or newly enhanced as a response to women's gains in public life, male belief in women's greater emotionality took on greater significance in a culture that officially insisted on uniform restraint and allowed for no recognition of distinctively feminine emotional qualities. Women, ultimately, would learn to return the favor in arguing that men remained disproportionately (and unacceptably) aggressive. Again, this was not an entirely new charge, except for the terms employed, but it was newly significant given the lack of official sanction for male use of angry impulses. In sum, men and women may well have reacted to the new emotional culture differently, at least on average. They may have used it to create a new set of mutual accusations. Gender relations were by no means magically smoothed by the new culture, and it was no accident that popular features on the "Battle between the Sexes" emerged in precisely the same decades when twentieth-century emotionology was being defined and disseminated.

The fact remains, however, that both genders were exposed to cultural change and that the new culture erased, at least officially, most of the classic gender definitions that had been central to Victorian emotionology. Men and women might forge gender-specific variants, in part through selective retention of Victorian ideals, but neither personnel experts nor family advice experts acknowledged significant differentiation in emotional requirements. Indeed, after some transitional confusion in the 1920s, when mothers were singled out for attack, most experts also retreated from the notion that males and females were emotionally different by nature. Thus, in the childrearing literature, children—not boys or girls—became the problem category, with the same emotional management techniques required for both genders. Likewise, in the personnel literature, after some initial discussions of women's unfavorable reactions to an emotionally harsh male work environment (or of a uniquely female backbiting jealousy on the job), emotional control advice and manipulation were targeted at workers, not one gender or the other. Here we see that the efforts to achieve uniformity, across gender, region, and to an extent social class, developed partly from the new emotional norms themselves. Men were asked to tone down the anger—to become good salesmen, for example. Women were asked to reduce claims based on motherlove—to become effective professionals as well as really adequate mothers. In terms of desired results, the genders grew closer. Everyone could learn to be nice.

While twentieth-century emotionology reduced some traditional differentiations, including not only those of region or gender but also those between home and work, it inevitably generated important internal strains. Victorian tensions were in principle alleviated, as in the decline of separate emotional standards for men in the family and on the job, but the general public's actual reception of the new standards is not certain. Moreover, the new emotionology itself established at least three largely novel tensions.

The first, already discussed, involved the increasing distinction between negative and positive emotions. This clear differentiation was one of the major shifts away from Victorian standards, according to which emotions perceived as dangerous could nevertheless, in appropriate circumstances, serve as vital motivators. Twentieth-century redefinitions, in contrast, treated negative emotions very differently from their positive counterparts. To the negative emotions were applied the fear that they would fester and the anxiety that they would veer out of control. Correspondingly, the most careful strategies of ventilation and avoidance were applied to the negative emotions, for any expression beyond the purely verbal risked getting out of hand.

Yet, as we have seen, the negative/positive distinction, though vivid, was also incomplete. Several emotions, most notably grief, in fact hovered between the two categories, though there was a pronounced effort to judge them as effectively negative and therefore to apply the standard suppression and avoidance techniques. More important, the concern about excess applied to positive as well as negative impulses. Love, while good, could also get out of hand.

The emphasis on distinctions between bad and good emotions led to important differences between the American emotionology and that of other cultures. Americans in general were less willing to identify their emotional experiences and were particularly strong in their desire to conceal the negatives. With regard to certain emotions like anger, American culture did not reach the top of the repression scale, but its systematic blasts at negative emotions and the unusual concern for their concealment demonstrated the impact of the new good-bad categorization.[5]

Despite these distinctions, however, the uniform concern about excess and loss of control cut across the good-bad divide. It was perhaps no accident that shortly before the rise of the new emotional culture, concern about obsession made new headway in psychology and some resultant popularizations. While psychological research defined obsession carefully, popular treatments loosely associated loss of rational control to the point of compulsive thought and behavior with the power of emotion in excess. Thus a *Harpers' Monthly Magazine* story of 1906, entitled "The Obsession of Ann Gibbs," showed how the protagonist's grief leads directly to uncontrolled obsession over "fineries," and ultimately to stark insanity. A 1913 story in *The Outlook* used the word "obsession" to describe an intense emotion that could ultimately kill. While obsessive loss of control applied most readily to emotions like fear, it was increasingly extended to grief and even to certain forms of love, where intensity might burden not only the individual but also the others exposed, whose whole emotional balance might be thrown off by the effects of untrammeled passion.[6]

The new principles of emotional management, and particularly the underlying concern about intensity, also involved some subtle tensions between individual and group: here was the second implicit debate. The new emotional standards often seemed bent on defending individual autonomy. Control over fear or anger protected the individual's rational power to decide, while immunity from overweening love was explicitly portrayed as an essential step in the process of individuation. Hence twentieth-century culture is often, and not inaccurately, seen as a triumph of individual expression in which intensity is attacked precisely because it could limit this expression either from within or from without.[7] But the new culture also placed strong emphasis on smooth relations between the individual and others. Grief, as we have seen, earned new demerits not only because it unseated individual reason but also because it disturbed others. The same held true of jealousy, which was feared both for its all-consuming qualities and for the burdens it placed on the object of jealousy. Thus the culture was in no simple sense individualistic. Rather, it sought to combine apparent individual control with important promptings of group harmony. Again, the link was intensity itself, which worked against both goals. Ultimately, the burden that intensity placed on group harmony outweighed the apparent commitment to individuation in directing the new styles of emotion management. The desire not to feel obligated, and therefore to resent emotional intrusion by others, surpassed interest in maximizing one's own opportunities for expression, while the new concern about avoiding embarrassment added group pressure in a more direct sense.

Finally, the new management principles struck a subtle balance between regulation and independence. Attacks on Victorian standards frequently created an aura of new freedom. The decline of gender differences opened some new emotional areas, and the interest in reducing emotional enforcement of hierarchy—particularly the rejection of anger as a management tool—painted new vistas as well. More fundamentally still, the growing attack on guilt promised independence in a variety of directions; emotion could now be proclaimed as a no-fault domain. Emphasis on ventilation promoted a sense that any emotion could be discussed, with open communication guaranteed. Yet rules of another, perhaps more subtle sort formed an integral part of the new culture. Emotion must not get out of hand. Embarrassment must be avoided. Undue emotional commitment was wrong. Even open communication must not lead to dramatic or upsetting scenes. The underlying principle, clearly, was the systematic constraint on intensity. Emotions were fine as long as they stayed in check; old rules could be waived so long as the results did not become intrusive; muted communication must often substitute for full expression.[8]

Here was the most subtle of all the tensions embedded in the new standards. American periodicals and other prescriptive materials frequently trumpeted the triumph of individualism and spontaneity over real or imagined Victorian restraints. Advertisements offered enticing images of personal expression wherein "true" personalities could shine forth, shedding their purely institutional roles. As in the heralded shifts in fashionable dress during the 1920s, autonomy seemed to triumph over regulation. But, as we have seen, the conformist impulse gained new strength as well, and the necessity of fitting in with groups and with larger institutions put pressure on emotional independence. Muting of intensity was a vital precondition for reconciling group needs with apparent spontaneity; here was the crucial new rule.

The apparent emphasis on freedom explains why so many observers, then and since, have erred in heralding twentieth-century culture as an undiluted triumph of emotional deregulation. A more careful historical assessment, juxtaposing the new style with its Victorian predecessor and cutting beneath the somewhat misleading rhetoric, reveals the constraints that accompanied some personal latitude. While specific rules varied with professional context, and while individuals could negotiate some space precisely because the leading guidelines embraced antiregulatory language,[9] the room for maneuver did not include major opportunities for intense outpourings. This was the bedrock of the new emotional regime.

The tensions in the new culture—between a penchant for pleasant emotions but the desire to control them, between the individual and the group, and between real and apparent freedom from regulation—all revolved around the insistence on restraint. Thus one could "be oneself" only so long as one's maturity assured that one's emotions would remain in check and not bother others. Rules could be jettisoned as long as fear of embarrassment maintained the basic principles of control. Good emotions blurred with bad when excess threatened. The replacement of Victorian emotional culture raises a host of analytical issues, such as the need to assess the extent of acceptance of the new values. Yet we cannot fully understand the culture without first exploring the reasons for its existence, the combination of factors that rendered Victorian norms anachronistic and implicitly centered the goals of emotion management on the problem of intensity. A full celebration of a "cool" value system would await the 1960s, when the word emerged from its traditional service in describing an alternative to fiery passion to characterize the standards of a whole generation. But the bases for esteeming cool control had been set some decades before.[10]

7

"Impersonal, but Friendly":
Causes of the New Emotional Style

Victorian emotional culture was not replaced by accident. Beginning in the 1920s or a bit before, a variety of factors combined to undermine the nineteenth-century synthesis and build up a new aversion to emotional intensity. Simply put, the combination of economic and familial functionalism and the larger innovations that supported Victorian culture began to unravel. New economic forms redefined functional emotions. Cultural changes further pointed this redefinition in the direction of growing hostility to intense emotional experience. A new breed of experts translated these various factors into emotionology. Finally, alterations in family forms, and particularly parent-child relations, worked into the brew. In one sense, this mix of factors that caused the new emotionology was unsurprising. Emotional change reflected some of the developments associated with the maturation of American industrial society, which have been widely studied and which remain open to much discussion. Even here, however, the link with emotion helps identify the larger structural shifts in society, pinpointing their timing, and explaining their links with individual behavior. Furthermore, familiar themes like heightened consumerism or the reduced birthrate did not by themselves guide the shift in emotional standards. Their combination was vital, and they were supplemented by other changes in personal values, including new anxieties about health. New economic and familial structures required new emotional definitions, but the specific results were not inevitable, save as the cultural context shifted as well. The challenge is to fit the puzzle together with the mixture of novel and recognizable pieces. The result not only explains the changes already described, but explains why the second quarter of the century served as the real crucible of contemporary middle-class character in the United States.

Neither the disseminators nor the audience for the new emotional culture spelled out their overall motivations. As we have seen, some of the changes were almost unperceived, and no one explicitly captured the general movement against intensity. Many advice givers and advice receivers were almost surely unaware of exactly why they wanted to move away from the emotional culture of previous generations even when, as was the case by the 1940s, they did recognize that they wanted to behave differently and to socialize their children differently than in the past. This means that causation must be teased out from a variety of indications, with careful attention to the connections that can be demonstrated but no claim of rigorous proof.

Not surprisingly, shifts in emotionology responded to several basic changes in American society during the second quarter of the twentieth century. However, some major changes were not clearly involved. We will see, for example, that the state had no definable role in the new emotionology, except insofar as a growth of government functions gave some of the new breed of experts the backing of agencies such as the Children's Bureau. Leading events such as the world wars factor in, but only rather vaguely, while the experience of the 1930s depression seems oddly irrelevant to the ongoing reconsideration of emotional standards that began during prosperity and continued even amid economic dislocation.

As in the nineteenth century, specific factors combined with more general changes to promote redefinitions in emotionology, particularly where discrete emotions were concerned. A new stance toward grief, as we have seen, owed much to the radical decline in the infant mortality rate that occurred between 1880 and 1920 and that began to be perceived by the 1890s.[1] With less need to anticipate grief on the death of a child, with growing emphasis on successful measures to reduce many causes of death, and with valorization of medical personnel as heroic death fighters, grief almost inevitably declined in stature. New attention to problems of jealousy followed in part from changes in patterns of social interaction. During the Victorian era men and women spent much time in separate social spheres; young men roomed with their colleagues, participated in male lodges, and only in their later twenties began a process of active courtship.[2] By 1920 young men and women spent more and more time in each other's company as coeducation gained ground and novel practices such as dating reconfigured the social activities of high school and college-age youth. New prescriptions against jealousy were a necessary result of this increased heterosexual mingling. New levels of concern about anger and aggression followed in part from perceptions of heightened crime, including juvenile delinquency, and the results of untrammeled aggression in Nazism and then renewed world war. It was difficult, in this context, to view channeled anger as a safe or even useful emotional motivation. As parental control over adolescents became increasingly limited, attention to emotional guidance for younger children was heightened, and an effort was made to develop emotional enforcers that were less dependent on lifelong guilt, more attuned to the emerging peer culture.[3] Efforts to increase adult supervision of children and youth, widely noted as dividing the nineteenth-century experience of childhood (particularly for boys) from the new, more regulated environment of the early twentieth century, fed the revision of fear standards, for adults could justify their new claims of authority as coaches or scoutmasters in part from their need to attack Victorian "boy culture" and its use of dares and bravado. The simple fact of greater urbanization also affected fear, removing children from daily interaction with animals and thus making them more likely to be frightened by a neighbor's pet. Fear of animals quite probably increased (in contrast to the dominant nineteenth-century concern, which was cruelty to animals).[4] Certainly such fear became more noticeable, and this in turn helped spur the larger reevaluation of fear in boyhood. Changes concerning love, finally, owed a great deal to the growing acceptance of birth control devices in the middle class. Premarital sex was not immediately revolutionized as a result, but the idea of love rising above sex made far less functional sense by the 1920s, and as a result some of the more general ethereality vanished.[5]

This review of specifics could easily be extended, and existing studies of changes in individual emotions have already prepared a great deal of useful explanation. Some of the causes for these specific changes relate to the larger framework that must be developed to account for the more general attack on emotional intensity. It remains important to attend to shifts that bore particularly on a single emotion.[6] Among other things, specific contexts help explain some of the differences in timing already noted. By studying such contexts we learn, for example, that attention to grief preceded the more general reconsideration of Victorianism because of declining death rates—though in the long run the results merged with the larger twentieth-century emotional configuration. The general factors and especially the main lines of cultural and functional change transcended a mere accumulation of particulars. This is why, as was true in explaining Victorian emotionology, a larger analysis remains essential.

At the same time, it is vital to insist on the magnitude of the changes that were occurring, for while important continuities persisted from the previous culture—including the aversion to anger in families or the distinction between jealousy and love—it is still the case that the Victorian amalgam was jettisoned. Such a sharp change in standards sets a demanding analytical agenda, making it necessary to identify the causes that prompted such a substantial reworking of widely accepted norms. By the same token, the causation package that can be identified helps explain why so many Victorian staples—from emotional distinctions between the genders to the unprecedented attack on intensity—were replaced.

Yet, beguilingly, there is a line of argument, offered particularly by European scholars, that takes a different tack, and this must be assessed before the more elaborate alternative is presented. Several perceptive Dutch and German sociologists have stressed the emergence of a new emotional style in the twentieth century.[7] Much of their evidence is European, but their generalizations often range across the Atlantic. In some ways, in their fascination with growing informality and individualized adjustments in emotional presentation, they claim greater movement away from Victorian standards than may actually apply. As noted in the previous chapter, it is important at least in the American case to emphasize the real tension between individualism and regulation and not to assume that the former triumphed over the latter. I will return to the issue of European-American comparison in a concluding chapter, but at this point it is necessary directly to address the European theories of causation.

The most impressive work to date on emotional style has simultaneously portrayed a major twentieth-century shift and claimed substantial continuity in causation. Abram de Swaan, in describing the contrast between nineteenth- and twentieth-century approaches to emotional standards, notes a major shift from "management by command" to "management by negotiation." He insists that both phases constitute stages in a common civilizing process that began with the growing strength of national states as early as the seventeenth century. To reconcile his dual claims, de Swaan begins by stressing, correctly, that the "widely held assumption" that emotional restrictions were lessening "does not hold." His vision of management by negotiation assumes a great deal of self-control, which is why the appearance of freedom in the new emotional style "is so rarely experienced as liberating." This leads de Swaan and other analysts like Cas Wouters, who go somewhat farther in exploring innovation and informality, to the second reconciling claim: that precisely the success of Victorian impulse control—the nineteenth-century version of Norbert Elias's civilizing offensive—has allowed a relaxation of the most formal emotional rules in the twentieth century.[8] Precisely because most people have internalized appropriate controls of violence, sexuality, and emotional outburst, twentieth-century society can afford a much looser emotional regime, at least on the surface.

In these analyses, causation is not really an issue. De Swaan mentions changes in management hierarchies and Jürgen Gerhards addresses the impact of a consumer society, but according to these analysts, these contemporary efflorescences are ultimately generated by the inexorable civilizing process—the force, connected with state discipline and upper-class control of the lower orders, that launched greater impulse control even before the Victorian era itself. They admit that the civilizing process has become more complex in the twentieth century, as Elias himself noted in a final phrase and as his disciples discuss more elaborately; relaxation of sexuality and of earlier standards of bodily control, as in posture or dress, make this obvious. But the process itself remains ineluctable, almost beyond explanation.[9]

A claim that grants major change but makes no concerted effort to explain it provides an elusive target for alternative analysis. Obviously, emotional control continued in the twentieth century; in some ways, it increased. To this extent, it is accurate to draw a very general link between the present and past periods in which emotional regulation had also occurred. A few of the more simplified claims of direct continuity between Victorian and twentieth-century control approaches can be easily dismissed, but the overall change-within-common-process approach is harder to tackle. Those who believe in an ineffable civilizing offensive, tied however diffusely to a tangible entity such as the nation state, may well be unpersuadable. But this same ineffability must raise questions: Has a common underlying force guided emotional culture for the past four centuries? Is the twentieth century, with its undeniable shifts in focus, still part of the same fundamental period in emotional culture as the eighteenth century or the Victorian era?

I have argued that the change that began to take shape in the 1920s in the United States was profound, comprising a major part of a more general shift in American personality standards that has been noted by various scholars, from David Riesman onward.[10] Change is never complete. The new twentieth-century emotional style built on some of the standards that Victorians had also emphasized, and of course the larger similarity—that both cultures set forth emotional standards at all—must be granted as well. But the context for emotional culture was changing substantially, which means that new causation can and should be sought. It is not necessary to rely on an overarching civilizing process in order to unearth a new explanatory combination that, in addition, includes some factors mentioned only in passing in the European assessments. Nor is such reliance desirable, for it distracts from a full understanding of the new emotional signals themselves. Granting, then, that some momentum from past emotional management continued and that twentieth-century American society, like all modern societies, most definitely did seek to regulate impulse, it is essential to undertake a fresh look at causation.

In this effort, emphasis on innovation gains pride of place, for what took shape by the 1920s was a major reevaluation of intensities in personal expression. The Victorian relationship between sexuality and emotion, for example, was virtually reversed. During the nineteenth century sexual intensity was regarded with uniform hostility in middle-class culture, which prescribed that sexual pleasure be sought cautiously and in moderation. Emotions, in contrast, could be vigorously indulged in appropriate contexts. By the 1920s the reversal was underway; despite hesitations, sexual intensity won new approval. The principal new sexual constraint involved explicit identification of homosexuality as a warning that intensity must be directed appropriately, in the proper context. Emotional intensity, in contrast, now encountered some of the same blanket aversion that had described sexual intensity in the previous era. Emotion, not sex, became the field in which great management subtlety was required. Other constraints were reevaluated at the same time. Rigid costumes and corresponding injunctions about posture gave ground fairly steadily, though bodily discipline was still enforced by anxieties about weight and exercise. Still, on balance, greater physical freedom coincided with the new, if subtle, restraints on emotional expression. Fear of excess showed not only in the emotional sphere but also in the new definition of alcoholism as something more than a problem of moral discipline; here was another area in which some individuals, at least, needed to be warned that self-control must be bolstered.[11]

Beyond the major shifts in the rules governing specific emotions—the decline of channeled anger, attacks on excessive motherlove, the painful reevaluation of grief—the basic tone of twentieth-century emotions advice was transformed. As the growing reliance on embarrassment suggests, even the functions of emotions in maintaining human relationships were recast, with intensity now seen as a barrier rather than a bond.[12] The extent of the transformation calls for an explicit causal inquiry, whatever one's ultimate views about some underlying civilizing process might be. General factors must be identified that explain the overall directions of change and its concentration in the three to four decades after 1920. Such an exploration will not only account for the change but also deepen our understanding of its nature.

Sources of Standards: A Changing Intellectual Base

During the Victorian period the primary source of emotional advice to the middle class came from people whose authority rested on a combination of morality and common sense. Morality was in some instances bolstered by Protestant religious training, though this was not always the case and most advice after 1830 strove to avoid a sectarian tone. Thus Jacob Abbott, author of several family manuals and twenty-three books in the *Rollo* series, built not only on his training as a Protestant minister but also on his dissatisfaction with conventional theology in his effort to update and broaden a largely moral version of his religion—and to reach a varied middle-class audience outside any institutional setting. Such confidence in moral vision also predominated among many of the authors for popular periodicals like the *Ladies Home Journal,* as well as among other prolific advice writers like T. S. Arthur, who also mixed vaguely religious injunctions with specific emotional advice.[13] As we have seen, scientific claims began to intrude on the moral ground of advice by the end of the century, but they initially supplemented moralism in the area of emotional standards. Authorities like G. Stanley Hall largely echoed the claims made by the moralists when writing about such topics as the motivational importance of anger or the gender basis for natural emotions such as fear or jealousy.

Two kinds of challengers arose to contend with the Victorian moral authority, both of which blossomed fully in the 1920s. The first were the self-conscious moderns, who still argued morality but based their claims less on common sense and more on up-to-dateness. We have seen the impact of modernist thinking in the areas of grief, love, and jealousy particularly. More important still was the new appeal to science and related research studies as the basis for popularized emotional advice and as the most far-reaching alternative to moralism. A characteristic exemplar of the new-style advice writer was D. H. Thom, who trained as a physician and then moved into psychiatry and guidance work while also serving as a major author for the Children's Bureau in the Department of Labor. Social workers, doctors, psychologists—these were the people who were now entitled to define standards or whose theories other popularizers referred to in justifying their own approaches. As we have seen, new journals such as *Parents' Magazine* and *Esquire* eagerly turned to these new authorities in articles dealing with children's fears or the new standards of love. New subdisciplines got into the act, most notably with the rise of industrial psychology and the resulting zeal of personnel experts to prescribe appropriate emotional qualities at work.[14]

The new breed of popularizing experts both encouraged and reflected changes in dominant emotional standards. Their basic arguments shifted from training for moral standards toward encouragement of personal adjustment, simply as a function of the change in the disciplinary background of the advice setters whose authority and knowledge they drew upon. This change clearly provides part of the explanation for new concerns about emotional intensity, a quality that was far more appropriate when a person's main task was to live up to demanding standards than when that task was redefined in terms of demonstrating self-control and the ability to work and play well with others. The shift showed clearly, for example, in the recasting of fear from an occasion for moral challenge to a potential source of damaging trauma.[15] In essence, the new breed of experts was explicitly interested in challenging the wisdom of their elders—a feature particularly prominent among the modernist writers—and in the process they generated a definite direction for change that profoundly altered the goals of personality development.

The new bases of relevant expertise also brought other new factors into play. One of these involved, quite simply, data. Scientific experiments began to provide unexpected information, particularly about children, as early as the 1890s, when G. Stanley Hall and others sponsored studies of childhood emotions. While his own views on emotions reflected a firm Victorianism, the facts he uncovered shook Victorian foundations. Hall's findings on the frequency of night terrors among infants raised questions about the Victorian stiff-upper-lip approach to male courage, for as Hall himself noted, children's fears were both unpredictable and irrational. Soon after 1900 advice manuals sponsored by the Child Study Association, including Alice Birney's, began to introduce new cautions concerning fear even as Victorian standards were maintained in other respects. Birney stressed the emotional fragility of young children and the need for protective strategies, clearly forecasting the more general reassessments of the 1920s. She also ignored the Victorian tradition that distinguished boys from girls where fear was involved; scientific observation showed that children's problems with fear knew no gender. Other linkages between experiment and advice occurred in the area of children's jealousy, though here it seems likely that standards began to change even before scientists started measuring jealousy among young children. Nevertheless, the series of 1920s psychological studies seemed to confirm the prevalence of bitter rivalries among siblings—particularly, but not exclusively, girls—and this further fueled the effort to focus new socialization attention on this emotional problem. New data also entered into the current of advice about anger at work as Elton Mayo and others uncovered surprising levels of rage on the shop floor that, in their judgment, profoundly interfered with efficiency.[16] Here again, objective science did not reign supreme, given that Mayo and his colleagues interpreted worker anger in light of middle-class domestic standards; but new facts about emotional expression became available in the process and added to the sense that past emotional norms must be reassessed.

New expertise implicitly affected gender contours. Advice writers in both the Victorian era and the early twentieth century divided fairly evenly between males and females. But the women who penned popularizations or magazine articles after 1900 were increasingly professionals, caught up in the movement to justify their work not on grounds of special female emotional qualities but through objective science. Few of the new women writers professed active feminism. Nevertheless, although they wrote mainly during decades in which feminism moved into a less strident phase, many of the childrearing experts of the 1920s and 1930s illustrated the extent to which professionally trained women implicitly revised key elements of the Victorian system, including its gender divisions. Their new credentials were typically impressive. Dorothy Canfield Fisher, one of the early revisionists, held a doctorate (though in French literature); Alice Birney had attended Mount Holyoke and later became a professional child welfare worker. These two women were of course transitional, and both at least initially reflected some of Victorianism's continued hold. Slightly later women popularizers, born after 1890, had more explicit professional backgrounds. Caroline Zachary earned a doctorate in educational psychology, Dorothy Baruch a doctorate in psychology. Sidonie Gruenberg had advanced education, while Marian Faegre was an academic.[17] None of these women was actively partisan, but their standards almost inevitably challenged Victorian assumptions about female emotionality and the differences between men and women. And while many other popularizers were men, some of these, like D. H. Thom, worked closely with the women experts of the Children's Bureau in what was increasingly a coeducational field.

The new experts were also frequently aware of their role in helping to set common standards for a nation that had seemed, around 1900, dangerously fragmented by labor strife and diverse waves of immigration. The 1920s launched the period of new attention to Americanization, and many of the new popularizers played a role in educational and media efforts to move toward a common culture.[18] This mood did not require that Victorian standards be altered, but it did help generate a sense that older values might be reevaluated and that some innovation might forward the process of reducing divisions in American values.

Finally, the new experts were conduits through which the impact of certain striking events could affect advice about emotional standards. Advice in the 1920s and 1930s was colored by American reactions to the perceived irrationality and childishness of European warmongers, stirred initially by the fears roused during World War I and its aftermath. We have seen that some popularizations, particularly those dealing with grief, delighted in contrasting American rationality with European ungoverned impulse. Connections grew more explicit with the advent of Nazism and World War II, particularly with regard to growing concern about anger—or, more properly, about what was now termed "aggression"—in light of such sweeping evidence of what untrammeled rage could do to a civilized society.[19] It is hard to determine how much the atmosphere of the world war years colored basic changes in emotional standards, but there is no question that individual experts and whole schools of thought, such as behaviorism, were affected by a desire to define standards of socialization that would keep Americans free from the madness they thought they saw in other parts of the world.

Experts and popularizers alone do not an emotional culture make. There is a tendency among some historically minded students of changes in emotional culture to ignore issues of authorship, treating their sources as automatic reflections of larger and more interesting changes in the society around them. Indeed, the new breed of popularizers who were cutting their teeth in the 1920s largely mirrored developments in the economy and in wider culture that in turn serve as the principal explanations of why emotional standards shifted away from Victorianism. In addition, only these larger factors account for the growing audience for the experts—the people who thronged to the lectures of the marriage counselors, for example, or who gobbled up the stories in *Esquire* or the advice columns in *Parents' Magazine*. Furthermore, specific intellectual schools among the experts largely pale beside the broader changes that their theories mirrored. Behaviorism, as we have seen, played a role in some of the new emotional standards, though Watson's theories were not uniformly adopted and particularly affected revisions in the areas of fear and motherlove. By the 1940s the somewhat greater Freudian influence ushered in certain changes in popularized advice, while the growth of a more permissive attitude symbolized by the early Dr. Spock, which was deliberately directed against behaviorism, modified emotional norms in a few cases. In general, however, the new emotionological trends overrode the seemingly vital fluctuations in dominant psychological schools.[20] The attack on anger, the concern about sibling jealousy, even the substantial downgrading of motherlove, which had gained impetus from behaviorism, largely continued in the years of Spockian permissiveness. Again, we must not let attention to authorship of advice unduly simplify our understanding of causation or lead us into every fad and byway of expert enthusiasm. The fundamental trends ran deeper.

Still, shifts in expertise both reflect and help account for a number of features of the new approach to emotional standards. Secularization increased, with divine support and heavenly reward increasingly withdrawing from emotions of all sorts. New data helped generate the growing focus on emotional guidance for very young children. Concern about healthy personalities and smooth interpersonal relationships, the dominant themes in advice psychology, began to outstrip explicitly moral goals. This in turn played a role not only with regard to overall emotional intensity but also in the new aversion to guilt and the effort to use embarrassment to signal maladjustment in emotional expression. New kinds of training produced different views of the gender implications of emotional standards.[21] Thus, analyzing the new breed of experts helps explain the timing of the redefinition of basic emotional culture, and also some of the directions this new definition took.

Family

Two strands of change within the middle-class family fed into the growing preoccupation with intensity, and they most definitely help explain the almost desperate search for innovative guidance from the experts. The more familiar of these involved gender, but the more significant centered on parent-child relations.

By the 1920s social interactions between men and women were changing rapidly, both before family formation and during marriage. The Victorian life course had entailed a considerable period of separation between women and young men, who they moved away from their parents and into the company of other men while they decided on careers and launched their first efforts. This was the time when men formed intense emotional bonds with each other, sometimes as roommates, and when they joined the fraternal lodges that burgeoned during the nineteenth century. With marriage, typically around the age of thirty, more involvement with women occurred, but lodge activity might persist and contact was further limited by the sheer length of the working day, which was sometimes supplemented by periods of isolation in the male sanctuary upon return to the home. Even vacations frequently separated men from their families.[22]

Family time for men may have begun to increase as early as the 1880s. Certainly by the 1920s evidence of heightened paternal involvement with families began to proliferate. Meanwhile, dating activities brought men into social contact with women earlier, during high school or college. For the middle class, dating was a social and sexual activity removed from active thoughts of marriage, at least until the college years, but it represented a huge departure from the male-oriented socializing of the nineteenth century. Not surprisingly, lodge membership began to plummet during the 1920s.[23] Within marriage, there was an increase in social activities that joined husband and wife, as studies like that of Middletown suggested. Card playing and other home-based entertainments brought the sexes into contact with each other, reducing gender distinctions in social patterns. Parties that sometimes involved carefully, if subtly, regulated sexual games among husbands and wives from different families began to appear in the middle-class social scene from the 1920s onward.[24]

In a variety of respects, then, from the teen years onward, social contact between men and women increased rather strikingly over the levels of the Victorian era. The term "companionate marriage" has been coined to describe precisely these social patterns, which were also recommended by the new breed of marriage counselors.[25] This was no breakthrough toward gender equality, but it was nevertheless a substantial shift in the interactions between men and women. Even as the change confirmed women's domestic role by emphasizing family companionship, it also signaled the need to adjust some of the emotional disparities that had been fundamental to Victorian culture.

Obviously, new contacts increased the pressures against specific emotions like jealousy. Particularly before the rise of "steady" dating late in the 1930s, dating deliberately involved contacts with various individuals from the opposite sex, which burdened a jealous temperament almost unbearably. Increased socializing might also, as *Esquire* noted, have prompted some rethinking of love, on grounds that transcendent closeness amid daily socializing was too much of a good thing.[26]

The larger implications of these new social patterns affected overall judgments of intensity. Now that men and women socialized with each other on a more routine basis, efforts to define the genders in terms of radically different emotional styles almost inevitably came under question. This in turn altered the framework in which emotions such as fear or anger were evaluated, adding to research findings that also blurred distinctions between boys and girls. Insistence on special emotional courage for males made less sense when smooth relations between men and women headed the agenda. Motherlove, of course, fell victim to the same homogenizing impulse, as did channeled anger for men. Because many emotional intensities preached in Victorian culture had also served to define gender identity, the reduction of gender as a category in social relations inevitably reshaped consideration of passion as well. Love was no longer the intense emotion that enabled men and women to transcend their differences. Gender distinctions remained, and the attack on romantic love in one facet of male culture can even be seen as an innovative reaction against the dissolving of prior emotional divisions. But the Victorian staples no longer served, and with this there was a decline in openness to the kinds of intensities that would help men establish their particular qualities, would help women establish theirs, and would help both overcome their differences in love.[27]

Relations between parents and children changed at least as much as did social interactions between men and women. However, these changes are harder to trace if only because rhetoric could so obscure reality. Well into the twentieth century, middle-class readers liked to hear about how important children were and how well they were being treated in this enlightened age. The proclamation of the new era as the "century of the child" picked up on this whiggish theme of progress.[28] At this level Victorian fascination with children seemed to be gaining ground as more families realized the centrality of parent-child relations while casting aside some of the more brutal or heedless treatments of the past. In some respects, of course, as in child health, the proclamations of progress were true; but in descriptions of emotional standards they could easily mislead.

Advice givers were clearly urging parents to regard children, including very young children, as far more problematic, vulnerable, and downright difficult than their Victorian counterparts. Nineteenth-century belief in an innocent blank slate was declining in favor of implicit belief in a host of ingrained fears and hostilities. Parents must not only avoid giving bad examples; they must also actively organize emotional and material support systems to help children overcome innate jealousies or anxieties. Further, these same parents might not have quite the automatic fund of emotional virtues as had been available in the Victorian assumption of transcendent maternal love. In a variety of ways, then, parenting was becoming harder, at least according to the prescriptive literature. One explanation for this persistent complication of the parental task, this new view of children as problems, lay in the desire of the popularizers to get their rhetorical foot in the door, to persuade an audience that outside advice was essential. But real changes in parent-child contacts were in fact occurring. These changes, in turn, involved both shifts in adult caretaking and alterations in the emotional experiences of young children themselves.

Parents in the middle class had more direct contact with their young children by the 1920s than had been common previously. The use of live-in servants declined in the middle class from the 1890s onward.[29] Day servants were now often drawn from groups seen as even more different from the middle class than nineteenth-century domestics had been, and quite apart from the sheer reduction in servant availability, they were less likely to be used for child care. Beginning in the 1920s proper, coresidence by older relatives, particularly grandparents or maiden aunts, also began to decline steadily,[30] which further reduced the range of adults able to participate in daily child care. This weakening of the extended family in initial response to the growth of an urban, industrial society occurred after a century in which it had actually gained ground. The change was often compounded, at least on a day-to-day basis, by suburbanization, which absorbed more and more levels of the urban middle class from the 1880s onward.[31] Changes of this sort inherently increased the intensity of parent-child contacts and potentially also the burdens on the parents involved.

Continued reduction of the birth rate, while limiting the pressure on parents on a numerical basis, also compounded the starkness of parent-child interactions. There were fewer older children to help with later child care and to serve as buffers between young children and their parents. A second child, as a result, was likely to direct a great deal more emotional attention to parents than was common in larger broods. Certain kinds of emotional intensities, including sibling jealousy, tend to increase in small families, where children do not see themselves as part of a larger group with mutual responsibilities for their own maintenance, but rather focus directly on ties to parents.[32] With two- and three-child families becoming the norm in the middle class by 1900, and with the birth rate declining further thereafter, parental awareness and experience of distressing emotional signals from children readily increased. Emotions were more focused, and there were fewer intermediaries.

Finally, children's experiences also changed. Starting in infancy, they became more likely to sleep alone. Middle-class Victorian families routinely had children sleep together, which set patterns of physical and emotional relationship that extended to later friendships. This practice was abandoned beginning around 1900 and was actively disapproved by many experts between 1920 and 1940. Individuation, separate space and separate toys, became the key to proper socialization and avoidance of emotional complications.[33] At the same time, however, these new practices could increase the anxiety of very young children, now placed in a separate room at a very tender age. Growing reports of fears of the dark and of noise might well have sprung not only from new discoveries about childish irrationality but also from new stresses in the experience of childhood itself. The immaturity of children, their incapacity to behave "rationally," could gain new emphasis in this atmosphere, helping to make immaturity a badge of emotional incompetence when applied to adult behaviors as well.

The net effect of these changes clearly established some of the context for the growing perception of children as emotionally vulnerable, prone to ungovernable extremes unless carefully guided and manipulated. The resulting increase in pressure on adults may well have developed some new ambivalences about infants that, while normally repressed, may have added yet another ingredient to the desire to keep emotional levels down. The attack on intensity, in other words, reflected new tensions in the parent-child experience and some attempt on the part of parents to project their own turmoils onto their children, to cope with their own need to suppress by insisting that children learn early on to keep emotional burners on low. Parents afraid to acknowledge their own sexual jealousy, for example, could focus new attention on sibling squabbles. Parents tenser with children's emotions than they liked to admit could express some of their feelings by urging the kids to stop acting like babies and learn to keep cool.

Innovations in family life, particularly the rapid reduction of the birth rate, also influenced intellectual judgments on the family, in Europe as well as the United States. Rudolph Binion has highlighted the new hostility to the family in literature from the 1880s onward as authors began to focus on deviant sexuality, oppression of children and women, and the stifling effects of family life on all its members. He attributes this literary revulsion to two main factors: the anxieties resulting from the newly nonprocreative nature of sexuality attendant on birth rate reduction; and the rising emotional intensity within families attempting to realize Victorian norms within a smaller, more intimate framework. Certainly the literary current helped set the stage for the defiant modernism that in turn attacked conventions of jealousy and familial grief by the 1920s. It may also have mirrored deeper tensions within the middle-class family itself that moved toward deintensification in reaction to the guilts and uncertainties generated by unprecedented levels of birth control, as parents worried about the ethics of contraception and the goals of family life with the experience of parenthood reduced.[34]

Whatever the more pervasive psychological undercurrents for the literary attack on family might have been, there is no question that by the 1920s changes in parent-child contacts and in gender relations had departed from Victorian norms, often in directions participants did not fully or frankly grasp. These changes in turn helped spark reconsideration of specific emotional standards, making emotions such as jealousy and fear more problematic. More generally, they encouraged a redefinition of desirable emotional pitch. Shifts in family relations thus coincided, both in overall timing and in direction, with the factors that most clearly defined the new emotional culture. These factors emanated from economic structure and from new anxieties about the body.

The Consumer Society

More and more Americans were becoming entranced by the joys of consumerism in the decades around 1900—there is no historical mystery to uncover here.[35] Advertisements became more elaborate, department store displays more extravagant, the sheer delight in buying new items more pronounced. What consumerism meant in real, middle-class life is not, however, fully clear as yet. The emotional implications of consumerism help clarify its meaning, while rising consumer commitment in turn explains many of the changes in emotional culture. Some relationships between consumerism and emotion are fairly obvious,[36] but the crucial link with intensity, less visible on the surface, proves particularly revealing.

Consumerism was not new at the turn of the century. Elements of a new passion for goods, with emotional implications such as impulsiveness and a new tendency to define personal identity through things, have been traced back to the eighteenth century. However, consumerism took on a dramatic new shape in the twentieth century, not only because of the greater abundance of goods but also because of a deeper impact on personal meanings. The incorporation of attachments to things into emotionology was a symptom of this intensification. Several distinct changes in tone emerged in the early twentieth century, providing the context for heightened links with emotion. Commercial notices, for example, shifted from dry, largely informational headings to more frankly emotional appeals, suggesting that buyers could achieve better ways of life by purchasing particular products. Thus as late as the 1890s, advertisements for silk goods came in the form of statements of price and utility in newspaper product lists, but thereafter they stressed a carefree mood and more than a bit of sexuality. Increasingly, illustrative materials accompanied slogans such as a department store's lure, "To feel young and carefree, buy our silk." Department stores were also remodeled in the early decades of the twentieth century to stress larger, more evocative store windows and displays. Charged adjectives like "alluring," "bewitching," "enticing"—or, for more domestic products, "healthy," "sanitary," "warm"—became staples in promotional campaigns. The range of goods themselves steadily expanded. The bicycle served as the first relatively expensive mass sales item widely purchased in the middle class that was not fairly directly related to needs (however elaborately defined) of food, clothing, or shelter. The 1880s craze emphasized the recreational and pleasurable functions of bicycles. Cosmetics, automobiles, and a wealth of other products added to the list during the first decades of the twentieth century, while even more ordinary goods, like soap, were pushed well beyond any definable necessity.[37] The idea of a new stage of consumerism taking shape by the early 1900s seems well founded.

This heightened middle-class consumer interest, in turn, had several effects on emotional standards. First and most obviously, it encouraged the growing penchant to distinguish between pleasant and unpleasant emotions.[38] Consumers sought products that made them feel good and shunned those that did not; not surprisingly, emotional standards increasingly moved in the same direction. Thus emotions like grief, which clearly involved pain and in addition could promote relatively few goods outside the services of the undertaker, came in for reexamination, were held up to the new light of consumer pleasures and found wanting.

The decline of guilt was an obvious result of heightened consumerism. Advertisers explicitly contended with possible guilt at self-indulgence, urging buyers to take a kind of pleasure in acquisition that would be untainted by internal emotional warnings.[39] In a consumerist context, guilt clearly joined the list of bad emotions.

Growing consumerism also encouraged a new informality, a sense of loosening standards. Advertisers depended on impulse. A highly regulated atmosphere, in which firm social hierarchy prevailed, was not conducive to sales or to the open enjoyment of things, and so, as many sociologists of emotion have noted, this atmosphere gradually changed. Here was a clear source of the new emotional standards, which carried fewer firm prohibitions and claimed more expressiveness and openness. Certainly, consumer culture in the United States highlighted a strong democratic ingredient, emphasizing the wide availability of goods rather than rigid status groups,[40] and this in turn promoted reassessment of certain emotions, like anger, that could be associated with defense of hierarchy. Smooth relations—including of course customer relations—rather than divisions based on entitlements to emotions like anger gained new emphasis in harmony with consumer values.

Consumerism also promoted the use of goods to deflect emotional stress. Beginning in the 1920s emotional advice conveyed this compensatory strategy in a variety of different contexts. Jealous or potentially jealous children should be distracted by access to their own clothes, toys, and room. Grandparents were told to bring gifts for a jealous sibling when offering traditional presents to a new baby or a birthday child. Children's fears might be approached through the lure of things, as in the suggestion that candy be used to draw a reluctant child into a darkened room. Some anger advice suggested that directing rage at things (rather than people) was a possible outlet for emotions otherwise best kept under wraps. The evolution of *Esquire* magazine implied that things might even be used to replace excessive love, as the magazine turned men's attention away from debates over romance toward a diet of travel, records, cars, and gadgets.[41]

Finally, the use of goods as distractions could easily be transformed into a use of goods as a focus for intense attachments that were now no longer available in relationships. A logic of consumerism, indeed, involved winning satisfactions through acquisition that previously might have been won through passions like love or even anger. This point is no mere theoretical construct. Extremes such as the new disease of kleptomania showed how the passion for things could consume consumers in an atmosphere in which displays of goods gained a new place in the daily routine.[42]

Children, newly problematic in family and emotional life, were exposed to the new effort to equate emotions and things early on as part of the attempt to guide them away from emotional extremes. Toys were of course used as distractions in many distressing situations, and while the technique was surely not brand new, its frequency increased as the range and importance of manufactured toys steadily expanded. Most revealing in this connection was the advent of new kinds of dolls. Dolls, of course, were no innovation of the turn-of-the-century decades. During most of the nineteenth century, however, dolls had been rather expensive items and had been designed primarily for older children. Their functions, while not divorced from emotion, were defined primarily in terms of utility and aesthetics.[43] Dolls were intended to teach various kinds of learning and developmental skills and (particularly after the Civil War) an appreciation for fashion—the latter especially for the younger girls. By the 1890s an emotional role for dolls began to be suggested; comments were made to the effect that dolls might serve as objects of attachment to replace fathers absent at work. By this point also, girls were urged to use dolls for training in grief; doll funerals and other rituals were encouraged, as were such objects as doll coffins. Still, however, most dolls remained stiff, fragile creatures destined more for admiration and role playing than for deep affection, and the fascinating effort at grief involvement was designed for middle childhood, not the impressionable early years.

This situation changed in part because of new technology that allowed American manufacturers to displace European importers and to provide a succession of soft, cuddly creatures, including the famous American teddy bear, that were directed at infants of both sexes. In preventing German exports, World War I completed the process of converting doll production to domestic centers and to products designed for physical contact rather than fragile items designed for aesthetic admiration. Rag dolls of all sorts proliferated, and the conversion to dolls that looked like children (or young animals) rather than adults was completed.[44]

At the same time dolls for older children, increasingly varied and numerous, became enmeshed in a variety of fantasy productions. Children's stories supplemented the use of dolls by providing settings in which dolls expressed and received a variety of emotions. Children were encouraged to display attachment to dolls, and on their own they might also turn dolls into objects of rage or jealousy. Above all, dolls were increasingly designed to act as children or siblings, with their child owners being encouraged to feel parental or sisterly emotion toward them. Not surprisingly, in this new climate dolls began for the first time to receive comment from childrearing authorities and popularizers. Some objected to the kinds of fantasies that dolls stimulated: "Why foster a craving for novelty and variety that life cannot satisfy?" A minister blasted teddy bears as substitute objects of affection that corrupted the maternal instinct. More observers, however, commented on the positive roles dolls could play in emotional life. Thus teddy bears "may have robbed childhood of one of its terrors"—the fear of animals.[45] The importance of the new dolls' cuddly qualities was emphasized, both because they facilitated girls' acquisition of maternal instincts and, more generally, because they provided infants of both sexes with a concrete, reliable focus for attachments. A 1932 observer in *Hygeia* put the point directly, though stiffly: "With the realization of the psychologic importance of the child's early years, there has arisen a new need, that of definite toys of peace and a technic of presenting play material that will furnish the right background and associations for feelings."[46] Or, in an article of 1914: "Children's affections [have] come to center around the toys with which they have lived and played." For infants, parents were advised to "choose a soft animal; the affections as yet are very physical, and this is known as the 'cuddling' age."[47] The link between dolls and other toys and children's emotions, though not an invention of the twentieth century, was almost certainly expanding.

The early use of dolls and other toys as emotional focuses for young children, followed by the deliberate use of material objects to distract from emotional excess, linked consumerism to the socialization process and the perceived problems of children's lack of mature control. There was no plot here, no foul machinations by toymakers or other consumer gurus to ensnare minds and passions; rather, growing consumer interests, increasingly recognized by parents and childrearing authorities, were fit into the experience of growing up just as new questions about children's emotions were being posed. By the 1920s many middle-class Americans were being taught that intense emotion might more safely be directed toward artifacts than toward people and that acquisition might compensate for the limits to emotional spontaneity in other facets of life. And they began learning these lessons in infancy with the endearing toys that now crowded their cribs. In this sense consumerism went beyond its more obvious function of downgrading unpleasant emotions to undercut emotional intensity in interpersonal relations more generally.

Bureaucracy and the Service Sector: A New Functionalism

Changes in middle-class family life and the increasing emphasis on consumerism in American society helped reshape emotional culture. These factors explain major developments like the good-bad dichotomy and the growing focus on early childhood, and they contributed to the aversion to intensity. Trends in both areas, however, accumulated over several decades; they do not fully account for the emergence of the new emotional culture from the 1920s onward. Furthermore, while they are relevant to issues of intensity, they do not fully describe the new interest in self-control. Shifts in family patterns, for example, explain new concerns about children but not the growing emphasis on rationality. To achieve greater chronological precision and to account for a larger number of the actual directions of twentieth-century emotionology, we must consider other changes in economic structure that had accumulated by the 1920s.

The growth of managerial bureaucracies, particularly in corporations but also in sectors such as school administrations and other public agencies, called for new qualities that were different from the real or imagined virtues of the Victorian entrepreneur. Sports goals were redefined, for example, with football gaining on baseball in part because it seemed to inculcate teamwork more fully.[48] At the same time, the rise of the service sector, with a growing number of jobs in sales, clerical work, and the like, called for what came to be called "people skills," which had received far less emphasis in the production-oriented nineteenth century. On the whole, these skills were also required in bureaucratic hierarchies, at least in the middle ranks. Finally, though on a more subsidiary level, these developments also brought growing numbers of middle-class women into the labor force, at least briefly before marriage, and this had its own influence on the emotional tenor of work.[49]

These developments, maturing by the 1920s, undercut the previous functional basis for emotional norms. They called for new definitions, including new goals in the emotional socialization of children. They supported the kinds of experts who were beginning to voice defense of new standards.[50] Finally, the shifts in American economic structure generated an audience for the new goals: managerial and service-sector personnel would, at least by the 1930s and 1940s, take the lead in internalizing twentieth-century emotional strategies, including the implicit but pervasive interest in avoiding undue intensity.

Several of the landmark studies of emotion in the twentieth century have illustrated the link between changes in occupational structure and emotional standards. Arlie Hochschild's examination of employer manipulation of emotion focused on the service sector. She paid particular attention to female employees like flight attendants, who were enjoined to smile and avoid spontaneous emotional response regardless of provocation. She found that this injunction affected not only the employees' experiences of their jobs but also their emotional reactions in other relationships. The Dutch sociologists who have emphasized the new informality, in which emotions are presented carefully depending on context, have similarly highlighted the bureaucracies of the later twentieth century, where at least superficial democracy reduces detailed rules of emotional conduct but where the need to manifest appropriate responses and avoid embarrassment continues to define important constraints.[51]

In the United States the impact of new work settings became manifest during the 1920s. It was at this point that department store personnel programs increased their efforts to make sales clerks conform to middle-class norms in dress and demeanor. It was at this point that advice books for would-be secretaries (male as well as female) began to emphasize the need for emotional control, shifting away from the stress on honesty and punctuality that had dominated behavioral sections of corresponding manuals in the 1880s. And it was at this point that Elton Mayo, manifesting the middle-class aversion to undue anger that in the nineteenth century had focused almost exclusively on the home, began to apply his standards to shop-floor tactics, sketching the ventilationist approach that would spread widely in children's socialization as well as in work settings in subsequent decades. During the 1920s (with a bit of preparation during World War I) Mayo and other industrial psychologists also contended that new kinds of emotional restraint were needed in job areas where female employees were beginning to play a role, however subordinate. Women, so the new common wisdom argued, could not take the emotional rough-and-tumble that Victorian work had entailed, breaking down in tears at signs of anger on the part of supervisors. Moreover, women brought new jealous backbiting to the job floor, which must be nipped in the bud by an insistence on rational control.[52] It was at this point, finally, that Dale Carnegie and other business advice leaders began to stress the need for a combination of strict emotional control and an appearance of effusive bonhomie for salesmen or managers. Carnegie's approach in essence argued for manipulation of the salesman's emotional arsenal such that a less rational, more openly emotional customer would be completely disarmed, charmed, and ready to buy.[53] The 1920s, in sum, saw the inauguration on a variety of fronts of new standards for managing emotional intensity and a new group of experts eager to implement those standards because of the nature of job requirements in a bureaucratic, service-oriented environment. Revealingly, while some of the standards were also suggested for factory labor, they were never pushed as hard in the blue-collar sector as they were for managers, clerks, and salespeople.

In this new campaign, particular emotions that might interfere with smooth bureaucratic or customer relations received the most elaborate comment. Managers and salesmen must keep a lid on their anger lest they provoke subordinates or antagonize buyers. Thus many of the retraining courses and much of the personnel advice directed to the new clerical and managerial middle class from the 1920s onward focused on anger, with a few remarks on jealousy added in. But there was a larger theme of rationality that could call any threat to careful emotional control into question. Mayo, for example, argued in 1933 that modern industrial life does "predispose workers to obsessive response"—to precisely the kind of emotion-driven irrationality that could so disrupt smooth production and harmonious bureaucracies.[54] Mayo's response, which was to employ company psychologists to counsel emotionally fervent personnel, implied that emotions interfered with economic objectives much more than problems between labor and capital did and, further, that emotional intensity could be "cured." Aversion to intensity, then, followed from the work goals attached to dominant American business organization and occupational structure by the second quarter of the twentieth century.

The contrast with Victorian functionalism was marked. Victorian emotional standards were designed to separate work from family, whereas experts à la Mayo were eager to harmonize work and family under more general strategies of intensity control. The frequent contention that work problems most commonly resulted from domestic turmoil or poor upbringing revealed the new holistic approach, which in turn argued against any emotional locus for intense expressions whatsoever. Whereas Victorian standards had helped separate the genders, the growing service economy called for standards that would subsume both men and women, at least to the point where they could work smoothly together in the same space. Whereas Victorian standards emphasized emotional respectability as part of a definition of social class, twentieth-century work, in the broader context of consumerism, downplayed formal hierarchy in favor of wider emotional rules that would reduce intensity for all parties.[55] The only class factor still implicitly granted was the emphasis on training for the managerial middle class primarily. Finally, Victorian standards had highlighted emotions, particularly for men, that could serve as vibrant motivations, where fervor and controlled channeling could combine to prompt high achievement. The new economic setting, though never specifically belittling achievement goals, clearly placed smooth human relations at the forefront, again attacking emotional intensities that might make it harder for people to get along in the fast-growing offices and stores.

While work needs produced the functionalist pressure to redefine emotional goals, the resulting standards were felt in the home as well as on the job. Personnel counselors, trying to shift the blame for job tensions to the domestic front, implied the need to control intensity across the board. As Hochschild has shown, full-blown programs of workplace emotional management inevitably carried over into domestic life— though this extension was not necessarily present in the initial job campaigns of the 1920s and 1930s. Arguments for proper emotional social-ization of children—prevention of harmful accumulations of ungov-erned anger, fear, or jealousy—commonly mentioned the requirements of successful adjustment to work as one of the central adult realities that must be anticipated by careful parental strategies. This popularization, which began in the 1920s, stood in contrast to Victorian manuals that had connected socialization to work mainly through discussions of chan-neled anger or courage.

The childrearing advisers did not specifically articulate their aware-ness of a new economic structure, but their overall approach suggested a level of awareness that at times spilled over into actual vocabulary. In the first edition of his immensely popular baby book, Dr. Spock repeated essentially Victorian advice about anger, arguing that parents must help children learn that the emotion had no place in the home but also that, properly directed, it could be a useful spur. Spock noted that the competitive drive resulting from anger would be useful when children grew up to become hard-driving businessmen or farmers. A bit more than a decade later, and in all subsequent editions, Spock's advice changed, as did his career references. By the 1960s children's anger should be firmly controlled in all circumstances, for the emotion was both dangerous and valueless. Rather than teach children how to chan-nel their aggressive energies toward useful goals, parents should help children minimize intensity by harmless verbalizing; anger itself should have no place in the development of their emotional makeup. Reveal-ingly, when Spock now referred to the work goals for which children were being prepared, his examples came from the areas of management and sales, where smooth personalities and emotional control held pride of place.[56] Spock's conversion on this point, though helpfully explicit, was a bit late; others had realized earlier that the economic role models of the nineteenth century had faded from fashion, and with them the kinds of emotions in which children should be schooled. More generally, the growing emphasis on the need to overcome emotional immaturity resulted from the fact that children's innate emotional turmoil was recognized at the same time that modern work heightened the demand for systematic control of intensity. Small wonder that avoidance of intensity, not only in clearly disruptive categories like anger but also in more benign staples such as motherlove, became such a dominant theme.

Finally, evidence appearing by the late 1930s delineates the final puzzle piece in this functionalist approach to cultural change: the families that most eagerly bought into the new advice literature on emotional control came from the sectors of the middle class most involved in the managerial and service occupations. Arthur Jersild's polling data about levels of parental concern over children's emotional problems, including sibling jealousy, show that suburban families easily exceeded all others. The urban upper class and working class both lagged, rating other, nonemotional issues with children considerably more important. Miller and Swanson's 1950s survey of Detroit families similarly showed, with a more extensive database, that managerial families were most interested in the newer approaches to childrearing, paying particular attention to strict emotional control by parent and child alike. Older middle-class families and traditional blue-collar families were noticeably less interested. Parents from entrepreneurial families, for example, admitted that they were far more likely than their managerial counterparts to punish children when angry and were less concerned if their children were angry as a result of discipline.[57] That this same division generated a growing audience for the new standards was suggested in a number of other studies, particularly focused on the suburbs, of parents who explicitly sought (or claimed to seek) to counter the emotional guidelines their own parents had emphasized.[58] Again, persistent economic change forced the reconsideration of Victorian emotionology and the development of norms in which intensity played no legitimate role. The same change spread from the workplace to other sites, including the family and childrearing, and it also produced the sectors of the middle class (some newly risen from labor and immigrant ranks) most attuned to the advice that resulted. A new functionalism assured both a radical shift in standards and a basis for their dissemination.

The economic shifts persisted, gaining momentum over time and so increasing the pressure to redefine emotional norms and to accept the redefinitions first widely sketched in the 1920s. Managerial bureaucracies became ever larger and more visible in terms of defining probable adult economic roles. The service sector, with its ubiquitous people-pleasing requirements, grew still more rapidly, and by the 1950s television, staffed by service-sector workers par excellence, helped translate the ever-smiling models of service success into daily viewing. The fuller participation of women in the work force during the 1950s and 1960s extended this aspect of the service economy, adding female stereotypes of niceness and docility to the existing standards of emotional control and putting new pressure on men to master impulses that might seem troubling in a dual-gendered job environment.

Cultural Change: Anxieties over Health and Salvation

A functionalist approach to twentieth-century emotionology centers on the new job structure of an advanced industrial society and is supplemented by attention to shifts in family patterns and rising consumerism. This approach accounts for a great deal of the growing aversion to intensity in middle-class emotional culture. It targeted anger; it fed hostility to jealousy and concerns about the distorting effects of too much motherlove; it even contributed to the shifts in grief standards as part of the campaign to smooth over any emotional expression that could disrupt interpersonal harmony and the even flow of the daily routine.

Yet functionalism, even combined with consideration of other structural changes such as twentieth-century demography, should not be pressed too far. There is no reason to assume that the twentieth century poses an exception to previous episodes of major emotionological redefinition, such as the seventeenth–eighteenth centuries and then the Victorian era, when cultural factors conjoined with functional factors to account for new directions. More concretely, some facets of the twentieth-century aversion to intensity do not spring clearly from a functionalist framework. Although there is no clear proof that campaigns against anger actually improved productivity, and although some cultural assumptions were already involved in the reactions of Mayo and his colleagues, the attempts to suppress anger do seem largely functionalist. But the same does not so readily apply to the redefinitions of courage and fear. The attack on Victorian interest in courage was fully as important a part of the overall move against emotional intensity as any other change in the 1920s, yet its link to economic structures is at best remote.[59] With respect to fear of death specifically, given that society was rapidly accommodating to changes in the child mortality rate, functionalism of another sort might be adduced; and of course changes in the actual experience of children and their contacts with adults entered in, as we have seen. But for fear in general, and to an extent for grief and love, the concern about intensity, though not unrelated to functionalism, is most readily explained by shifts in middle-class culture away from the distinctive religious and medical amalgams of Victorianism. This broader cultural change also underlay some of the most vivid imagery of the new emotionology, with its anxieties about emotions that could fester, accumulating much like poison in the body and requiring the regulatory equivalent of lancing a boil.

Relevant cultural change, in turn, included two ingredients. One was fairly obvious in the gyrations of self-styled modernists and sober advice givers alike, the other much less transparent but probably more widely shared and certainly influential.

Discussions of grief and fear during the 1920s made it clear that many popularizers found religious certainties considerably diminished in the American middle class. From this stemmed contentions that assurances of a heavenly reunion might not be credible to alert children, who would sense that their parents no longer adhered to the Victorian formulas. Prayer was no longer invoked in mainstream advice as a means of dealing with fear. The decline of motherlove might also reflect a shift in the salience of semireligious imagery.[60] To the extent that confidence in a benevolent Victorian God declined, a need for greater caution in emotional intensity might well have followed: there was no divine hand to bring fervent expressions to a successful result, and individuals required greater circumspection in tailoring emotions to the reactions of others.[61] Professed religious belief may have altered less fully than the science-based experts contended, however. The factor is relevant, but its weight remains difficult to assess.

There is no question, however, that emotions were assessed in increasingly secular terms, without the moralistic and spiritualized backdrop standard in Victorian emotional discourse. Thus *Esquire*, attacking nineteenth-century love ideals, blasted their excessive spirituality. Efforts to associate love with religious reward now seemed silly, unmodern, given the new focus on physical attraction and mutual accommodation. Even as the middle class continued to profess some religious commitments, the effective utility of religion in helping to guide emotion waned noticeably.

Growing concern about the inner workings of the body was even more widely applicable to the heightened aversion to emotional intensity. Just as medical routines began to change for the middle class, popularizations increasingly highlighted the role of emotions in unseating physical equilibrium and even good health.

Belief in the salience of emotions for health was no new discovery, of course. Traditional humeral medicine had tended to view bodily changes as causing emotion; physical imbalance could prompt outbursts or even outright insanity. From Galen onward, however, Western physicians and medical commentators referred to the effect of emotion on the body, recurrently mentioning the role of love, fear, or grief in causing pains in the heart. In seventeenth-century England, William Harvey discussed the effect of repressed anger in causing "distressing pain in the chest" on the part of one patient. Eighteenth-century investigators still more commonly stressed the role of specific emotional states, notably anger, in causing angina and other heart problems. Learned articles frequently cited the onset of temper as a cause of death.[62]

While this line of argument continued into the nineteenth century, most Victorian physicians, at least until the 1870s, focused more on diagnosis than on explanation. Physical symptoms held center stage with the introduction of new instruments such as the stethoscope. In the popular imagination, judging by dominant emphases in the middle-class press, environmental dangers to health easily prevailed over emotional links. Until the germ theory was assimilated and serious contagious disease began to recede, attention to emotional factors, and particularly the idea that emotional intensity could cause bodily harm, remained at most a subordinate theme. Moralistic fiction did sometimes punish emotional excess with death, though just as commonly a victim of emotional misbehavior died or fell ill, causing guilt and remorse on the part of the miscreant. The most obvious manipulation of health anxieties to regulate middle-class behavior focused not on emotion per se but on sex, with the widely disseminated belief that sexual excess or premature indulgence could result in ailments ranging from acne through sterility to lunacy.[63]

This thinking began to change in the 1870s as earlier medical ideas about emotional causation began to blend with growing public concern about the pressures of modern life. Two articles appeared in the *Popular Science Monthly* in 1874–1875 on "Induced Disease from the Influence of the Passions." "The passions which act most severely on the physical life are anger, fear, hatred, and grief." Love, it was argued, sustained life until it deteriorated into grief or unless it stimulated unduly strenuous exertion. Rage disturbed both the "organic nervous chain" and the heart, causing major disturbance and in some instances death. The brain could also be paralyzed from rage, leading to "a congestion of the vessels of that organ." Fear and grief could have similar effects, grief for example frequently producing irregularity in heartbeat and also stomach distress. Worst of all were the occasions in which "the passions, excited in turn, injure by the combined influence of their action." The health message was clear: "Whenever, from undue excitement of any kind, the passions are permitted to overrule the reason, the result is disease; the heart empties itself into the brain; the brain is stricken, the heart is prostrate, and both are lost." Popularizers were also at pains to cite new instruments, like the cardiograph, that permitted unprecedented measurement of these sometimes unseen inner effects of emotion. At the same time, Darwinian work on the evolutionary functions of emotion, including preparation for flight or fight, encouraged the revival of interest in the impact of emotion on the body.[64]

Victorian emphasis on bodily restraint for the purpose of avoiding undue sexuality or contagion certainly did not disappear, but the new concern for emotional control in the interest of physical well-being began to gain ground. The body might still be seen as a machine, but now it was perceived as a machine that might break down, often insidiously, from within, with unchecked emotions being a major source of damage.

The widely popular commentary on nervous disorders, or neurasthenia, formed an initial result of this anxiety about the impact on physical health of intangible pressures—of what in the later twentieth century would be called stress. From the 1880s past 1900, middle-class Americans were regaled with accounts about the deleterious impact of fast-paced modern life on the heart, on the circulation, and on sanity.[65] Diagnosis of neurasthenia for the middle class focused on tension or dissipation, whereas for lower-class women it was sheer overwork that could prompt nervous disorder. Nervous force was seen as human capital that must be economized, with caution required to avoid "depleting waste."

Thus generalized anxieties about trends in modern life helped account for the neurasthenia craze. Thereafter, between 1900 and 1930, the pace of popular accounts of the ominous link between emotions and health stepped up—literally quadrupling over levels in the 1890s. The rise of psychology both reflected and fueled the growing effort to see emotional control as central to physical well-being. But other, more prosaic factors were also involved; more focused beliefs about the vulnerability of internal organs played a role as well. After 1900 the concept of blood pressure reached public awareness, with appropriate warnings soon attached. Relatedly, the sphygmomanometer was invented in 1896, and its increasing use in routine medical checkups brought home to middle-class Americans the important mystery of internal conditions within their bodies. Attention to inner, organic degeneration increased as well, as common contagious diseases came under greater control particularly after the influenza epidemic of 1919. While phobias about germs persisted, the growing significance of degenerative diseases won public notice. Not coincidentally, efforts to popularize fundraising for and awareness of cancer gained ground rapidly in the 1920s and 1930s, generating the first instance of a successful public campaign over a degenerative ailment.[66] In sum, with the widespread awareness of the nervous pressures of modern society as a backdrop, practical changes in medical routines and disease patterns, supported by wide public discussions, set the stage for a much more specific use of health as a measurement of appropriate emotional standards.

As attention shifted from general nervousness to emotionality, initial popular commentary focused on the increasingly suspect emotions. An article in 1896 described the results of fear: "When under fear's sway the heart beats quickly and violently, and palpitates or knocks against the ribs, thus the heart's action becomes disturbed." Anger received similar attention in 1900 in the *Scientific American:* "The heart bounds or beats rapidly and several cases of death due to cardiac lesion are ascribed to anger. Some people have peculiar feelings in the throat and mouth, others become dizzy or faint . . . , and in twenty cases attacks called bilious are ascribed to anger." One book linked the emotions to the growing concern about infants, stating that "children often died of violent, mental excitement." *Living Age* returned to fear in 1907: "We are now informed that the emotion of fear may produce paralysis, jaundice, sudden decay of the teeth, erysipelas, eczema and even death." *Current Literature* discussed the poisons produced by excess passion, arguing that hate produces enough chemicals in the body "to cause the death of perhaps fourscore persons." Another 1907 article summed up the increasing agreement: "Now it is the emotions that are the most obvious meeting ground of the flesh and the spirit."[67] Similarly, the *Saturday Evening Post* told its middle-class audience that "by the time an emotion has fairly got us in its grip . . . the blood-supply of half the organs in our body has then powerfully altered, and often completely reversed."[68]

While blood and heart commanded the most attention, suggesting links between new theories about the impact of powerful emotions and growing concerns about cardiac awareness, popular articles by 1914 also noted links to gastric distress. For example, *Harper's Magazine* brought this new area to public attention: "Not only are the secretory activities of the stomach unfavorably affected during strong emotions; the movements of the stomach as well, and, indeed, the movements of almost the entire alimentary canal, are wholly stopped during excitement." The range of damaging emotions expanded as well, an editorial in the *Independent* dryly noting, "We often hear of people dying of grief." The article went on to comment that the literary device of perishing from heartbreak turned out to be quite accurate in many cases, particularly when strong emotion joined with outright physical decay. Grief could, in sum, "corrode" internal organs. Extending the same thought, "love-sickness" was noted as a real malady and no mere poet's fancy; love could produce loss of appetite, dysfunction of the heart, and ailments of the lungs and liver. The public also was treated to increasingly specific comments on emotion's chemical effects. *Living Age* discussed the production of adrenalin under the sway of emotion, which "raises the blood pressure, constricts the smaller blood-vessels . . . and increases the sugar-content of the blood."[69] And again, the general point continued to be hammered home, as in a 1913 essay in *Harper's Bazaar*:

It is now a fact recognized by scientific experts that many nervous disorders are the product of emotions which years before the onset of the illness had not been properly controlled, but only repressed or allowed to disguise themselves in other forms of self-gratification.

In the light of what has been said we can understand how to manipulate our thoughts and emotions so that we may live healthy and therefore useful lives.[70]

By the 1920s, along with ongoing commentary on the deleterious impact of intense emotions on heart, blood, and stomach, popular magazines increasingly emphasized the lessons to be drawn from the new wisdom. "The general law is that all peaceful, tranquil, undisturbing types of thought tend to act beneficently and helpfully upon all bodily organs and functions. . . . while all of the opposite nature have disturbing and destructive influences, and tend to produce bodily disorders." In commenting on the role of strong emotions in the poor health of war-devastated Europe, the *Literary Digest* described how people "overcome by their emotion, would . . . perform all sorts of antics, the subjective mentality gaining the ascendancy over the higher centers of judgement." A few comments made an exception for joy, arguing that it revived the organism, but otherwise strong passions seemed uniformly bad for the health. Thus a 1926 piece on blood pressure in the *American Magazine* argued that even love could damage the system, as opposed to a calmer, cheerful but more controlled approach to romance.[71]

Both religious and secular authorities found support for their claims in the growing belief in the need for emotional control. Serene faith might be a remedy, "allowing our bodies to recover from many ills." John Watson argued in *Harper's* that the same result would be achieved by a scientifically sound childrearing strategy that would prevent durable disruption of the nervous and digestive systems by teaching children how to avoid strong emotion, enabling them to "get a grip" on their own emotional behavior. In *Harper's* in 1922, a Harvard medical school professor chimed in with a cautionary essay on "What Strong Emotions Do to Us." After detailing all the standard circulatory, digestive, and cardiac issues, Dr. Cannon turned to the proper preventatives: solid rational control. "The wise man" is he who accepts problems "philosophically, and so far as possible, turns his attention to other affairs. Thus the futile emotional disturbance may be aborted." A proper mental attitude can allow "emotional factors" to be "diverted and minimized to insignificance."[72]

The early decades of the twentieth century thus saw what one historian has termed the "somaticization" of psychological tensions. Another historian, more vaguely but quite accurately, speaks of a transition from fears of forces in the outer world, which were dominant in Western culture through the eighteenth century, to fears of inner forces, which gained ground during the twentieth century.[73] The growing anxieties about emotion that developed during the initial phases of the shift away from Victorian emotionology expressed both the somaticization process and the heightened concern about unseen but menacing currents in the body's interior. A new nervousness about health, all the greater for uncertainties about the afterlife, helped regulate emotional norms as shifts in emotionology participated in other fundamental changes in middle-class beliefs. Awareness of the many facets of organic deterioration contributed strongly not only to the growing aversion to intense emotional experience but also to some of the specific imagery that viewed damaging emotion in terms of inward accumulation and virtual poison. This same approach explains why even emotions not particularly related to smooth management coordination came under the general attack on emotional intensity. Functionalism and a new health culture neatly meshed to urge that the passions be kept under strict control.

Conclusion

Most of the factors that prompted reconsideration of Victorian emotional formulas and the generation of a new emotionology predicated on more systematic avoidance of intensity gained momentum from about 1920 onward. Consumerism and the demands of a management-based service economy established an increasingly pervasive framework. Shifts in gender roles and concerns about children's behavior continued to affect emotional formulas, with post–World War II changes, including dramatic loosening of parental supervision over adolescents, adding important ingredients. The trajectory of cultural change was perhaps more complex. The interwar theme of religious uncertainty waned somewhat, and increased recognition of the strength of American religions promoted some revision of the expert proclamations of the 1920s and 1930s, particularly concerning such emotions as grief. At the same time, many secularizing trends continued, including heightened sexuality, making most Americans uncomfortable with religiouslike passions as opposed to calmer statements of belief. The fascination with health as a barometer of emotional control persisted strongly. Magazine articles on the subject declined in number as what had been a set of novel pronouncements between 1900 and 1930 became part of a common fund of wisdom about strategies to avoid high blood pressure or ulcers. These beliefs persisted and provided dramatic enforcement to warnings about emotional excess. Commentary on the deleterious effects of anger recurred, for example, in the 1980s fascination with "type A" personalities and their proneness to heart attacks.[74] The American preoccupation with cardiovascular disorder gave rise to theoretical formulations about the relationship between a society's prohibitions and its preferred disease emphasis. By the 1970s and 1980s, indeed, health culture and corporate functionalism easily conjoined. Training sessions for flight attendants, for example, argued not only that anger must be avoided in order to please customers; it must also be avoided in the interests of attendants' health, for not only lack of control of levels of anger but the mere fact of the emotion itself could damage the heart. "I'd like to talk to you about being angry. I'm not saying you should do it for the passengers. I'm saying do it for *yourselves*."[75]

The combination of factors that emerged by the 1920s to produce a new emotional culture called on various kinds of change in American life. The combination was complex. It guided a new type of popularizing expert and motivated a growing audience to seek new directions in emotional advice. The combination developed early in the United States; a comparable mixture would affect Europe only in the 1960s, and even then would lack some specific ingredients such as the particular American fascination with heart disease.[76] The combination explains both the need to reformulate Victorian standards and the persistence of the new amalgam. It generated powerful changes in what Americans thought they should seek in emotional behavior and what anxieties they had when they considered deviations from the norm. The same combination of causes, finally, explains not only why many Americans were ready to listen to new advice but also why this advice was internalized in many ways and incorporated in many facets of American life. Because it responded to important trends, the new emotional culture had a wide array of impacts; it received from the wider society, but it also gave, in turn helping to reshape aspects of this society.

8

The Impact of the New Standards: Controlling Intensity in Real Life

Most of the disciplines that study emotion in social contexts note the relevance of norms to emotional reality.[1] The evidence from the Victorian era yields the same conclusion: standards count, even though individuals vary around the norm and in general accept innovation gradually at best. People work to adjust their expressions of emotion, even their self-reports, according to cultural standards, though of course they continue to differ in temperament and may also find ways to manipulate the cultural system to their personal emotional advantage. Even young children pick up emotional cues offered by adult caregivers, which means that cultural standards are transmitted as part of a process that helps children select among the emotional options available to them.[2]

If it is to have more than passing significance, any analysis of emotional standards must be able to demonstrate that cultural materials have real-life impact. It is tempting to assume as much, but to do so would be fraudulent; the assumption must be demonstrated for any cultural area or period. The first historians who dabbled explicitly in the study of emotion drew oversharp contrasts between one period and the next because they did not examine the complexities of impact. Certainly it is difficult to determine "actual" emotions in the past, and thus to discern how much they shifted to accord with a new emotional culture. Evidence is often sketchy, particularly where inner feelings are concerned. Even where indications of attitudes exist, people frequently claim to adhere to one set of standards while behaving quite differently. This is a common problem, for example, in assessing the extent to which parents really change their childrearing styles as opposed to learning what to tell outside observers, sometimes with the utmost sincerity.[3]

But the new standards that developed during the second quarter of the twentieth century did have consequences. They changed, at least in some measure, the way many Americans thought about various kinds of emotional intensities—and/or they reflected these changes. They altered the ways in which many Americans responded to other people's emotions, creating such a significant bias against strong emotional expressions that it was often the emotional individual, not the object of his or her emotion, who was seen as requiring remediation. The new standards, finally, affected a number of social institutions and conventions, altering them to reflect a new desire to avoid what was increasingly pejoratively regarded as emotionalism. Indeed, the idea of emotionality carried a new taint, as the 1960s fascination with the word "cool" suggested; more than in the nineteenth century, when the focus had been more subtly directed toward inappropriate use or target, open emotion now could convey an embarrassing vulnerability.[4]

So the requirement for a study of emotional culture can be fulfilled in this case. It can be shown that the standards put forward to replace Victorianism had impact; the culture counted, and it helps explain a variety of changes in American life, from opinion to law. No single study can do justice to the range of possible results of a growing aversion to intensity, and many areas must be sketched tentatively at best. However, enough can be demonstrated to justify recognizing a new set of emotional signals as a powerful factor for change in middle-class life over the past seven decades.

Aside from the need to acknowledge insufficient evidence and individual variation around norms, three issues complicate this final part of the analysis of emotional transformation: continuities from the past must be acknowledged; problems of timing must be reviewed; and a special complexity concerning institutionalization of the new standards must be invoked, for certain public outlets deliberately defied the new norms in the very process of adjusting to their impact.

Victorianism did not die overnight. We have seen its persistence in periodic reassertions of older grief values, for example, or in the long attachment to channeled anger in some of the most popular childrearing manuals. Victorian standards that were susceptible to deintensification proved particularly hardy. Thus there was no general movement against the idea of love; rather, love was subtly redefined toward reduced fervor. Beliefs about gender and emotion easily survived a host of changes, not only in culture but also in actual expression; into the 1990s Americans reported believing that women were naturally more loving than men, men naturally more often angry. Advertising continued to play up a special kind of motherlove, at least as it might be expressed in a desire to have clean kitchens or satisfied child eaters; this was not the powerful Victorian version, to be sure, but it maintained some of the trappings.[5] Continuities from earlier periods had also bedeviled Victorianism— there was no sudden conversion to the idea of avoiding anger in punishing children, for example. But aspects of Victorianism had been prepared by previous shifts in emotional culture reaching back to the seventeenth or eighteenth century, which had begun to create firmer standards against domestic anger and to promote new ideas of love. In contrast, the twentieth-century attack on intensity was a more abrupt shift of gears away from earlier standards. It is hardly surprising, then, that a host of apparent anomalies persisted, even as the new standards were in many respects gradually assimilated.

A new emotional culture yields consequences only over time. While parents hastened to assimilate some of the new wisdom about children's fears and jealousies by the later 1920s, a full set of results had to await at least a generation, at which point children raised under some attempt to incorporate new standards could demonstrate their impact in adulthood and in their own childrearing practices.[6] Thus our focus shifts from the 1920s and 1930s to the 1940s and beyond, in some cases reaching into quite recent times. This extension of the time frame is untidy, but it is entirely logical given the slow process required to internalize highly personal new beliefs. My emphasis on the word "cool" is in this sense deliberate. "Cool" became a widespread term for an appropriate emotional style only in the 1960s, for the full measure of the culture occurred thirty to forty years after its effective inception. Indeed, the fact that the term has maintained standard popularity among youth into the 1990s may plausibly suggest not only the culture's ongoing potency but also the continued elaboration of its results.

As argued earlier, it is necessary to demonstrate that an emotional culture translated into major public institutions and practices in order to show that it was more than a meaningless fad. As we have seen, Victorian emotional culture meets this test fairly readily, whatever the variations in individual acceptance might have been. The same holds true for twentieth-century culture, but modern middle-class life introduced an interesting division. There is evidence that important facets of public life reflected the new standards, but it also appears that the very inculcation of a cool culture created a need for alternative outlets in which quite different emotional values, including Victorian symbols, could at least be vicariously experienced. Discussion of this complexity must await the following chapter, which will explore the divided world that made the new cautiousness endurable by creating an aura of greater freedom. The present chapter will set the stage by examining the most straightforward public translations of the new standards.

Beliefs

Between the late 1920s and the late 1940s, a growing audience developed for new-style advice about emotion. The establishment and popularity of magazines in which this advice featured prominently, like *Parents' Magazine* (1927) and *Esquire* (1933), provide strong evidence of this audience (though it is always possible that audience interest focused on other content and merely tolerated the novel emotionology). Explicit appeals for formal advice on marriage and spouse selection, as in the popularity of advice columns or the efforts to establish college courses in the subject from 1927 onward, suggest a similar uncertainty about older standards and a desire for clarification of new norms. The sheer volume of new childrearing manuals from the mid-1920s through Dr. Spock suggests the same, as do family studies and polling data from the 1930s through the 1950s. Relevant findings emphasized the extent to which emotional problems were seen as crucial by parents newly worried about excessive temper or sibling rivalry; by adults worried about their own jealousy (particularly after about 1950, when sexual jealousy replaced sibling tensions in acknowledged prominence); or by spouses rating each other (men worried about women's emotional nagging, women about men's emotional unresponsiveness). Polls indicated that the new, suburban, managerial-service middle class was particularly eager to jettison outdated emotional standards. By the 1940s a series of studies more widely suggested particular interest in establishing a new pattern of childrearing, deliberately different from that of parents or grandparents in terms of disciplinary style and emotional goals. Use of therapy, finally, again reflected a growing audience for innovation or at least for guidance at a time when emotional standards were shifting and the importance of emotional conformity was in many ways increasing.[7] By the 1930s child guidance clinics, initially established for troubled working-class families, found themselves increasingly preoccupied with middle-class clients who were, in turn, eager for help in controlling unacceptable childish anger or jealousy.[8] By the 1940s a growing number of therapists for adults began to report issues relating to anger and other areas of emotional intensity—and these issues involved not only cases of unwanted excessive emotion but also inability to express emotion after a childhood of sedulous suppression.

The new emotional culture fed this growing audience interest and almost surely reflected it as well. Experts worked hard to sell their wares; they had a vested interest in innovation, particularly as the basis for expertise shifted toward scientific popularization.[9] But from the 1920s onward experts also reported their own need to respond to the kinds of problems parents or others brought to them; for example, parental requests for advice on new sibling jealousies preceded the experiments that provided scientific basis for expert concern. The establishment of a new emotionology set the stage, then, for wider changes in actual emotional beliefs, but it also reflected some of these changes as well. The internalization of twentieth-century emotional culture was not a one-way street.

The process of innovation did not yield a blanket statement of concern about undue intensity. The experts were not explicit on this point; rather, the attack on intensity accumulated through specific comments on the dangers of romantic love as the basis for marriage or the hazards of anger in the workplace. Neither was the middle-class audience fully aware of the overall consistency of new emotional reactions. Yet the combined impact of specific shifts of belief concerning individual emotions and emotional relationships clearly suggests increasing agreement on the need to keep emotions under careful wraps.

Surveys indicate clearly, for example, a general middle-class consensus on the embarrassing childishness of jealousy by the 1960s. Whether or not this had in fact developed earlier cannot be fully determined, but the new common wisdom clearly reflected the long process of socialization in this direction since the 1920s. Initially it emphasized standards for children (conceived with an eye toward adult emotional behavior and probably translating adult concerns), then adult jealousy per se. Some extreme manifestations, like the jealousy workshops of the 1970s, were atypical and followed from the particular tenor of the sexual revolution decades, but the larger agreement had wider and deeper roots. While some Americans fell back on a temperament argument, implying that they were jealous by nature, an increasing number either denied jealousy or admitted deep personal responsibility for the emotion, proving "more likely to try and change, or else get out of, relationships where they feel unhappy and insecure." Comparative analysis from the same period, around 1970, indicated that Americans were far more likely to profess great discomfort with jealousy than were people from most other cultures (50 percent more likely than their closest competitors, West Indians). About a third of all middle-class Americans claimed freedom from jealousy, and others expressed uneasiness with this facet of their emotional makeup; both self-reports worked against intensity, requiring in its place nonchalance or concealment or both. And while jealous Americans tended to argue that their emotional style resulted from insecurity, the animus against the emotion had reached such proportions that some authorities argued that the reverse equation might in fact hold: that people with unduly intense emotions such as jealousy might become insecure because of their anxiety and embarrassment over their intense reactions.[10]

The bias against manifesting jealousy fed new social patterns as well as difficult self-evaluations. As early as the 1920s parties held by middle-class couples began to emphasize some controlled spouse swapping as couples shifted partners for games or, in some cases, even in seemingly sedate small towns, for a bit of kissing and fondling. With increasingly overt sexual experimentation and some outright commitments to open marriages by the 1960s, tests of jealousy control expanded. Again, only a minority pushed to the extremes, but the pressure to avoid expressions of jealousy unquestionably mounted as spouses moved toward more diverse interactions and in some instances unconcealed infidelity. Jealous reactions among swinging couples were disapproved: "I think it comes from possessiveness and I'm trying to grow away from that." From the 1920s onward, growing pressure to control jealousy was a vital precondition for women's new public contacts and for more permissive sexual standards.[11]

At the same time, the hostility to jealousy could produce new institutions designed to minimize it. Dating, for example, moved fairly quickly from its initial "polygamous" form, in which youth were expected to date multiple partners, to more controlled arrangements that would among other things offer a greater protection against jealousy. From the late 1930s onward teenagers frequently moved from playing the field to seeking a steady dating partner (or, in the middle class, a series of steady dating partners). The greater "security" cited in this growing movement meant many things, including the mere convenience of not having to worry about finding a partner, but it undoubtedly reflected a desire to avoid the jealous discomforts of uncontrolled dating. Then, as dating began to decline in the 1960s, it was replaced by larger peer groupings in which pairing was less emphasized and pressures against jealousy were routinely enforced by group conformity. A cool emotional style, including avoidance of jealousy, became a vital part of the new social code.[12]

Middle-class Americans did not find a perfect solution to their own strict codes concerning manifestations of jealousy. Steady dating, for example, reduced jealous onslaughts for a time but opened the way for tension-filled breakups or subsequent jealousy about a partner's previous involvements. A majority combined profound disapproval of jealousy with some admitted pangs, an uncomfortable amalgam that provoked real embarrassment and a consistent effort to control both excessive internal passion and overt display. Private battles against jealousy as heterosexual social contacts widened provided an important ingredient for twentieth-century emotional life and a recurrent setting for the larger war against intensity.

A new current of psychological research on jealousy underscores the ongoing importance of jealousy in American life and its potentially constructive consequences. Researchers mention a pronounced effort to ignore jealous responses as one coping mechanism for individuals and, above all, a distinctive American impulse to check others' reactions when jealousy does emerge. In contrast to jealous Frenchmen, who tend to get mad, or Dutchmen who get sad, jealous Americans, when they cannot conceal, tend to canvass friends and acquaintances both for support and for assurance that the emotion has not emerged too strongly. Amid great individual variations in the personal capacity to minimize jealousy, then, the anti-intensity culture continues to have impact.[13]

New standards applied to fear had more ambiguous results, though the effort to avoid intense confrontation—or to stage-manage childhood toward this end—was widespread. The spate of parental letters to child-rearing authorities from the late 1920s onward suggested widespread agreement on the newly problematic status of fear. Fears loomed large among the emotional issues parents cited as real worries by the late 1940s, particularly in the suburban middle class. Some inconsistency developed, with some older gender distinctions being maintained. Fa-thers worried about boys' fears less than mothers did, and continued interest in competitive contact sports like football encouraged demon-stration of courage even for many middle-class boys. On the other hand, some nineteenth-century fear rituals declined under growing adult supervision; amateur boxing for middle-class boys was a case in point. Overall, despite lags and disagreements, the goal of limiting deliberate contact with fear in childhood almost certainly gained ground.[14]

As for middle-class adults, there is no way to demonstrate that they grew more likely to try to avoid fear than had their counterparts in the nineteenth century. To be sure, military service became less popular in the middle class and less likely to produce personal accounts of courage in the fashion common during the Civil War. A variety of factors con-tributed to this shift, but the declining validity of fear encounters might have been one of them. Verbal admission of fear, ironically, became somewhat more acceptable by midcentury. Because it was thought that fear should not be experienced too intensely and because ventilation was a widely recommended means of reducing intensity, discussions of fear in battle or in anticipation of battle became more open and were even recommended as part of therapy. At the same time, however, lesser fears were commonly given other terms, like "nervousness" or "anxiety," lest undue intensity be implied. To this extent, some authorities argued, fear became less "available" as an emotional experience by the later twenti-eth century.[15] Finally, the vocabulary used to describe emotionally in-tense confrontations with fear clearly declined, as courage—despite John F. Kennedy's adoption of the term—began to take on slightly anachronistic connotations.

Application of the anti-intensity theme to grief also produced ambiguous results. Many people continued to grieve as they had in the nineteenth century, mourning the deaths of children or young adults with great sorrow. Here, the biggest change may have been not culture but demographic reality, as child death rates declined greatly and thus greatly reduced the occasions for grief manifestations. At the same time, awareness of new grief rules spread, making some people comfortable with relatively little show of outward sorrow and causing others who were genuinely grief-stricken to question or criticize their own reactions. Therapists reported problems with patients who adamantly insisted that there must be something wrong with them because their grief "cures" did not occur as rapidly as the general culture urged or simply because they occurred in less recognizable phases. "I feel like I am just at a standstill in my life, really, just kind of stopped there," said one patient actively fighting her deep grief. The need for therapy itself, though not unprecedented, was a sign of growing discomfort with spontaneous emotional reactions to sorrow. Many marriages now split apart during grief over the death of a child, and this newly common family disruption reflected not only hostility to the grief of others but also confusion over one's own reaction; shared grief, that staple of Victorian culture, became harder to achieve.[16]

Adult efforts to disclaim intense anger were more clear-cut than was the case with grief and, particularly, with fear. The new emotionology did not, after all, deny the possibility of intense fear if it was provoked by something from the outside world; it merely argued that the intensity was risky and undesirable. The new standards of restraint did not prohibit either adults or children from experiencing or to some extent expressing fear. As for grief, though it was regarded more ambivalently than fear, it could not entirely be denied. Anger, however, was another matter; like jealousy, this was an emotion to be controlled even in response to outside stimuli.

By the 1950s, surveys of middle managers noted a widespread interest in claiming temper control as a common characteristic. And while angry supervisors remained a problem for many workers, the extent of the problem almost certainly declined. By the 1970s, less than 10 percent of all workers listed emotional tensions with supervisors as a significant job issue. Correspondingly, strikes over issues of management style declined steadily from the 1940s through the 1970s; statistical categories are crude, but they suggest almost a 50 percent drop. And the fact that strikes and strikers themselves declined in relation to the size of the labor force after a peak in the 1950s suggests, among other things, a growing worker embarrassment at organized displays of anger as part of job life.[17] Trade unions began to join employers in urging emotional restraint. As a United Auto Workers booklet argued in the mid-1940s: "A lost temper usually means a lost argument." In the early 1970s workers of various sorts told Studs Terkel about their internalization of anger control. "You always have to be pleasant—no matter how bad you feel." "You can't say anything back. The customer is always right." Foremen, who dealt with underlings rather than customers, boasted of their ability to create an atmosphere of positive cheer, using their own acceptance of the new emotional rules to affect those around them.[18] As with jealousy, then, increasing numbers of Americans on the job either argued that they had mastered an unpleasant emotional tension and could avoid intensity spontaneously or that they imposed control on their intense feelings, even at some internal cost. The new rules won widespread adherence, even if claims undoubtedly exceeded real achievement.

Parental standards for anger also changed. Parents increasingly vowed to gain control over anger in dealing with children, and even more revealingly, they expressed less pleasure in children's anger as a sign of spirit, though this decline occurred more slowly among fathers than among mothers or school authorities. Anger was increasingly a problem, pure and simple—one of the "adjustment problems" widely noted by school guidance counselors, replacing sexual transgressions as the leading category by the 1940s.[19] An array of surveys from the 1940s onward revealed discomfort, and sometimes even deeper depression, when control slipped and anger was expressed in the family. This was not necessarily novel, as Victorian culture had preached against the angry quarrel, but it may have gained ground particularly among men, who, despite some conventional wisdom to the contrary, were now as likely to be upset with their own display of anger in a marital spat as were wives. By the 1970s marriage authorities, cleverly but not necessarily inaccurately, argued that reactions to one's own anger had surpassed anger itself as a cause of disputes and even breakups. "Their [the spouses'] problem isn't that they are angry with each other; it's that they think they shouldn't be angry with each other." By the early 1950s surveys reported that an overwhelming majority of couples felt bad if they became emotional in quarreling with each other, and the bad temper of a spouse was rated as one of the leading problems in marriage.[20] Victorian promptings to control anger in the family, now overlaid by the more general warnings against emotional intensity, worked to restrain the emotion or to create complex reactions when the restraint broke down, including, ironically, yet more anger that could not be directly expressed.

As with jealousy, finally, the desire to conceal anger, to claim that it did not exist, spread in American culture.[21] Here was one of the important "secrets" of modern society, which comparative studies suggested was particularly prevalent in the United States. Despite the absence of similar analysis for the Victorian era, the strong likelihood, given the new emotional norms, is that this secretive reaction was a twentieth-century artifact, especially for men and especially in public encounters such as those of the workplace.

Quite apart from individual variations in temperament, other factors prevented uniform commitment to anger avoidance within the American middle class. Fundamentalist Christians from various social classes seemed to encourage the anger-avoidance code: "The Christian response is to put our anger at a distance" because anger indicates reluctance to trust in the guidance of the Lord. "Don't get mad. Hang on. Jesus is coming. Be patient." On the other hand, however, the fundamentalist method of anger control involved repressing anger in the family but actually encouraging its expression against outside targets. This differed from the blander but more systematic evisceration of anger intended by the ventilationist approach. Historian Philip Greven has argued that even in the later twentieth century, this approach to anger harked back to a pre-Victorian evangelical tradition that allowed for an underlying rage that could burst out against evildoers.[22] By the 1970s some of this anger began to fuel new protest movements directed, for example, against legalized abortion.

Youth protesters in the 1960s demonstrated intense anger, as did many feminists in the ensuing decade. Yet here the general anger control formulas did have a bearing, if an incomplete one. Feminists carefully maintained the control theme in their own groups, though this did not prevent expressions of deep anger against male opponents. Youth in the 1960s, with their emphasis on love over war, liked to think of themselves as apostles of gentleness, which meant that their own anger often disconcerted them (or led to denial); this discomfort with anger may even have inhibited a more durable or ideological commitment to protest. Anger control had its impact, in other words, even on certain middle-class groups that flirted with considerable intensity at least during a particularly vibrant protest period.

Even aside from important subcultural or chronological variations, anger by no means disappeared from middle-class life. Many people, as we will see, professed a tension between controlling their own anger and feeling compelled to absorb or mediate the anger of others. As the new anger standards took hold, some individuals continued to claim a positive use for anger in dealing with others. For example, a foreman in the 1930s acknowledged the new advice to use sensitivity in reacting to angry workers but reacted tersely: "Well, even if it is true, what of it? I've got to do something with such birds." Even in the 1970s service workers might claim that a healthy temper was a sign of "red-blooded" Americanness. These arguments on behalf of anger, however, did not set forth an alternate standard in which certain kinds of angry intensity might be justifiable or useful. Instead, as in the case of the foreman, they recognized the new norms even while professing impatience with them or, as with the service workers, they were accompanied by parallel claims of a capacity normally to keep cool. A pro-anger stance was progressively discredited. This is why the temptation to veil or prevaricate increased. This is why the emotional basis for certain institutional expressions of anger, like fire-breathing unions or strikes, steadily eroded. This is why older workers themselves measured change: "The younger workers don't even know how to take the crap we took."[23] Of course the decline in strikes was by no means total, and of course emotional factors were only one element in the complex shift in the accessibility of protest. But it remains true that the new movement against intensity undermined the passions that could in turn undergird expressions of moral outrage, at least around the workplace. Conversions to the new standards thus linked personal expectations to wider social trends.

Unlike anger, love was not systematically denied. However, its locations were narrowed, its language was moderated, and in some instances its ambivalence increased—all under the spur of the new cautions about intensity.

Men and women still sought love, but their vocabulary moved away from the soaring, religiouslike fervor of the Victorian era. At the same time, the centrality of sex in describing and measuring love advanced. By the 1950s, many courting couples and marriage partners emphasized the same combination of personal and sexual compatibility in defining what they meant by love. They talked of identifying marital success by a capacity to "work and play together successfully" for years. They replaced boundlessness with a desire for good sense: "Our marriage should be rational and controllable." Even when seeking permanence, they often prided themselves on their ability calmly to acknowledge the possibility of divorce.[24]

Men began to talk of love more casually. By the 1920s the institution of dating privileged sexual contacts over Victorian transcendence. A 1920s fraternity phrase captured the new mood: "If a girl doesn't pet, a man can figure he didn't rush her right." The whole practice of dating introduced a recreational element into heterosexual contacts, at least from the male side, that squeezed out love. By the 1940s high school boys talked in terms of pushing petting as far as their dates would allow, describing the experience as "having fun" or "taking them for a ride." Similar though less crudely put concepts suffused marriage, with increased interest in defining marriage in terms of sexual satisfaction (particularly on men's part). Polls in the 1930s suggested considerable complaint by wives about husbands' failure to express love verbally, while husbands responded with a critique of wives' tendency to manifest hurt feelings.[25] There was no direct dispute about love here but also no widespread ability to describe the emotion in terms of transcendence. Even wives who might comment on their husbands' emotional reticence were no longer describing the kind of descent from spiritual love that had appeared in Victorian evaluations.

Women also experienced new conflicts in defining love. A recent analysis of the 1920s diary of a Western Pennsylvania woman, though reflecting some purely personal psychodynamics, illustrates some of these conflicts. Gladys Bell harbored late-nineteenth-century ideals of intense love, which she found reflected in the books she read and the movies she saw. She even shared the characteristic late-Victorian dilemma about the balance between religion and love. But unlike the late Victorians, she held back from admitting love, lest she be engulfed by it, adding notes like "I'm losing my grip on myself" when she could not control her emotions to her satisfaction. She saw new sexual interests and even new career interests (she was a teacher) as reasons for her failure to find the love she professed to want. "Funniest thing of my life is that I never 'fell in love.' " A brief engagement left her feeling that "love in some form or other has taken possession of me" while at the same time she lamented, "I seem to have lost a part of myself." Ultimately she married a man she hesitated to love, moved to do so because, among other reasons, she worried that his own love might "turn to something harmful." She never managed a Victorian-like faith in romantic passion. Her case demonstrates a clearly transitional situation, in which older definitions persisted but were reevaluated in terms of threat, above all because of the paralyzing effects of intensity on individual will.

The whole genre of love letters declined, partly because new means of communication developed but partly perhaps because of the more prosaic and/or more overtly sexual phrasing that many couples found appropriate to express their emotional ties. The same trend affected writings among friends. Discoveries of throwbacks to Victorian vocabulary in the letters of women friends—particularly in letters by people like Eleanor Roosevelt who were raised in the transition decades between Victorian and twentieth-century emotional culture—evoked startled incomprehension or accusations of lesbianism or both. Obviously a new language did not necessarily mean a different emotional experience where love or intense friendship was involved, and it is true that a history of the content of modern friendship has yet to emerge. But the altered vocabulary suggested a substantial change in the ability to express a nineteenth-century style love (and perhaps the very idea of love among friends), or at least in the sense of the appropriateness of such expression.

Greater caution toward love continued into the 1970s and beyond. A number of observers noted changes in middle-class dating patterns. Steady dating declined in favor of looser alliances among many peers; or if steadies developed, they were typically treated less intensely than their counterparts had been a generation before. Love-struck couples wandered around high school corridors less often than in the 1950s. Many observers found the same emotional loosening among adults. As Alan Bloom put it, even the replacement of the phrase "in love" with the word "relationship" suggested greater tentativeness. The exact tenor of heterosexual love remains to be fully captured by research, and as always there was variety, but agreement on change was widespread.[26]

Several factors prompted this further shift away from intensely romantic love. Economic pressures, beginning with the later stages of the baby boomers' maturation, prompted marriage at older ages. New sexual habits, particularly the normalcy of premarital sex, removed certain mysteries from love. For some teenagers who preferred to delay their sexual initiation, the new sexual habits also reinforced a certain reserve that could replace standardized rules like "good girls say no." These new factors added to the ongoing culture of emotional reticence, allowing this culture in essence to implement the limitations on mutual devotion that were generated by economic changes. Love, already in process of redefinition by the 1930s, came to take on different meanings for young people, becoming either more purely sexual or more cautious or both, as economic and sexual realities prompted fuller acceptance of post-Victorian standards in generating real emotional life.

Friendship as well as love reflected the effects of new adult constraints and of new vocabulary. Male friendship changed decisively. The loving attachments that young middle-class Victorian men had openly sought and described disappeared. Some may have survived through the collegiate years, yielding only in early adulthood to less intense male contacts, but even before full adulthood, growing fear of homosexuality significantly reduced men's willingness to talk or write about their emotions for each other or to combine emotion with open physical contact. As homosexuality gained new definition and more open disapproval, the male dilemma became in some senses a special case, but it also fit the larger pattern of downgrading intense emotional bonds. While male friendship was partially replaced by new social contacts with women, a certain guardedness often carried over into those contacts.[27]

Children still loved their mothers, but here too signs of altered emotional experience began to surface by the 1930s. A study of mother-daughter relationships notes a more relaxed, even flippant tone in daughters' letters after the 1920s.[28] A young woman thus wrote from camp: "It was nice to hear from you, to put it mildly. I'd like to write often very much . . . but alas and alack, when I have two minutes to sit down and write, I must write reports." This letter actually resulted from the promptings of the young woman's father. Women, apparently less intensely or at least more ambivalently attached to their mothers, became not only more nonchalant about staying in contact but also more likely to express open annoyance at interference. A diabetic wrote her concerned mother, who had sent a maid to accompany her home from boarding school: "I think its [sic] selfish when you let your responsibility for me run away to such an extent that it seriously hampers my life. . . . I had a few hopes that you would have out grown [sic] some of this since I have been away, but maybe that's hoping to [sic] much from you." Attention to peers and boys began to replace some of the intimacies previously focused on the mother-daughter tie. This could simply transfer intensity to another target, but it certainly suggested some experiential impact of the growing cautions against motherlove as the quintessential female emotional focus. Thus a girl might wonder about love in general, while simultaneously noting that "I very seldom think of Dad & Mom though I'm of course fond of them."[29] Patterns varied, to be sure, and nineteenth-century–style fervor might still emerge. But the language and general tone changed, leading to the increasing frankness young women gained by the 1960s and 1970s in discussing their relationship with their mothers in terms of problems more than rewards.[30] To be sure, the problems were rooted in undeniable emotional links, but these links now had to be broken or reforged in the interests of personal independence and reduced intensity.

The general aversion to emotional intensity significantly changed the way middle-class Americans described their own emotional goals and even the way they defined desirable emotional experiences. Concerning many negative emotions, deception gained ground—self-deception in some cases, concealment from the outside world in others. It was no accident that, by the 1960s, sunglasses became a badge of American cool, for they hid emotions the eyes might disclose. While ventilationist strategies in principle promoted some willingness to put certain emotional tensions into words—"it made me so mad"—even this release was often constrained by embarrassment. Not surprisingly, advice about venting emotions often emphasized the need for complete privacy, like shouting in a closet. Far more frequently and systematically than in the nineteenth century, emotionality took on unfavorable connotations, suggesting an inability to maintain proper control. Middle-class Americans worked to restrain themselves.

The Emotions of Others

The new emotional culture significantly reduced tolerance for other people's intensity. To be sure, the culture harbored an important inconsistency in this respect. On the one hand, people were trained to identify their emotions and verbalize them lest they fester, and this ventilationist strategy implied some willingness on the part of others to listen to an emotional experience. Friendship might be defined, to use a 1980s phrasing, in terms of "being there" for someone else's emotional outpourings. On the other hand, intense emotion was also a sign of immaturity, and it could be shunned on that basis even when a given individual was too overwhelmed to be properly constrained by embarrassment. While parents were enjoined to listen to their children's venting as part of the effort to socialize them toward appropriate emotional control in adulthood, many parents unquestionably found even this exposure to others' emotion somewhat wearing. Children became more problematic because they needed an emotional audience that adults should not require, and parental pleasure in dealing with children declined measurably, at least between the 1950s and the 1970s, in part for this reason.[31]

Impatience with others' emotions applied clearly to jealousy and anger. Lewis Terman's 1930s marriage survey disclosed a definite resentment against spousal jealousy, primarily among husbands. According to most married men, jealousy had become an intolerable emotional intrusion. Sexual experimentation like open marriage, as it spread by the 1960s, was often initiated by one partner on the assumption that it was up to the other partner to handle any ensuing jealousy. In other words, jealousy became the problem of the person who felt it, not a cue to a partner to offer systematically reassuring behavior. Apology might be expected more from a jealous spouse than from the partner who had flirted or strayed even further into the growing opportunities for sexual promiscuity. Paul Popenoe cited an impulse on the part of targets of spousal jealousy to wish to retaliate—to give their partner "something to be jealous about." Even in the 1930s in conventional Middletown, the Lynds noted a widespread sense that concealment of affairs had become less essential than before—a theme that carried easily into the 1980s, when many couples found frankness, with its accompanying demand for control over jealousy, a legitimate test of a mate's emotional maturity.[32]

The anger of others became increasingly unattractive. In colleges the growing practice of soliciting student evaluations encouraged comments on grumpy professors, and open displays of faculty temper were readily condemned. On the job, standards reflected a certain complexity for a few decades; middle managers were taught in the 1930s and 1940s that a certain amount of worker anger might have to be accepted, not because it was justified but because workers had so many domestic problems or simply lacked appropriate breeding. Middle management thus involved turning the other cheek, accepting (though immediately diluting) emotional outbursts that supervisors themselves must avoid. Over time, expectations of middle-class control mounted steadily. Workers became accustomed to foremen who kept their temper in check—one of the key reasons for a declining rate of personal tensions with supervisors—while blithely advising less controlled supervisors to catch up with the times: "He should use some psychology." By the 1970s a few employees even argued that their supervisors had become so eager to avoid confrontation, so reluctant to criticize, that guidelines for improved performance had become impossibly fuzzy.[33]

Revealingly, training for middle managers moved increasingly away from techniques for dealing with angry customers or subordinates to assumptions that such strategies would not be necessary. The sensitivity-training groups (T-groups) that gained wide popularity in the 1950s and 1960s differed from earlier management retraining efforts in shifting away from explicit lessons in temper control or in defusing the reactions of others. In keeping with the widespread (if somewhat cosmetic) promptings toward more open communication, T-groups also advocated such communication, in the process revealing their assumption that negative emotions would be held in check. "Effectiveness decreases and emotionality increases." T-groups argued against strict hierarchy or firm repressiveness with the clear expectation that anger would no longer enter in; only positive feelings, desirable for management loyalty, would emerge when frank exchanges were encouraged. Thus when T-group advocates spoke of "more authentic" personal relationships on the job, they assumed that anger had no place in authenticity; only affection would emerge in an open environment. Movements of this sort, though eager to embrace a nonrepressive language, constituted a clear escalation of the anger-control goals, and particularly a growing intolerance for expressions of temper on the part of others, at least within management ranks. Just as there was no longer any clear reason to spend much time listening to another proclaim jealousy, so anger now discredited its bearer; few if any occasions seemed to require listening to someone else talk about his or her rage.[34]

The clearest victim of the growing intolerance for emotional intensity on the part of others was grief. We have seen that the etiquette manuals, picking up on the new aversion to intense grief, argued in terms of the emotion's unpleasantness for other people, "who might find it difficult to function well in the constant company of an outwardly mourning person." Stories also dealt with the problems of peer reactions—"her friends were again feeling a little critical of her, saying to one another that it would be a pity if poor Marian should allow grief to make her 'queer.' " From the 1920s onward formal mourning declined. Special clothes were abandoned except for funerals themselves, and increasingly even for funerals. Markings on homes progressively disappeared. Employers became increasingly reluctant to allow time off for mourning apart from a funeral day or half-day. And, always granting variety in personal reactions, many Americans became impatient with the need to listen to the grief of others, particularly after an initial this-should-do-it exchange. The removal of death to hospitals, where few people were allowed to participate in the receipt of the final news, was not directly caused by the new aversion to handling grief, but it certainly furthered the process. Avoidance of grief situations seemed to make the new emotionology work well.[35]

But grief itself did not decline as rapidly as did public tolerance for it. Stories might note the decline of conventional mourning and of sacred symbols of the departed, but their recommendations for alternatives remained rather vague: "Slowly, slowly we come out of all this. Slowly we learn that the one way to keep our own forever with us, is to lift into the aura of his spiritual permanence." By the 1950s certain categories of grief-stricken Americans, such as people who lost a child or spouse at an untimely age, began to form voluntary groups of kindred souls, providing emotional support for each other on the basis of their shared experience and their common realization of the lack of extensive sympathy from the wider society. Support groups like Theos and the Compassionate Friends spread to most American cities.[36] This new bond elevated strangers to a position of emotional importance simply on the basis of the unavailability of sympathetic others, including, often, friends. The bond might fill the void, but it also testified to the growing distaste for other people's intensities even at times of crisis. The pressure to maintain control of oneself and the convenient belief in the immaturity of others' outbursts supported a major change in emotional interactions in many middle-class families and acquaintance groups. Here the "impersonal" portion of the "impersonal but friendly" tandem could shine through.

Impatience with others' emotion applied also to sadness. A major study in the 1980s showed a pronounced difference between assessment of one's own sadness and reactions to other people's. One's own sadness was perceived as a legitimate problem that called forth strategies for resolution. Sadness in others, however, was a form of whimpering incapacity that was at best an annoyance, at worst a cause for avoidance. The study was not, to be sure, historical, and there is no evidence to prove that past reactions to sadness in American culture had been more generous. Nevertheless, the correspondence between this study's results and reactions in other emotional instances is striking. Here, too, strong emotions might force efforts to find acquaintances based on shared emotional state, an odd alignment produced by the twentieth-century sense that emotions should not normally intrude. Or they might prompt a turn to therapy, the other contemporary remedy for emotions that had no audience.

The growing aversion to dealing with the emotions of others was in fact one of the most powerful effects of the new emotional culture. It sustained a growing sense of individualism as people became emotionally more separate,[37] and it supported the enforcement of emotional control through embarrassment, for the belief that strong emotions might unfavorably affect peers' reactions was often quite accurate.

Like beliefs about one's own emotions, reactions to others' varied, of course, by individual temperament. We are talking about changing norms, not a set of uniform patterns. Further, an important gap also opened between men and women in their respective interpretations of the new emotional culture. Men most clearly moved toward a distaste for emotional exchange on the grounds that individuals should exert self-control, while many women preferred to seek and provide an audience for the verbal venting of intense sentiments. Here the quarrel was not about the need to control emotions but about the role of others in facilitating this process. The movement toward greater uniformity in emotional standards had itself carried some antifemale implications, particularly in the attacks (by many professional women as well as men) on motherlove and excessive romantic love. A tone was set by the 1930s in which living up to the gender-neutral standards of emotional control seemed to require particular redress on women's side. Differences in expectations about support from others added to this new, subtle but potentially bitter gender gap. By the 1960s, women's claims of men's excessive coldness became commonplace, both within and without the growing feminist movement; and women were echoed by many in the small band of "men's liberationists." Men, so this argument went, were too rigidly closed to their own emotions and too intolerant of others' needs for emotional expression; women were no more emotional in fact, but they were more aware and certainly more mutually supportive. Aside from the liberationist wing, men largely seemed to ignore these jeremiads, and polls in the 1970s and 1980s revealed men's strong belief that women were too emotional and too dependent on an audience for their emotional experiences. This was in fact one of the chief grievances men manifested against women, so the difference was far from trivial.[38]

The most pervasive emotional gender gap of the twentieth century thus differed considerably from the Victorian statement of differences in emotional traits, though it had some similar resonance. It could produce bitter disputes over response to emotional distress and particularly over conversation concerning emotional issues. This gap widened even as many aspects of men's and women's lives grew closer together—perhaps, indeed, precisely because they drew closer together, requiring or promoting some new differentiations in order to preserve identities on new bases.

Yet women's emotional expressiveness should not be exaggerated. Not only because of continued male influence but also because many women were eager to dissociate themselves from Victorian traditions of maternalism, the overall context for reacting to the emotions of others did narrow. Women might share more than men on average, but they too lost Victorian opportunities in experiences such as mourning. Though the theme of self-sacrifice persisted in women's definitions of love, the decline of motherlove and redefinitions of romance both worked against the kinds of selfless devotion popular in Victorian women's culture and enacted by some women. By the 1960s a new insistence in women's literature on greater assertiveness further assailed altruistic love even in this final bastion, at least in principle. Again, the new emotional culture's promotion of increased separateness among individuals stands out, though men probably internalized this standard more commonly than women. Worry about emotional "contagion" limited tolerance for the angry, the grief-stricken, the depressed. This trend helped generate new needs (though again more widely among women than among men) for professionals whose job it was to listen to intense emotions that might find no other audience. The rise of therapy in the American middle class, though deriving from a number of factors, including the decline of fervent religion, owed much to the need to find listeners as the more traditional pool dried up.[39]

Declining tolerance for emotional intensity in others had other effects that marked its fairly steady progress between the 1920s and the 1980s. Two developments in particular delineated the changes in the audience for emotion. The first marks a growing need to identify real emotional sharing as a special rather than a normal trait. The second suggests ways in which some individuals tried to develop alternatives to serious support from the outside world.

The word "empathy" was coined early in the twentieth century, in part to provide an English equivalent for the German word *Einfühlung*. The word initially gained currency only among experts in psychology and kindred fields and was not directed toward normal social interactions. By the 1920s it was particularly applied to the capacity for deep appreciation of works of art or music. The word gained public usage only in the 1950s and 1960s in the United States, where it described individuals able to share deeply in the feelings of others. By the 1980s it was dubbed a "vogue word," open to some confusions but most commonly denoting a capacity for emotional sharing.[40] The coining, progress, and changing emphases of the word suggest that an emotionally altruistic quality needed to be identified because it stood out from what were becoming the most common reactions to the feelings of others. Empathy involved more than a negotiated willingness to listen briefly to the emotions of others in the expectation that the same service would be provided in return—the most common ventilationist strategy. The quality was praised, but more significantly it was reified and granted terminology because of its scarcity value. Finding an empathic listener when in emotional need or even a truly empathic moment on the part of a reasonably sensitive other became an achievement clearly to be distinguished from normal experience. Finding an explicit term for such an unusual experience became equally necessary.

It is not surprising that as the audience for emotion narrowed its range, some emotions were increasingly described in terms of isolation. In the twentieth-century debates on the function of sadness, American authorities have exhibited a pronounced tendency to label as useful the kind of sadness that allows an individual to withdraw in order to assess and retool before emotional reentry to a full range of activity. Sadness as a means of appealing to others for help has won less approval, and the kind of empathy with sadness developed in other cultures, and possibly in the Victorian past even within the United States, has become less common as well. Small wonder that the most common deviant emotional state in the twentieth century, depression, involves pronounced withdrawal from emotional interaction, in contrast to many qualities of the most widely noted deviance of the Victorian era, hysteria.[41] Emotions work well, even to express dysfunction, when they call for little reaction or when they emphasize withdrawal from interaction.

As the context for emotional response shifted and individuals struggled to gain appropriate control, the role of totally private emotional expression changed. A need to find emotionally kindred spirits, as in the grief support groups, was not abandoned. But many people also needed to seek some release without expecting anyone else to respond or share. Shouting in the closet or in the privacy of a car may have served this purpose, as some authorities recommended.[42] At least as interesting, and a bit more traceable, was a shift in the nature of adult diaries.

Diaries in the nineteenth century and earlier were often relevant to emotional expression. But their main function was to record emotional reactions in terms of the standards desired; the diary became a record of success or failure in living up to emotional goals, a moral account. Thus diarists documented their struggles with temper or the grief they shared with others. Rarely did a diary explicitly serve as a form of release in absence of social support. Twentieth-century diaries, in contrast, moved in precisely this direction. Moral self-evaluation continued, but the trend was toward use of the diary directly to state emotional experiences that could not otherwise be vented, to express emotions that were recognized as too intense for an audience but that required release from the personal interior. Maintaining multiple diaries served as one outlet that allowed emotional expression to be subdivided so that its intensity would not seem overwhelming, even to the lone author-reader. Thus a woman kept an "angry journal" that she felt must be separated from comments on marriage or on spiritual yearnings because "it's just too full of nasty ugly things." A mild-mannered professional, proud of never displaying temper, deliberately maintained a journal filled with all his "negative emotions . . . feelings of remorse and loss . . . jealousy, anger and swearing come out in unabashed tones. . . . When I write, I can get much rawer . . . I don't have to worry, Am I hurting somebody? Am I inflicting pain?" By the later twentieth century other individuals used diaries precisely because they found themselves too emotional and their emotions too overwhelming to, and unwelcomed by, significant others.[43]

New technologies might also have provided additional, if more muted, forms of release. For example, when computer mail was developed, individuals used it to express much more emotional reaction than they would venture either in speech or in normal writing. The novelty of the medium and the anonymity of the audience reduced the normal constraints imposed by the twentieth-century standards of self-control and the usual awareness of an unsympathetic audience.[44]

The decline of a sense of obligation to respond to others' emotions, and the echoes of this decline in individual efforts to seek compensatory release, form one of the leading impacts of twentieth-century emotionology, clearly differentiating emotional relationships from Victorian patterns. This trend led not only to acceptance of reduced intensity in one's own expressions but also to changes in the nature of friendship and to some new uncertainties surrounding expectations within the family. The new atmosphere could work well for individuals who normally had their emotions in appropriate check or for whom the impulse to conceal was not a strain. But the same atmosphere might also leave certain emotional needs unanswered in times of crisis, or it might limit the outlets available to individuals who, correctly or not, judged themselves more emotional than the times allowed. Again, shifts in responsiveness to others, based on the growing disapproval of intensity, heightened emotional individualism. But successful navigation of the new environment also required some combination of considerable individual self-control, private release, and concealment; individualism should not be confused with spontaneity, despite recurrent rhetoric directed against repression. The preoccupation with one's own emotional control, in turn, contributed to the limited tolerance for the intrusions of others. Victorian selflessness, not to mention the emotional collaboration discovered in other cultures— like the shared sadness conveyed by the word *fago* in Ifaluk society[45]—

became increasingly rare, except as it was specially reinvented by groups of initial strangers united by some pressing need to manufacture emotional support.

Institutional Reactions to the New Culture

The emotional culture that began to form in the 1920s produced some rapid changes in public institutions. Shifts in corporate programs were part of the emerging culture itself, particularly in the campaign against intense anger. Corporations that set up retraining classes, tests to help weed out hotheads, and personnel counseling were responding to the new standards while also defining and disseminating them. Over time, additional corporate initiatives flowed from the larger implications of twentieth-century emotionology. By the 1950s job interviews were characteristically restructured to reduce emotional anxiety. The idea of using emotional cues to test character gave way to a desire to promote calm, since vigorous emotion would simply distract. The same style applied to the increasingly common exit interview, where departing employees were encouraged to discuss problems but also to gain a more balanced mood; insofar as possible, no one should go away mad.[46]

Work life might still stir deep emotion; we have seen that many workers responded to the new standards not by avoiding emotion but by restraining or concealing it. Public impact is not the same thing as institutional ability actually to control emotional experience. Corporate manipulation did confuse some workers about what their "real" emotions were, but it did not control emotional experience completely. This same uncertainty applies to the military efforts to curtail intense emotion by providing a more understanding approach to fear during World War II and then subsequently reducing hazing exercises in training, for their success can hardly be measured.[47]

On the other hand, attempts to regulate the activities of children and youth, particularly prominent during the early decades of the twentieth century, had more consistent implications for emotional socialization. Adult groups sought to limit boy culture, to reduce the fights and the risky dares that had translated ingredients of Victorian emotionology into daily life.[48] Adult initiatives were not entirely successful, but many historians agree that the autonomy of boys was curtailed to some extent into early adolescence by activities such as scouting and by the extension of after-school programs. Some of the resultant organizations, to be sure, maintained a Victorian tone—like the sports teams that worked on channeling anger. Others, however, sought more fully to regulate intense interactions; cub scout programs, for example, emphasized crafts that might substitute busy work with inanimate objects for some of the emotional liveliness of Victorian boyhood.

Schools participated actively in the attempt to develop new policies that would limit emotionality. Success may have been elusive because for each emotion-reducing policy, other developments, such as racial integration, may have provided new reasons for fear or anger in the school setting.[49] But explicit school policies did shift under the new emotionological aegis, and these policies had significant consequences in their own right.

By the 1930s, school authorities began urging reduction of fear-inducing situations. One authority noted: "Many junior high schools, by eliminating home work and stressing day-by-day preparation at school, have done much to banish the fear of semester examinations." By the 1940s education officials increasingly emphasized positive reinforcements rather than fear-inducing punishments and comparisons, to the point that some educators came to believe that only kindness, not stressful criticism, was worth conveying as a response to classroom work. The flunking of students declined in favor of more lenient acknowledgments of minimum quality or improvement such that students could be spared the anxiety, and teachers the resultant student anger, of being held back. Schools worked also to limit hazing practices by student organizations. The decline of new introductions of honor codes was a response to concerns about the stress of intense guilt, and by the 1960s students themselves proved increasingly loath to report violations of codes lest they betray their peers and involve themselves in unwanted settings of intense emotion.[50] Competitiveness was downplayed by new policies designed to keep grades private. By the 1980s identifiable posting of grades, by which students might learn their comparative ranking and risk the resultant envy and jealous resentment, had become not only uncommon but illegal (though in this case students often rejected the system by immediately discussing their grades anyway, in part to demonstrate their ability to rise above emotional tensions among friends). Schools also developed the use of guidance counselors in part to deal with children—particularly angry children—who did not live up to appropriate emotional codes. And by the 1950s teachers themselves, like other middle-class workers, were being urged to adopt more "psychological" techniques in dealing with students—including careful control over their own tempers.[51]

Most indicative of the new desire to defuse the emotional atmosphere of the classroom was the progressive shift in grading policies. By the 1950s, school authorities—including teachers—began to participate in a massive escalation of average grades, which often yielded a majority of students earning honors marks in suburban high schools and prestigious colleges, despite evidence that objective student performance levels were deteriorating. Higher grades were thought to reduce student anxiety and anger and thus help teachers curtail emotional confrontations with students or their parents (this trend largely continues into the 1990s). For their part, many students seemed not illogically to assume that a friendly personality and controlled emotional behavior largely sufficed to merit good marks. American schools—and particularly those dominated by the middle class—showed the stamp of a new set of emotional goals as strong emotion came to be seen as a distraction from, even a deterrent to, educational performance rather than a spur to achievement.[52]

American colleges and universities participated enthusiastically in the new emotional climate, particularly from the 1950s onward. They attacked emotionally threatening (and sometimes physically dangerous) fraternity hazing practices in favor of milder initiations. They joined in the upward grading curve and provided a growing array of counseling services and friendly student affairs personnel to make students feel less emotionally threatened. Evaluations of faculty encouraged students to comment on the personality attributes of faculty, promoting a sense that traditional aloofness or invocations of fear should be replaced by a more relaxed, at least apparently affable manner. "Quality of life" became a campus watchword as a moderate and supportive emotional atmosphere replaced traditional points of stress. As campus supervision of sexual habits declined amid 1960s attacks on the doctrine of in loco parentis, efforts to monitor emotional styles in the direction of a pleasant mildness ironically increased.

The new emotionology increasingly informed the law and some uses of the law. The same held true for Victorian emotional culture, but the new directions were even more dramatically novel. As early as the

1890s, American states began to turn against the jealousy defense as an excuse for homicide, as they increasingly disallowed the invocation of the "unwritten law" as a form of insanity. Even with this shift, however, state legislatures and juries continued to reduce the charge of murder to that of manslaughter when the "heat of passion" could be invoked by a man. Southern states in particular maintained their regional tradition of supporting jealousy. By the 1970s, however, passion was finally struck down. Texas withdrew its statute in 1974 while Georgia rescinded its tolerance in 1977. "In this day of no-fault, on-demand divorce, when adultery is merely a misdemeanor . . . any idea that a spouse is ever justified in taking the life of another—adulterous spouse or illicit lover—to prevent adultery is uncivilized."[53] Public or at least legal sanction for this intense emotional act had been revoked. Other states moved in the same direction, even limiting jury flexibility in delivering verdicts on manslaughter.

Jealousy and even intense love were also attacked by the abrupt termination of alienation-of-affection suits, which flourished in the United States from the late nineteenth century until the 1930s. Alienation-of-affection actions had been based on the idea that engagement gave each partner some ownership of the other—such that proprietary rights were violated if one partner was wooed away—and also on a recognition of the intense suffering that withdrawal of love might cause. Emotional distress must be soothed, usually by substantial monetary awards from a well-to-do fiancé. By the 1930s, however, the emotionological basis for these "heart balm" suits, as they had been dubbed, had eroded. Jealousy was now tawdry and embarrassing, and people should either not love too intensely or lick their wounds in private. The rate of suits plummeted, and in the 1970s state governments (with rare exceptions) put an end to the category by formal legislation.[54]

The most striking and general legal incorporation of the growing hostility to emotional intensity applied to the growing currency of no-fault actions. Just as the rise of mental cruelty provisions had symbolized the application of Victorian culture to marriage law, which was intended to sanctify intense family bonds and punish their violation, so no-fault actions translated the desire to avoid emotional entanglements into an even wider-ranging set of legal innovations. No-fault worked toward a simplification of divorce whereby neither party would have to proclaim particular emotional or other damage and whereby both parties could, for the public record at least, proclaim their ability to agree without requiring legally sanctioned emotional (or material) hostage taking. As no-fault spread out from California by the late 1960s, the percentage of men filing for no-fault divorce increased gradually. This indicates the reduced stigma of being divorced, to be sure, but it was also a sign that the emotionally "cooler" gender now found a legal proceeding that matched its emotional self-image.[55] No-fault also mirrored the decline in the need to proclaim guilt, not only in divorce but also in automobile accidents. The legal provision unquestionably concealed continued anger, grief, and guilt, but concealment was part of the new culture, certainly preferable to direct, intense confrontation with emotion.

The advent of no-fault legislation responded to many factors. Concerning car insurance, reduction of legal costs and delays served as primary motivation, but an emotional culture that discouraged adversarial attitudes was also relevant. The more prosaic changes in insurance law prepared the way for no-fault divorce reforms. They also reflected growing dissatisfaction with the lies and delays attendant on most fault-based divorce, which required couples who had agreed to a divorce to trump up charges of cruelty or adultery. Nevertheless, the new emotional culture was central to the no-fault divorce movement. It was no accident that discussions of divorce by consent dated back to the years around 1920, when the new emotionology was itself being installed. Proponents of no-fault in the 1960s and 1970s argued explicitly in terms of avoidance of emotional stress: divorcing couples had experienced enough "emotional trauma" without having to "endure a legal trauma as well." The whole adversarial nature of conventional divorce seemed anachronistic in an increasingly therapeutic atmosphere. Divorcing couples should be encouraged to consider counseling but should also be free, perhaps after additional counseling, to undertake a new relationship undamaged by a bruising emotional experience in the interim. The elite divorce lawyers who initially spearheaded the no-fault movement in California were explicitly bent on humanizing the divorce process by decreasing the conflict level—and emotional ingredients were central in these considerations. California testimony from 1964 onward placed the new emotional standards directly on the table (though the novelty was not acknowledged). Thus a psychiatrist argued that all divorce was the result of "gross emotional immaturity. . . . Emotional immaturity is a state of decadence or regression . . . because somehow or another, in this pattern of growth, he [the relevant spouse] was not able to develop better solutions, better emotionality, better emotional solutions to problems."[56] Adding intense emotional conflict to this brew was, it seemed, nonsensical; it was better to let people cut their losses and start afresh. No-fault provisions also affected the costs of litigation and could have implications for property settlement, but the response to new emotional standards—and above all, the desire to facilitate escape from intensity without imposing additional emotional stress in the process—lay at the center of this broad legal current. A basic pillar of the legal system involving family law and conceptions of responsibility had been reconstructed to fit altered beliefs about emotional propriety.

During the 1970s one state after another raced to catch up with California. The speed with which no-fault legislation spread, and the relative lack of controversy, further suggest the wide agreement on the goals of avoiding unnecessary intensity. One scholar has emphasized lobbying and legislative process as the keys to this "silent revolution," but a larger public concern about conflict and the burdens of passion drove the process as well.[57]

American law also served emotional goals in other, more indirect ways, though here patterns may have been less novel. Rates of litigation remained high in the later twentieth century, and many observers commented on the aggressive, angry style of many courtroom suits. Yet beneath the surface, a different emotional reality could be played out. Despite, or perhaps because of, the adversarial approach of courtroom attorneys, many Americans were drawn to minor lawsuits as a way of expressing their anger (or grief) over an accident or malfeasance through some sort of small claims action—along with some hope of monetary gain, though studies suggested that this was often a minor motivation. As one litigant who was suing a store noted: "I was really angry. I'd been gypped and there was nothing I could do . . . I think that suing him made me feel better. I guess I did it just to let off steam." But a large minority of individual litigants never actually appeared in court, sometimes because out-of-court settlements were made but also, in almost as many instances, because they felt that launching the suit was sufficient to serve the purpose of venting. There was no need to follow up and no interest in sustaining the emotional basis of the suit intensely enough to go to further trouble, particularly amid long trial delays. Claims suits thus allowed a modest ritual expression of emotion, but the act of bringing suit often sufficed to defuse the intensity, and many litigants actually depended on the no-show system to excuse them from the need for outright confrontation. Thus an apparently direct outlet for aggression became increasingly modified as the emotional culture encouraged a gap between initial claims and willingness to persist or to express intense emotion in an open court. Furthermore, even among individuals who did pursue their claims, many were at pains to identify their goals as righting an injustice, not as indulging a "fit of anger." Finally, by the later 1970s, even preliminary adversarial action was losing ground to arbitration procedures, which provided a counterpart to no-fault laws in the divorce arena. Again, not only the law itself but also some of its uses translated a widespread desire to restrain passion, even though the adversarial elements in the legal system reflected older standards.[58]

Advice about emotion thus fed into efforts by employers, youth authorities, jurists, and legislators to reduce the settings in which strong emotion need be expressed or, in the case of legal claims action, to provide ritual outlets that might limit the expression. Vivid emotion was no longer a useful test of or motivation for people; rather, people deserved protection from its onslaught, whether in divorce action or military training or school examinations. Gradually and incompletely but unquestionably, American institutions moved toward translating a culture of mildness into a host of standard routines, with impacts ranging from grading policies to the unprecedented effort to dissociate the emotion-laden concept of fault from wide stretches of the law.

Conclusion: The Broader Consequences

The impact of a changing emotionology took shape from the 1930s onward. It appeared in the three areas that constitute the crucial tests of a link between culture and consequence: personal belief and self-judgments, reactions to others, and institutional context. However, it was not confined to these three areas, for these impacts, in turn, fed a variety of new behaviors, facilitating if not actually causing them. New sexual patterns, as we have seen, unquestionably depended on a decline in the legitimacy of felt jealousy. Not only growing promiscuity but also increasing opportunities for wide heterosexual social contacts and attendant flirting demanded a relaxation of Victorian beliefs not only about women but also about jealousy and intense love. Obviously, some Americans remained uncomfortable with the new formulations precisely because their values or personalities did not adequately adjust. But overall, new beliefs about the need for mature control and new institutional practices, including declining legal sanction for jealousy, pushed the new values and thus opened the way to altered behaviors. The decline of open grief affected more than mourning rituals. Rapidly increasing separation and divorce also caused pain, and again some outright maladjustment, but they were carried out on the assumption that most Americans would know how either to control or to conceal their grief, with perhaps some sporadic and uncertain emotional support from friends so long as the intense reactions were neither too great nor too long. Decline of anger linked, as we have seen, to shifts in protest movements, reaching well beyond the emotional sphere per se into broader reaches of power and politics.

The impact of the new emotional culture spread to other areas as well, though I will leave a full assessment of these wider consequences for the conclusion. Political styles expressed the assimilation of the new standards despite a few nostalgic gestures to the livelier political culture of the past such as the manufactured exhilaration of presidential nominating conventions. The emotional edge of political debating declined in comparison with nineteenth-century levels or with ongoing patterns in parliamentary formats such as those of Great Britain or Canada. Nastiness may well have increased; several observers suggested that outright lying rose from the 1960s onward.[59] But direct encounters among candidates, and particularly the so-called debates that became obligatory after the late 1950s, featured largely separate statements blandly devoid of any overt anger or passion. Self-presentation rules remained complex. Absence of affect was unacceptable; Michael Dukakis discovered this in 1988 in response to a question about how he would react to a rape of his wife, which launched him into a dry, rational discourse on his philosophy of punishment and convinced many observers that he was a political robot. But public displays of intense emotion, and particularly negative emotion, were now signs of vulnerability, not desirable fervor. Subcultural styles that retained a higher degree of emotionality, as in African American politics, remained interesting but also somewhat foreign, outside the middle-class mainstream. Not surprisingly, the self-control and plasticity widely noted as being required for television coverage blended readily with the emotional culture that had already been taking shape: public figures must be ready to display emotional control and a meaningless smile at the drop of a camera button.

On the more personal level, declining intensity affected issues of emotional commitment in friendship and family life. By the 1950s a sense of growing reservations about deep emotional involvement between parents and children, among friends, and in courtship became widespread and persisted into the 1990s. The theme was easily trivialized and exaggerated, but it had some measurable manifestations. The shift from reliance on dating to wider peer associations pointed in the direction of looser emotional (though not sexual) involvements among teenagers after 1960. The rise in the marriage age in the middle class from the early 1970s onward, along with increasing divorce, translated new tensions about commitment into the statistical realm. A looser style of address from children to parents was matched between the 1950s and the 1970s by the measurable decline in parental satisfaction with children. Fathers and mothers alike reported a decreasing sense of reward in dealing with their children. In 1976, for example, less than half as many American parents rated children as providing a major goal in life as had their counterparts twenty years before. Thus a decline in parents' moral authority over children was matched by declining emotional rewards. According to the same polling data, the importance of the marital bond did rise, but this conclusion stands in some contradiction to actual rates of marriage and divorce, and it is notable that good marriages were defined more in terms of shared consumption goals and leisure patterns than in terms of emotional interactions where, as we have seen, men and women often evinced sharp disagreements.[60] Overall, while the family institution remained varied and viable, attention to individual needs, including as we can now see the complex task of emotional self-control and self-presentation, increasingly overshadowed strong emotional bonds with others.

The impacts of twentieth-century emotional culture need further study. This is true even in areas where definite conclusions can already be drawn. In some respects twentieth-century impacts are less well explored than their Victorian counterparts, for greater familiarity with the Victorian culture and greater perspective on its interactions have facilitated recent findings concerning the intertwining of emotionology with courtship, workplace environment, and law. This chapter's tentative sketch of consequences had to await the analysis central to the earlier chapters, that is, the clear definition of the twentieth-century standards that replaced Victorianism and establishment of the major causes involved. The same definition also invites further work that will take this new culture seriously as a factor among a variety of other developments in American society. Some of the contours of emotional relationships within the twentieth-century family, for example, remain elusive. Certainly additional work on friendship and other centers of emotional response to others remains highly desirable, for generalizations and laments have outpaced data on change.

What, for example, was the impact of the new emotional culture on relationships among siblings after early childhood? Declining family size reduced early sibling ties and encouraged a focus on parents. The new emotional standards warned against too much intensity among siblings because it was likely to turn sour, perhaps even dangerous. Hence siblings were urged to separate, to emphasize individual rather than shared space, and to develop activities that would discourage intense rivalries. Probably, this pattern fostered looser sibling relationships in subsequent adulthood. Certainly twentieth-century imagery, in which adult brothers and sisters play only bit parts in most middle-class lives, contrasts markedly with Victorian ideals of lifelong bonds emanating from the emotionally vivid family of origin.[61] Here might be one more area in which the effort to downplay intensity has undercut a potentially vigorous human relationship—always recognizing, of course, individual variations around the norm. But because the actual history of ties among brothers and sisters has yet to be sketched, any plausible conclusion about trends that would link this emotional relationship to somewhat clearer shifts in friendship and parenthood must remain hypothetical, awaiting further work that can utilize the framework provided by the historical findings on emotionological change.

The nature of variations around the new norms also deserves attention. Regional factors are less important than in the nineteenth century, which seems logical, but the South continues to stand out in certain areas of impact—even in rates of homicide provoked by jealousy. Religious and ethnic subcultures also demand attention where emotional standards are concerned. Gender variations emerge more clearly but amid great complexity in comparison with the clear-cut principles of the nineteenth century. Gender standards for emotional expression merged;

this was one of the leading trends from the 1920s onward, well in advance of a full revolution in ascribed roles. Both males and females were called upon to reduce their special areas of emotional intensity in favor of a common pattern of control. However, this same movement generated special attacks on emotional women and on women's Victorian traditions, whereas men were called to change with far less editorializing. This differentiation, in turn, along with the striking distinctions in the prior tradition, generated some real dispute, not so much over the basic new standards but rather over the ways in which they were incorporated. Women's links to a special maternalism attenuated but did not disappear. Women remained more likely to think of love than men—by the 1980s they were almost twice as likely to associate sex with love, for example—and they continued to associate love with self-sacrifice, in contrast to the most heralded male variants of the modern love theme. Even more generally, women responded to new emotional rules with frequent interest in discussion, whereas men disproportionately preferred to leave the subject off their conversational agendas (beginning even in boyhood, when excited talk of sports served as the main topical gambit).[62] Thus conventional images of emotional differentiation persisted, often in contrast to a more common shared reality. The new culture, in sum, redefined gender distinctions, but despite some homogenizing impulses, it hardly eliminated them and may actually have exacerbated potential misunderstandings about how emotions were to be handled. Add to region, gender, class, and ethnicity the factor of personal variations, and the complexities of adjustments to the new emotional standards inevitably require further analysis.

Change occurred nevertheless, and it moved many segments of the American middle class in some common directions. Public tolerance of strong emotion declined. Embarrassment frequently checked emotional intensity and led to claims of a uniformly cool, controlled personality.[63] Increasing numbers of people concealed their emotional reactions when dealing with objectionable acts, or loss, or rivalry, or even the tug of family ties, for they were rightly aware that they could not count on much active support from others or were even persuaded that their reactions were their fault in the first place. Intense emotions still occurred, if only because the environment delivered new challenges that could not be fit into a culture of control, but they fit the revised American context badly.

9

The Need for Outlets: Reshaping American Leisure

Some societies may manage almost complete control of at least one strong emotional category, like anger. The Hutterite religious sect in Canada discouraged aggression by providing no rewards for angry behavior and no examples of adult anger. As a result, despite severe discipline and many frustrations, it avoided almost any kind of interpersonal aggression. Zuni Indians prohibited not only outward signs of anger but the inner feeling as well, a standard that children learned as part of their initiation into religious adulthood. The Utku Inuit group tolerates anger only in infants; beyond that, it provides neither vocabulary nor behavior that could encourage anger, and manages to remain apparently anger free.[1]

These examples of extensive expunging raise some questions, of course. First, they involve small, unusually cohesive cultures; such thorough repression may be unimaginable, even for a single social class, in a larger society. Second, they involve a single reproved emotion, not the recent American pattern that seeks to control intensity across the board. And finally, they may not actually have succeeded in fully repressing the emotion in question. While the Utku resolutely avoid anger, they kick their dogs viciously and, when encountering frustration, they frequently cry; emotion may have been successfully diverted, but it has hardly been expunged.

Although it was averse to intensity, twentieth-century American emo-

264

tional culture did not attempt a full repression of major emotions. Popularizers urged verbal identification of the emotions, and assumed that, while successful socialization would reduce their strength and avoid "festering," they might well persist. The trick was to control or conceal, not to escape altogether. The culture itself, then, raised the issue of what might happen to emotions that could not be openly indulged but that endured nevertheless.

In fact, the twentieth-century standards raise issues important to emotions research in general. Both the possibility of basic emotions and observable historical continuities in human emotion suggest that people may have a common range of emotions or affects that are biologically or psychologically programmed in. If this is the case, then culturally constructed efforts to constrain emotions may well affect overt expression, but the emotions will also demand compensatory outlets—as with the Utku and their dogs. Thus the new attempt to restrain certain emotions and emotional intensity in general forces some inquiry into potential outlets. As we will see, emotional constraint not only served as a direct cause of new laws and habits; it also served as an indirect cause of approved surrogates.

Apart from the possibility that certain emotions are basic, the sheer power of Victorian values made it probable that, especially during the first generation of cultural change, considerable continuity would persist from the past even as some shifts began to take hold. The potency of the imagery of motherhood, or transcendent love, or righteous masculine anger clearly might live on, possibly merging with the new standards in a durable amalgam. Here, too, there may have been an attempt to compensate for the new values, and this attempt may have constituted part of the larger impact of the new emotionology. Several observers have, for example, noted a tendency for emotional nostalgia in the later twentieth century as contemporaries look back on real or imagined past images of motherhood or channeled anger and wish they could somehow be recaptured. Nostalgia might cause complexity in its own right, helping to create some alternatives to the straightforward translation of the now-dominant standards into middle-class life.[2]

Three issues, then, prompt a brief consideration of some ambivalent qualities in the larger impact of twentieth-century emotionology. First, because complete suppression was not envisaged, many Americans may actively have sought surrogate channels beyond secretive diary writing, not to challenge the more fundamental standards but to relieve the resultant tensions slightly. Second, to the extent that basic impulses exist, an approach so much more systematically suppressive than its Victorian predecessor (particularly for men) may have prompted unforeseen changes that would provide outlets outside the most official culture. And third, the sheer power of Victorian impulses (some of them relating to even earlier Western norms) may have required some compromises with Victorianism, even as the new standards largely won the day; nostalgia for past expressions could enter into this mix.

In the analysis that follows, we will see that the results of twentieth-century emotional culture involved an increasing reliance on partially symbolic alternatives to day-to-day emotional restraint, some of them expressive of Victorian standards, some of them serving even more obviously as raw release. Tracing the emotional functions of familiar twentieth-century staples in such areas as leisure and vocabulary gives deeper meaning and explanation to facets of emotional life that lie largely outside work and family. It also extends the causal power of the ascending emotional culture itself—though in some unexpected directions.

Outsiders provided one form of symbolic alternative. As with many cultures, Americans in the twentieth century sometimes looked to them as legitimate targets for otherwise dubious intensities. Some picked internal targets, like minority groups, but on the whole the public use of these groups for venting suppressed emotion declined in favor after the 1920s. Foreign enemies were another matter; Hitler and then Soviet Russia provided outstanding symbols against which fear and anger could be directed. Whether American emotional culture encouraged more symbolic enmity than was otherwise likely merits consideration. Anger, fear, and grief partially constrained at home could pour out in hostility to foes abroad, even more than is usual in the arena of international conflict. The Soviet atomic threat, which generated fear that Americans had been taught they should be able to avoid, may thus have generated unusually strong reactions against Communist evil, in this case at home through McCarthyism as well as abroad.[3] As the Soviet threat faded in the later 1980s, efforts to find new targets for intense hostilities—as in likening Iraq's Saddam Hussein to Hitler—might also suggest emotional needs that made foreign villains particularly welcome. Proving an unusual employment of outside emotional targets would admittedly be difficult, but the possibility is real.

More obvious, and more clearly related to the peculiarities of twentieth-century emotional culture, was the use of more accessible cultural symbols to relieve emotional pressures imposed by the new norms. Revealingly, whereas the word "cool" was a standard invocation in daily exchanges, the word "hot" began to apply to leisure goods such as intense music, or sex, or consumer sales items, or any new popular-culture icon. Revealingly also, while "hot" might have been good in these symbolic connections, it never came to rival "cool" in standard vocabulary. Hot qualities remained not only separate from but also more dangerous than the approved cool.

Balancing standard norms with outlets was a difficult task in twentieth-century America. Individuals and at times the larger society could come close to explosion when suppressed emotions were unmatched by suitable releases. Individual tantrums, and collective hysterias directed for example at feared minorities or foreign devils, suggested the fragility of the balance. Nevertheless, outlets did help, and the emotional culture defined a wide array of usages for watching displays of intensity by others.

Release through Power: An Emotional Upper Class

Because of personality traits of Victorian heritage or some other complex set of factors, many individuals in the middle class defied the pervasive injunctions against emotional intensity. A marriage partner might still try to dominate through anger or compel attention through intense grief. The new norms affected the range of emotional experience, but there were hosts of variations.

One of these variations stemmed from status. Individuals of high status could still release types of emotional intensity that were normally disapproved. The corporate work environment was democratic in tone, but at least in the United States, some limits applied. Thus the T-group movement, while generalizing recommendations about calm and control, rarely evoked participation by top management. Correspondingly, executives were far less likely to emphasize smooth personalities and more likely to stress aggressive traits than were middle managers. After a prior career in middle management, some executives doubtless maintained a controlled, superficially friendly style, but this was far from the norm.[4]

Furthermore, precisely because intensity was normally shunned, the impact of a temperamentally manipulative executive could be confusing. Outbursts that would usually bring discredit to their presenters were less clear cut when combined with power. Small wonder that many middle managers commented on how "frazzled" they were; in addition to meeting their own requirements of emotional control, they also had to mediate between demanding working-class subordinates and angry bosses. By the same token, chief executives could escape from a work life of emotional caution by capping successful promotion with a relaxation of the twentieth-century emotional rules.[5]

By 1990 a new phrase denoted both the temptation of those atop the hierarchy to indulge in more spontaneous emotion and the tension that this habit could evoke. American leaders began to speak, or be spoken of, in terms of "going ballistic." Thus in 1992 President Bush was reported as "going ballistic" over information leaks in his administration. Or as the same president had disclosed in 1988, with characteristic verbal felicity, he might at times go "a little ballistic—which is only part true—semi-ballistic." This exaggerated missile terminology suggests both an attempt to recognize the unusual, extreme quality of anger even at this level and a desire to make sure the emotion drew attention by subordinates. Emotional life, newly constrained at most middle-class levels, was definitely not yet egalitarian.[6]

The Therapeutic Approach

The constraints of the new emotional culture were clearly reflected in the growing use of formal therapy, wherein individuals sought to release their grief, anger, or fear in the privacy of a professional office. Talking out intense emotions became a central therapeutic mechanism that fit the wider notions of verbal venting while also serving as an acceptable, because confidential, outlet.[7]

Along with individual sessions, group therapy movements built on the dominant culture and its attendant constraints. In 1959, to take one widely publicized example, Synanon was established in California to provide self-help for heroin addicts. The organization was founded on the assumption that addicts were unaware of their own realities, using drugs to escape bottled-up emotions that must be effectively released in order to restore proper functioning. Given a lifetime of self-deceit and emotional evasion, "truth" required open expressions of verbal violence and hostility. Cathartic sessions promoted foul language, shouts, and violent gestures in order to achieve two purposes: realistic self-confrontation and draining of the accumulated emotion. Release was essential, not to arouse anger but to avoid festering. Insults and other provocations built up confrontations during the catharsis, for lashing out was a vital, though early and temporary, phase in the emotional healing process.[8]

The Need for Outlets: Family

Unlike some top executives, most middle-class people could not count on bending the rules or finding occasions in the daily routine to set off emotional missiles. Nor did most rely on therapy groups. Therefore many people experienced a new need for alternative settings in which a different emotional vision could be indulged.

For some, one such setting was the family. Though it was technically against the emotional norms to do so, many people allowed emotions carefully bottled up on the job to spill out at home. Even though they knew that their outbursts were inappropriate, they could not contain themselves—and their guilt could actually add fuel to the fire. By the 1960s some authorities were suggesting that the family be used as a release, "providing a place where one can safely drain off hostility that has accumulated in the outside world." This was described as "one of the important mental health functions of a good marriage." Some husbands, particularly, adopted this tack. One commentator described a man who "had no difficulty keeping his small-boy side locked away while he was at work." But his immaturity could not fully be stifled: "To him, 'relaxing' at home had come to mean letting the small boy call the shots and bully everybody." Yet for most people this outlet, if used at all, provided scant relief; polls revealed growing discomfort, with oneself or with a spouse, when hostile emotions burst forth. "I'd get so upset, I'd throw up and not be able to eat." "When she comes after me like that, yapping like that, she might as well be hitting me with a bat." And there is evidence, further, that middle-class couples in particular worked hard to restrain emotions, even in times of economic tension, that other American families might release more freely.[9]

The strict rules many people tried to impose on themselves could certainly prove counterproductive. It is possible, even in some middle-class families, that the absence of regular opportunities to express vigorous, hostile emotions drove some individuals to greater extremes when they passed the breaking point. Family abuse was of course no invention of the twentieth century, but it may have been exacerbated by the very effort of emotional constraint. Parents who carefully learned that even mild expressions of anger against children were damaging might in some instances have prepared for an episode of more extensive abuse by their curbs on daily spontaneity. Jealousy, sedulously denied by most men, could trigger beatings and worse, and some authorities contended that the very act of denial intensified the anger and made the ultimate conflagration worse.[10]

Yet extensive use of the home as a place for emotional release was not common, precisely because it so clearly deviated from long-standing emotional rules. The larger impact of twentieth-century emotionology was to support a growing array of symbolic emotional alternatives that in turn described a large part of the leisure life of the growing middle class.

The Need for Outlets: The Culture of Leisure

Many cultures offer channels for deviation from standard social constraints. One example is the often-noted role of approved drunkenness and some sexual license in what otherwise seems a straitened Japanese middle-class existence. Certainly Victorian culture had its escape hatches. Vigorous moral reform could provide women with occasions for righteous anger normally reserved for men, while men could seek alternatives to sexual regulations through pornography, use of prostitutes, and the like. Even women could find opportunities for mild sexual titillation in stories of aristocratic derring-do, like du Maurier's tales of Trilby. Where emotional norms were concerned, however, most Victorian leisure culture abided by the rules. Stories of transcendent love or successful battles with jealousy or fear were written in ways that seem naively exaggerated today, but they were in full harmony with desired intensities. Sports helped boys and young men carry out injunctions to preserve but channel anger and to cultivate courage.

How well this harmony between leisure and mainstream values worked may be questioned. Many middle-class people, even aside from "hysterical" women, may have been too constrained by emotional norms that not only regulated their work and family relationships but also ruled their available reading matter and leisure-time activities. On the other hand, the fact that both leisure and real life allowed for opportunities for emotional intensity may have made the amalgam work for many people. While spontaneity was discouraged, blandness could also be avoided by people who formed intense attachments to friends or family, who prided themselves on the passion that impelled them in work or on a playing field, and who sought reading matter and other entertainment that would help them imagine themselves in other emotional excursions that seemed challenging extensions of real life.

Beyond reinforcing approved emotional intensity, elements of nineteenth-century leisure culture provided undeniable excitement. With new forms of fiction, like hard-hitting detective novels of the Nick Carter genre, and with growing use of sports and some frequenting of lower-class amusement centers, the excitement potential accelerated in the final two decades of the century. Some leisure historians and theorists, building on these developments, have assumed a straight-line trajectory between Victorian amusements and more contemporary patterns. However, despite undeniable links in both form and excitement function, the twentieth century added important new ingredients, based not only on more ample time and resources but also on growing needs for emotional alternatives.[11]

It is hardly a secret that middle-class leisure began to diverge strikingly from Victorian patterns by the 1920s, with some limited innovations taking shape even before 1900. Popular fiction and then films moved away from straightforward moralisms into a variety of escapist ploys, featuring new levels of adventure, violence, and implied sexuality. Sports gained growing audiences, and while they embodied some key Victorian values, their role began to change for the middle class in important ways. Heightened consumerism poured new passions into the acquisitions of things. Middle-class people, in sum, began to seek experiences and imagery that would allow them to use leisure safely to compensate for the growing stringency of their emotional life. Much leisure became deliberately separate from, almost deliberately antagonistic to, the norms of daily life.

Attempts to explain the dramatically novel tone of twentieth-century leisure have often floundered. New technology such as movies and, later, television provided a new framework for leisure but hardly accounts for the form it took. After all, Victorian moralisms could have been translated to the new media, and they sometimes were, to a limited extent. Commercial manipulation by the new capitalist captains of professional entertainment clearly helped prompt a growing emphasis on impulse and also a certain passivity within the target audience. Appealing to widespread human interests literally around the world in the twentieth century, commercial manipulation does help explain some of the new leisure currents, but it does not fully account for audience response in the United States; there is a gap to be filled. Many authors have also pointed to growing middle-class interest in lower-class and ethnic entertainment forms that provided alternatives to middle-class inhibitions. Entertainers from outside the mainstream middle class acquired new roles, and some middle-class youth deliberately went "slumming" in order to experience new forms of music, looser language, and more open sexuality. Criminal elements associated with leisure interests such as gambling gained new influence in the process. But even granting an increase of democratic impulse in a consumer society and a modification of Victorian snobberies, it is not clear why middle-class people found new uses for alternative cultures in their leisure lives. Gambling impresarios may have benefited from the new quest for excitement, but they did not cause it.[12]

The development of new emotional constraints, particularly the new barriers against intensity, helps account for crucial directions of twentieth-century leisure in the growing American middle class and for the meaning of this leisure. The new emotionology also contributes directly to an understanding of the timing involved; after all, some of the possibilities, including lower-class contact, had been available long before they were actually taken up. Correspondingly, the new leisure, broadly construed, helps explain how Americans could accept the new emotional rules in their daily lives: by seeking a realm of imagination now explicitly different from their actual emotional routines. Leisure was not life, as some advocates of a new leisure ethic mistakenly argued.[13] Its divergence from normal rules was precisely its emotional function. Commercial promoters seized on these new leisure needs and perhaps extended them, but they did not create them. Influences from lower-class social and ethnic groups fed into the leisure patterns, but only because middle-class people found in them some of the symbolic alternatives they now required. As leisure time grew, the relationship between leisure and daily reality changed dramatically. Emotional needs served as the intermediary between several developments such as corporate work and the new direction of leisure.

Growing interest in sexuality, particularly but not exclusively among men, formed one vital channel. By the 1920s groups like fraternity brothers began to talk more openly about sex, to seek sexual pleasure more consistently, and to think about sex more often or at least more consistently than their Victorian counterparts had done. Where actual sexual opportunities fell short, an increasingly charged world of fiction and advertising extended the imagination. Sex or sexual musings provided an intensity that emotional life might now lack, an ability briefly to lose oneself without directly violating the emotional code.[14]

Language loosened in the new leisure culture. Cursing became more common, first among men and then among aspiring women in the middle class. The growing openness of swearing has been widely noted in histories of twentieth-century middle-class culture but is hard to explain. Contacts with lower-class elements that had never accepted Victorian shibboleths about profanity fed into the new pattern, but they hardly account for middle-class acceptance. The same holds true for media promotion of looser language; while shock value helped sell certain books and movies, it was responsible more for furthering a new middle-class impulse than for creating it. Beginning in the 1920s some new expressions, like the popular and ambiguous exclamation "nuts," followed from the growing effort to pursue sexual interests more openly. But acceptance of swearing, including women's growing tolerance even before their own widespread indulgence, allowed more than sexual allusion. It permitted a verbal jolt at a time when standard emotional rules were tightening. The same people who were learning to mask their anger, or even to claim they had none, might now openly say "hell" or "damn" or, still later, even "fuck." The words were not intended to convey deep anger, and it was a task of middle-class auditors to learn not to take the words seriously—a test of their own participation in a charade in which strong words were meant to be divorced from strong emotion. Saying the words might provide some release, but their utterance was often accompanied by a carefully reassuring grin designed to confirm that no real emotional rules violation had been intended.[15]

Sports, shopping, and escapist fiction provided three other outlets, often combined with more open sexuality and looser language, in which intensity could be sought outside normal emotional life. These outlets tended to promote a growing quest for the excitement that Victorians had sought in passion. And by being disconnected from the usual rules, they also fostered a certain passivity in which acts and products offered by others might substitute for direct experience.

Consumerism was hardly new in the twentieth century. Elements of it surely date back to the first uses of economic surplus in human life, particularly in emerging upper classes, and a modern form of more extensive, expressive consumerism has been plausibly traced to the eighteenth century, when acquisition of things like stylish clothing began to play a new role in Western society.[16] In the twentieth century, however, consumerism became more widespread, commanding new uses of time and fostering new environments like shopping centers and then malls. It also became, in its own way, more intense. The new emotional culture deliberately fostered surrogate attachment to objects as a means of preventing emotional intensity among people. Thus, as a means of curbing sibling jealousy, children were taught to turn to their own things and to expect new ones. Adult men were offered consumerism as a preferred alternative to intense romantic love, and the newly touted companionate marriage emphasized shared enjoyment of acquisitions. The act of shopping began to acquire a potential passion of its own, particularly for middle-class women. At an extreme, the passion could turn to kleptomania, in which the intense yearning for goods surpassed both any real economic need and the law itself.[17] Theft aside, it was now permissible to invest emotional meaning in the act of acquisition and in the objects acquired. American advertising and merchandising carefully stressed ultimate equality of access, and as a result consumerism was not seen as violating democratic standards or directly leading to envy.[18] This further legitimized an attachment to things that might easily surpass the newly constrained attachments to people. Revealingly, new emotional involvements with pets accompanied the growing interest in things. Surely the vital connection between consumerism and emotional culture helps explain consumerism itself, a dominant phenomenon of twentieth-century American life but one whose meaning—as opposed to its utility to its capitalist promoters—has been difficult to penetrate.

Like consumerism, sports also appeared in modern form before the twentieth century but took on additional meanings because of new kinds of emotional needs. Whereas shopping may have served women more fully than men, sports involved men more than women, though gender distinctions were not absolute.

The emergence of new sports emphasis in the nineteenth century formed part of Victorian emotionology. It largely differentiated boys from girls. It helped teach boys not only physical fitness (an interest that girls might also acquire) but also the manly emotional qualities of channeled anger and control of fear. Sports served many other functions as well, including recalling more traditional, preindustrial community solidarity—there is no need to push emotionological explanations too far. But the relationship to Victorian values was obvious, and it was often noted in prescriptive literature about how boys could be trained to be men.[19]

Victorian-traditional qualities in sports persisted through the twentieth century, a phenomenon that provides one of the real complexities in dealing with the actual incorporation of newer emotional standards. Although boys were taught in early childhood to be emotionally similar to girls, for many decades access to sports was exclusively theirs. As in Victorian times, they were still told that sports allowed men emotionally to prove themselves. In sports activities they were allowed physical contacts and embraces with friends now denied in other settings. They were told to conquer their fear and to deliberately seek aggression. Emotion remained good in sports, and sports were still touted—Victorian style—as providing valuable training in emotion.

Yet because of the larger changes in emotional culture, including the new emotional rules that were urged on men at work in their capacities as middle managers or salesmen, sports integrated less fully with men's lives than had been the case in the nineteenth century. Sports now provided occasions for nostalgic indulgence that were vital not so much to train men as to help them endure the new emotional rules that corporate manhood entailed. The symbolic functions of sports changed precisely in the decades in which they began to gain vast new popularity. They explicitly became emotional outlets, and this new function often overwhelmed more traditional purposes:

I watched the Steelers lose football games every way you could think of and I never bitched. And I ain't no gambler neither. Never bet a penny on the football game, I just used to go to old Forbes Field every Sunday when the Steelers were home and it just brought out a lot of emotion in me I couldn't get rid of no other way.

Those are men. Giants. And they're down there strugglin' and sweatin' and bleedin' and doin' a little war right there between those little chalk stripes on the grass and I just found out I could whoop and holler my guts out and nobody would think I was nuts. It didn't make no difference to anybody else what I was really hollering about. People around me were all hollering too. I mean, it really helps you, brother, to reach down to your toes and pull out a yell you been keepin' bottled up inside you for Christ knows how long.[20]

Twentieth-century men watched games that recalled physical skills they had shared or wished to share, but above all they watched games that reflected different emotional rules from those they lived with. They could watch ritualized, in-your-face arguments with referees, open exhilaration, emotional comradery in victory or loss, courageous play through pain and violent clashes on the playing fields or hockey rinks— they could watch, in sum, Victorian-style intensity writ large. While most of the sports that gained spectator popularity had been regularized in the nineteenth century, through provision of standardized rules and settings, they moved away from stiff-upper-lip amateur sportsmanship toward more emotionality during the twentieth century. They also gained a wider and more emotional audience as a result of new technology and new American needs. American sports crowds remained relatively orderly, but as they shouted, raged, and cavorted, they allowed emotional release and a sense of emotions shared with strangers. Even home audiences could join in loud celebrations or laments in which emotions overflowed normal bounds. The African American crowds that rejoiced over radio broadcasts of Joe Louis bouts in the 1930s were not unique; raucous parties and even solitary shouting attended the steady spread of sports presentations over the airwaves.[21]

Direct spectatorship also soared. For major league baseball it tripled during the first two decades of the twentieth century. The rise of professional football dates from the 1920s and was thus coincident with the full development of the new emotional culture. Annual rituals like the Army-Navy football game or the major New Year's bowl games were also enshrined in the same period and were followed by a wide array of professional and college tournaments. Not only national leagues but also local teams, including high school and club performers, provided outlets for emotional crowds. The importance and meaning of sport changed, particularly for spectators, as the emotional ramifications increased along with new media reportage and greater leisure time. The word "fan" gained currency from its inception in the mid-1890s to its solidification in the language by the 1920s. Apparently an American abbreviation of "fanatic," the word appropriately suggests the kind of intensity now applied to, and found in, the act of sports spectatorship.[22]

Furthermore, the emotional representations of the players themselves expanded beyond the Victorian version of channeled male passions. By the 1970s and 1980s the open emotionality of athletes reached new levels. Even staid sports like tennis saw a new kind of contentiousness that offended purists but attracted viewers who enjoyed a blend of performance and vivid feelings—even outright immaturity. Players in several sports developed new levels of taunting and new displays of triumph—while men in ordinary life were being enjoined to conceal such sentiments more fully than ever lest they rouse the resentment of others in the workplace, including a growing group of sensitive women. Taunting "trash talk" and dancing celebrations over fallen athletes became commonplace, to the apparent delight of partisan crowds. "The truth of the matter is, spectator sports are more fun now *because* athletes are willing to let their emotions show. . . . Athletes lead cheers, milking the crowd for emotional support." And, one might add, crowds themselves gained ever greater levels of release.[23]

Thus sports gained stature among men as symbolic expressions of emotions now largely excluded from ordinary life—just as jousting tournaments in the late Middle Ages had for a century or more recalled earlier forms of contest. For many players, even in strictly amateur matches, and for the even larger spectator throngs, sports allowed a relaxation of the normal rules of feeling and expression—and almost surely made the rules easier to accept when ordinary life resumed.

For an even wider array of Americans, fiction and media representations, including popular music, came to serve the same function, presenting emotions that were far stronger and less alloyed than their audience could allow themselves to experience in the daily routine—or offering excitement without specific emotional representations. The variety of formats was great, and their service to dominant emotional culture provides only one source of explanation for the overall tenor of American leisure life.[24] Other family and personal needs, commercial pressures, and technological opportunities must be factored in. Nevertheless, understanding the use of leisure as a form of emotional alternative provides some unifying explanations otherwise lacking. Furthermore, the trend away from portrayals of surrogate emotional intensity toward audience-rousing excitement with less explicitly emotional overtones suggests an evolution that paralleled the growing hold of the culture of constraint in daily middle-class life. Nostalgia for elaborate emotions was still served, but gut-wrenching though not explicitly emotional violence or terror gained ground.

Gothic novels and soap operas, for example, did not provide their largely female audience with Victorian versions of spiritual love; rather, they offered an intense mixture of emotions in which women were represented as passive victims of passions beyond their control. The Gothic motif often had love conquer accomplished women, after which fear predominated as women remained powerless. Harlequin romances moved in the opposite direction, from fear to love, with women becoming somewhat more potent as love began to triumph. Soap operas emphasized the power but also the complexities of love, which ultimately, if briefly, won out over other relationships, including those based on power or money. Here, obviously, the "new love" theme of accommodation and careful planning was turned on its head, for love was deliberately portrayed as blind and compelling. Soap operas might also showcase other intense emotions, including anger. By the 1980s angry people were portrayed as heroes up to 82 percent of the time—again in deliberate, cathartic contradiction to anger standards in the ascending emotional culture. The audience for soap operas and romance novels was by no means exclusively middle class, to be sure, but the release they provided extended to this group as well, from the housewives tuned in to radio pathos in the 1930s to the fashionable audiences for prime-time television soap operas in the 1980s.[25]

Films offered a variety of emotional messages, including both support for the new culture and surprisingly literal, nostalgic representations of Victorian values. Early on movie stars recognized their role as emotional/sexual idols feeding the fantasy life of an audience pressed by routine and seeking some vicarious alternative to daily emotional constraints. Stephan Stills told a Harvard Business School panel in 1925 that he knew what he meant, as a symbol of masculinity, to the bored, unchallenged men of his generation.[26] Ironically, the increasing regulation of noise and other spontaneous expressions in anonymous movie theaters added to the regulations of twentieth-century life, in contrast to the livelier traditions of vaudeville. But this very repression increased viewer involvement with the emotional meaning presented by the vivid lives on the screen. Emotionally as well as sexually fervent personalities contrasted with the bureaucratic routines of everyday existence—and with the subdued atmosphere of the movie house itself.

In addition to romantic passions, movies, radio, and related fiction developed other revealing emotional styles. One, building particularly on the literature and comic strips offered to adolescent boys, featured the emotionless hero who experienced great excitement while displaying no passion of his own. The Superman comic strip, conceived in 1938, represented a young male fantasy of overwhelming strength and flight—and attendant ability to attract female interest that was completely ignored—unencumbered by emotional complexities. Jerry Siegel, one of the creators, talked of his inspiration: "As a high school student . . . I had crushes on several attractive girls who . . . didn't know I existed. . . . It occurred to me: What if I had something special going for me, like jumping over a building or throwing cars around or something like that?" Superman's defense of virtue and "the American way" was a Victorian throwback, but his immunity to fear and other emotions made him representative of a new kind of hero appropriate for a culture of greater emotional control. Some of the same qualities, including imperviousness to emotion (leavened occasionally by a certain compassion, but more often by hostility to women), would enter other hero genres, including even the Rambo films of the 1980s.[27]

Sometimes accompanying the emotion-free hero, another film and fiction motif involved a growing interest in provoking audience terror. From Frankenstein films to teenage exploitation movies and the gratuitous violence of the 1970s and 1980s, shock scenes elicited, as one viewer put it, "an intensity rarely if ever encountered" in ordinary life. Use of stories to elicit fright was not novel, of course. Monsters inhabited the folktales of premodern cultures, and Victorian fiction had offered a terror genre. But the theme escalated in popular American fare after the 1930s and was shorn of some of the more obvious religious, guilt-infested connotations of its predecessors. Along with other fear-provoking experiences, such as the more challenging amusement park rides and staged "fright nights" on Halloween, terror films provided another interesting contrast to—another catharsis for—the dominant emphases of the new, real-life emotional culture being installed in the same decades. This was fear as pure sensation, not as a call to courage or to other, more complex emotional intensities. It provided what by the 1980s was intriguingly labeled a "rush"—a passing, spontaneous intensity separate from one's normal emotional personality. Except for aficionados of daredevil stunts, escapist terror was experienced passively by people safely ensconced in movie houses or roller-coaster rides. It was a release from the normal rules, not an extension of them, and it was popular for that reason. As with professional sports, emotionally escapist fare sold well, adding a vital ingredient to a consumer culture that in other respects supported a more restrained emotional style.[28]

In addition to fiction and film, popular music provided its own intensities that also frequently contrasted with more explicit emotionality. An emotional singing genre persisted, particularly in the "country" movement, that lamented the throes of love and jealousy and celebrated manly courage; again, leisure outlets appealed to diverse tastes. More interesting, however, was the music that was either purely instrumental or whose lyrics carried little overt message; this music drove home an intense beat and, aided by new technologies, featured increasing physical volume. Aspects of jazz, and even more of rock and roll, celebrated intensity with no explicit emotional strings, and the addictive popularity of the new styles suggested an audience search for leisure forms that could overwhelm, that were exciting but did not require elaborate emotional expression. In some instances by the 1960s, deliberately antiestablishment lyrics expressing raging cynicism about love and the sweeter emotional snares added passionate words to the overwhelming sound. Hostility, like terror, may have served as an emotional surrogate. As in sports, music audiences screamed and jumped, turning spectatorship into an emotion-draining crowd activity. As in sports also, the intense musical performers often featured racial minorities whose presumed freedom from constraint provided symbolic outlet for a middle-class, though in this case also largely youthful, audience.[29]

Sports, terror films, amusement parks, rock music, sex (particularly with the growing emphasis on orgasm)—all had the capacity temporarily to block out other impulses and provide a moment of exhilaration. All might cancel out rational restraint, usually without imperiling emotional control once the moment had passed or the leisure setting had been abandoned. The contrast between the quest for excitement, usually vicarious, and the growing hostility to emotional intensity offered no real contradiction. The two movements fed each other, as cathartic cultures have always done. The result, nevertheless, was a fascinating duality in many American lives, between the bland emotions lived and the soaring excitement witnessed and perhaps shared with roaring crowds. It was also a testimony to the real power of the emotional culture, which was strong enough to force these channels of release. For the theme of symbolic alternative ran through an array of leisure representations from the 1920s onward, from childhood fright fare through the sports thrills that comforted graying middle-aged men. The passivity of much American leisure—the growth of spectatorship, culminating with the ascendancy of television—was consistent with the emotional needs that bore on entertainment. People wanted more to witness emotion than to experience it; removal from participation, except for an anonymous shout or two, was precisely the point, for active participation would contravene the dominant emotional rules. Of course passivity resulted from other factors too, including available technology and commercial pressure; but it served its audience, who wanted forms of release that were quite separate from reality.

Conclusion

The driving need for surrogate emotional outlets fed a series of developments in American leisure during the twentieth century. It translated general pressures into specific leisure forms, rivaling and perhaps surpassing the importance of commercial manipulation or contact with the lower classes. A quest for excitement—usually vicarious—created new interests for middle-class Americans, contrasting markedly with the Victorian emphasis on the desirability of calm havens. Twentieth-century leisure placed a premium on "action," as in the Gamblers' World banner, "For the Individual Who Enjoys Action," or the ever-renewed action-adventure category of police movies and violent television shows. From the popularity of rock stars to that of the mean-spirited mockers on hate-radio shows in the 1980s, leisure forms increasingly stressed bombastic style over content, providing a thrill without emotional involvement.[30]

The importance of emotional release through leisure highlighted the role of actors in twentieth-century American culture. Deft at taking on others' emotions without venturing their own, actors represented emotional vigor and thus provided contrast with normal constraint. In the new emotional culture, the idea of acting also appealed to the strong impulse to conceal. Indeed, acting was built into normal emotional interchange.[31]

Emotional release also depended heavily on strangers, in complex ways. Increasing reliance on sports and entertainment for emotional release provided new opportunities for cultural "otherness." The stereo-typed roles for actors of Mediterranean origin as steamy lovers or for African Americans as exuberant, emotionally spontaneous athletes and musicians contributed to the rise of these groups in the world of emo-tional symbolism—a rise that could easily eclipse their gains in many other spheres. Strangers in this sense performed a new emotional service for the middle-class mainstream. Strangers of another kind also provided a setting for more direct emotional release; anonymous crowds allowed demonstrations of anger or exhilaration that many people would deny themselves in other contexts. Max Weber's dictum that modern societies imposed uniform rules for acquaintances and strangers alike was not true for Victorian society, given the domestic-public division, and it was even less true for the twentieth century. Emotional control applied to acquaintances and, in most respects, the family, but greater intensity might be ventured, fleetingly, among strangers. This standard applied to other encounters with strangers aside from that of anonymous crowds. For example, fingered or shouted displays of rage while driving were surely intensified by the strains of commuting, but they also served as a more general release that often differed sharply from middle-class emo-tional behavior in other settings.[32]

Growing use of vicarious outlets also called additional emotions into play. Media and sports could represent intense grief, anger, sadness, or fear. Nostalgia for Victorian emotions featured strongly in fiction and film, differentiating this emotion in the twentieth century from Victorian reminiscence of the real or imagined physical qualities of bucolic scenes. Further, surrogate emotional attachment to the acquisition of things opened the way to greater envy as an intense emotion appropriate for a consumer society. Envy was not officially countenanced; indeed, it came under the same strictures against intensity as did the other major emotions, which was one reason why Americans began to call it "jealousy" and to attach the same sense of opprobrium or embarrassment to it.[33] Envy was an immature emotion that should at least be veiled. American advertising (unlike European) usually avoided explicit appeals to envy, preferring the democracy-of-buying-opportunity approach instead. Nevertheless, though envy has not been well studied, the emotion almost certainly found new outlets. Attachment to things included attention to one's neighbor's things—keeping up with the Joneses, in the popular midcentury phrase—and this invited implicit envy as a partial substitute for other kinds of emotional fervor. At the same time, however, envy was characteristically less intense than more reproved emotions such as jealousy.[34] Again, escapism remained compatible with real-life anti-intensity.

On yet another front, shock entertainment of the sort purveyed in teenage exploitation films by the 1960s appealed to a growing fascination with disgust that was signaled by the rising use of the word "gross" to designate a revulsion that was not however entirely unpleasant. Disgust is another emotional area that invites exploration in the history of twentieth-century passions.[35] Attraction-repulsion reactions to vicarious objects of disgust—gigantic insects, or slime, or simulated gore—often combined with vicarious fear. Finally, sports and some media portrayals also catered to exhilaration at a time when direct displays of exhilaration on the strength of one's own accomplishments were increasingly discouraged as vain and unsocial. By invoking additional emotions—again, usually vicariously—the growing role of outlets multiplied their functions in the realm of feelings without, however, directly contradicting the basic anti-intensity norms in daily life.

How well the outlets served is of course questionable. Twentieth-century emotionology raises fascinating questions about the extent to which emotions can be transferred to different and less direct settings. It is incontestable, however, that the transfer was attempted, and that it generated a pervasive new impulse in the shaping of American leisure life.

Vicariousness, however, was not the only innovation as the new leisure culture responded to twentieth-century emotionology. A strong movement to substitute sensation for emotion (at least, emotion as defined in Victorian terms) also emerged. Instead of cognitive musings on the courageous conquest of fear, films, amplified music, and amusement parks called on an ability to enjoy, or survive, brief bombardments of shock and surprise. As with the growing intrusion of sexuality on what had been emotional ground, the emphasis on sensation introduced greater physicality to the arenas where indulgence contrasted with normal restraints.

The need for representations of a different, more vivid, and more sensational set of emotional standards to contrast with the new constrained normalcy created a dual middle-class culture not unlike the more famous two cultures that emerged in contemporary intellectual life.[36] To be sure, the American middle class did not directly embrace all the fancies of modern art, which in turn continued, often deliberately, to defy bourgeois taste in a battle that had begun in the nineteenth century. Nevertheless, the alternatives that modern artists threw up against scientific and social-scientific rationalism emphasized some of the same spontaneity and excitement that the middle class sought in spectatorship. The subdued restraint of actual emotional life was balanced out by the exuberance of professional athletes or rock stars, just as science was challenged by the efforts of antirepresentational artists to portray the irregularities of a world gone mad. Unlike the artists, the bulk of the middle class held back from direct participation in its alternative emotional world, preferring to pay entertainers (handsomely) to act it out; but the middle class did not commit fully to a single reality.

10

Pre-Conclusion:
Prospects? Progress?

Two issues inevitably arise from analyzing recent changes in emotional culture. Neither permits a definitive answer in the context of this study, but both warrant comment before we return to the more definitive findings for a real, if brief, conclusion. The first issue involves the relationship between the standards established between 1920 and 1950, with expanding impact into the 1970s, and more recent trends: Are we operating within the same basic framework, or has some other major shift intervened? The second issue involves some editorializing: Were the emotional characteristics of twentieth-century middle-class America good or bad in relation to Victorian or other precedents? Few comments on shifts in national traits can avoid some value judgments, and it is better directly to admit as much than to mislead by implicitly claiming objectivity.

Present and Recent Past

The new emotional culture that replaced Victorianism was well established by 1950, with consequences that gained ground, for the most part, at least through the 1970s—as in the case of law. As for the past decade or so, we have no reliable models to suggest how often significant, directional changes in emotional culture ought to be anticipated. We know that no formulation lasts forever, and we know that very frequent, once-a-decade or even once-a-generation shifts do not normally occur, despite contemporary impressions of great change. For example, childrearing fads oscillated back and forth between permissiveness and strictness from 1900 to 1950, but these short-term shifts did not undo the more fundamental framework in which child socialization was being transformed toward regulation of emotional intensity and preparation for goals in school and corporate work. Even the upheavals of the 1960s, so strikingly iconoclastic at the time, yielded only modest durable changes in American culture; indeed, in certain respects, as we have seen in connection with the discomfort over anger and jealousy, they actually confirmed mainstream standards.[1]

Thus we know that directional changes occur fairly rarely (witness the long duration of essentially Victorian standards, with some slight modifications in the 1840s that then lasted into the twentieth century). We know that short-term deviations, though sometimes widely touted by contemporary media eager to show how everything is changing around us, do not necessarily deflect the more important standards. But we do not know the exact duration of an emotionology. Therefore, perhaps the most honest way to deal with the problem of contemporary standards would be to stress lack of perspective and let it go at that. Certainly, I do not wish to join those historians who establish a pattern in the past and then leap to the present to assert continuities or stark contrasts without noting the need for serious examination of intervening developments. Yet our story takes us so close to the present that some straws in the wind might be swatted at.

There have certainly been some modifications in the culture that began to take shape seventy years ago. These modifications, along with a media-fed propensity to assume that we have just witnessed a particularly sharp rupture with our past a couple of minutes ago, might lead some to make a case for a new, "postmodern" period different from the framework that operated until recently. Let us briefly examine some of these modifications.

Beginning in the 1960s, concerns about the limitations of "modern" grief standards began to circulate, spearheaded by gurus like Elisabeth Kubler-Ross. As death and dying courses proliferated for a time on college campuses, it became fashionable to assert that contemporary Americans had lost the ability to die well or to mourn well. Much of the criticism was directed at doctors and hospitals wedded to a death-fighting stance, but grief came in for comment as well. According to some experts, contemporary society, having removed death from home and family and become focused on the shallow joys of work and material acquisition, had shunted grief, not only damaging the process of dying but also leading to severe psychological stress among those left behind, perhaps even causing unnecessary depression and even suicide. New movements like the creation of hospices attempted to reintegrate the family with death, allowing more "natural" grief in the process. Therapists began to rethink their penchant for damping down grief, wondering if the emotion should not be encouraged instead. There was no full revolution in standards, and indeed a steady increase in the use of cremation in the United States reflected a continued wish to handle death in an emotionally unobtrusive fashion. But there is no question, either, that grief had been turned into a problem case in which the overall impulse against emotional intensity might have to be rethought, and was being rethought in some quarters.[2]

To some observers by the late 1980s, Americans were becoming too free in expressing their anger. Unpleasant encounters with rude sales clerks and hostile strangers—including highway drivers—fed the impression that emotional controls were breaking down. Carole Tavris wrote a popular book on this subject, and her views were echoed in a number of editorials. Apparently growing rates of violence, including family abuse, seemed to support the notion that anger was breaking out of its previous bounds. Anger seemed to be reintroduced into the political arena with the rise of feminism in the 1970s and then other ardent protest movements organized around issues such as abortion or gay rights. Here were groups that made no bones about their grievances and their right, even their responsibility, to be deeply angry at their opponents—be they men, intolerant heterosexuals, or prochoice advocates.[3]

Impressions of new outpourings of anger deserve serious assessment. Obviously, not all Americans agreed on standards, and unquestionably some new movements consciously strove to modify blanket constraints. At the same time, the cautions against anger—such as the editorials on civilized people's responsibility to remove anger from public exchange—reinforced the larger anti-intensity culture. Further, some of the scare stories—about family abuse, for example—correctly identified problems but tended to exaggerate their incidence or at least their novelty.

Increases were claimed without full evidence, and some kinds of abuse were cited as frequent that were in fact quite rare (or, in not a few instances, completely fabricated). These dramatic new cautionary tales constituted a means to gain additional support for constraints on anger and aggression, reinforcing middle-class anger standards. It is not clear that the standards themselves were being modified.[4]

By the late 1980s a few observers began to talk of some positive uses for jealousy. With growing emphasis on sexual fidelity under the impact of AIDS and persistent concern about family stability, a few popular magazine articles began to take a second look at this "negative" emotion, arguing that a bit of jealousy might be socially useful and that an individual need not feel hopelessly guilty upon discovering some jealousy in his or her bosom.[5] As for guilt itself, scattered comment bemoaned its decline in what seemed to be an amoral, corrupt society during the 1980s.

Symbols of intensity also crept into daily life through the back door of the new leisure outlets. Signs of exhilaration—the clenched fist and dramatic exclamation—used for sports successes like a tennis win or a football touchdown spread into television shows, where they applied to sexual triumphs or simply to getting a good grade on a test. From television these signs migrated into "real life," with young middle-class Americans using these gestures to express great joy over often modest accomplishments. Whether this interesting interpenetration of leisure culture with daily emotional life had much meaning—in particular whether it indicated some significant new acknowledgement of intensity rather than a labored stab in that direction—is debatable.

Changes in gender roles based on the growing movement of women into the labor force generated increasing discussion of emotion in the 1970s and 1980s. Feminists and male liberationists tried to put additional pressure on middle-class men to restrain anger and aggressiveness and to display greater empathy and affection. Women were called upon to express more assertiveness—as carefully distinguished from anger—and to moderate any impulse toward self-sacrificing love. Some middle-class men became more active as fathers, and researchers busily discovered that men could nurture children as well as mothers could. Few men, however, attempted to rival women in child care, and in general, given the declining per capita birthrate, emotional attention to children probably declined. These important developments affected emotional standards but did not clearly redefine them in fundamental ways, except insofar as they pressed further in the direction of greater gender uniformity, a trend that had been established a half-century before. Men's ongoing complaint that women were too emotional also reflected an earlier trend that continued to complicate not only relations between the sexes but also the implementation of the basic emotional standards.[6]

A number of indicators suggested a reversal of the trend toward homogenization that had been active in emotional culture and other areas between the 1920s and the 1950s. Americans became more diverse in terms of class and ethnic divisions. Some of the trends underlying the new diversification patterns were the rapid growth of immigration, largely from non-European sources; the increasing assertiveness of African Americans; and the emergence of new economic divisions between the broad middle class and the unskilled as the economy continued to move away from a manufacturing base. By the 1980s, of course, diversity itself was being celebrated as a major political and educational goal. But even before this point reading materials, including popular magazines, moved away from attempts to feed on growing consensus toward representation of more specialized interests. Diet, which had become more uniform, now splintered into a growing variety of taste groups. Some of this diversification inevitably affected the middle class itself, creating opportunities for certain groups to distance themselves from mainstream standards—as in the commune-based youth movements of the 1960s and early 1970s. More important was the inescapable fact that emotional habits still dear to the middle class did not describe some other categories in American society, some of whom were more obviously angry, more prone to open grief, or in other ways divergent from the anti-intensity norms still embraced, in the main, by the middle class itself.[7]

Modifications of the anti-intensity standards—increasing disagreement in groups outside the middle class and occasionally amid groups within it—have clearly added some new complexity to the twentieth-century framework during the past decade or so. Fundamental change, however, has probably not yet occurred and may not even be foreshadowed by the developments outlined above. The principal causes that generated the anti-intensity emotionology in the first place continue to operate: the requirements of a corporate, service-oriented economy and management structure; small family size, with emphasis on leisure and sexual compatibility between spouses; consumerism; and anxiety about hidden forces within the body that might be disturbed by emotional excess. Reliance on key outlets for release from emotional constraint, particularly through leisure, have if anything accelerated. And the American middle class is still in a relatively early phase of assimilation of the new culture; it would be unusual to see a replacement model taking definite shape just forty years after the culture reached full articulation.

Furthermore, there is considerable evidence of continuity from the established framework. During the 1960s and 1970s the greeting card industry that had grown up around Victorian emotional sentiments in the nineteenth century began to diversify. Victorian-style emotions still figured prominently, now more comfortably purchased commercially than written directly. But a new genre appeared—the humorous, somewhat mocking card that so clearly expressed a common discomfort with too much intense emotion. Jokes, for many trendy buyers, were more appropriate than mushy sentimentality on occasions such as Valentine's Day. Joke cards themselves evolved. They became increasingly accessible, and by the 1990s they increasingly emphasized sexual innuendo and prowess—another suggestion that combinations first established in the 1920s are still alive and well.

The ongoing decline of Victorian-style love has already been noted. Teenage dating and adult vocabulary about relationships continued to change from the 1970s onward, and a series of popular films about murderous romantic obsessions, in which women (particularly) became fatally emotionally attracted by passing romances, drove home the point that intensity might be dangerous.

Attacks on intense anger persisted. Popularized articles repeated most of the old formulas, in which anger builds up blood pressure and speeds up heartbeat, "and you become a pressure cooker waiting to explode." Suppression of anger was bad, but having anger in the first place was in many ways even worse. To be sure, popularizers acknowledged that anger might exist; as with grief, though to lesser degree, recognition of some real problems attached to restraint may have increased. But while release might be essential, it should not burden relations with others; here, the anti-intensity standards remained in force. People were advised to allow a cooling-off period—"I don't want to argue with you at this time, because I'm not going to be rational"—and then to solve the problem calmly. Or they should throw a tantrum when no one else is around—"punch the sofa pillows and yell or shake your fists and jump up and down." And if all else failed, and there was still anger that could not be harmlessly expressed, they should "seek professional help."[8]

Anti-anger campaigns continue to grace corporate programs. In the early 1990s the Total Quality Management movement swept through American businesses and even academic sanctuaries. Borrowed from Japan, it had originally been sketched by American psychologists soon after World War II. Not surprisingly, it actively furthers the agenda of emotional restraint, urging that emotions play a role at work only insofar as they promote loyalty and motivation (does the organization's "vision" provide a "strong EMOTIONAL PULLING FORCE?"). Otherwise, along with detailed procedures for running meetings and coordinating projects, the TQM movement stresses emotional pruning as one of its three major goals. "Interactive skills" training involves teaching workers and managers labels for supportive behaviors that will avoid provoking others and thus disrupting contacts along with strongly negative terms for various types of emotional interference. Defensive or attacking stances that involve strong emotions are taboo: "Defending/Attacking behavior is seen as making personal attacks, moving away from issues, and becoming emotional." "Tempers become frayed. These spirals are easy to start but hard to stop." "These behaviors usually involve value judgments and contain emotional overtones." Elaborate, if somewhat childish, exercises take trainees through situations in which they are supposed to apply the correct tag and the correct judgment. Retraining is considered necessary when emotionality has not been properly noted or, even worse, has actually been approved.

The TQM movement is interesting in three respects. First, in its emotions component it literally repeats hosts of training attempts of the sort first launched in the late 1920s. Second, to the extent that it innovates, it extends the assumptions of general emotional control. Whereas the first wave of corporate guidance taught people to control their own emotions but to be prepared to deal with other people's, TQM, like the T-groups in the 1960s, assume that everyone should share responsibility. Once properly trained, everyone should be able to avoid intense feelings, though it might be necessary to deliver an occasional clucking reminder that colleague X seems to be a bit "attacking." Furthermore, high-level executives are asked to join others in this emotional constraint program, though some still hold out for greater personal latitude while urging their subordinates to toe the line. Finally, the sheer popularity of TQM, though based on several factors, reveals the ongoing currency of anti-intensity assumptions. Along with some better problem-solving skills and more focused committee meetings, keeping rationality at the forefront will make all well with the American economy. Correspondingly, an effort to keep work criteria central to the larger emotionology also persisted.

On another front, graders began to be urged to keep emotion out of their assessments of students' work. Not only anger but even annoyance was not to sully marginal comments on an essay, for example, no matter how stupid the error in usage or how often repeated. This directive, reflecting the wider effort to make education friendly, not only extended the emotional control theme to graders. It also assumed that students had internalized the new standards, such that the intrusion of any but the most supportive emotions would put them off—in contrast to earlier periods when teacher anger, however unpleasant, could be motivational.[9]

A final case for continuity arises from the movements to encourage more active fathering that were in force by the 1980s. These movements were only partly novel, for in fact they built on the greater approval of fathers that had developed from the 1920s onward. Fathers were urged to express more supportive emotions as part of their new role in child care, but no one expected or recommended great emotional intensity. Fathers could be careful monitors and good friends to their children— the fathers-as-pals approach, launched in the 1920s, was given greater latitude—and affection for children remained essential, but the all-out devotion of the ideal Victorian mother receded ever further from memory.

American language continued to reflect incorporation of a pleasant but nonintense emotionality. "Niceness" became a watchword for sales clerks and others in casual contact. "Have a nice day" struck many foreigners—even neighboring Canadians—as a remarkably insincere phrase. At the same time, though, they noted that Americans did seem "nice," an attribute that includes unusual discomfort with emotional outbursts on the part of those raised in different cultures where displays of temper might be more readily accepted. In American culture, "nice" did have meaning—it connoted a genuine effort to be agreeably disposed but not deeply emotionally involved while expecting pleasant predictability from others.

Because we are so close to recent developments, it is obviously easy to exaggerate continuity or change. A fuller study, and more time in which to evaluate some of the modifications that clearly have entered in, like the new approach to grief, might yield conclusions different from those sketched here. Tentatively, however, a verdict can be offered: key trends have persisted, gaining new expressions in several areas, and alterations have largely operated within the established framework. Even some of the warning signals, like the periodic jeremiads about growing anger and abuse, have served in fact to reinforce the basic norms of restraint within the middle class rather than to herald some new emotional anarchy. Whatever the future might hold, at the end of the twentieth century middle-class Americans continue to value cool—as the ever-ascending popularity of the word itself suggests.

Progress or Deterioration?

Histories that deal with changes in human characteristics or intimate activities almost invariably raise questions about the quality of the changes. Were they good or bad? Should we somehow work for a restoration of past values instead of debased modern currency? My principal purpose in evoking this inescapable topic is twofold. First, I find it difficult to offer firm judgments in this area, not so much because I recognize that the objectivity of this book's historical findings is disputable as because tastes vary, and one person's gains may be another's loss. Second, it is vital, whatever tastes are involved, to stress complexity; twentieth-century standards were not necessarily worse than their Victorian counterparts, but rather offered a different pattern of advantages and disadvantages.

A few observers have argued for progress, and many of the early proponents of the new standards certainly thought they were advancing clearly over the confusions of their predecessors. They believed that restraint of intensity would produce less violence, better personal adjustment (recall the good results anticipated from reducing smothering mothering), better relationships on the job, and so on. Ex post facto praise for the new standards has particularly focused on the benefits of liberation and candor. Cas Wouters thus writes of American pilots in the Gulf War who spoke freely of their fears before undertaking bombing missions, correctly noting that this open venting of emotion would have seemed unmanly in the Victorian code. Presumably, mental health is better served by this verbal openness, which does not diminish soldiers' ability to drop bombs on hapless Iraqis. In the 1970s several scholars praised the new liberation from jealousy, arguing that less possessive love freed people for more genuine relationships and better sex.

The problem with these arguments is that they involve potential misuse of the idea of liberation, at least in the U.S. context. As we have seen, in many ways constraint actually increased. Thus, for example, freedom from jealousy was great for some people, who felt little of the emotion themselves and enjoyed promiscuity or the prospect of it, but it was hell on wheels for those who did experience the emotion but were urged to deny its validity. Furthermore, although greater verbal openness might well be a gain, in certain cases, as with grief, even this opportunity declined in comparison with Victorian usage.[10]

The more common tone adopted in discussions of the decline of Victorianism and the rise of a different, twentieth-century personality is one of lament. David Riesman's contrast between inner-directed, highly motivated nineteenth-century types and other-directed, peer-influenced, less achieving contemporaries, though carefully balanced, inclined strongly to a sense of loss. This sense is clearer still in Christopher Lasch's update on this account, which contrasts highly motivated if somewhat neurotic nineteenth-century Americans with indulgent, narcissistic, standardless contemporaries, open to the whims of outside experts and consumer gurus. According to Lasch, things were better back then: kids were given clear standards, parents had confidence in their values, people worked harder and with more sense of meaning, and so on. Not coincidentally, Professor Lasch was invited to converse with former President Carter during the latter's crisis-of-values phase at the end of the 1970s, though by that point Americans generally were not interested in learning about how they had jumped the moral rails. Other sweeping assessments have chimed in, some quite recently. Robert Bellah's ambitious inquiry into the tension between family cohesion and individualism shows that the latter is clearly gaining and offers some pessimistic judgments about the results for the larger society, though Bellah does acknowledge some positive potential for the family. Barrington Moore laments the decline of the basis for moral outrage, which has led to a decline of really challenging social protest that might in turn keep the wielders of power at least partially honest. Charles Sykes zeroes in on the decline of guilt and the associated collapse of a sense of personal responsibility; individuals have become insatiable, in his view, and their reluctance to experience intense guilt leads them constantly to blame others and to seek redress from the outside world. Even Warren Susman's heralded contrast between nineteenth-century emphasis on character and twentieth-century emphasis on personality seems to denigrate the more recent patterns, showing personality to be more manipulative, more shallow than the Victorian character that, as we have shown, was meant to develop around the management of intense emotions.[11]

Evaluations of this sort do not, of course, pick up all the facets of emotional change. Sykes, for example, may overdo rampant individualism by failing to note the number of constraints, both bureaucratic and emotional, under which modern Americans labor. Lasch's claim of rising narcissism has not been widely accepted as an empirical statement, though it seemed challenging for a time. But the studies of American character that contrast it with the Victorian past do overlap with the findings of the present study of emotional standards, and their uniform pessimism might certainly apply to my findings as well.

It is easy to join the distinguished scholars who have already pointed out the drawbacks to twentieth-century emotionology. Because of our own nostalgia for aspects of Victorianism, itself a part of contemporary emotional culture, it is hard to avoid some sense of things gone awry. The very process of change causes problems; adjustment of standards can be confusing, even if the new goals are just as acceptable as the previous goals had been to the prior culture. Men, for example, who faced new pressures to curb anger at work, might find the transition difficult, even despite the symbolic outlets provided through sports. The same applies to women denied such easy claims to the powers of intense motherlove. Too much challenge to emotional standards can cause anxiety in itself, and it is possible that this result has been part of the twentieth-century condition for the American middle class.[12]

Beyond the difficulties of transition, the new culture had some unquestionable drawbacks. It did place important constraints on certain types of emotion, causing individuals to feel guilty when they experienced impulses such as jealousy. Inability to express these impulses might actually have heightened anger or frustration even as direct outlets for anger and frustration declined. This was not of course a brand-new problem: Victorianism had its strict rules as well, particularly for women, but the level of constraint did rise after 1920 for the middle class overall. Noting another, related conflict between rules and impulses, Hochschild has described the extent to which work-based requirements for emotional suppression could confuse reactions off the job as well.[13]

The drawbacks of twentieth-century emotionology were not simply personal. They also affected interpersonal relationships and the society as a whole. Intense bonds, particularly in friendship, were harder to maintain; along with other factors, such as changes in residential patterns, this result of the new emotional culture yielded new potential for a sense of loneliness. On the societal level, the emotional basis for middle-class protest, or at least acknowledgment of the validity of intense grievance, eroded to some extent even as the occupational structure became increasingly middle class; this could be judged a significant deterioration in American political life. Even protest movements that did surface seemed to lack full sustaining power, in part perhaps because their middle-class participants grew embarrassed about their own anger. This is a plausible ingredient (among others) in the collapse of student rebellion in 1973 (interestingly, a collapse much more complete than occurred in Europe) and perhaps in the oscillations of feminism. More generally, the new culture encouraged a certain amount of passivity, with the strong reliance on acting out by means of watching others perform, the use of embarrassment to enforce careful rules on intensity, and the emphasis on fatigue as a legitimate reason to pull away from normal emotional performance. It was safer to be tired than to be emotionally upset, and the sequence of terms generated to describe the need to withdraw—"stressed out," "burned out"—along with probable new emphasis on sadness as a means of pulling back, highlighted the cautious aspects of the new emotional culture.[14]

The impact of twentieth-century emotionology on families is harder to pin down. Obviously, overt family instability increased during the decades in which the new rules were installed. Less intense emotional commitments may have played some role in this complex process. According to polling data, appreciation for children declined, at least between the 1950s and the 1970s, and greater impatience with immature emotional outbursts may well have entered into this important process. On the other hand, reported satisfaction with spouses increased, and men's satisfaction with marriage remained high and even grew at points, which might mean that, for some key groups, a focus on a less emotionally intense but companionate marriage paid off.[15]

Furthermore, there were some definite advantages to the new culture. Differential gender standards declined despite persistent beliefs about love or anger that reflected older patterns. This change facilitated new kinds of feminist arguments on behalf of greater equality, though a tension remained between claiming equality on the basis of shared human worth and emphasizing distinctive feminine virtues. As we have seen, less rigid emotional differentiation between the sexes may have heightened contentiousness, providing men and women with new ways to complain about each other's interpretation of the new rules. But it is possible to argue that, on the whole, greater equality was served. By the same token, some of the specific pressures of Victorianism on women lessened, and with this came a decline of tensions that had resulted in disproportionate female hysteria.

New sexual interactions gained from the twentieth-century rules on jealousy, though these can be variously evaluated. Some men may have benefited from less rigid rules about masculine intensities; the possibility of admitting fear rather than claiming courage, of relying on professionals to act out some of the more demanding masculine rituals, and of emphasizing charm over channeled anger surely offered relief to many men. The fact that certain men's groups demanded even greater changes by the 1970s may have reflected some of the flexibility already acquired through the replacement of Victorian stereotypes; the earlier improvements may have made it possible to envisage more improvements in the same direction. Even the new rules on grief may have pleased some people, freeing them from elaborate ceremony and a kind of compulsory emotional routine. While "liberation" is the wrong word for a new pattern of constraint, there were some emancipating qualities for many individuals.

The greatest potential gains from the new emotionology involved relationships with other people. Despite variety and complexity, many workers did report fewer emotional hassles with supervisors by the 1940s and 1950s. The pressures to offer smiling courtesy to customers— the impersonal-but-friendly motif—may have improved the experience of shopping. As McDonald's and other chains spread in the 1980s, efforts by American companies to teach Russian employees to treat customers pleasantly highlighted U.S. standards and suggested some ways in which they might yield a more pleasant daily existence (always depending on one's value system, to be sure, and recognizing that some strain for workers was attached). It seemed "nicer" to be a customer in the United States than in Russia. Not everyone lived up to the new rules, and the need for outlets prompted some rough edges, but it is not fatuous to claim measurable improvements. In general, as many sociologists have argued, emotional inequality decreased in the twentieth century despite some hesitations in the upper reaches of management. Emotional abuse of subordinates probably declined and certainly could be more readily identified and complained about.[16]

The main point is not to argue a clear case of progress or deterioration but to stress the impossibility of such a case against those who have exhibited undue optimism and the even greater number who have greeted twentieth-century emotionology with pessimism. The new culture functioned, and its strengths and weaknesses were simply different from those that had prevailed in Victorian culture. Some emotional cultures, to be sure, might be rated less adequate than average; a few societies that seem to encourage high levels of anger, with resultant interpersonal conflict, may not work too well.[17] But the labeling game is risky, and certainly the balance sheet of twentieth-century emotionology defies easy bottom lines.

There was definitely a somewhat manipulative quality about contemporary emotional culture that might be noted without slipping back into the change-as-deterioration syndrome. Particularly in the past few decades in the United States, when the basic constraints have persisted along with a vocabulary of therapeutic mental health, some misleading signals have been offered. Middle-class people have been treated to a rhetoric of impulse and spontaneity while being told simultaneously to keep emotions damped down, to avoid public displays or impingements on others. The effect can be an image of freedom, particularly when contrasted with simplistic images of past repression, that is belied by the ongoing injunctions against real intensity. Thus new concern about grief does not yet affect actual rituals of mourning, and anger can be described, but only calmly or privately, and it should not be indulged. We have not, in sum, been treated to many honest appraisals of our actual emotional values, which is one reason for tracing the origins and causes of these values, as this book has done.

Whether or not better understanding will produce better personal or social results is anyone's guess, but I have a bias in favor of understanding. It is also important to remember not only that contemporary emotional culture has real advantages but also that any society imposes restraints on impulse. A problem with some pessimistic descriptions of the twentieth century is that they suffer from the false impression that social controls are new and evil inventions; such controls have always existed in some form, and ours may not be the worst imaginable.

One point seems quite clear. The causes of the emotional standards that replaced Victorianism were neither frivolous nor short lived. Thus there is no prospect of recapturing Victorianism whole, even if to do so were desirable. Nostalgia may usefully highlight some current shortcomings, but it may also be a misleading guide. We may be able to modify the emotional culture so solidly established a half-century ago; someday, also, Americans will surely move to another framework. With better understanding of what our rules really are, some individuals may choose to carve out slightly richer options. But we have been dealt a powerful cultural hand, and indications are that most middle-class Americans are still playing it.

Conclusion:
A Cautious Culture

The argument that runs throughout this study can be summarized briefly. An emotional culture that developed deep roots in the nineteenth century, affecting a variety of behaviors in the family and in public life, yielded to a decisively new style during the second quarter of this century. This new culture was far more consistently cautious where emotion was concerned, and like its Victorian predecessor, it had a wide range of impacts in private behaviors and expectations and in institutional arrangements. It resulted from a concatenation of several shifts in American society, including familiar developments such as the rise of corporate management and consumerism but also important new anxieties about bodily health in an age when fears turned inward. The new culture, finally, did not move in exactly the directions many Americans imagined. It was not entirely liberating, not simply an individualistic alternative to some uniform Victorian repression that in fact had not applied. The culture imposed significant new stress in middle-class life and evoked new needs for secret or symbolic release.

Victorian emotional culture had served more overt class and gender purposes than its twentieth-century replacement did, though the newer standards continued to allow groups to judge each other and opened new areas for gender dispute. Victorians valued emotions as motivators, as the sources of energy in work and politics and as a crucial cement for family life. The twentieth-century emotional style tolerated certain emotional interests as part of leisure life and personal identity, but urged overall restraint as part of the need to present a pleasing, unobtrusive front to others. Emotions were recognized as inevitable but were seen as more risky than useful, except as they were dissipated in harmless chatter or spectator symbolism. The departure from Victorian fervor was considerable.

These points recalled, it remains to offer a final assessment of significance, to suggest opportunities for further research, and to redraw connections with theories of emotion—three interrelated tasks that can be accomplished on the basis of points already made.

A major change in emotional culture is a significant development in a society's history.[1] Real redirections, so far as we know, occur rather rarely, though short-term adjustments that maintain basic trajectories may be more common. Victorian emotional culture built on trends, such as heightened familial affection, that had been developing for at least a century, adjusting them to the initial apparent requirements of industrial life. Thus the fundamental shifts that began early in the twentieth century attacked some long-standing emotional patterns, and this inevitably had substantial, sometimes confusing effects. The shifts came as quickly on the heels of Victorianism as they did because of the need to react more fully to the emotional demands of industrial society, which had now also achieved more mature organizational form and generated growing anxiety about attendant nervous and somatic stress.

The results spilled over into a variety of aspects of American life. Not only family relationships but also patterns of leisure and the motivations used in school and work shifted in accordance with the growing aversion both to the so-called negative emotions and to intensity of any sort, resulting in a need for ritual outlets. As a principal conduit through which structural changes in American society were translated into personality goals, emotional culture forms one of the leading facets, and one of the most tangible ingredients, of the kind of character transformation that many scholars have sought to define for this same period. Goals shifted from vigorous motivation to people pleasing, and the redefinition of emotional standards was central to the shift.[2]

Along with specific adjustments in emotional reactions, such as the revision of mourning practices or the new middle-class concern about the immaturity of jealousy, the new emotionology entered into a series of larger alterations in interpersonal style. Beginning in the 1950s and 1960s, use of first names became increasingly common in dealings with college students or business customers. Because contact was meant to convey uninvolved friendliness, some of the traditional distinctions in naming that had been based on varying degrees of emotional intensity as well as social hierarchy fell into disuse. Childhood was redefined, in ways that remain open to further exploration, as emotional maturity became an increasingly important goal amid relaxation of certain other conventional restraints. Fatigue—an extreme of emotional disengagement—became an increasingly acceptable complaint, replacing other forms of deviance, such as hysteria, that had involved a more active emotional performance. The new tension between openness to emotional venting and a sense that emotional issues were childish signs that need not be dignified by much attention became a characteristic twentieth-century sore point, dividing gender values in new ways.

Language itself mirrored the shifts in culture, furthering them in the process. The word "passion" was increasingly confined to the sexual sphere, and use of the word declined. Dictionary definitions of "emotion" itself became increasingly bland. Noah Webster had spiced his definition with terms like "vivid" and "passionate," but by the 1950s his heirs were equating emotion with the blander word "feelings" and were noting that varying strengths of feeling might be involved in emotion. The adjective "emotional" began to take on overtones of excess by the early twentieth century. Previously a fairly neutral term, in that people could be described as insufficiently as well as unduly emotional, the word began to connote lack of adequate control, at least when applied to individuals. Being described as an "emotional person," or accused of "emotionalism," was no compliment, even with no qualifying adjectives attached. By the 1920s another new combination entered in with the concept "emotionally disturbed," a label most frequently attached to children. It clearly reflected firmer categories of emotional deviance and a new set of parental anxieties. By the 1950s, when the phrase was common in child development studies, it was explicitly defined as a lack of "inner control" and attributed to as many as a quarter of all grade school children on the basis of a host of prosaic symptoms. Here was another way to make emotion a problem.[3]

Historians have long seen the 1920s or even the ensuing quarter-century as a crucial period of change in American life.[4] Obviously, many factors impelled adjustments besides the redefinition of emotional culture. But this redefinition now warrants a prominent place among the various forces to be assessed in explaining how contemporary life and institutions differ from their counterparts in the Victorian era. The subject of emotional change is, to be sure, still an innovation in the historical lexicon, and it would be folly to expect standard textbooks immediately to be rewritten to give the emergence of a twentieth-century emotional style its due. Even earlier attempts to define character change, like David Riesman's justly famous hypothesis, fit with difficulty into the conventional ways of viewing American history—even on the part of social historians, who pride themselves on openness to innovation. Nevertheless, the challenge is clear. At some point between 1920 and the 1950s most middle-class Americans moved toward emotional values rather different from those of their parents. Some were aware of the change, some not; some were troubled by the decline of older values, others leapt gleefully toward this aspect of modernity. The process not only brought some of the larger alterations in American society into personal compass; it also took on its own power, altering the kind of treatment many Americans expected from others and creating the demanding standards they imposed on themselves.

Much remains to be done as the contours of the emotionological transformation emerge more fully. A host of loose ends must be left dangling after any attempt to convey a phenomenon as complex and as hard to pin down as a sea change in emotional style. Readers will doubtless pick up a number of pathways that I have barely glimpsed. Be that as it may, because assessing a cultural shift should orient further research as well as mark progress already achieved, I would like to issue six specific invitations for additional study.

The first asks simply for ongoing attention to recent developments, oriented toward fuller testing of the previous chapter's claim that, despite adjustments, the twentieth-century emotional style remains essentially intact. In this effort historians but particularly sociologists and social psychologists imbued with genuine historical perspective can utilize understanding of the new culture as a litmus for change. Sorting out ephemeral shifts or mere adaptations from genuine and durable new directions is no easy task, but the emotionological findings of the present study provide some measurement standards.

The second research need involves assessment of a wider range of emotions during and after the transition period. Anger, love, fear, grief, guilt (plus shame and embarrassment), and jealousy do not constitute an entire emotional palette. Implications for other emotions have been offered here. For example, we have seen that new uses for sadness, and possibly a new if somewhat convoluted popularity of this emotion, fit the overall pattern of emotional change, including the reduced availability of more intense grief; but the topic invites further inquiry. Nostalgia may have changed to include real or imagined recollections of earlier emotional bonds conveyed, among other things, as part of media fare. Exhilaration may have been toned down in keeping with the general reduction of intensity, except as conveyed through recreational fare and spectatorship. Even joy, or at least expressions of joy, may have become more circumspect. Envy seems to have increased in complexity, having been encouraged by consumerism but placed under constraints as the concept merged with jealousy in popular belief. But these are suggestions based on the larger framework, not real investigations. Other recently studied emotions, like gratitude or expectations of gratitude, may also have changed, but apparently without much connection to the general style.[5]

Shifts in the balance among emotions under the general impulse of reducing intensity warrant attention as well. As jealousy, for example, received particular reproval, anger may have taken up some of the slack, even though it too was discountenanced.[6] Efforts to deny or conceal the "green-eyed monster" easily generated anger at the provoking beloved, and while anger also required restraint, it may have seemed more respectable, less childish than jealousy. Even with emotions that clearly fit under the anti-intensity rubric, additional analysis remains desirable.

The coherence and outreach of the middle class constitutes the third field for further study suggested by an understanding of Victorianism and the transition toward deintensification. Most emotions history has focused primarily on the middle class, and this study is no exception. Victorian emotional culture set standards that other social groups might aspire to or might fabricate as part of an effort at respectability. It was deliberately introduced to marginal middle-class segments like department store clerks. It was also used by the solid middle class itself to judge and condemn inadequate emotional behavior by social inferiors—

including not only outbursts of unwonted spontaneity but also inadequate intensities in such areas as grief, courage, or maternal affection. All of this does not constitute a history of emotional cultures for non–middle-class groups, but it does provide some guidelines.

In the twentieth century, we have less to go on. The new emotional culture was urged on the working class, particularly in such areas as anger control; as the middle class imposed new constraints on its own members, it became even less tolerant of emotional diversity. In this sense twentieth-century emotionology played a key role in the daily subtleties of middle-class hegemony. But we have also seen signs that workers were not expected fully to assimilate middle-class niceties. On the other hand, the rapid expansion of the middle class, through self-identification and the rise of the service sector, implied new needs to acquire a middle-class emotional veneer. How various working-class groups, some with distinct ethnic cultures, reacted to growing middle-class hegemony constitutes a vital area for further study. Modification of mainstream standards, unusual utilization of certain outlets, including ethnic celebrations, or outright rejection of key standards all are active possibilities, even as middle-class authorities labored to create emotionally controlled work personalities and a more uniform pattern of child-rearing. The addition of new immigrant groups after the 1950s adds to the complexity inviting attention. African American assertiveness, celebrated in highly emotional crowd scenes, and a bristling individual resentment at certain white standards suggest an obvious disharmony in recent decades. Among many employment barriers to inner-city blacks, unwillingness to live up to middle-class definitions of emotional decorum, particularly in service-sector jobs, plays a definite role. This divide in emotional cultures can be exacerbated by white assumptions about African American passions, which are regarded as entertaining on a playing field but inappropriate, even frightening, at closer range.[7]

In sum, examining class and ethnic variations and divisions over emotional culture forms one of the ways to investigate living social structure in any historical period. Ironically, we have made less use of this opportunity for our own era than for periods in the past.[8]

Range of impact constitutes the fourth area open to further analysis. One of the crucial findings about both Victorian and twentieth-century emotional culture is that they affected not only self-evaluations and private relationships but also areas of public life such as work or even political styles. Emotional standards allow the social constructionist, through history or anthropology or sociology, to relate individual values and socialization to a much wider realm. This is why, despite social historians' common preference for assumptions of mass rationality, the subject of emotion has such important potential for investigations of the past. We can easily see implications of changing standards for law[9] or for protest potential—in combination, of course, with other factors—but to date we have only broken the surface of this subject. Does the increasing American interest in an emotional style that appears friendly but not unduly engaged relate to diplomatic efforts to identify friends abroad and to worry (excessively, in European eyes) about whether we are "liked"? Does the same interest help explain the eagerness of individual negotiators, like Franklin Roosevelt at Yalta or George Bush with his horseshoe games with foreign dignitaries, to elicit superficially friendly expressions from their interlocutors (including, for FDR, the stony-faced Stalin)? These clearly tantalizing extensions of the new emotional style may be unwarranted, but they are worth examining as we continue the process of figuring out how long a shadow the anti-intensity culture cast.

The fifth direction for future study lies in the obvious desirability of comparative inquiry. Both Victorianism and the transition toward a more complex set of constraints were shared between the United States and Western Europe. But sharing is not equivalence, and further work on both time periods is necessary to establish greater comparative precision. For the twentieth century, the research of Dutch and German sociologists suggests some trends very comparable to those in the United States, as well as similar causes, including new employment structures and growing consumerism.[10] But the timing was different, with the European break occurring more in the 1960s than earlier. Different timing suggests a somewhat different pattern of causation, manifestation, and results. Some of the confusions that have appeared in definitions of twentieth-century emotional style have resulted from unwarranted assumptions of transatlantic equivalence, as opposed to considerable similarity. An obvious if challenging task is to begin to sort this out. Exploration of the American transition helps refine the questions to ask: Why the 1960s as a starting point rather than the 1920s? Did Europeans share some of the health concerns that helped direct American cool? Did Europeans end up embracing spontaneity more fully (as some of the Dutch studies suggest), and if so, why? Why did Americans seem disproportionately eager to conceal?

Finally, fuller understanding of our recent emotional history may help improve interdisciplinary inquiry into the constructionist aspects of emotion itself.[11] History is a newcomer amid explicit studies of emotion. In introducing a more self-conscious attention to the process of change, it fleshes out many of the theoretical claims made by constructionists. For the twentieth century, history employs many recent findings and explanations developed by the growing breed of sociologists of emotion. Thus a certain amount of interdisciplinary crossover is built into our growing ability to define and explain recent patterns in emotional standards. But history also challenges students of emotion to tackle some new complexities. Anthropologists, the most empirically successful constructionists to date, have not usually dealt with change. Psychologists, the kings of the hill in emotions research, tend to seek constants. They do share some sympathy with constructionist claims, in terms, for example, of investigating culturally specific emotions functions rather than some grand evolutionary scheme, but they do not inquire into change directly. Their causation focus involves microlevel, proximate relationships rather than more sweeping phenomena such as bureaucratization.[12]

In principle, the establishment of a new emotional culture toward the mid–twentieth century sets up topics for psychologists to investigate from their own vantage point; they might, for example, test different generational values or standards held by different segments of the occupational structure. Examination of childrearing styles in light of an overarching, if implicit, attempt to curtail intensity could readily blend psychological and historical approaches. Social psychologists have already contributed to the task of exploring the anti-intensity culture, but have not yet wedded this essentially historical outline to the actual developmental processes. Psychologists and historians have also joined in identifying the emergence of a newly playful style with children on the part of middle-class fathers beginning in the 1920s. This parental strategy, designed to build bonds through shared entertainment rather than more traditional moral or emotional intensity, provides another framework for exploring the actual operation of new parental tactics in a socialization process; but the next, more strictly psychological step has yet to be taken.[13] Interdisciplinary bridges of this sort are immensely difficult, but they do follow from a growing understanding of some of the kinds of changes that have enmeshed our society.

For students of emotion generally, of whatever disciplinary stripe, the exploration of twentieth-century emotional culture already contributes to a theoretical understanding of what emotion is all about. History and historical sociology, along with cultural comparisons, provide the clearest empirical basis for constructionist approaches to emotion. The sweep of the movement away from Victorian culture and the causes that intertwined to shape a new culture constitute a major case study in the constructionist mode. To be sure, the study does not resolve the nature-versus-nurture debate, that hardy perennial in emotion theory. On the one hand, the avid twentieth-century search for outlets for constrained emotions supports attention to basic or "natural" passions such as anger or fear, or to more general "vital affects" that are biologically based but shaped through parental care into more precise emotions.[14] On the other hand, the shift from Victorianism to a more cautious emotional culture demonstrates that culture counts for a great deal in directing emotional responses and evaluations according to changing social needs, though it does not specify exactly how much.

The real contributions of this kind of inquiry into emotional change lie beneath the most conventional nature-versus-cultural-construction controversy. Constructionists have too often ventured theories about the kinds of social functions that can shape emotion without offering sufficient empirical grounding. Or, in anthropology, they have demonstrated vivid cultural contrasts without determining precisely what caused them. In the case of the twentieth-century transition, causation can be explored. It can be demonstrated that although new economic forms redefined the functions an emotional culture was to serve, they did so in combination with new cultural forces, particularly beliefs about physical health. This precise pattern is surely unique, but the basic model of seeking a combination of functional factors and examining how they were shaped by new beliefs may well apply in other instances.[15]

More systematic attention to causation also leads to considerations of timing, another key factor in a historical approach to the construction of emotions. In this area we have too few cases thus far to venture a theory of timing. However, we have seen that there was a lag between initial indications of a new emotional culture—which actually preceded the 1920s in expressions such as grief—and evidence of wider incorporation of the standards a generation later, followed a bit later still by institutional reactions in some areas of the law or school regulations. This twentieth-century pattern establishes a baseline that should be tested in other historical frameworks.

Debates about emotion have also tended to narrow assessments of the results of particular emotional styles. Biological and psychological determinists tend to emphasize the functions of an emotion for the individual: grief is a signal for help, sadness an opportunity to withdraw and regroup, etc. Apart from the culturally specific limitations of this approach, it simply does not capture the wider social impact of emotional values. Constructionists have been more sensitive to emotions' effects, for example in dealing with the responses an emotion elicits, but they may limit inquiry to a largely private or familial sphere. Exploration of the twentieth-century emotional style furthers an inquiry into the wider ramifications of changing standards. Individual experience and function remain relevant, but so do the signals given to others about how to deal with an individual's self-presentation—one of the most sensitive barometers of the twentieth-century uneasiness over intensity—and so do the results of emotional standards in arrangements at the workplace or in public law. Here, too, an explicit historical synthesis helps define some of the subordinate theoretical issues in the constructionist approach to emotion.

Finally, historical inquiry into emotional culture inevitably addresses theoretical issues in history itself. The present study provides additional ammunition to the numerous critics of modernization theory as applied to the emotional realm, showing that a simple repression-liberation contrast between Victorianism and the twentieth century is profoundly misleading. Understanding the actual emotional style that emerged from the 1920s onward, and its causes, also casts doubt (at least for the United States) on a second common formulation that sees recent change as somehow continuing a "civilizing process" of emotional restraints that began several centuries back. Without totally disproving this approach, I have argued that the twentieth century is quite different from the nineteenth in the area of emotional standards, and that this difference was caused by very new factors in social organization and popular beliefs. Both the differences themselves and their deep-seated causes indicate that it is not useful to explain recent patterns in terms of some overarching process that cuts across definable historical periods, including our own. Indeed, in certain respects twentieth-century culture recalled some pre-Victorian emotional qualities, particularly in urging against undue emotional intensity within the family—though it would be misleading to conclude, as Willmott and Young have implied, that Victorian delight in appropriate intensity constituted a historical oddity that contrasts with an emotional caution bounding Victorianism at both chronological ends.[16]

For the aversion to intensity that emerged among middle-class Americans in the twentieth century translated the apparent needs of an increasingly managerial, health-conscious society into the emotional realm. The resulting emotional standards were at least as unusual as Victorianism had been, and they were decidedly modern. Just as they differed from earlier American precedent, so they also contrasted with emotional cultures in other parts of the world, particularly in the pressure they placed on Americans to conceal reactions. The cool, chilled-out character popular among American teenagers was matched by the businessman claiming control of his life and his passions, eager to fit into new campaigns like Quality Management that called for careful monitoring of emotions during meetings (no "attacking or defending" behaviors, please). In the culture of the twentieth century, undue emotion, whether anger or grief or love, meant vulnerability as well as childishness. By the 1990s, several generations had been schooled in the desirability of keeping most emotions buttoned up and expecting other people to do the same. American cool still prevails.

Notes

1. Introduction

1. Arlie R. Hochschild, "Emotion Work, Feeling Rules, and Social Structure," *American Journal of Sociology* 85 (1979): 551–75. On cool, see "The Executive Life," *New York Times,* 28 Feb. 1993.
2. Peter N. Stearns and Deborah C. Stearns, "Historical Issues in Emotions Research: Causation and Timing," *Social Perspectives on Emotion* 2 (1994), forthcoming.
3. Roger Chartier, "Intellectual History or Sociocultural History? The French Trajectories," in Dominick LaCapra and Steven Kaplan, eds., *Modern European Intellectual History* (Ithaca, N.Y., 1982), 13–46; Robert Darnton, "Intellectual and Cultural History," in Michael Kammen, ed., *The Past before Us* (Ithaca, N.Y., 1980), 327–54; James A. Henretta, "Social History as Lived and Written," *American Historical Review* 84 (1979): 1293–1333; Patrick H. Hutton, "The History of Mentalities: The New Map of Cultural History," *History and Theory* 20 (1981): 237–59.
4. "Emotionology" is a term developed to provide a convenient label, convertible to adjectival form, for emotional culture or feeling rules. It has won a certain audience, though is here used interchangeably with the other terms preferred by some. See Peter N. Stearns and Carol Z. Stearns, "Emotionology: Clarifying the History of Emotions and Emotional Standards," *American Historical Review* 90 (1985): 813–36.
5. Robert L. Griswold, *Family and Divorce in California, 1850–1890: Victorian Illusions and Everyday Realities* (Albany, N.Y., 1982); Robert M. Ireland, "Insanity and the Unwritten Law," *American Journal of Legal History* 32 (1988): 157–72; and "The Libertine Must Die: Sexual Dishonor and the Unwritten Law in the Nineteenth-Century United States," *Journal of Social History* 23 (1989): 27–44.
6. M. C. Clark and A. M. Isen, "Toward Understanding the Relationship between Feeling States and Social Behavior," in A. H. Hastorf and A. M. Isen, eds., *Cognitive Social Psychology* (Elsevier/North Holland, 1982), 73–108.
7. For a spirited defense of the basic emotions concept, and an attack on constructionism, see several articles in Theodore Kemper, ed., *Research Agendas in the Sociology of Emotions* (Albany, N.Y., 1990), particularly the essay by the editor. See also

Carroll E. Izard, "Emotions in Personality and Culture," *Ethos* 11 (1983): 305–12; and Theodore D. Kemper, "Social Constructionist and Positivist Approaches to the Sociology of Emotions," *American Journal of Sociology* 87 (1981): 336–62.

8. Claire Armon-Jones, "The Thesis of Constructionism," in Rom Harré, ed., *The Social Construction of Emotions* (Oxford, 1986), 32–56, and "The Social Function of Emotion," in ibid., 57–83; Rom Harré, "An Outline of the Social Constructionist Viewpoint," in ibid., 2–14; Nancy Scheper-Hughes, "Culture, Scarcity, and Maternal Thinking: Maternal Detachment and Infant Survival in a Brazilian Shantytown," *Ethos* 13 (1985): 291–317; Catherine Lutz and G. White, "The Anthropology of Emotions," *Annual Review of Anthropology* 15 (1986): 405–36; Catherine Lutz, *Unnatural Emotions: Everyday Sentiments on a Micronesian Atoll and Their Challenge to Western Theory* (Chicago, 1988); Owen Lynch, "The Social Construction of Emotion in India," in Owen Lynch, ed., *Divine Passions: The Social Construction of Emotion in India* (Berkeley, Calif., 1990).

9. Harré, "Outline;" Errol Bradford, "Emotions and Statements about Them," in Harré, *Social Construction of Emotions*, 15–31; Lutz and White, "Anthropology;" Kemper, *Research Agendas*.

10. Kevin White, *The First Sexual Revolution: The Emergence of Male Heterosexuality in Modern America* (New York, 1993), chaps. 3 and 4; Gilbert Barnes and Dwight Dummond, eds., *Letters of Theodore D. Weld, Angelina Grimke Weld, and Sara Grimke, 1822–1844* (New York, 1934), 600; Peter N. Stearns, "Girls, Boys, and Emotions: Redefinitions and Historical Change," *Journal of American History* 80 (1993): 36–74.

11. For background on the modern middle class, see Stuart M. Blumin, *The Emergence of the Middle Class: Social Experience in the American City, 1760–1900* (New York, 1989); on cultural hegemony, in addition to the classic work by Antonio Gramsci (*Selections from the Prison Notebooks* [New York, 1971]), John Hargreaves, *Sport, Power, and Culture* (New York, 1986).

12. Edward Shorter, *The Making of the Modern Family* (New York, 1975); Lawrence Stone, *The Family, Sex, and Marriage in England, 1500–1800* (New York, 1977); Randolph Trumbach, *The Rise of the Egalitarian Family: Aristocratic Kinship and Domestic Relations in Eighteenth Century England* (New York, 1978).

13. Stanley Coben, *Rebellion against Victorianism: The Impetus for Cultural Change in 1920s America* (New York, 1991); Roland Marchand, *Advertising the American Dream: Making Way for Modernity, 1920–1940* (Berkeley, Calif., 1985); Daniel T. Rodgers, *The Work Ethic in Industrial America, 1850–1920* (Chicago, 1978); Steven Seidman, *Romantic Longings: Love in America, 1830–1980* (New York, 1991); Warren Susman, *Culture as History: The Transformation of American Society in the Twentieth Century* (New York, 1985); Leonard J. Moore, "Historical Interpretations of the 1920s Klan: The Traditional View and the Populist Revision," *Journal of Social History* 24 (1990): 341–58; and *Citizen Klansmen: The Ku Klux Klan in Indiana, 1921–1928* (Chapel Hill, N.C., 1991).

14. Peter N. Stearns and Carol Z. Stearns, *Anger: The Struggle for Emotional Control in American History* (Chicago, 1986); Peter N. Stearns, *Jealousy: The Evolution of an Emotion in American History* (New York, 1989); Peter N. Stearns and Timothy Haggerty, "The Role of Fear: Transitions in American Emotional Standards for Children, 1850–1950," *American Historical Review* 96 (1991): 63–94.

15. Karen Lystra, *Searching the Heart: Women, Men, and Romantic Love in Nineteenth-Century America* (New York, 1989); Jan Lewis, "Mother's Love: The Construction

of an Emotion in Nineteenth-Century America," in Andrew E. Barnes and Peter N. Stearns, eds., *Social History and Issues in Human Consciousness* (New York, 1989): 209–29; Seidman, *Romantic Longings*.

16. Francesca M. Cancian and Steven Gordon, "Changing Emotion Norms in Marriage: Love and Anger in U.S. Women's Magazines since 1900," *Gender and Society* 2 (1988): 303–42.

17. Lynn Lofland, "The Social Shaping of Emotion: The Case of Grief," *Symbolic Interaction* 8 (1985): 171–90; Phillipe Ariès, *The Hour of Our Death*, trans. Helen Weaver (New York, 1981). Ariès's survey of death practices has massive implications for a history of grief, as do other studies of changes in funerals and monuments; interestingly, however, an explicit history of grief, beyond general survey level, has not been attempted. See Paul C. Rosenblatt, *Bitter, Bitter Tears: Nineteenth-Century Diarists and Twentieth-Century Grief Theories* (Minneapolis, Minn., 1983) for an interesting, but in my view flawed effort in that direction.

18. Norbert Elias, *The Civilizing Process: The History of Manners,* trans. Edmund Jephcott (New York, 1978); John F. Kasson, *Rudeness and Civility: Manners in Nineteenth-Century Urban America* (New York, 1990); Alain Corbin, *The Foul and the Fragrant: Odor and the French Social Imagination* (Cambridge, Mass., 1986); Arthur Mitzman, "The Civilizing Offensive: Mentalities, High Culture, and Individual Psyches," *Journal of Social History* 20 (1987): 663–88; Peter Burke, *Popular Culture in Early Modern Europe* (New York, 1978); Rhys Isaac, *The Transformation of Virginia, 1740–1790* (New York, 1982); Stearns and Haggerty, "Fear;" Jean Delumeau, *La peur en Occident, XIVe–XVIIe siècles: Une cité assiégée* (Paris, 1978), and *Sin and Fear: The Emergence of a Western Guilt Culture, Thirteenth–Eighteenth Centuries,* trans. Eric Nicholson (New York, 1990); Stearns and Stearns, *Anger*; Roger Wertheimer, "Understanding Retribution," *Criminal Justice Ethics* 2 (1983): 19–38.

19. Jean-Louis Flandrin, *Families in Former Times* (New York, 1979); Stearns, *Jealousy*; John Demos, "Shame and Guilt in Early New England," in Carol Z. Stearns and Peter N. Stearns, eds., *Emotion and Social Change: Toward a New Psychohistory* (New York, 1988), 69–86; Trumbach, *The Rise of the Egalitarian Family*; Lofland, "The Social Shaping of Emotion"; Rosenblatt, *Bitter, Bitter Tears.*

20. David Riesman, with Nathan Glazer and Reuel Denney, *The Lonely Crowd: A Study of the Changing American Character* (New Haven, Conn., 1961); Christopher Lasch, *The Culture of Narcissism: American Life in an Age of Diminishing Expectations* (New York, 1979).

21. Gordon Clanton and Lynn G. Smith, eds., *Jealousy* (Lanham, Md., 1987); for a summary of the modernization argument, see Cancian and Gordon, "Changing Emotion Norms in Marriage"; Arlie R. Hochschild, *The Managed Heart: Commercialization of Human Feeling* (Berkeley, Calif., 1983), and, with Anne Machung, *The Second Shift: Working Parents and the Revolution at Home* (New York, 1989); Francesca M. Cancian, *Love in America: Gender and Self-Development* (New York, 1987).

22. Jürgen Gerhards, "The Changing Culture of Emotions in Modern Society," *Social Science Information* 28 (1989): 737–54; Cas Wouters, "Developments in the Behavioral Codes between the Sexes: The Formalization of Informalization in the Netherlands, 1930–85," *Theory, Culture, and Society* 4 (1987): 405–27, and "On Status Competition and Emotion Management," *Journal of Social History* 24 (1991): 699–717; Abram de Swaan, "The Politics of Agoraphobia: On Changes in Emotional and Relational Management," *Theory and Society* 10 (1981): 359–85; see also Mitz-

man, "The Civilizing Offensive," for a related historical argument about the recrudescence of spontaneity.

23. C. Brinkgreve and M. Korzer, "Verhaeltnisse in der niederlaendischen Gesellschaft (1938–1977). Analysis und Interpretation der Rategeber Rubrick einer Illustrierten," in P. Gleichmann, ed., *Materielen zu Norbert Elias' Zivilisationstheorie* (Frankfurt, 1979), 399–410; Wouters, "On Status Competition."

24. James Benton, "The New Sensibility: Self and Society in the Post-Industrial Age," Ph.D. diss., University of California at Los Angeles, 1981.

25. R. Gordon Kelly, *Mother Was a Lady: Self and Society in Selected American Children's Periodicals, 1865–1890* (Westport, Conn., 1974); Bernard Wishy, *The Child and the Republic: The Dawn of Modern Child Nurture* (Philadelphia, 1968); Philip J. Greven, Jr., ed., *Childrearing Concepts, 1628–1861* (Itasca, Ill., 1973). Evaluation of the history of childrearing advice on anger, in this and subsequent chapters, is based on a combination of studies of advice—often quite good, though not directed to the subject of emotion—and primary materials. Inquiry into nineteenth-century approaches is facilitated by several excellent histories of childrearing in general, such as those cited above. These studies help establish the representativeness of the primary materials consulted. For the twentieth century, secondary treatments have focused primarily on infant care and on Dr. Spock (see Leone Kell and Jean Aldous, "Trends in Child Care over Three Generations," *Marriage and Family Living* 22 [1960]: 176–77; Jay Mechling, "Advice to Historians on Advice to Mothers," *Journal of Social History* 9 [1977]: 44 ff.; Celia B. Stendler, "Sixty Years of Child Training Practices," *Journal of Pediatrics* 36 [1950]: 122–34; Thomas Gordon, *Parent Effectiveness Training* [New York, 1970]; Martha Wolfenstein, "Trends in Infant Care," *American Journal of Orthopsychiatry* 23 [1953]: 120–30; and Stephanie A. Shields and Beth A. Koster, "Emotional Stereotyping of Parents in Child Rearing Manuals, 1915–1980," *Social Psychology Quarterly* 52 [1989]: 44–55). Here I have undertaken wider reading, testing for representativeness by picking up major examples of "schools" such as the Watsonians and by using materials issued from major parent-guidance groups and publications, including the journal *Parents' Magazine*. Representativeness is also tested through analysis of internal consistency on key points within each period and through juxtaposition with some children's literature and school advice. There is no denying the fact that a study of childrearing literature that goes beyond mere summary to claims of changes in tone and of some connection with wider social values exceeds the most rigorous standards of evidence. This limitation imposes caution on both the researcher and the reader. It is at least partially compensated for by the importance of advancing a richer historical context for the understanding of emotional life.

26. Frank Luther Mott, *A History of American Magazines,* 4 vols. (Cambridge, Mass., 1957–1968). On selecting etiquette books, Kasson, *Rudeness and Civility.*

27. Choice of magazines was made by using Frank Luther Mott's assessment of what was most popular (*A History of American Magazines*). *Godey's Ladies Book* was used from 1840 to 1855 (see Mott, 1:581). *Peterson's Magazine* was used for 1860–1895 (see Mott, 1:593, 2:309–11). The *Ladies Home Journal* was used for the twentieth century (see Mott, 4:540 ff.). Lest it be objected that these magazines were consumed by women only, Mott has demonstrated that they were widely read by men, too, the *Ladies Home Journal,* in fact, being the magazine third most in demand by soldiers during World War I (1:590, 4:550).

28. Peter N. Stearns, "Anger and American Work: A Twentieth-Century Turning Point,"

in Stearns and Stearns, eds., *Emotion and Social Change*, 123–50; Lystra, *Searching the Heart*; Linda W. Rosenzweig, " 'The Anchor of My Life': Middle-Class American Mothers and College-Educated Daughters, 1880–1920," *Journal of Social History* 25 (1991): 5–26; Arthur T. Jersild, et al., *Joys and Problems of Child Rearing* (New York, 1949); Daniel Miller and Guy Swanson, *The Changing American Parent* (New York, 1958).

29. Colin Campbell, *The Romantic Ethic and the Spirit of Modern Consumerism* (New York, 1987).

30. This is a point made by Steven Gordon in "The Socialization of Children's Emotion: Emotional Culture, Competence, and Exposure," in Carolyn Saarni and Paul Harris, eds., *Children's Understanding of Emotion* (New York, 1989), 319–49; George Rudé, *The Crowd in History: A Study of Popular Disturbances in France and England, 1730–1848* (New York, 1964). For a recent version of the rationalist social history of protest, see Charles Tilly, *Contentious French* (Cambridge, Mass., 1986); other researchers have granted some role for emotional display in the protest process. See Michelle Perot, *Les ouvriers en grève: France, 1871–1890*, 2 vols. (Paris, 1974). On emotion and cognition, see Clark and Isen, "Toward Understanding the Relationship between Feeling States and Social Behavior"; Izard, "Emotions in Personality and Culture."

31. Riesman, *Lonely Crowd*; Robert Bellah, et al., *Habits of the Heart: Individualism and Commitment in American Life* (Berkeley, Calif., 1985).

2. The Victorian Style

1. Cas Wouters, "On Status Competition and Emotion Management," *Journal of Social History* 24 (1991): 699–717, and "Developments in the Behavioral Codes between the Sexes: The Formalization of Informalization in the Netherlands, 1930–85," *Theory, Culture, and Society* 4, nos. 2–3 (1987): 405–27; John F. Kasson, *Rudeness and Civility: Manners in Nineteenth-Century Urban America* (New York, 1990); D. H. Thom, *Guiding the Adolescent* (Washington D.C., 1935), and *Child Management* (Washington, D.C., 1925); Gordon Clanton, "Jealousy in American Culture, 1945–1985: Reflections from Popular Culture," in David Franks and E. D. McCarthy, eds., *The Sociology of Emotions* (Greenwich, Conn., 1989).

2. Catharine Sedgwick, *Home* (Boston, 1834); Felix Adler, *The Moral Instruction of Children* (New York, 1901); Peter N. Stearns, *Jealousy: The Evolution of an Emotion in American History* (New York, 1989), 49–58.

3. Jean Strouse, *Alice James: A Biography* (New York, 1980); Arthur Mitzman, "The Civilizing Offensive: Mentalities, High Culture, and Individual Psyches," in Peter N. Stearns, ed., *Expanding the Past: A Reader in Social History* (New York, 1989); Lloyd DeMause, ed., *History of Childhood* (New York, 1974); William G. McLoughlin, "Evangelical Child-Rearing in the Age of Jackson: Francis Wayland's View on When and How to Subdue the Willfulness of Children," *Journal of Social History* 9 (1975): 234.

4. Bernard I. Mursten, *Sex and Marriage through the Ages* (New York, 1974); R. P. Neuman, "Masturbation, Madness, and the Modern Concepts of Childhood and Adolescence," *Journal of Social History*, 1975, 1–27.

5. Patricia Branca, *Silent Sisterhood: Middle-Class Women in the Victorian Home* (Pittsburgh, 1975); Peter Gay, *Education of the Senses*, vol. 1, *The Bourgeois Experience: Victoria to Freud* (New York, 1984); Carl Degler, *At Odds: Women and the Family*

in America from the Revolution to the Present (New York, 1980); Carol Z. Stearns and Peter N. Stearns, "Victorian Sexuality: Can Historians Do It Better?" Journal of Social History 18 (1985): 625–34.

6. Karen Lystra, Searching the Heart: Women, Men, and Romantic Love in Nineteenth-Century America (New York, 1989); Steven Seidman, "The Power of Desire and the Danger of Pleasure: Victorian Sexuality Reconsidered," Journal of Social History 24 (1990): 47–68. For a larger comparison with sexuality, applying some of the same ideas of dominant discourse I direct to emotionology, see Michel Foucault, History of Sexuality, vol. 2 (New York, 1990).

7. Presbyterian Banner, 14 July 1880. My thanks to Charles Hachten for the reference; Anne C. Rose, Transcendentalism as a Social Movement (New Haven, Conn., 1986).

8. Anne L. Kuhn, The Mother's Role in Childhood Education: New England Concepts, 1830–1860 (New Haven, Conn., 1947); Mary Ryan, Cradle of the Middle Class: The Family in Oneida County, New York, 1790–1865 (Cambridge, Mass, 1981).

9. Sedgwick, Home.

10. See, for example, Reverend John S. C. Abbott, The Mother at Home; or, The Principles of Maternal Duty (Boston, 1834), 66; "Hints for Maternal Education," Mother's Magazine, Aug. 1834, 113, 114; S. F. W., "Woman's Sphere," American Ladies' Magazine, May 1835, 264; Sarah W. Gordon, "It Should Be Love," Mother's Assistant and Young Lady's Friend, March 1849, 53; Reverend V. Clark, "The Ruined Son," Mother's Assistant and Young Lady's Friend, Oct. 1845, 74; "The Beginning," American Ladies' Magazine, Jan. 1829, 4; "On Early Domestic Education," Mothers' Monthly Journal, 1837, 6; Mrs. [sic] C. Sedgwick, "A Plea for Children," American Ladies' Magazine, Feb. 1835, 95; Virginia Cary, Christian Parent's Assistant; or, Tales for the Moral and Religious Instruction of Youth (Richmond, Va., 1829), x; G. W. H., "The Disadvantages of Childhood," Mother's Magazine, 1867, 7; "What Virtue Is," Mother's Magazine, Aug. 1834, 115; D. M. L., "Early Habits of Industry," Mother's Magazine, Feb. 1834, 17; "Let Reason Dictate," Mothers' Monthly Journal, Nov. 1837, 170–71.

11. Reverend John Todd, "Address to Mothers," Mother's Magazine, Nov. 1839, 219; E. L., "The Mother's Affections," American Ladies' Magazine, July 1833, 320; Lydia H. Sigourney, Letters to Mothers (Hartford, Conn., 1838), 47; "Family Government Essential to Material Property," Mother's Monthly Journal, 1833, 36.

12. Stearns, Jealousy, 45–58; Peter N. Stearns and Timothy Haggerty, "The Role of Fear: Transitions in American Emotional Standards for Children, 1850–1950," American Historical Review 96, no. 1 (1989): 63–94.

13. Reverend Daniel Wise, Bridal Greetings . . . (New York, 1852), 122; Nancy F. Cott, The Bonds of Womanhood: "Woman's Sphere" in New England, 1780–1835 (New Haven, Conn., 1977).

14. Lydia Child, The Mother's Book (Boston, 1831), 28–32; Stearns and Haggerty, "The Role of Fear," 66–68; T. S. Arthur, Mother's Rule (Philadelphia, 1856), 289–90; John Demos, "Shame and Guilt in Early New England," in Carol Z. Stearns and Peter N. Stearns, eds., Emotion and Social Change (New York, 1988), 69–86; Philip J. Greven, Jr., The Protestant Temperament: Patterns of Childrearing, Religious Experience, and the Self in Early America (New York, 1977).

15. Peter Gregg Slater, Children in the New England Mind: In Death and in Life (Hamden, Conn., 1977); Bernard Wishy, The Child and the Republic (Philadelphia, 1968), 11–12.

16. Horace Bushnell, Views of Christian Nurture (Hartford, Conn., 1847), 253–55;

Child, *The Mother's Book,* 37; Louisa Hoare, *Hints for the Improvement of Early Education and Nursery Discipline* (Salem, Mass., 1826), 70–71; Helen Lathrop to Amy Aldis Bradley, 15 Feb. 1894, Bradley Family Papers, Arthur and Elizabeth Schlesinger Library on the History of Women in America, Radcliffe College. See also John S. C. Abbott, *The Mother at Home* (London, 1834), 68–69.

17. William B. Moore and Stephen C. Davies, "Rosa Is an Angel Now," *Western Pennsylvania Historical Magazine* 58 (1975): 221, 226, 336.

18. Hoare, *Hints for the Improvement of Early Education,* 67–70.

19. Carol Z. Stearns and Peter N. Stearns, *Anger: The Struggle for Emotional Control in America's History* (Chicago, 1986), chap. 3.

20. *Godey's* 34 (1846): 5–7; William Alcott, *The Young Husband* (Boston, 1840), 231; Orson S. Fowler, *Fowler on Matrimony* (New York, 1842), 105; Wise, *Bridal Greetings,* 23.

21. *Godey's* 47 (1853): 138–39; *Godey's* 47 (1853): 397; *Godey's* 28 (1843): 214; *Peterson's* 47, no. 6 (June 1865): 405–7; *Godey's* 2 (1840): 77–81; Stearns and Stearns, *Anger,* 44–49.

22. Martha Jane Jewsbury, *Letters Addressed to Her Young Friends* (Boston, 1829); see also John Angell James, *The Family Monitor* (Concord, N.H., 1829), 83; Hoare, *Hints;* Horace Bushnell, *Views of Christian Nurture* (Boston, 1847), 47. See also Catharine Beecher, *Treatise on Domestic Economy* (1841; repr. New York, 1871); R. Gordon Kelly, *Mother Was a Lady: Self and Society in Selected American Children's Periodicals, 1865–1890* (Westport, Conn., 1974), 74–75; Abbott, *Mother,* 51; T. S. Arthur, *Home Scenes* (Philadelphia, 1854), 54; Stearns and Stearns, *Anger,* chap. 3.

23. Stearns, *Jealousy,* chap. 2.

24. Max O'Rill, *Her Royal Highness, Woman* (New York, 1901); "Thoughts on Married Love," *Godey's Lady's Book,* Jan. 1847, 5; "Editor's Table: Wedded Love," *Godey's Lady's Book,* Aug. 1861, 170; Mary Rosemund, "Amiability vs. Jealousy," *Godey's Lady's Book,* Aug. 1876, 146–56; Mrs. E. B. Duffy, *What Every Woman Should Know* (Philadelphia, 1873), 64–65.

25. G. Stanley Hall, *Adolescence,* 2 vols. (New York, 1904) 1:357. Hall did admit, though vaguely, that if jealousy were considered more broadly, beyond the confines of romance alone, men might be as susceptible as women. T. S. Arthur, *The Young Wife* (Philadelphia, 1846); William A. Alcott, *The Young Husband* (Boston, 1841), 271; Mrs. Clarissa Packard [Caroline Howard Gilman], *Recollections of a Housekeeper* (New York, 1834), 53, 54–58.

26. Wise, *Bridal Greetings,* 122; James Bean, *The Christian Minister's Affectionate Advice to a Married Couple* (Boston, 1832), 17.

27. Alcott, *Young Husband,* 41; *Peterson's* 47, no. 6 (June 1865).

28. T. S. Arthur, *Advice to Young Ladies* (Boston, 1848); T. S. Arthur, *Advice to Young Men* (Boston, 1848; repr., Philadelphia, 1860); Stearns and Stearns, *Anger,* chap. 4.

29. American Institute of Child Life, *Problem of Temper* (Philadelphia, 1914), 1–5; *The Handbook of the Man of Fashion* (Philadelphia, 1847), 86; Cecil B. Hartley, *The Gentlemen's Book of Etiquette and Manual of Politeness* (Boston, 1873), 11, 155.

30. See for example Horatio Alger, *Luck and Pluck* (New York, 1869); G. Stanley Hall, "A Study of Anger," *American Journal of Psychology* 10 (1899): 683; American Institute of Child Life, *Problem of Temper,* 1–5; Hall, *Adolescence,* 1:221; Edwin Kirkpatrick, *Fundamentals of Child Study* (New York, 1903, repr., 1919), 136; Alice Birney, *Childhood* (New York, 1904), 66–67, 96.

31. Hall, "Anger," 638; American Institute of Child Life, *Problem of Temper,* 10–11.

32. Bushnell, *Views of Christian Nurture*, 253–55; Arthur, *Mother's Rule*, 288.
33. Oliver Optic [William Taylor Adams], *Now or Never* (Boston, 1856); Harry Castlemon, *George at the Wheel; or, Life in the Pilot-House* (Philadelphia, 1881), and *Frank on the Lower Mississippi* (Boston, 1868), 74–76.
34. "The Boy of Chancellorville," *Carleton* 1 (1865): 601–2; "Winning His Way," *Carleton* 1 (1865): 159; Edmund Kirkpatrick, "The Little Prisoner," *Our Young Folks*, 1885, 35; on the mother theme, see Jan Lewis, "Mother's Love: The Construction of an Emotion in Nineteenth-Century America," in Andrew E. Barnes and Peter N. Stearns, eds., *Social History and Issues in Human Consciousness* (New York, 1989), 207–29.
35. Stearns and Haggerty, "Role of Fear," 70–74.
36. *Oxford English Dictionary* (London, 1989), s.v. "sissy."
37. Felix Adler, *The Moral Instruction of Children* (New York, 1901), 194–95.
38. "Summing Up of John Graham, Esq., to the Jury, on the Past of the Defense, on the Trial of Daniel McFarland, May 6 and 9, 1878" (New York, 1870), 13; John D. Lawson, ed., *American State Trials* (St. Louis, Mo., 1928), 12:731–32.
39. "Family Government Essential to National Prosperity," *Mothers' Magazine*, 1833; see Lewis, "Mother's Love," 209–29; "The Connection between Piety and Usefulness in Mothers," *Mothers' Monthly Journal*, Jan. 1837, 12; see also "Maternal Influence," *Mothers' Magazine*, April 1841, 84; "The Mother's Power," *Mothers' Magazine*, 35, 1867, 221; L. E., "Home," *American Ladies' Magazine*, May 1830, 218, 217, 218; "The Happy Family," *Mothers' Magazine*, May 1839, 111; John A. Bolles, "The Influence of Women on Society," *American Ladies' Magazine*, June 1831, 256; Maria J. McIntosh, *Woman in America: Her Work and Her Reward* (New York, 1850), 77.
40. Reverend E. H. Chapin, "A Mother's Love," *Mother's Assistant and Young Lady's Friend*, July 1845, 9; Frederick, "Maternal Affection," *Casket*, April 1827, 134; "Extracts from Reports of Maternal Associations," *Mothers' Magazine*, Feb. 1841, 46; McIntosh, *Woman in America*, 25; Fanny Fern [Sarah P. Parton], *Ruth Hall and Other Writings*, Joyce W. Warren, ed. (New Brunswick, N.J., 1986), 24; Abbott, *The Mother at Home*, 6.
41. Lewis, "Mother's Love," 218–19.
42. Fanny Fern [Sarah P. Parton], "A Mother's Influence," in *Fern Leaves from Fanny's Port-Folio*, 2d ser. (Auburn and Buffalo, N.Y., 1854), 252, 256; Eliza Duffey, *The Relations of the Sexes* (New York, 1876), 91; Henry Chavasse, *Physical Life of Man and Woman* (Cincinnati, Ohio, 1871), 39; Orson Fowler, *Love and Parentage* (New York, 1856), 68.
43. Duffey, *Relations of the Sexes*, 219.
44. Karen Lystra, *Searching the Heart: Women, Men, and Romantic Love in Nineteenth-Century America* (New York, 1989), 35–43; Peter N. Stearns and Mark Knapp, "Men and Romantic Love: Pinpointing a Twentieth-Century Change," *Journal of Social History* 26 (1993): 769–96; Richard Henry Davey, *The Idle Man* (New York, 1822), 22; Frederick Saunders, *About Women, Love, and Marriage* (New York, 1868), 105, 143, and passim; Paoli Montegazza, *The Art of Taking a Wife* (New York, 1896), 217; Arthur, *Advice to Young Ladies*, 131, 164, and *Advice to Young Men*; see also T. S. Arthur, *The Young Husband* (Boston, 1841), for parallel sentiments addressed specifically to men.
45. "Two Lovers," *Presbyterian Banner*, 17 June 1875.
46. Paul C. Rosenblatt, *Bitter, Bitter Tears: Nineteenth-Century Diarists and Twentieth-Century Grief Theories* (Minneapolis, Minn., 1983). The Civil War brought expres-

sions of a more controlled approach to grief, with northern soldiers writing of the need for restraint on their part and that of the families back home. "Do not grieve too much," Michael Barton, *Good Men: The Character of Civil War Soldiers* (University Park, Pa., 1981). This theme, echoed also in World Wars I and II (see below, chap. 5), suggests an interesting emotional impact of war; but, in contrast to the twentieth-century experiences, it did not produce a lasting impulse toward control; Victorian culture reasserted itself in subsequent decades.

47. Nathaniel Hawthorne to Sarah Peabody, 15 March 1840, Hawthorne Collection, Harvard University; Lystra, *Searching the Heart,* 50; Reverend J. R. Miller, *Home-Making* (Philadelphia, 1882), 299.

48. Daniel Fiore, "Grandma's Through: Children and the Death Experience from the Eighteenth Century to the Present," unpublished honors paper, Carnegie Mellon University, 1992.

49. *McGuffey's Fourth Eclectic Reader* (1866); Richard Evans, "The Golden Stein," *Analytical Fourth Reader,* 1888; Martha Finley, *Elsie's Girlhood* (New York, 1872), 156; Louisa May Alcott, *Little Women* (New York, 1868), 472, 488.

50. Words by George P. Morris, music adapted from "Long Time Ago," a "blackface" song by Charles E. Horn (who also wrote "Rocked in the Cradle of the Deep"), in William R. Ward, ed., *The American Bicentennial Songbook* (New York, 1975), 2:155. In addition to songs and schoolbook references, a vast amount of popular art, including school paintings and samplers, was devoted to mourning themes between 1820 and the late nineteenth century. See Teresa M. Flanagan, *Mourning on the Pejepscot* (Lanham, Md., 1992).

51. Nicholas E. Tawa, *Sweet Songs for Gentle Americans: The Parlour Song in America, 1790–1860* (Bowling Green, Ohio, 1980), 134; "Literary publications developed a near obsession with the grave," writes Lewis O. Saum in "The Popular Mood of Pre–Civil War America," *Contributions in American Studies,* no. 46 (Westport, Conn., 1980), 90. L. Covey, in *The American Pilgrimage: The Roots of American History, Religion, and Culture* (New York, 1961), quotes a poem written by Abraham Lincoln in 1846, "My Childhood Home I See Again," which ends: "Till every sound appears a knell, / And every spot a grave." See also David Stannard, *Death in America* (Philadelphia, 1975); Charles Jackson, ed., *Passing: The Vision of Death in America* (Westport, Conn., 1977); *Christy's Plantation Melodies #2* (Philadelphia, 1858); *Buckley's Ethiopian Melodies* (New York, 1853–1857).

52. *Buckley's Ethiopian Melodies.*

53. Philip J. Greven, Jr., *Spare the Child: The Religious Roots of Punishment and the Psychological Impact of Physical Abuse* (New York, 1991); John Spurlock, "The Free Love Network in America, 1850 to 1860," *Journal of Social History* 21 (1988): 765–80, and *Free Love: Marriage and Middle-Class Radicalism in America, 1825–1866* (New York, 1989).

54. Lystra, *Searching the Heart;* Judith Ann Dulberger, "Refuge or Repressor: The Role of the Orphan Asylum in the Lives of Poor Children and Their Families in Late-Nineteenth-Century Urban America," Doctor of Arts diss., Carnegie Mellon University, 1989.

55. Jan Lewis, *The Pursuit of Happiness: Family and Values in Jefferson's Virginia* (New York, 1983); Suzanne Lebsock, *The Free Women of Petersburg: Status and Culture in a Southern Town, 1784–1860* (New York, 1984).

56. Steven Stowe, in *Intimacy and Power in the Old South: Ritual in the Lives of the Planters* (Baltimore, Md., 1987), deals explicitly with the "deep, tense rivalry among

men" (2), though without treating jealousy directly. See also Bertram Wyatt-Brown, *Southern Honor* (New York, 1982), especially chaps. 8 and 12; Dickson Bruce, Jr., *Violence and Culture in the Antebellum South* (Austin, Tex., 1979), 67–89; Daniel Blake Smith, *Inside the Great House: Planter Family Life in the Eighteenth-Century Chesapeake Society* (Ithaca, N.Y., 1980), 61–76; and, on the growing stress on romantic love, Lewis, *The Pursuit of Happiness*.

57. Michael Barton, *Goodmen: The Character of Civil War Soldiers* (University Park, Pa., 1981).

58. But see Stephen Frank, " 'Rendering Aid and Comfort': Images of Fatherhood in the Letters of Civil War Soldiers from Massachusetts and Michigan," *Journal of Social History* 26 (1992): 5–32.

59. Rhys Isaac, *The Transformation of Virginia, 1740–1790* (Chapel Hill, N.C., 1982); Kenneth Lockridge, *On the Sources of Patriarchial Rage: The Commonplace Books of William Byrd and Thomas Jefferson and the Gendering of Power in the Eighteenth Century* (New York, 1992); see also Philip J. Greven, Jr., *Protestant Temperament: Patterns of Childrearing, Religious Experience, and the Self in Early America* (New York, 1977) on regional differences in the colonial period.

60. Bruce, *Violence and Culture in the Antebellum South*; Jay Mechling, "National Character and Adult Personality Consequents of American Child-Rearing Practices, 1794–1830: The Southern Subset," unpublished paper, 1968. I am grateful to Professor Mechling for sharing this paper.

61. Frank, " 'Rendering Aid and Comfort.' "

62. Peter N. Stearns, "Girls, Boys, and Emotions: Redefinitions and Historical Change," *Journal of American History* (1993): 36–74; Hall, *Adolescence*, vol. 1, passim; Howard R. Garis, *Uncle Wiggily's Story Book* (New York, 1921), 4 (I am grateful to Clio Stearns, who called this passage to my attention); *Ladies Home Journal*, Sept. 1905, 40; *Ladies Home Journal*, March 1905, 10; *Ladies Home Journal*, Feb. 1910, 30.

63. Arthur, *Mother's Rule*, 168–71; Arthur, *Advice to Young Ladies*; Jay Mechling, "Courage and Heroism in Everyday American Life, 1890–1930," paper presented to American Studies Association Annual Meeting, New Orleans, Nov. 1990. Note that women's courage was cited in dealing with misfortune. The *New York Times* in 1801 talked about women's superior "courage and patience" as a reason they committed suicide less often than men. *New York Times*, 17 Jan. 1861, 2:1; see Howard Kushner, "Suicide, Gender, and the Fear of Modernity in Nineteenth-Century Medical and Social Thought," *Journal of Social History* 26 (1993).

64. Lydia Sigourney, *Girl's Reading Book* (Newburgh, N.Y., 1847), 217; Alcott, *Little Women* (1868; repr., New York, 1984), 318–27; Jacob Abbott, *Rollo at Play* (New York, 1860). For general discussion of the Rollo series, see Wishy, *Child and the Republic*, 47.

65. Robert M. Ireland, "Insanity and the Unwritten Law," *American Journal of Legal History* 32 (1988): 157–72, and "The Libertine Must Die: Sexual Dishonor and the Unwritten Law in the Nineteenth-Century United States," *Journal of Social History* 23 (1989).

66. Lewis, "Mother's Love," 217–19; *Mother's Magazine*, 1833, 23–24; "Report of the Philadelphia Union Maternal Association," *Mothers' Monthly Journal*, June 1837, 93; "The Satin Pelisse," *American Ladies' Magazine*, Dec. 1830, 540; Abbott, *Mother*, 66.

67. John Starrett Hughes, "The Madness of Separate Spheres: Insanity and Masculinity in Victorian Alabama," in Mark Carnes and Clyde Griffen, eds., *Meanings for Man-*

hood: *Constructions of Masculinity in Victorian America* (Chicago, 1990), 67–78; Fern, *Ruth Hall*, 24.

68. Stearns and Knapp, "Men and Romantic Love"; Saunders, *About Women, Love, and Marriage*; T. S. Arthur, *Advice to Young Men.*

69. Demos, "Shame and Guilt in Early New England," 69–86.

70. Charles J. Hoadly, ed., *Records of the Colony and Plantation of New Haven*, 2 vols. (Hartford, Conn., 1867–1868), 2:136; *Essay Court Records* 8:303; J. K. Hosmer, ed., *Winthrop's Journal*, 2 vols. (Boston, 1908), 1:283.

71. Sedgwick, *Home.*

72. A good example of this plot line can be found in the immensely popular story by T. S. Arthur, *Ten Nights in a Bar-Room* (1854; repr., Donald A. Koch, ed., Cambridge, Mass., 1974); solitary confinement quotation from David Rothman, *The Discovery of the Asylum: Social Order and Disorder in the New Republic* (Boston, 1971), 83.

73. Kasson, *Rudeness and Civility*, 114; Elias, *Civilizing Process* (New York, 1978), makes the same point about "civilization's" expansion of embarrassment—as behavioral rules increased, so did opportunities for feeling shamed or embarrassed in certain settings. See Susan Miller, *The Shame Experience* (New York, 1985); David Ausubel, "Relationships between Shame and Guilt in the Socializing Process," *Psychological Review* 62 (1955): 378–90; Janice Lindsay-Hartz, "Contrasting Experiences of Shame and Guilt," *American Behavioral Scientist* 24 (1984).

74. Anne Vincent-Buffault, *The History of Tears: Sensibility and Sentimentality in France* (New York, 1991).

75. Amariah Brigham, "Statistics of Suicides," *American Journal of Insanity* 4 (1848): 2437. See Kushner, "Suicide, Gender, and the Fear of Modernity"; Thomas Haskell, "Capitalism and the Origin of Humanitarian Sensibility," *American Historical Review* 90 (1980): 339–61, 517–60; William Ellery Channing, "The Demands of the Age in the Ministry" (1838), in *Works* (Boston, 1848), 3:147. The importance of intensity in Victorian culture is a key theme in Peter Gay's recent book, *The Civilization of Hatred* (New York, 1993).

76. Wishy, *Child and the Republic*; Kelly, *Mother Was a Lady*. For the various sources of adult standards for socialization in the nineteenth century and how they could move in complementary, even when not identical, directions, see Daniel T. Rodgers, "Socializing Middle-Class Children: Institutions, Fables, and Work Values in Nineteenth-Century America," *Journal of Social History* 13 (1980): 354–67; Gillian Avery, "Two Patterns of Childhood: American and English," *Hornbook Magazine* 60 (1984): 794–807. See also R. Gordon Kelly, "American Children's Literature: A Historiographical Review," *American Literary Realism* 6 (1975): 89–107; and "Literature and the Historian," *American Quarterly* 26 (1974): 141–59; Patrick Dunae, "Penny Dreadfuls: Late Nineteenth-Century Boys' Literature and Crime," *Victorian Studies* 22 (1978): 133–50; and Gillian Avery, *Childhood's Pattern: A Study of the Heros and Heroines of Childhood Fiction, 1770–1950* (London, 1975). On choice of magazines and childrearing manuals, see chap. l, n. 25 and 26 above.

77. Hall, *Adolescence*, passim; see also G. Stanley Hall, "A Study of Anger," *American Journal of Psychology* 10 (1899): 615–91, and "A Study of Fear," *American Journal of Psychology* 8 (1897): 147–249; Carl Degler, "Darwinians Confront Gender," in D. L. Rhode, ed., *Theoretical Perspectives on Sexual Differences* (New York, 1990), 33–35; and Karen Offen, "Feminism and Sexual Difference in Historical Perspective," in ibid., 13–20.

78. Birney, *Childhood.*

79. Kasson, *Rudeness and Civility,* 34–146; *Handbook of the Man of Fashion,* 83; Hartley, *Gentlemen's Books,* passim.
80. Only women needed outlets that circumvented the emotional culture to some degree, because of the greater repression required of them. Illness might respond to limitations on anger and sexuality alike. Fierce commitment to reform movements, often based on public manipulation of the maternal and domestic role, allowed many women after 1870 to express anger, including anger at men as drunkards or sexual reprobates. But this outlet, though contrary to gender rules, simply transposed to reform-minded adult women some of the same targeting urged on men; to this extent even maverick women could fit into the larger culture of intensity. The fact remains that the need for approved releases from most normal emotional rules was much less great than that required for the physical and sexual restrictions—and much less than would develop in the twentieth century in response to a very different emotionology.

3. Evaluating the Victorian Emotional Style

1. Arthur Mitzman, "The Civilizing Offensive: Mentalities, High Culture, and Individual Psyches," *Journal of Social History* 20 (1987): 663–88. One important complication needs attention, though it is peripheral to the present analysis. Nineteenth-century middle-class culture was not the same throughout the Western world, though it contained some similar ingredients. French culture, for example, never developed the angel-in-the-house view of women. Continental European emotionology may have been more formal and repressive than American, just as chaperonage and other restrictions were more common in crucial personal relationships. Excessive generalization about Victorianism creates part of the misleading simplification of the nineteenth-century pattern in any particular Western society.
2. Peter N. Stearns and Deborah C. Stearns, "Historical Issues in Emotions Research: Causation and Timing," *Social Perspectives on Emotion* 2 (1994), forthcoming; Claire Armon-Jones, "The Thesis of Constructionism," in Rom Harré, ed., *The Social Construction of Emotions* (New York, 1986), 32–56, and "The Social Functions of Emotion," in *Social Construction of Emotions,* 57–83; Arlie Russell Hochschild, "Emotion Work, Feeling Rules, and Social Structure," *American Journal of Sociology* 85 (1979): 551–75.
3. Stearns and Stearns, "Historical Issues in Emotions Research"; James R. Averill, "A Constructivist View of Emotion," in R. Plutchick and H. Kellermar, eds., *Theories of Emotion,* vol. 1, *Emotion: Theory, Research, and Experience* (New York, 1980), 305–39. Hochschild, "Emotion Work," 551–75.
4. Stearns and Stearns, "Historical Issues in Emotions Research"; Robert V. Wells, "Family Size and Fertility Control in Eighteenth-Century America: A Study of Quaker Families," *Population Studies* 25 (1971): 73–82; Peter N. Stearns and Timothy Haggerty, "The Role of Fear: Transitions in American Emotional Standards for Children, 1850–1950," *American Historical Review* 96, no. 1 (1991): 63–94.
5. Lynn Lofland, "The Social Shaping of Emotion: The Case of Grief," *Symbolic Interaction* 8, no. 2 (1985): 171–90; Steven Seidman, *Romantic Longings: Love in America, 1830–1980* (New York, 1991); Ellen K. Rothman, *Hands and Hearts: A History of Courtship in America* (Cambridge, Mass., 1987); E. Anthony Rotundo, "Romantic Friendship: Male Intimacy and Middle-Class Youth in the Northern United States, 1800–1900," *Journal of Social History* 23 (1989): 1–25.
6. Phillipe Ariès, *The Hour of Our Death* (New York, 1981); David Edward Stannard,

The Puritan Way of Death: A Study in Religion, Culture, and Social Change (Ann Arbor, Mich., 1975).

7. Jan Lewis, "Mother's Love: The Construction of an Emotion in Nineteenth-Century America," in Andrew E. Barnes and Peter N. Stearns, eds., *Social History and Issues in Human Consciousness* (New York, 1989), 209–29; Barbara Welter, "The Cult of True Womanhood, 1820–1860," *American Quarterly* 18 (1966): 151–74.

8. Benjamin N. Nelson, *The Idea of Usury, from Tribal Brotherhood to Universal Motherhood* (Princeton, N.J., 1949); Edmund Leites, *The Puritan Conscience and Modern Sexuality* (New Haven, Conn., 1985), and "The Duty to Desire: Love, Friendship, and Sexuality in Some Puritan Theories of Marriage," *Journal of Social History* 15 (1982): 383–407; Peter Burke, *Popular Culture in Early Modern Europe* (New York, 1978); Norbert Elias, *The Civilizing Process: The History of Manners,* trans. Edmund Jephcott (New York, 1978); Rhys Isaac, *The Transformation of Virginia, 1740–1790* (Chapel Hill, N.C., 1982); Philip J. Greven, *The Protestant Temperament: Patterns of Child-Rearing, Religious Experience, and the Self in Early America* (New York, 1977).

9. Christopher Clark, *The Roots of Rural Capitalism: Western Massachusetts, 1780–1860* (Ithaca, N.Y., 1990).

10. Daniel T. Rodgers, "Socializing Middle-Class Children: Institutions, Fables, and Work Values in Nineteenth-Century America," *Journal of Social History* 13 (1980): 354–67.

11. Richard L. Bushman and Claudia L. Bushman, "The Early History of Cleanliness in America," *Journal of American History* 74 (1991): 1213–38; John F. Kasson, *Rudeness and Civility: Manners in Nineteenth-Century Urban America* (New York, 1990).

12. Oliver Optic [William Taylor Adams], *On the Staff* (Boston, 1896), 398–400. The changing response of boys and boys' literature to the Civil War has been commented on by Sam Pickering in "A Boy's Own War," *New England Quarterly* 48 (1975): 362–77; see also Oliver Optic, *On the Blockade* (Boston, 1890), and *The Soldier Boy* (Boston, 1863).

13. Robert L. Griswold, "The Evolution of the Doctrine of Mental Cruelty in Victorian American Divorce, 1790–1900," *Journal of Social History* 20 (1986): 127–48.

14. Isaac, *Transformation of Virginia*; Kasson, *Rudeness and Civility*.

15. Kasson, *Rudeness and Civility*.

16. Peter N. Stearns, *Be A Man! Males in Modern Society* (New York, 1991); Mark C. Carnes and Clyde Griffen, eds., *Meanings for Manhood: Constructions of Masculinity in Victorian America* (Chicago, 1990).

17. Robert C. Solomon, *About Love: Reinventing Romance for Our Times* (Tampa, Fla., 1989). Randolph Trumbach, *The Rise of the Egalitarian Family: Aristocratic Kinship and Domestic Relations in Eighteenth-Century England* (New York, 1978); William J. Goode, "The Theoretical Importance of Love," *American Sociological Review* 24 (1959): 38–47; W. J. Walter, "The Jealous Lover," *Godey's Lady's Book,* Nov. 1841, 193; Mary Rosemund, "Amiability vs. Jealousy," *Godey's Lady's Book,* Aug. 1876, 156, 146–56.

18. Barbara Duder, "Medicine and the Healing of the Body," in J. Lachmund and Gunna Stollberg, eds., *The Social Contruction of Illness* (Stuttgart, 1992), 39–53. See also Roger Smith, *Inhibition: History and Meaning in the Sciences of Mind and Brain* (Berkeley, Calif., 1992), chap. 2. At the scientific level, new beliefs in the mind regulating a bodily machine encouraged study of inhibition—including the introduction of the word itself in 1858. Catherine Gallagher and Thomas Laqueur, eds., *The*

Making of the Modern Body: Sexuality and Society in the Nineteenth Century (Berkeley, Calif., 1987).

19. Kasson, *Rudeness and Civility.*

20. Lewis, "Mother's Love"; Ann Douglas, *The Feminization of American Culture* (New York, 1978); Philip G. Slater, *Children in the New England Mind* (Hamden, Conn., 1977); Paul Charles Hachten, "From Wicked Philosopher to Moralist Poet: Pittsburgh's Presbyterian Mentality and the Rise of Pleasure-Seeking," undergraduate honors thesis, Carnegie Mellon University, 1991.

21. Mary P. Ryan, *Cradle of the Middle Class: The Family in Oneida County, New York, 1790–1865* (New York, 1981); Richard Rabinowitz, *The Spiritual Self in Everyday Life: The Transformation of Personal Religious Experience in Nineteenth-Century New England* (Boston, 1990); Philip J. Greven, Jr., *Spare the Child: the Religious Roots of Punishment and the Psychological Impact of Physical Abuse* (New York, 1991).

22. Lewis, "Mother's Love"; Karen Lystra, *Searching the Heart: Women, Men, and Romantic Love in Nineteenth-Century America* (New York, 1989); Steven Seidman, "The Power of Desire and the Danger of Pleasure: Victorian Sexuality Reconsidered," *Journal of Social History* 24 (1990): 47–68; Byron Caldwell Smith, *The Love-Life of Byron Caldwell Smith* (New York, 1930); Gilbert Barnes and Dwight Dumon, eds., *Letters of Theodore D. Weld, Angelina Grimke Weld, and Sarah Grimke* (New York, 1934), 588, 625.

23. Peter N. Stearns and Mark Knapp, "Men and Romantic Love: A Twentieth-Century Transition," *Journal of Social History* 26 (1993), 769–96.

24. Andrew Carnegie, "Deed of Trust—Carnegie Hero Fund Commission," in *Annual Report of the Carnegie Hero Fund Commission* (Pittsburgh, Pa., 1930), 9–11.

25. Gustav Kobbe, "Every-Day Heroism," *Century* 55 (1897–98): 401; Jay Mechling, "Everyday Heroism and the Real Self in America, 1890–1930," paper presented to the American Studies Association, New Orleans, 1990.

26. G. Stanley Hall, *Adolescence: Its Psychology and Its Relations to Physiology, Anthropology, Sociology, Sex, Crime, Religion, and Education,* 2 vols. (New York, 1904); Benjamin G. Rader, *American Sports: From the Age of Folk Games to the Age of Spectators* (Englewood Cliffs, N.J., 1983); Anthony M. Platt, *The Child Savers: The Invention of Delinquency* (Chicago, 1969); Martha H. Verbrugge, *Able-bodied Womanhood: Personal Health and Social Change in Nineteenth-Century Boston* (New York, 1988).

27. Robert M. Ireland, "The Libertine Must Die: Sexual Dishonor and the Unwritten Law in the Nineteenth-Century United States," *Journal of Social History* 23 (1989); Joshua Dressler, "Rethinking Heat of Passion: A Defense in Search of a Rationale," *Journal of Criminal Law and Criminology* 73 (1982): 421–34; Rex v. Greening (1913) 23 Cox Crim. C. 601, 603; Scroggs v. State, 94 Ga. App. 28, 93 S.E. 2d 583 (1956); Jeremy D. Weinstein, "Adultery, Law and the State: A History," *Hastings Law Journal,* Nov. 1986, 219–38; Texas Penal Code, art. 1220 (1925).

28. Steven Stowe, *Intimacy and Power in the Old South: Ritual in the Lives of the Planters* (Baltimore, Md., 1987), deals best with the "deep, tense rivalry among men" (21), though without treating jealousy directly. See also Bertram Wyatt-Brown, *Southern Honor* (New York, 1982), esp. chaps. 8 and 12; Dickson Bruce, Jr., *Violence and Culture in the Antebellum South* (Austin, Tex., 1979), 67–89.

29. George G. Killinger, ed., *Penology: The Evolution of Corrections in America* (St. Paul, Minn., 1978); Kermit Hall, ed., *Police, Prison, and Punishment* (Hamden, Conn.,

1987); Blake McKelvey, *American Prisons: A History of Good Intentions,* 2d ed. (New York, 1974); Roger Wertheimer, "Understanding Retribution," *Criminal Justice Ethics,* 1983, 15–36.

30. Ireland, "The Libertine Must Die."
31. Lawrence M. Friedman and Robert V. Percival, "Who Sues For Divorce? From Fault through Fiction to Freedom," *Journal of Legal Studies* 104 (1982): 79; Griswold, "Evolution of the Doctrine of Mental Cruelty," 127–48.
32. Sheffield v. Sheffield, 3 Texas Reports 87 (1848). Some judges even went so far as to insist that a guarantee of virtual marital indissolubility not only brought moral order but also promoted personal happiness. Drawing once again from Lord Stowell's 1790 decision, an Ohio court in 1859 and a Massachusetts court in 1867 quoted approvingly the English jurist's assumption "that the general happiness of the married life is secured by its indissolubility. When people understand that they must live together, except for a very few reasons known to the law they learn to soften by mutual accommodation, that yoke which they know they cannot shake off. They become good husbands, and good wives, for necessity is a powerful master in teaching the duties which it imposes." See Duhme v. Duhme, 3 Ohio Decisions 99–100 (1859); and Bailey v. Bailey, 97 Massachusetts Reports 381–81 (1867).
33. Bailey v. Bailey, 97 Massachusetts Reports 381–81 (1867).
34. Carpenter v. Carpenter, 30 Kansas Reports 744 (1883); other decisions picked up on this interpretation: Avery v. Avery, 5 Pacific Reporter 418–22 (Kansas, 1885); Lyle v. Lyle, 86 Tennessee Reports 372–76 (1887); and Mason v. Mason, 131 Pennsylvania State Reports 161–65 (1890).
35. Barnes v. Barnes, 30 Pacific Reporter 299 (California, 1892).
36. Viviana Zelizer, *Pricing the Priceless Child* (New York, 1985); Vivian Fox and Marten Quilt, *Loving, Parenting, and Dying: The Family Cycle in England and America* (New York, 1980).
37. Ralph Houlbrooke, ed., *Death, Ritual, and Bereavement* (Boston, 1989). On the importance of ritual in handling and expressing grief, Robert V. Wells, "Taming the 'King of Terrors': Ritual and Death in Schenectady, New York, 1844–1860," *Journal of Social History* 27 (1994), forthcoming; Maris Vinovskis, "Angels' Heads and Weeping Willows: Death in Early America," *American Antiquarian Society, Proceedings* 86 (1976): 273–302.
38. Lewis O. Saum, "Death in the Popular Mind of Pre–Civil War America," in David E. Stannard, ed., *Death in America* (Pittsburgh, 1975), 33, 38; David E. Stannard, *The Puritan Way of Death: A Study in Religion, Culture, and Social Change* (Ann Arbor, Mich., 1976), 247–55, 258; Stanley B. Burns, M.D., *Sleeping Beauty: Memorial Photography in America* (Altadena, Calif., 1990), 107; Kenneth L. Ames, "Ideologies in Stone Meanings in Victorian Gravestones," *Journal of Popular Culture* 14 (1981): 641.
39. Henry Adams, *Democracy: An American Novel* (New York, 1952), 144.
40. Joan Jacobs Brumberg, *Fasting Girls: The Emergence of Anorexia Nervosa as a Modern Disease* (Cambridge, Mass., 1988); Edward Shorter, "Paralysis: The Rise and Fall of A 'Hysterical' Symptom," in Peter N. Stearns, ed., *Expanding the Past: A Reader in Social History* (New York, 1988), 215–48.
41. Elizabeth Fox-Genovese, *Within the Plantation Household: Black and White Women of the Old South* (Chapel Hill, N.C., 1989), 250–51; Elizabeth Parsons-Channing, *Autobiography* (Boston, 1907); Lydia Howard Sigourney, *Lucy Howard's Journal* (New York, 1858), 6–7; Lloyd DeMause, ed., *History of Childhood* (New York,

1974); Patricia Branca, *Silent Sisterhood: Middle-Class Women in the Victorian Home* (Pittsburgh, 1975), 95–113; Margaret Elizabeth Sangster, *An Autobiography* (New York, 1909), 143 ff. For a modern statement that anger not expressed causes self-alienation, see Jean Baker Miller, "The Construction of Anger in Women and Men," Stone Center for Developmental Services and Studies, Work in Progress, no. 83-01 (Wellesley, Mass., 1983). Charlotte Gilman, *Recollections of a Southern Matron* (New York, 1852), 296–98. See also Stearns and Stearns, *Anger: The Struggle for Emotional Control in America's History* (Chicago, 1986), chaps. 3 and 4; Ethan Smith, ed., *Memoirs of Mrs. Abigail Bailey* (1815; repr., New York, 1980), 14 ff., 17.

42. Winnifred Babcock, *Me: A Book of Remembrance* (New York, 1915), 231, 276, 349–50; Michael P. Weber and Peter N. Stearns, eds., *The Spencers of Amberson Avenue* (Pittsburgh, 1983), 121–24.

43. David M. Katzman, *Seven Days a Week: Women and Domestic Service in Industrializing America* (New York, 1987); Daniel E. Sutherland, *Americans and Their Servants: Domestic Service in the United States from 1800 to 1920* (Baton Rouge, La., 1981); Catherine E. Beecher, *Treatise on Domestic Economy* (1841; repr., New York, 1970), 134, 122, 139–40.

44. C. B. Zachary, *Personality Adjustments in School Children* (New York, 1929); John W. M. Whiting and Irwin L. Child, *Child Training and Personality* (New Haven, Conn., 1953); James R. Averill, *Anger and Aggression; An Essay on Emotion* (New York, 1982); M. R. Yarrow, J. D. Campbell, and R. V. Burton, *Child-Rearing: An Inquiry into Research Methods* (San Francisco, 1968), 80. Jerome Kagan and H. A. Moss (*Birth to Maturity: A Study of Psychological Development* [New York, 1962]) argue that unpredictability is particularly salient for girls, whose anger is most fully repressed in childhood but who may turn out to be quite aggressive later in life.

45. Weber and Stearns, *Spencers*, 121–22.

46. Linda W. Rosenzweig, " 'The Anchor of My Life': Middle-Class American Mothers and College-Educated Daughters, 1880–1920," *Journal of Social History* 25 (1991): 5–25. See, for example, Dummer Papers, Schlesinger Library, Radcliffe College, letters to Katharine Dummer Fisher, box 45, folder 925; letter to "Happy" (Etherl) Dummer Mintzer, July 8, 1920, box 10, folder 165a; letters from Katharine Dummer Fisher, box 45, folder 895; letters from Frances Dummer Logan, box 12, folder 185; and letters from "Happy" (Ethel) Dummer Mintzer, box 10, folder 162.

47. Smith, *Love-Life*, 4, 9, 49, 73–74, 141–42; see also Seidman, "Power of Desire and Danger of Pleasure," 47–67; Smith, *Love-Life*, 9, 49, 73–74, 141–42; Barnes and Dumon, eds., *Letters of Theodore D. Weld*, 554, 583.

48. Karen Lystra, *Searching the Heart: Women, Men, and Romantic Love in Nineteenth-Century America* (New York, 1989); Ellen K. Rothman, *Hands and Hearts: A History of Courtship in America* (Cambridge, Mass., 1987); Seidman, *Romantic Longings;* Clelia Duel Mosher, *The Mosher Survey: Sexual Attitudes of Forty-Five Victorian Women*, James Mahood and Kristine Wenburg, ed. (New York, 1980).

49. Carroll Smith Rosenberg, *Disorderly Conduct: Visions of Gender in Victorian America* (New York, 1985); Sarah Butler Wistar, London, to Jeannie Field Musgrove, New York, 18 June. See also 3 August 1870, all cited in Smith Rosenberg; Mary Hallock (Foote) to Helena Dekay, 23 September 1873, cited in Smith Rosenberg, 56; Mary Grew, Providence, R.I., to Isabel Howland, Sherwood, N.Y., 27 April 1892, Howland Correspondence, Sophia Smith Collection, Smith College.

50. Rotundo, "Romantic Friendship," 1–25; Peter Gay, *The Tender Passion* (New York,

1986), 207–9; James Barnard Blake, Diary, 10 July 1851; see also Blake's entry for 13 July 1851, cited in Rotundo, "Romantic Friendships."

51. Mary Hallock (Foote) to Richard Gilder, 14 December 1873, cited in Smith Rosenberg, *Disorderly Conduct,* 56.

52. See for example Nancy Schrom Dye and Daniel Blake Smith, "Mother Love and Infant Death, 1750–1920," *Journal of American History* 73 (1986): 329–53; Laurel Thatcher Ulrich, *Good Wives: Images and Reality in the Lives of Women in Northern New England, 1650–1750* (New York, 1982); Jan Lewis, *Pursuit of Happiness: Family Values in Jefferson's Virginia* (New York, 1983), chaps. 3 and 5; Sylvia D. Hoffert, " 'A Very Peculiar Sorrow': Attitudes toward Infant Death in the Urban Northeast, 1800–1860," *American Quarterly* 39 (1987): 601–16.

53. Paul C. Rosenblatt, *Bitter, Bitter Tears: Nineteenth-Century Diarists and Twentieth-Century Grief Theories* (Minneapolis, Minn., 1983), 21, 38, 93 and passim; Diary of Nellie Wetherbee, unpublished manuscript, Bancroft Library, University of California, Berkeley, 1860.

54. Wells, "Taming the 'King of Terrors.' " It is of course important not to exaggerate differences in nineteenth-century *private* reactions from earlier grief expressions, but the volume and relative openness of expression point to some common distinctions.

55. E. Anthony Rotundo, "Boy Culture: Middle-Class Boyhood in Nineteenth-Century America," in Mark C. Carnes and Clyde Griffen, eds., *Meanings for Manhood* (Chicago, 1990), 15–36; Mark C. Carnes, *Secret Ritual and Manhood in Victorian America* (New Haven, Conn., 1989); Joseph F. Kett, *Rites of Passage: Adolescence in America, 1790 to the Present* (New York, 1977).

56. Lew Wallace, *Lew Wallace: An Autobiography* (New York, 1906), 122; see also John Doane Barnard, "Journal of His Life, 1801–1858," MS, Essex Institute, 3–4; Daniel Carter Beard, *Hardly a Man Is Now Alive: The Autobiography of Dan Beard* (New York, 1939), 47; Alphonso David Rockwell, *Rambling Recollections: An Autobiography* (New York, 1920), 56; Henry Seidel Canby, *The Age of Confidence: Life in the Nineties* (New York, 1934), 44; Charles Dudley Warner, *Being a Boy* (Boston, 1897), 50; Rotundo, "Boy Culture"; "Mrs. Manners," *At Home or Abroad; or, How to Behave* (New York, 1853), 112–13.

57. David Leverenz, *Manhood and the American Renaissance* (Ithaca, N.Y., 1989); Stephen Frank, " 'Rendering Aid and Comfort': Images of Fatherhood in the Letters of Civil War Soldiers from Massachusetts and Michigan," *Journal of Social History* 26 (1992): 5–32; Daniel J. Elazar, ed., "Working Conditions in the Early Twentieth Century: Testimony," *American Jewish Archives* 21 (1969): 163; L. G. Lindahl, "Discipline One Hundred Years Ago," *Personnel Journal* 28 (1949): 246; Tamara K. Hareven and Randolph Langenbac, *Amoskeag: Life and Work in an American Factory City* (New York, 1978), 352 and passim; see also Michael Santos, *Iron Workers in a Steel Age: The Case of the A. M. Byers Company, 1900–1969,* D.A. diss., Carnegie Mellon University, 1981.

58. Weber and Stearns, eds., *Spencers,* 123–24; Peter G. Filene, *Him/Herself: Sex Roles in Modern America* (New York, 1975).

59. M. M. Bradley and Peter Lang, "Emotional Processing: Perception, Imagery, and Memory," paper presented to the International Society for Research on Emotion, August 1992.

60. Ireland, "The Libertine Must Die," 27–43; "Thoughts on Married Love," *Godey's Lady's Book,* Jan. 1847, 6; Peter N. Stearns, *Jealousy: The Evolution of an Emotion*

in *American History* (New York, 1989), chap. 2; *The Art of Letter Writing in Love, Courtship, and Marriage* (New York, 1846).

61. Kenneth A. Lockridge and Jan Lewis, "Sally Has Been Sick: Pregnancy and Family Limitation among Virginia Gentry Women, 1780–1830," *Journal of Social History* 22 (1988): 5–19.

62. John Demos, "Shame and Guilt in Early New England," in Carol Z. Stearns and Peter N. Stearns, eds., *Emotion and Social Change: Toward a New Psychohistory* (New York, 1988), 69–85.

63. Rotundo, "Romantic Friendship"; Smith Rosenberg, *Disorderly Conduct*, 53–76; Mary Hallock (Foote) to Helena Gilder, 23 September 1873, cited in Smith-Rosenberg, *Disorderly Conduct*.

64. *The Art of Pleasing; or, The American Lady and Gentleman's Book of Etiquette* (Cincinnati, Ohio, 1855); Wells, "Taming the 'King of Terrors' "; *The Handbook of the Man of Fashion* (Philadelphia, 1847), 85; Cecil B. Hartley, *The Gentleman's Book of Etiquette and Manual of Politeness* (Boston, 1873), 80; Rosenblatt, *Bitter, Bitter Tears*; Ariès, *Hour of Our Death*.

65. Carol Z. Stearns, "Sadness," in Jeanette Haviland and Michael Lewis, ed., *Handbook of Emotions* (New York, 1993).

66. Stearns and Stearns, *Anger*, chap. 5; Jed Dannenbaum, *Drink and Disorder: Temperance Reform in Cincinnati from the Washington Revival to the WCTU* (Urbana, Ill., 1984).

67. Kasson, *Rudeness and Civility*, chap. 5; Thomas Embley Osmun [Alfred Ayres], *The Mentor: A Little Book for the Guidance of Such Men and Boys as Would Appear to the Advantage in the Society of Persons of the Better Sort* (New York, 1884); [Delano, Mortimer, and Reginald Harvey Arnold], *Simplex Munditiis* (New York, 1891); *Bad Breaks in Good Form* (New York, 1897).

68. Aaron Ben-Ze'ev, "Emotional Intensity," paper presented to the International Society for Research on Emotion, August 1992; N. H. Frijda, J. Ortony, J. Sonnemans, and G. Clore, "The Complexity of Intensity: Issues Concerning the Structure of Emotional Intensity," in M. Clark, ed., *Review of Personality and Social Psychology* (Beverly Hills, Calif., 1992).

4. From Vigor to Ventilation

1. Stephanie A. Shields and Beth A. Koster, "Emotional Stereotyping of Parents in Childrearing Manuals, 1915–1980," *Social Psychology Quarterly* 52 (1989): 44–55; William Byron Forbush, *The Character-Training of Children* (New York, 1919), 2:179–87.

2. Oliver Optic [William Taylor Adams], *On the Staff* (Boston, 1896), 389–400. The changing response of boys and boys' literature to the Civil War has been commented on by Sam Pickering in "A Boy's Own War," *New England Quarterly* 48 (1975): 362–77; see also Oliver Optic, *On the Blockade* (Boston, 1890), and *The Soldier Boy* (Boston, 1863); Felix Adler, *The Moral Instruction of Children* (New York, 1901), 72; Mrs. Theodore [Alice McLellan] Birney, *Childhood* (New York, 1904), 24–29.

3. Forbush, *Character-Training*, 2:157–66, 162–63.

4. Adler, *Moral Instruction*, 213–14.

5. G. Stanley Hall, "A Study of Fear," *American Journal of Psychology* 8 (1897): 147–248; Birney, *Childhood*, 24–29. The present section is not intended as a systematic inquiry into the evolution of formal psychological or psychiatric theories of fear

over the past century. This might be a useful additional project. Hall's article on fear, though less theoretical than is his wont, accumulated a hodgepodge of data on childish fears and sparked interest among both scholars and popularizers. See *American Journal of Psychology* 8–18 (1897–1917). The concentration on fear specified children, with occasional excursions into adult phobia. French work on the frequency of infant fears was also widely cited: thus the *American Journal of Psychology* reported Binet's study on infant fear (*Année psychologique,* 1895, 223) in *American Journal of Psychology* 7 (1896): 577. In all this, the emphasis was highly empirical, with little attention to causation.

6. Ben B. Lindsay and Wainwright Evans, *The Companionate Marriage* (New York, 1927), 72, 73, 86, 90.

7. Harold Anderson, *Children in the Family* (New York, 1937), 76.

8. Allan Fromme, *The Parents Handbook* (New York, 1956), 101; Peter N. Stearns and Timothy Haggerty, "The Role of Fear: Transitions in American Emotional Standards for Children, 1850–1950," *American Historical Review* (Feb. 1991); Ada Hart Arlitt, *The Child from One to Twelve* (New York, 1931), 113; Mary A. Boucquet, "Baby Fears," *Parents' Magazine* 21 (June 1946): 96; Gladys Groves, *Marriage and Family Life* (New York, 1942), 69.

9. Groves, *Marriage*, 69; John B. Watson, *Psychological Care of Infant and Child* (New York, 1928), 45; Forbush, *Character-Training,* 2:163.

10. Winnifred De Kok, *Guiding Your Child through the Formative Years* (New York, 1935), 76, 58–77. For a slightly more academic statement urging revision of parental reactions to children's fears, see Dorothy Canfield Fisher and Sidonie Gruenberg, *Our Children: A Handbook for Parents* (New York, 1932), 134–37.

11. U.S. Department of Labor, Children's Bureau, *Are You Training Your Child to Be Happy?* (Washington, D.C., 1930), 32.

12. D. H. Thom, *Child Management* (Washington, D.C., 1925), 12–15.

13. De Kok, *Guiding Your Child,* 76; Sidonie Gruenberg, ed., *Encyclopedia of Child Care and Guidance* (New York, 1952), 845–52.

14. Watson, *Psychological Care,* 45–68, 54, 68; see also M. C. Jones, "The Elimination of Children's Fears," *Journal of Experimental Psychology* 7 (1924): 382–90. Uses of Watsonianism permitted some interesting Victorian throwbacks. If children could be entirely manipulated, they might be taught mild versions of fear as the basis for forming subsequent courage; people did need to face risks. One popularizer boldly offered a subheading to her article, arguing that the new methods of teaching fear control should produce "a generation of young people braver than their elders." In other words, even as newly explicit attention was given to young children and to manipulative strategies, an ultimate goal of courage—including the use of the word itself—might persist, even though this was not characteristic of most statements of the 1930s. See Fisher and Gruenberg, *Our Children,* 137; Ruth Sapin, "Helping Children to Overcome Fear," *Parents' Magazine* 8 (1 May 1933): 14–16. The 1930s manuals that used Watsonian ideas without expressing a larger goal of courage (as opposed to a more limited, ad hoc prevention of fear) include D. Russel, *Children: Why Do We Have Them?* (New York, 1933); Arlitt, *Child from One to Twelve;* and E. R. Groves and G. H. Groves, *Wholesome Childhood* (New York, 1931).

15. "What to Do When Your Child Is Afraid," *Parents' Magazine* 2 (March 1927): 25–27. Helen L. Schulz, "Mother's Conquest of Fear," *Parents' Magazine* 10 (April 1935): 29–31; Boucquet, "Baby's Fears," 94–96; Lois Greenwood Howard, "What

to Do about Fear," *Parents' Magazine* 22 (March 1947): 175–77; Groves, *Marriage*, 69–72, reproduces Watsonian advice on fear almost literally.

16. Benjamin Spock, *The Common Sense Book of Baby and Child Care* (New York, 1945), 196–97, 283–97, 284, 295.

17. Fromme, *Parents Handbook*, 102–8. For a more representative statement, see Gruenberg, *Encyclopedia*, 845; Norma Cutts and Nicholas Moseley, *Better Home Discipline* (New York, 1952); V. von Valler Gilmer, *How to Help Your Child Develop Successfully* (New York, 1951). For *Parents' Magazine*'s adjustment to the new, more complex parental strategies, see Martin W. Piers, "Who's Afraid?" *Parents' Magazine* 24 (June 1949): 6, 95–99.

18. Arthur T. Jersild, et al., *Joys and Problems of Childrearing* (New York, 1949), 215 and passim; note that parental concerns were heightened through World War II's impact on children, although Jersild and his colleagues allowed for directly war-inspired fears in a separate category.

19. "Childhood Problems" section in *Parents' Magazine* 21 (March 1946): 34; 21 (May 1946): 46; 22 (October 1947): 35; 23 (May 1948): 34; 23 (July 1948): 42; and "Now This Is What I'd Do," *Parents' Magazine* 4 (January 1929): 24. See also Children's Welfare Federation of New York City, *Child Care Questions and Answers* (New York, 1948), 103–7, for a series of common parental concerns and appropriately anxious supportive strategies.

20. Arnold Gesell, Francis Ilg, and Laura Ames, *Youth: The Ages from Ten to Sixteen* (New York, 1956), 51, 65, 192.

21. Rupert Wilkinson, *American Tough: The Tough-Boy Tradition and American Character* (Westport, Conn., 1984).

22. Available studies on American children's fiction support the idea of a shift in tone during the 1920s, including a decline in heroic idealizations, but they have not developed a full characterization—partly because of a tendency to focus on literary quality and adult appreciation more than popularity and children's reactions. Still, a helpful guide is Sally McNall, "American Children's Literature, 1880–Present," in Joseph M. Hawes and N. Ray Hiner, eds., *American Childhood: A Research Guide and Historical Handbook* (Westport, Conn., 1988), 377–411, esp. 391–92. See also Deirdre Johnson, *Stratemeyer Pseudonyms and Series Books* (Westport, Conn., 1982). Although it focuses on England, Kristen Drotner's *English Children and Their Magazines, 1751–1945* (New Haven, Conn., 1988), aids in evaluating American patterns in the absence of a definitive study; see also Gillian Avery, *Childhood's Pattern: A Study of the Heroes and Heroines of Childhood Fiction, 1770–1950* (London, 1975), passim.

23. Franklin W. Dixon, *The Secret of the Lost Tunnel* (New York, 1950), 183, 206, and *The Mystery of Cabin Island* (New York, 1929), 198.

24. Paul Fussell, "The Real War, 1939–45," *Atlantic Monthly* 264, no. 2 (August 1989): 33–40. For a provocative discussion of fear in World War II, see Paul Fussell, *Wartime: Understanding and Behavior in the Second World War* (New York, 1989); D. L. Kirkpatrick, "How to Select Foremen," *Personnel Journal* 47 (1968): 262–70; Silas Warner, "Spotting the Neurotic—Helping the Maladjusted," *Personnel Journal* 36 (1957): 136–39. For the evolution of recommendations on job interview atmosphere, see *Personnel Journal*, 1940–1970. A lag of a few decades in institutionalization of new emotional standards is historically normal.

25. Sybil Foster, "A Study of the Personality Makeup and Social Setting of Fifty Jealous Children," *Mental Hygiene* 11 (1927): 533–71; Mabel Sewall, "Some Causes of

Jealousy in Young Children," *Smith College Studies in Social Work* 1 (1930–31): 6–22; Ruth E. Smalley, "The Influence of Differences in Age, Sex, and Intelligence in Determining the Attitudes of Siblings toward Each Other," *Smith College Studies in Social Work* 1 (1930–31): 23–44; D. M. Levy, "Studies in Sibling Rivalry," *American Orthopsychiatry Research Monograph,* no. 2 (1937); D. M. Levy "Rivalry between Children of the Same Family," *Child Study* 22 (1934): 233–61; A. Adler, "Characteristics of the First, Second, and Third Child," *Children* 3, no. 5 (1938): 14–39. Only one of these studies, but an interesting one, ran counter to the pessimistic findings about jealousy, noting the diversity of reactions among children and the frequency of intense affection: M. B. MacFarland, "Relationship between Young Sisters as Revealed in Their Overt Responses," *Journal of Experimental Education* 6 (1937): 73–79. But MacFarland's conclusions were ignored among the welter of findings that jealousy was a major problem and that its resolution depended on careful parental policy—almost certainly an exaggerated perception of a common (though decidedly not uniform) childhood response. See Judy Dunn and Carl Kendrick, *Siblings: Love, Envy, and Understanding* (Cambridge, Mass., 1982), passim.

26. Gordon Clanton, "Jealousy in American Culture, 1945–1985: Reflections from Popular Literature," in D. Franks and E. D. McCarthy, eds., *The Sociology of Emotions* (Greenwich, Conn., 1989), 179–93.

27. Beverly Cleary, *Ramona Forever* (New York, 1984), 176, 182. I am grateful to Clio Stearns and Julie Wiener for guidance in this literature; Peter N. Stearns, "Gender and Emotion: A Twentieth-Century Transition," in David D. Franks, ed., *Social Perspectives on Emotion* (Greenwich, Conn., 1992), 127–60.

28. Dorothy W. Baruch, *New Ways in Discipline: You and Your Child Today* (New York, 1949), 123; John C. Montgomery and Margaret Suydam, *America's Baby Book* (New York, 1951), 123; Spock, *Common Sense,* 2d ed. (1957); see also Brian Sutton-Smith and B. G. Rosenberg, *The Sibling* (New York, 1979), 260; David Black, "The Jealous Lover," *Mademoiselle* 89 (1983): 116; Margery Wilson, *How to Make the Most of a Wife* (Philadelphia, 1947), 131; Dorry Metcalf, *Bringing Up Children* (New York, 1947), 105; Bibi Wein, "Dealing with Jealousy," *Harper's Bazaar,* 1983, 207.

29. Thom, *Child Management,* 9–12; Children's Bureau, *Training Your Child,* 31; Child Study Association of America, *Guidance of Childhood and Youth* (New York, 1926), 100–101. This approach was repeated verbatim in a number of other manuals, though without attribution, perhaps because other, uncited authors might be jealous. Arlitt, *Child from One to Twelve;* Gruenberg, *Encyclopedia;* B. Harlock, *Child Development* (New York, 1954); Herman Vollmer, "Jealousy in Children," *American Journal of Orthopsychiatry* 16 (1946): 187.

30. Fromme, *Parents Handbook,* 93; Sidonie Gruenberg, *We the Parents* (New York, 1939), 90; Baruch, *New Ways,* 124, and *Understanding Young Children* (New York, 1949), 41; Montgomery and Suydam, *Baby Book,* 123; Daniel M. Levy, *Maternal Overprotection* (New York, 1943), 22–23; Haim Ginnott, *Between Parent and Child* (New York, 1965); Luella Cole and John J. B. Morgan, *Psychology of Childhood and Adolescence* (New York, 1947); Edmund Zilmer, *Jealousy in Children: A Guide for Parents* (New York, 1949); Mary M. Thomson, *Talk It Out with Your Child* (New York, 1953), 112; Foster, "Personality Makeup of Jealous Children," 53–77; Ruth Fedder, *You: The Person You Want to Be* (New York, 1957), 69.

31. De Kok, *Guiding Your Child,* 176.

32. Zilmer, *Jealousy in Children,* 85; Baruch, *New Ways,* 122–23; Joseph Teich, *Your Child and His Problems* (Boston, 1953), 101.

33. Montgomery and Suydam, *Baby Book,* 123–25; Spock, *Common Sense,* 272–79; Fromme, *Parents Handbook,* 251.

34. Teich, *Your Child,* 98; Margaret McFarland, *Relationships between Young Sisters* (New York, 1938), 67; "Family Clinic," *Parents' Magazine,* June 1955, 26; *Parents' Magazine,* 1954–59; Jersild, et al., *Joys and Problems,* 28–30, 87, 94; Gesell, Ilg, and Ames, *Youth,* passim.

35. Frank Caplan and Theresa Caplan, *The Second Twelve Months of Life* (New York, 1977); Carole Calladine and Andrew Calladine, *Raising Siblings* (New York, 1979), 31 and passim.

36. Lindsay and Evans, *Companionate Marriage,* 72.

37. Gordon Clanton and Lynn G. Smith, eds., *Jealousy* (Englewood Cliffs, N.J., 1977), 126; P. A. Sorokin, ed., *Explorations in Altruistic Love Behavior* (Boston, 1970), 18; Kingsley Davis, "Jealousy and Sexual Property," *Social Forces* 14 (1936): 395–405; Theodore Reik, *A Psychologist Looks at Love* (New York, 1944); Peter N. Stearns, *Jealousy: The Evolution of an Emotion in American History* (New York and London, 1989).

38. Edmund S. Conklin, *Principles of Adolescent Psychology* (New York, 1935), 254; see also Jerome M. Seidman, ed., *The Adolescent* (New York, 1953), 755–61; Francis S. Miller and Helen Laitern, *Personal Problems of the High School Girl* (New York, 1945), 72; Elizabeth B. Hurlock, *Adolescent Development* (New York, 1949).

39. Evelyn Duvall, *Facts of Life and Love for Teenagers* (New York, 1950), 210, 231.

40. Alexander Magoun, *Love and Marriage* (New York, 1956), 301, 304, 306; see also Judson T. Landis and Mary G. Landis, *A Successful Marriage* (Englewood Cliffs, N.J., 1958), 82; Evelyn M. Duvall and Dora S. Lewis, *Family Living* (New York, 1955), 19; Paul Popenoe, *Marriage Is What You Make It* (New York, 1950), 17 and passim; Paul Popenoe, *Marriage: Before and After* (New York, 1943), passim; Lear J. Saul, *Fidelity and Infidelity, and What Makes or Breaks a Marriage* (Philadelphia, 1961), 73; John Levy and Ruth Monroe, *The Happy Family* (New York, 1962), 89.

41. Nena O'Neill and George O'Neill, *Open Marriage: A New Life Style for Couples* (New York, 1984), 239, 240; Warren Mintz, review of *Open Marriage* by Nena O'Neill and George O'Neill, *Society* 2 (1974): 291–92; Clanton and Smith, *Jealousy,* 181, 195.

42. Carl R. Rogers, *Becoming Partners* (New York, 1972), 142, 181; Gay Talese, *Thy Neighbor's Wife* (New York, 1981); Carolyn Symonds, "Sexual Mate-Swapping: Violations of Norms and Reconciliation of Guilt," in J. M. Hensher, ed., *Studies in the Sociology of Sex* (New York, 1971), 87–88; Clanton and Smith, *Jealousy,* 181, 195; Lewis Terman, *Psychological Factors in Marital Happiness* (New York, 1938), 98–101; Ayala Pines and Eliot Aronson, "Antecedents, Correlates, and Consequences of Sexual Jealousy," *Journal of Personality* 51 (1983): 126–40; John Masterson, "Pretty Eyes and Green, My Love," *Psychology Today* 18 (1984): 71; Clanton, "Jealousy in American Culture."

43. Peter N. Stearns, "Anger and American Work: A Twentieth-Century Turning Point," in Carol Z. Stearns and Peter N. Stearns, eds., *Emotion and Social Change: Towards a New Psychohistory* (New York, 1988), 123–50; Faye E. Dudden, *Serving Women: Household Service in Nineteenth-Century America* (Middletown, Conn., 1983).

44. L. S. Gilbreth, *The Psychology of Management* (New York, 1919), 259; Robert F. Hoxie, *Scientific Management and Labor* (1915; repr., New York, 1966); August M. Kelley, *Shop Management* (New York, 1911); Frederick W. Taylor, *The Principles of Scientific Management* (New York, 1911); Judith A. Merkle, *Management and Ideol-*

ogy: *The Legacy of the International Scientific Management Movement* (Berkeley and Los Angeles, 1980).

45. Elton Mayo, *The Human Problems of an Industrial Civilization* (New York, 1933), 84 ff.; F. J. Roethisberger and William J. Dickson, *Management and the Worker* (Cambridge, Mass., 1941), 180 ff.; Walter Dill Scott, et al., *Personnel Management: Principles, Practices, and Point of View* (New York, 1941).

46. Harry W. Hepner, *Human Relations in Changing Industry* (New York, 1938), 96; Annette Garrett, *Counseling Methods for Personnel Workers* (New York, 1945), 71; Dale Carnegie, *How to Win Friends and Influence People* (New York, 1940), 2, 27, 68, 70, 156; R. C. Borden and Alvin Busse, *How to Win a Sales Argument* (New York, 1926), 7.

47. Ordway Teal, *Human Nature and Managers* (New York, 1933), 40; Hepner, *Human Relations*, 96; Nathaniel Cantor, *Employee Counseling: A New Viewpoint in Industrial Psychology* (New York, 1945), 64; Garrett, *Counseling Methods*, 71; see also Loren Baritz, *The Servants of Power: A History of the Use of Social Science in American History* (Middletown, Conn., 1960); C. S. Slowcombe, "Good Technique in Negotiating," *Personnel Journal* 14 (1935): 49; see also Lester Tarnopol, "Personality Differences between Leaders and Non-Leaders," *Personnel Journal* 37 (1958): 57–64; John B. Miner, *Personnel Psychology* (New York, 1969), 194; Erwin H. Schell, *The Techniques of Executive Control* (New York, 1934), 101.

48. Edward Kilduff, *The Private Secretary* (New York, 1915), 50, 57; see also later editions to 1935; see also Margery W. Davies, *Woman's Place Is at the Typewriter: Office Work and Office Workers, 1870–1930* (Philadelphia, 1982), 95. The routinization of claims of emotional control as part of professional competence in industrial psychology can be traced through standard textbooks (Hepner, *Human Relations*) and journals.

49. Roethisberger and Dickson, *Management and the Worker*, 212, 348; Joseph Tiffin and E. J. McCormick, *Industrial Psychology* (Englewood Cliffs, N.J., 1965), 188 ff.; Rexford Hersey, *Better Foremanship* (Philadelphia, 1961), 10; Glenn Gardiner, *Better Foremanship* (New York, 1941), 53–54; Charles C. Smith, *The Foreman's Place in Management* (New York, 1946), 119; W. E. Baer, "Do's and Don't's in Handling Grievances," *Personnel* 43 (1966): 30.

50. Burleigh B. Gardner and David G. Moore, *Human Relations in Industry* (Homewood, Ill., 1955), 272; Garrett, *Counseling Methods*, 120, 151 ff.; Helen Baker, *Employee Counseling* (Princeton, N.J., 1944), 40.

51. R. A. Sutermeister, "Training Foremen in Human Relations," *Personnel* 20 (1943): 13; Burt Scanlan, "Sensitivity Training: Clarification, Issues, Insights," *Personnel Journal* 50 (1970): 549.

52. Garrett, *Counseling Methods*; Baritz, *Servants of Power*, passim; Tiffin and McCormick, *Industrial Psychology*, 90, 188; Theodore Hewlett and Olive Lester, "Measuring Introversion and Extroversion," *Personnel Journal* 6 (1928): 352–610; Doncaster Humm, "Skill, Intelligence, and Temperament," *Personnel Journal* 22 (1943): 80–90; Stanley M. Herman, *The People Specialists* (New York, 1968), 245 ff.; Sutermeister, "Training Foremen," 13; Roethisberger and Dickson, *Management and the Worker*, 542; Baker, *Employee Counseling*, 40; William R. Spriegel, et al., *Elements of Supervision* (New York, 1942), 116; Cantor, *Employee Counseling*, 66.

53. Paul Johnson and J. C. Bledsoe, "Morale as Related to Perceptions of Leader Behavior," *Personnel Psychology* 26 (1973): 48–49; Guy W. Wadsworth, "Temperament Tests as Personnel Aids," *Personnel Journal* 15 (1937); Humm, "Skill, Intelligence,

and Temperament," 80–90; D. G. Humm and G. W. Wadsworth, "Temperament in Industry," *Personnel Journal* 21 (1942): 314–22; Baritz, *Servants of Power*, 155 ff.; Hewlett and Lester, "Measuring Introversion and Extroversion"; Donald A. Laird, *The Psychology of Selecting Men* (New York, 1927); G. W. Wadsworth, "How to Pick the Men You Want," *Personnel Journal* 14 (1935): 344.

54. Sutermeister, "Training Foremen," 13; Brian Kay, "Key Factors in Effective Foreman Behavior," *Personnel* 36 (1959): 28.

55. "The Humm-Wadsworth Temperament Scale," *Personnel Journal* 13 (1934): 322; on the evolution of testing to screen out hard-driving supervisors and specific programs as in Pillsbury Mills, see M. L. Gross, *The Brain Watchers* (New York, 1962); William H. Whyte, Jr., *The Organization Man* (New York, 1956), 140, 276 ff.; Robert M. Guion, *Personnel Testing* (New York, 1965); Ludwig Huttner and D. M. Stone, "Foreman Selection," in *Personnel Psychology* (1958); Laurence Siegel, *Industrial Psychology*, (Homewood, Ill., 1969), 165; John D. Cook, et al., *The Experience of Work: A Compendium and Review of LYP Measures and Their Use* (New York, 1981).

56. W. B. Dominick, "Let's Take a Good Look at the Foreman's Job," *Personnel* 21 (1944); Chris Argyris, *Interpersonal Competence and Organizational Effectiveness* (Homewood, Ill., 1962), 137, 174 ff., 255 ff.; Scanlan, "Sensitivity Training," 549–52.

57. W. Lloyd Warner, *American Life: Dream and Reality* (Chicago, 1962), 108.

58. Arlitt, *Child from One to Twelve*, 93; John Anderson, *Happy Childhood: The Development and Guidance of Children and Youth* (New York, 1933), 101; Emily Post, *Children Are People* (New York, 1940), 259.

59. Mayo, *Human Problems*, 84ff.; Garrett, *Counseling Methods*, 39.

60. John Dollard, et al., *Frustration and Aggression* (New Haven, Conn., 1939); Donald A. Laird and Eleanor Laird, *The Strategy of Handling Children* (New York, 1949), 78; Harold W. Bernard, *Toward Better Personal Adjustment* (New York, 1951), 170; B. E. Schwarz and B. A. Ruggieri, *Parent-Child Tensions* (Philadelphia, 1958), 48.

61. Schwarz and Ruggieri, *Parent-Child Tensions*, 89.

62. Esther Lloyd-Jones and Ruth Fedder, *Coming of Age* (New York, 1941), 35; Baruch, *New Ways*; William C. Menninger, ed., *How to Be a Successful Teenager* (New York, 1954), 141.

63. Anderson, *Children in the Family*, 106.

64. Baruch, *New Ways*, 7, 45, 61; De Kok, *Guiding Your Child*, 78ff.; Teich, *Your Child*, 142; Marion J. Radke, *The Relation of Parental Authority to Children's Behavior and Attitudes* (Minneapolis, Minn., 1946), 11–12; Metcalf, *Bringing Up Children*; Sidonie Gruenberg, *The Parents' Guide to Everyday Problems of Boys and Girls* (New York, 1958), 94.

65. Martin Bax and Judy Bermal, *Your Child's First Five Years* (New York, 1974); Irma S. Black, *Off to a Good Start* (New York, 1946), 140; Anna W. M. Wolf and Suzanne Szasz, *Helping Your Child's Emotional Growth* (New York, 1954); Grace Langdon and J. W. Staub, *The Discipline of Well-Adapted Children* (New York, 1952). Langdon had earlier written in the channeling mode (*Home Guidance for Young Children* [New York, 1931]); her conversion to greater rigor, like Dr. Spock's a bit later, is particularly interesting.

66. Susan Aukewa and Marilyn Kostick, *The Curity Baby Book* (New York, 1977), 12–13; Robert A. Baron, *Human Aggression* (New York, 1977), 269; Baruch, *New Ways*, 239; Florence Powdermaker and Louise Grimes, *Children in the Family: A*

Psychological Guide for Parents (New York, 1940), 240; Fritz Redl, *When We Deal with Children* (New York, 1966); Spock, *Common Sense*, 13, 48, 349; Violet Broad-ribb and Henry F. Lee, *The Modern Parents' Guide to Baby and Child Care* (Philadel-phia, 1973), 204; see also William E. Martin and Celia Stendler, *Child Behavior and Development* (New York, 1959), 221; Berthold E. Schwartz and B. A. Ruggieri, *You CAN Raise Decent Children* (New Rochelle, N.Y., 1971).

67. Lurre Nicholson and Laura Torbet, *How to Fight Fair with Your Kids . . . and Win!* (New York, 1980), 139; see also 18, 22, 32–33, 130–31, 287, 296.

68. *Ladies Home Journal*, Oct. 1955, 46; and June 1970, 102; Carol Zisowitz Stearns and Peter N. Stearns, *Anger: The Struggle for Emotional Control in America's History* (Chicago, 1986), chap. 7; Popenoe, *Marriage: Before and After*, 210–11.

69. Stearns, "Gender and Emotion."

70. William E. Blatz, "How to Deal with Anger and Fear," *Parents' Magazine*, 1932: 14.

71. Cas Wouters, "On Status Competition and Emotion Management," *Journal of Social History* 24 (1991): 699–717.

72. Baruch, *New Ways*.

73. American Psychiatric Association, *Diagnostic and Statistical Manual of Mental Disor-ders*, 3d ed. (Washington, D.C., 1980).

5. Dampening the Passions

1. Shula Sommers, "Adults Evaluating Their Emotions: A Cross-cultural Perspective," in Carol Zander Malatesta and Caroll E. Izard, eds., *Emotion in Adult Development* (Beverly Hills, Calif., 1984), 23–44; Joseph Veroff, Elizabeth Douvan, and Richard A. Kulka, *The Inner American: A Self-Portrait from 1957 to 1976* (New York, 1981), 106–21.

2. Carl Renz and Mildred Renz, *Big Problems on Little Shoulders* (New York, 1934), 84, 86–87; Robert I. Watson, *Psychology of the Child* (New York, 1959), 156.

3. Ruth Benedict, *The Chrysanthemum and the Sword* (Boston, 1946).

4. Dorothy Canfield Fisher and Sidonie Gruenberg, *Our Children* (New York, 1932), 119, 177; Renz and Renz, *Big Problems*, 86.

5. Benjamin Spock, *The Common Sense Book of Baby and Child Care* (New York, 1946), 195–96; Renz and Renz, *Big Problems*, 84, 86–87.

6. Renz and Renz, *Big Problems*, 87; Fisher and Gruenberg, *Our Children*, 119, 177; see also Arthur Jersild, *Child Psychology* (Englewood Clifs, N.J., 1960), 263, 287, 408; Martha Reynolds, *Children from Seed to Sapling* (New York, 1951), 89.

7. Renz and Renz, *Big Problems*, 84.

8. Fritz Redt, *When We Deal with Children* (New York, 1966), 136–37.

9. Robert Watson, *Psychology*, 460; Renz and Renz, *Big Problems*, 84.

10. Brian Melendez, "Honor Code Study," *Harvard University Report*, Sept. 1985. The vast majority of honor codes, where they exist, rode the final crest of Victorianism, from the 1890s to the 1920s. My thanks to Professor Ted Fenton for this information.

11. Peter N. Stearns, "Suppressing Unpleasant Emotions: The Development of a Twenti-eth-Century American Style," in Andrew E. Barnes and Peter N. Stearns, eds., *Social History and Issues in Human Consciousness: Some Interdisciplinary Connections* (New York, 1989); E. Goffman, "Embarrassment and Social Organization," *Ameri-can Journal of Sociology* 62 (1956): 264–71.

12. Phillipe Ariès, *The Hour of Our Death* (New York, 1981); Ralph Houlbrooke, ed., *Death, Ritual, and Bereavement* (London, 1989); Elisabeth Kubler-Ross, ed., *Death:*

The Final Stage of Growth (New York, 1975); Ivan Illich, Medical Nemesis (London, 1976).

13. Peter Uhlenberg, "Death and the Family," in N. Ray Hiner and Joseph M. Hawes, eds., Growing Up in America: Children in Historical Perspective (Urbana, Ill., 1985), 243–46.

14. Andrew White, The Warfare of Science with Theology (New York, 1894).

15. Lymon Abbott, "Christ, Secret of Happiness: The Joys of Sorrow," Outlook 83 (11 August 1908): 837–38; "Heart of Sorrow," Outlook 72 (6 December 1902): 775; see also "The Reality of Sorrow," Outlook 73 (24 January 1903): 197; Charles F. Dole, "Of Sorrow and Pain," Current Literature 29 (Deccember 1900): 694.

16. Rev. W. R. Inge, "The Vesper Hour," Chautauqua 62 (April 1911): 260; "The Great Adventure," Outlook 103 (22 March 1913): 605; Jane Belfield, "The Passing: An Emotional Monotone," Lippincott's Magazine 80 (September 1907): 374; "At the End of the Journey," Outlook 70 (25 January 1902): 216.

17. "Euthanasia: The Pleasures of Dying," New Englander and Yale Review 55 (September 1891): 231, 232–41.

18. H. B. Marriott-Watson, "Some Thoughts on Pain and Death," North American Review 173 (October 1901): 540–53; "The Dying of Death," Fortnightly Review 72 (August 1899): 246–69; "A New Medical Conception of Death," Current Literature 47 (October 1909): 453; see also Elie Metchnikoff and Dr. Henry Smith, "Why Not Live Forever?" Cosmopolitan 44 (September 1910): 436–46; "Pain, Life, and Death," Living Age 281 (May 1914): 368–70; "The Conquest of Love and Death," Current Literature 53 (August 1912): 1968.

19. Richard Fisguill, "Death and La Mort," North American Review 199 (January 1914): 95–107; "The German Idea of Death," Living Age 286 (August 1915): 523–29; "Editor's Diary," North American Review 186 (October 1907): 307–8; Arthur Reeves, "The High Cost of Dying," Harper's Weekly 52 (January 1913): 15; Graham Taylor, "Pioneer Inquiries into Burial Lots," Survey 28 (September 1911): 815–24.

20. "The Psychology of Sudden Death," Literary Digest 47 (December 1912): 1120; "Grieving," Independent 64 (1908): 476–77.

21. "Grieving," 476–77.

22. "The New Mien of Grief," Literary Digest 52 (February 1916): 292; see also "The Presence of Death," New Republic 11 (May 1917): 45–47; "Poor Death," Living Age 290 (September 1918): 360; "The Abolition of Death," Current Opinion 62 (April 1917): 270–71; "The Unseemliness of Funerals," Literary Digest 54 (April 1917): 1170; "And the Mourners Go about the Streets," Unpartizan Review 12 (July 1919): 176; Corra Harris, "Politics and Prayers in the Valley," Independent 71 (1916): 195.

23. "Agreeable Physical Aspects of Death," Current Opinion 72 (June 1922): 797; Sidney Lovett, "The Vocalism of Grief," Atlantic Monthly 130 (December 1922): 758–66; Sarah N. Cleghorn, "Changing Thoughts of Death," Atlantic Monthly, Dec. 1923, 812.

24. Geoffrey Gorer, Grief and Mourning in Contemporary Britain (New York, 1965).

25. H. A. Dallas, "What Is Death?" Living Age 332 (February 1927): 354–59; "The Tranquility of Death," Reader's Digest 56 (February 1950): 124–26; Marian Castle, "Decent Christian Burial," Forum 91 (April 1934): 253–55.

26. Merrill Clarke, "Instead of a Funeral," Christian Century 51 (July 1934): 894–95; see also Joshua Liebman, "Grief Is Slow Wisdom," Reader's Digest 51 (October 1947): 87–90; James Dabbs, "Give Sorrow Words," Christian Century 54 (February 1937): 247–49.

27. M. Beatrice Blankenship, "Death Is a Stranger," *Atlantic Monthly* 154 (December 1934): 649–57; Mabel S. Ulrich, "What of Death in 1931," *Scribner's Magazine* 89 (June 1931): 559–60; Milton Weldman, "America Conquers Death," *American Mercury* 10 (February 1927): 216–27; "Problems of Living," *Scholastic* 36 (April 1940): 31.

28. Dora K. Antrim, "Tragedy: With a Happy Ending," *Rotarian* 77 (October 1950): 26–28; Roy Dickerson, "Sorrow Can Be Faced," *Saturday Evening Post* 217 (July 1944): 17, 101; Ina May Greer, "Grief Must Be Faced," *Christian Century* 62 (February 1945): 269–70; Leslie Holman, "The War Department Report," *Ladies Home Journal*, July 1944, 142; see also James Gilkey, "If He Isn't Coming Back," *Woman's Home Companion* 70 (April 1943): 23.

29. Margaret Stroebe, et al., "Broken Hearts in Broken Bonds," *American Psychologist* 47 (1992): 1205–12; I am grateful to Baruch Fischoff for this reference. H. Lopata, "On Widowhood: Grief Work and Identity Reconstruction," *Journal of Geriatric Psychiatry* 8 (1975): 41–58.

30. Stroebe, "Broken Hearts;" James R. Averill and E. P. Nunley, "Grief as an Emotion and as a Disease; A Social-Constructionist Perspective," *Journal of Social Issues* 44 (1988): 79–95; J. Bowlby, *Attachment and Loss,* 3 vols. (Harmondsworth, England, 1971–80).

31. Cas Wouters, "Changing Regimes of Power and Emotion at the End of Life," *Netherlands Journal of Sociology* 26 (1990): 151–55.

32. D. A. Thom, *Child Management* (Washington, D.C., 1925), 14; Daniel Anthony Fiore, *"Grandma's Through": Children and the Death Experience from the Eighteenth Century to the Present,* unpublished honors paper, Pittsburgh, 1992; Peter Stearns and Timothy Haggerty, "The Role of Fear: Transitions in American Emotional Standards for Children, 1850–1950," *American Historical Review,* Feb. 1991; S. M. Gruenberg, ed., *The Encyclopedia of Child Care and Guidance* (New York, 1954), 170.

33. Ruth Sapin, "Helping Children to Overcome Fear," *Parents' Magazine* 8 (August 1933): 16; see also Donald A. Laird and Eleanor C. Laird, *The Strategy of Handling Children* (New York, 1949), 77; C. W. Hunicutt, *Answering Children's Questions* (New York, 1949), 22; Harold H. Anderson, *Children in the Family* (New York, 1941), 104–5.

34. Letter to Mrs. Frances Tuttle, Lucile, and Stephen, 9 August 1943, Tuttle Family Papers, Arthur and Elizabeth Schlesinger Library on the History of Women in America, Radcliffe College.

35. Allan Fromme, *The Parents Handbook* (New York, 1956), 66; Mrs. Theodore [Alice McLellan] Birney, *Childhood* (New York, 1905), 28, 239; Dorry Metcalf, *Bringing Up Children* (New York, 1947), 62–63; see also Sapin, "Helping Children," 16.

36. "In the Midst of Life," *Parents' Magazine* 20 (September 1945): 142; see also Lynn Chaloner, "When Children Ask about Death," *Parents' Magazine* 7 (April 1932); Sophie Falis, "When Children Confront Death," *Parents' Magazine* 18 (April 1942): 34; Mary M. Green, "When Death Came to School," *Parents' Magazine* 22 (April 1947): 20.

37. Jack London, *The Call of the Wild* (New York, 1903), 180–81; see also Evelyn J. Swenson, "The Treatment of Death in Children's Literature," *Elementary English* 49 (1972): 402.

38. Emily Post, *Etiquette: The Blue Book of Social Usage* (New York, 1934; 1st ed., New York, 1922), 413–17, 496.

39. Amy Vanderbilt, *New Complete Book of Etiquette* (New York, 1952), 121, 126.
40. Linda W. Rosenzweig, " 'The Anchor of My Life': Middle-Class American Mothers and College-Educated Daughters, 1880–1920," *Journal of Social History* 25 (1991): 5–25; E. S. Martin, "Mothers and Daughters," *Good Housekeeping* 64 (May 1917): 27; Ruth Ashmore, *Ladies Home Journal* 11 (September 1894): 16; "Antagonism between Mothers and Daughters," *Independent* 53 (26 September 1901): 2311; Gabrielle Jackson, *Mother and Daughter* (New York and London, 1905), 3, 63, 81, 85–86, 104, 114, 129.
41. Jan Lewis, "The American Doctrine of Motherhood in the Nineteenth and Twentieth Centuries," paper presented at the eighth Berkshire Conference on the History of Women, Douglass College, June 1990; Charolotte Perkins Gilman, *The Home, Its Work and Influence* (New York, 1903).
42. G. Stanley Hall, *Youth, Its Education, Regimen, and Hygiene* (New York, 1907), 303–61; S. Josephine Baker, *Child Hygiene* (New York, 1925), 22–27; James C. Fernald, *The New Womanhood* (Boston, 1891), 235–36.
43. Walter D. Edmonds, *Matchlock Gun* (1937; repr. New York, 1971); Franklin W. Dixon, *The Secret of the Lost Tunnel* (New York, 1950), 183, 206, and *The Mystery of Cabin Island* (New York, 1929), 198.
44. Regina G. Kunzel, "The Professionalization of Benevolence: Evangelicals and Social Workers in the Florence Crittenden Homes, 1915 to 1945," *Journal of Social History* 22 (1988): 21–40; Marion E. Kenworthy, "The Mental Hygiene Aspects of Illegitimacy," *Mental Hygiene* 5 (July 1921): 501.
45. Katherine P. Hewins, "A Study of Illegitimacy," *Survey* 46 (23 April 1921): 115; Amey Eaton Watson, "The Illegitimate Family," *Annals of the American Academy of Political and Social Science* 77 (May 1918): 103.
46. Stuart Alfred Queen and Delbert Martin Mann, *Social Pathology* (New York, 1925), 171; J. Prentice Murphy, "What Can Be Accomplished through Good Social Work in the Field of Illegitimacy?" *Annals of the American Academy of Political and Social Science* 92 (November 1921): 129–35; Hewins, "A Study of Illegitimacy," 115; Kunzel, "Professionalization."
47. Smiley Blanton, "Discipline," in R. O. Beard, ed., *Parent Education* (Minneapolis, 1927), 113–26.
48. Stephanie Shields, Pamela Steinke, and Beth Koster, "Representation of Mothers' and Fathers' Emotion in American Popular Literature," unpublished paper, Department of Psychology, University of California, Davis, 1990; M. V. O'Shea, *First Steps in Child Training* (Chicago, 1920), 128.
49. Lillian Evelyn Gilbreth, *Living with Our Children* (New York, 1928), 106–7; John B. Watson, *Psychological Care of Infant and Child* (New York, 1928), 6, 12, 86, and chap. 3; Anna W. M. Wolf, *The Parents' Manual: A Guide to the Emotional Development of Young Children* (New York, 1941), 81.
50. Ernest R. Groves and Gladys Groves, *Wholesome Childhood* (Boston, 1931), 12–13, 98–101.
51. Simon Grolnick, *The Work and Play of Winnicott* (Northvale, N.Y., 1990).
52. Spock, *Common Sense*, 3, 19; see also Elizabeth Bradford, *Let's Talk about Children* (New York, 1948), 49; Angelo Patri, *How to Help Your Child Grow Up* (Chicago, 1928), 7–19; L. Raymond, *Adoption and After* (New York, 1955); Judith Modell, "Meanings of Love: Adoption Literature and Dr. Spock, 1946–1985," in Carol Z. Stearns and Peter N. Stearns, eds., *Emotion and Social Change: Toward a New Psychohistory* (New York, 1988).

53. Hilde Bruch, *Don't Be Afraid of Your Child: A Guide for Perplexed Parents* (New York, 1952), 66; Thomas Gordon, *Parent Effectiveness Training: The No-Lose Program for Raising Responsible Children* (New York, 1970), 290.

54. Sidonie Gruenberg, et al., *Parents' Questions* (New York, 1949), 104–7; Winifred Paul, Mary Sweeney, and E. Lee Vincent, *Growth and Development of Your Child* (Philadelphia, 1942), 401.

55. Paul, Sweeney, and Vincent, *Growth and Development,* 403.

56. Willard Waller, *The Old Love and the New* (New York, 1930), 52; Shields, et al., in "Mothers' and Fathers' Emotion," cite prescriptive literature on the impossibility of either spouse showing too much love; S. L. Katzoff, *Why Marriage?* (San Fransisco, 1932).

57. Mrs. Havelock Ellis, *The New Horizon in Love and Life* (London, 1921), 27; see also Bertrand Russell, *Marriage and Morals* (New York, 1929); Mikhail Arttzybasheff, *Jealousy* (New York, 1923); Ben B. Lindsay and Wainwright Evans, *The Companionate Marriage* (New York, 1927), 72–73.

58. Steven Seidman (*Romantic Longings: Love in America, 1830–1980* [New York, 1991]) describes the whole debate opening up around 1900; see also Nancy Cott, *Grounding of Modern Feminism* (New Haven, Conn., 1987). On Lindsay, Lindsay and Evans, *Companionate Marriage,* 65; Margaret Sanger, *Happiness in Marriage* (New York, 1926).

59. Noah Webster, *American Dictionary of the English Language* (1828; repr., New York, 1970), vol. 2; *Oxford English Dictionary,* 2d ed. (Oxford, 1989), 9:59–60.

60. Arnold Gingrich, "Editor's Page," *Esquire,* autumn 1933.

61. On *Esquire* circulation, *Esquire,* Sept. 1936; on "new love," *Esquire,* Jan. 1934.

62. Peter Stearns and Mark Knapp, "Men and Romantic Love: Pinpointing a Twentieth-Century Change," *Journal of Social History* (Summer 1993); Carlton Smith, "Women as Creator," *Esquire,* March 1936, 75; Stanley Jones, "Last Stand of Man," *Esquire,* Nov. 1934, 64, 143.

63. Henry Morton Robinson, "This Brave New Love," *Esquire,* Feb. 1934, 56.

64. Alfred Adler, "Love Is a Recent Invention," *Esquire,* May 1936, 56.

65. Joseph Kessel, "Sleepless Night," *Esquire,* May 1936, 69.

66. André Maurois, "Forgive Me, Irene," *Esquire,* Jan. 1934, 33; John Cournos, "Second Honeymoon," *Esquire,* Oct. 1935, 58.

67. Robert T. Souter, "Boys Will Be Boys," *Esquire,* Feb. 1938, 120; Rion Bercowich, "Call Me Up," *Esquire,* Oct. 1934, 45.

68. G. T. Sweeter, "A Note from the Publisher," *Esquire,* Jan. 1950, 6; Betty South, "The Trouble with Women Is Men," *Esquire,* April 1952, 72.

69. Beth L. Bailey, "Scientific Truth . . . and Love: The Marriage Education Movement in the United States," *Journal of Social History* (Summer 1987): 711–32.

70. Ernest W. Burgess, Proposal for Marriage Study, handwritten draft, n.d., Burgess papers, University of Chicago, box 31, 11b–12.

71. Burgess, Proposal for Marriage Study, 16.

72. Data from Lewis M. Terman, *Psychological Factors in Marital Happiness* (New York, 1938), 142–66, quoted in Judson T. Landis and Mary G. Landis, *Building a Successful Marriage* (New York, 1948), 90–91. This scale also was reproduced, in part, in the *Woman's Home Companion* as a "quiz" on "popular fallacies" now debunked by sociologists, statisticians, educators, and psychologists. Judith Chase Churchill, "What Do You Know about Marriage?" *Woman's Home Companion,* Sept. 1950, 42.

73. Theodore Van de Velde, *Ideal Marriage: Its Physiognomy and Technique* (1930;

repr., Westport, Conn., 1950), 6. For a fuller discussion of the new near-equation of sex and love, see Steven Seidman, *Romantic Longings: Love in America, 1830–1980* (New York, 1991), chap. 3; L. T. Woodward, *Sophisticated Sex Techniques in Marriage* (New York, 1967), 11; Maxine Davis, *Sexual Responsibilities in Marriage* (New York, 1963), 184; William Robinson, *Woman: Her Sex and Love Life*, 17th ed. (1917; repr., New York, 1929), 363.

74. Davis, *Sexual Responsibilities*, 33.
75. Nena O'Neill and George O'Neill, *Open Marriage* (New York, 1972).
76. Tania Modleska, *Loving with a Vengeance: Mass-Produced Fantasies for Women* (Hamden, Conn., 1982); Francesca Cancian, *Love in America: Gender and Self-Development* (Cambridge, England, 1987).
77. On modern love as mere negotiation, Robert C. Solomon, *About Love: Reinventing Romance for Our Times* (New York, 1968), 19. For early identification of the "New Love" theme, Waller, *Old Love and the New*, 7. On increasing self-interest in love, Neil Smelser and Erik Erikson, eds., *Themes of Work and Love in Adulthood* (Cambridge, Mass., 1982), 127ff.

6. Reprise

1. Carl F. Kaestle and Helen Damon-Moore, *Literacy in the United States: Readers and Reading since 1890* (New Haven, Conn., 1991). On homogenizing advice, Urie Bronfenbreunner, "Socialization and Social Class through Time and Space," in Eleanor Macroby, T. M. Newcombe, and E. L. Hartley, eds., *Readings in Social Psychology* (New York, 1958). On new division, for example in family forms, see John Modell, "Suburbanization and Change in the American Family," *Journal of Interdisciplinary History* 9 (1979): 621–46.
2. Philip Greven, *Spare the Child: The Religious Roots of Punishment and the Psychological Impact of Physical Abuse* (New York, 1991); Roger Finke, "An Unsecular America," in Steve Bruce, ed., *Religion and Modernization* (Oxford, 1992), 145–69.
3. Cas Wouters, "On Emotion Management and the Integration of Classes and Sexes: A Report of Some Changes in Twentieth-Century Etiquette Books," paper presented at the Tenth Anniversary Conference, Theory, Culture, and Society, August 1992; Peter N. Stearns, "Girls, Boys, and Emotion: Redefinitions and Social Change," *Journal of American History* (1993): 36–74.
4. Stephanie Shields, Pamela Steinke, and Beth Koster, "Representation of Mothers' and Fathers' Emotions in American Popular Literature," unpublished paper, Department of Psychology, University of California, Davis, 1990.
5. Shula Sommers, "Adults Evaluating Their Emotions: A Cross-Cultural Perspective," in Carol Zander Malatesta and Carroll E. Izard, eds., *Emotions in Adult Development* (Beverly Hills, Calif., 1984).
6. Margaret Potter, "The Obsession of Amy Gibbs," *Harper's Monthly Magazine* 113 (September 1906): 583–91; Charles Howard Shinn, "The Mountaineer and the Obsession," *Outlook* 103 (February 1913): 408–11.
7. Robert N. Bellah, et al., *Habits of the Heart: Individualism and Commitment in American Life* (New York, 1983), 90 ff. See Richard Müller-Freienfels, *The Evolution of Modern Psychology*, trans. W. B. Wolfe (New Haven, Conn., 1935), 356.
8. Christen Brinkgreve, "On Modern Relationships: The Commandments of the New Freedom," *Netherlands Journal of Sociology* 18 (1982): 147–56.
9. James Beuler, "The New Sensibility: Self and Society in the Post-Industrial Age,"

Ph.D. diss., University of California at Los Angeles, 1981); Jürgen Gerhards, "The Changing Culture of Emotions in Modern Society," *Social Science Information* 28 (1989): 752. For a perceptive comment on apparent liberation but actual constraint in interwar fashion changes, see Mary Louise Roberts, "Samson and Delilah Revisited: The Politics of Women's Fashion in 1920s France," *American Historical Review* 98 (1993): 659–84.

10. On early uses of the word "cool" in emotions, going back to Beowulf, see the *Oxford English Dictionary*, 2d ed. (Oxford, 1989).

7. *"Impersonal, but Friendly"*

1. Peter Uhlenberg, "Death and the Family," in Ray N. Hiner and Joseph M. Hawes, eds., *Growing Up in America: Children in Historical Perspective* (Urbana, Ill., 1985), 243–46; on grief functionalism, James B. Averill and Elena Nunley, "Grief as an Emotion and as a Disease: A Social Constructionist Perspective," *Journal of Social Issues* 44 (1988): 79–95.

2. Peter N. Stearns, *Jealousy: The Evolution of an Emotion in American History* (New York and London, 1989); E. Anthony Rotundo, "Romantic Friendship: Male Intimacy and Middle-Class Youth in the Northern United States, 1800–1900," *Journal of Social History* 23 (1989); Mark Carnes, *Secret Ritual and Manhood in Victorian America* (New Haven, Conn., 1989).

3. John Modell, *Into One's Own: From Adolescence to Adulthood in America, 1920–1975* (Berkeley, Calif., 1989); Beth Bailey, *From Front Porch to Back Seat: Courtship in Twentieth-Century America* (Baltimore, 1988); Carol Zisowitz Stearns and Peter N. Stearns, *Anger: The Struggle for Emotional Control in America's History* (Chicago, 1986).

4. E. Anthony Rotundo, "Boy Culture: Middle-Class Boyhood in Nineteenth-Century America," in Mark C. Carnes and Clyde Griffen, eds., *Meanings for Manhood: Constructions of Masculinity in Victorian America* (Chicago and London, 1990); Peter N. Stearns and Timothy Haggerty, "The Role of Fear: Transitions in American Emotional Standards for Children, 1850–1950," *American Historical Review* (Feb. 1991): 63–94.

5. James Reed, *The Birth Control Movement and American Society: From Private Vice to Public Virtue* (Princeton, N.J., 1984); Steven Seidman, *Romantic Longings: Love in America, 1830–1980* (New York, 1991).

6. Peter N. Stearns and Deborah Stearns, "Historical Issues in Emotions Research: Causation and Timing," *Sociological Perspectives on Emotion* 2 (1994), forthcoming; John Demos, "Shame and Guilt in Early New England," in Carol Z. Stearns and Peter N. Stearns, eds., *Emotion and Social Change: Toward a New Psychohistory* (New York and London, 1988).

7. Abram de Swaan, "The Politics of Agoraphobia: On Changes in Emotional and Relational Management," *Theory and Society* 10 (1981); Jürgen Gerhards, "The Changing Culture of Emotions in Modern Society," *Social Science Information* 28 (1989); Cas Wouters, "On Status Competition and Emotion Management," *Journal of Social History* 24 (1991).

8. De Swaan, "Politics of Agoraphobia," 383; Norbert Elias, *The Civilizing Process* (New York, 1978).

9. John Kasson, *Rudeness and Civility: Manners in Nineteenth-Century Urban America* (New York, 1990). For an alternative European approach mentioning a rich array of

new causes of the sort this chapter details more elaborately, see Christen Brinkgreve, "On Modern Relationships: The Commandments of the New Freedom," *Netherlands Journal of Sociology* 18 (1982): 147–56. For a fuller description of the Elias issue, Peter N. Stearns, "Problems of Causation in Historical Emotion Research," *Amsterdam Sociologiche Tijdsshrift*, 1993.

10. David Reisman, *The Lonely Crowd: A Study of the Changing American Character* (New Haven, Conn., 1961); Christopher Lasch, *Culture of Narcissism: American Life in an Age of Diminishing Expectations* (New York, 1978).

11. Seidman, *Romantic Longings*; George Chauncey, Jr., "Christian Brotherhood or Sexual Perversion? Homosexual Identities and the Construction of Sexual Boundaries in the World War One Era," in Peter N. Stearns, ed., *Expanding the Past: A Reader in Social History* (New York and London, 1988); John D'Emilio and Estelle B. Freedman, *Intimate Matters: A History of Sexuality in America* (New York, 1988); Wouters, "On Status Competition"; James K. Martin and Mark E. Lender, *Drinking in America: A History* (New York, 1982).

12. Peter N. Stearns, "Suppressing Unpleasant Emotions: The Development of a Twentieth-Century American Style," in Andrew E. Barnes and Peter N. Stearns, eds., *Social History and Issues in Social Consciousness: Some Interdisciplinary Connections* (New York and London, 1989); Mark Leary, "Social Functions of Embarrassment and Blushing," paper presented at the International Society for Research in Emotion Conference, Pittsburgh, August 1992.

13. Helen Waite Papashvily, *All the Happy Endings: A Study of the Domestic Novel in America, the Women Who Wrote It, the Women Who Read It in the Nineteenth Century* (New York, 1956); R. Gordon Kelly, *Mother Was a Lady: Self and Society in Selected American Children's Periodicals, 1865–1890* (Westport, Conn., 1974); Bernard Wishy, *The Child and the Republic* (Philadelphia, 1968).

14. Loren Baritz, *The Servants of Power: A History of the Use of Social Science in American History* (Middletown, Conn., 1960).

15. Warren I. Susman, *Culture as History: The Transformation of American Society in the Twentieth Century* (New York, 1985); Stearns and Haggerty, "Role of Fear"; as we have seen, the first explicit invocation of science for new cautions on fear was Mrs. Theodore [Alice McLellan] Birney, *Childhood* (New York, 1904).

16. G. Stanley Hall, "A Study of Fear," *American Journal of Psychology* 8 (1897); Birney, *Childhood*; Peter N. Stearns, "Girls, Boys, and Emotion: Redefinitions and Historical Change," *Journal of American History* (1993): 36–74; Elton Mayo, *The Human Problems of an Industrial Civilization* (New York, 1993). See also chap. 4, n. 25 above.

17. Nancy F. Cott, *Grounding of Modern Feminism* (New Haven, Conn., 1987). See relevant entries in Jennifer S. Uglow, ed., *The Continuum Dictionary of Woman's Biography* (New York, 1989); John William Leonard and Albert Nelson Marquis, eds., *Who Was Who in America, 1897–1942*, vol. 1 (Chicago, 1943).

18. Carl F. Kaestle and Helen Damon-Moore, *Literacy in the United States: Readers and Reading since 1890* (New Haven, Conn., 1991).

19. I am grateful to Steven Schlossman for suggestions about the impact of World War I. On World War II and aggression concerns, see Robert A. Baron, *Human Aggression* (New York, 1977); William C. Menninger, ed., *How to Be a Successful Teen-ager* (New York, 1954), 141; R. J. Havighurst and Hilda Taba, *Adolescent Character and Personality* (New York, 1949); Arnold Gesell, et al., *Youth: The Years from Ten to*

Sixteen (New York, 1956), 339; John Dollard, et al., *Frustration and Aggression* (New Haven, Conn., 1939).

20. Beth L. Bailey, "Scientific Truth . . . and Love: The Marriage Education Movement in the United States," *Journal of Social History* (Summer 1987); Stephanie A. Shields and Beth A. Koster, "Emotional Stereotyping of Parents in Childrearing Manuals, 1915–1980," *Social Psychology Quarterly* 52 (1989): 44–55.

21. Stearns, "Girls, Boys, and Emotion."

22. Rotundo, "Romantic Friendship"; Carnes, *Secret Ritual.* For an interesting case of male solitude at home after work, see Edith Spencer, *The Spencers of Amberson Avenue: A Turn-of-the-Century Memoir,* Michael P. Weber and Peter N. Stearns, eds. (Pittsburgh, 1983).

23. Margaret Marsh, "Suburban Men and Masculine Domesticity, 1870–1915," in Carnes and Griffen, *Meanings for Manhood;* Peter N. Stearns, *Be a Man! Males in Modern Society,* 2d ed. (New York, 1991), chap. 6; Willard Waller, "The Rating and Dating Complex," *American Sociological Review* 2 (1937): 727–34; Beth Bailey, *Front Porch;* Carnes, *Secret Ritual.*

24. Robert Lynd and Helen M. Lynd, *Middletown: A Study in Contemporary American Culture* (New York, 1929); Willard Waller, *The Family: A Dynamic Interpretation* (New York, 1938); Robert L. Griswold, *Fatherhood* (New York, 1993).

25. Bailey, "Scientific Truth."

26. Stearns, *Jealousy,* chap. 6, 365; Peter Stearns and Mark Knapp, "Men and Romantic Love: Pinpointing a Twentieth-Century Change," *Journal of Social History* 26 (Summer 1993): 769–96.

27. Stearns, "Girls, Boys, and Emotion."

28. Lloyd DeMause, ed., *History of Childhood* (New York, 1974); Viviana Zelizer, *Pricing the Priceless Child* (New York, 1986).

29. David M. Katzman, *Seven Days a Week: Women and Domestic Service in Industrializing America* (New York, 1978).

30. Daniel Scott Smith, "Accounting for Change in the Families of the Elderly in the United States, 1900–Present," in David van Tassel and Peter N. Stearns, eds., *Old Age in Bureaucratic Society* (Westport, Conn., 1988).

31. Kenneth T. Jackson, *Crabgrass Frontier: The Suburbanization of the United States* (New York, 1985); Richard Sennett, *Families against the City* (Cambridge, Mass., 1970), makes this point vividly for turn-of-the-century Chicago.

32. Stearns, *Jealousy,* chap. 3; Judy Dunn, *Sisters and Brothers* (Cambridge, Mass., 1985), 98–99; Jane S. Bossard and E. S. Boll, *The Large Family System: An Original Study in the Sociology of Family Bahavior* (Philadelphia, 1956), 186–87.

33. Rotundo, "Romantic Friendship"; D. H. Thom, *Child Management* (Washington, D.C., 1925); Benjamin Spock, *The Common Sense Book of Baby and Child Care* (New York, 1946), chap. 1.

34. The displacement of new adult anxiety about jealousy onto children is explored in Stearns, *Jealousy,* chap. 4; Rudolph Binion, "Fiction as Social Fantasy: Europe's Domestic Crisis of 1879–1914," *Journal of Social History* 27 (1994), forthcoming.

35. Lizabeth Cohen, *Making a New Deal: Industrial Workers in Chicago, 1919–1939* (Cambridge, Eng., 1990); Francis G. Couvares, *The Remaking of Pittsburgh: Class and Culture in an Industrializing City, 1877–1919* (Albany, N.Y., 1984). One clear sign of intensifying consumerism was the rise of kleptomania from the 1880s onward.

36. Roland Marchand, *Advertising the American Dream: Making Way for Modernity,*

1920–1940 (Berkeley, Calif., 1985). For a theoretical statement, a bit sweeping in chronology, see Colin Campbell, *The Romantic Ethic and the Spirit of Modern Consumerism* (London, 1989).

37. Campbell, *Romantic Ethic*; Jonathan Katz, "The Invention of Heterosexuality," *Socialist Review* 77: 13; Couvares, *Remaking of Pittsburgh*; Marchand, *Advertising*; Vincent Vinikas, *Soft Soap, Hard Sell: American Hygiene in an Age of Advertisement* (Ames, Iowa, 1992).

38. Shula Sommers, "Adults Evaluating Their Emotions: A Cross-Cultural Perspective," in *Emotions in Adult Development,* Carol Zander Malatesta and Carroll E. Izard, eds. (Beverly Hills, Calif., 1984).

39. Ruth Benedict, *The Chrysanthemum and the Sword* (Boston, 1946).

40. Gerhards, "Changing Culture"; Wouters, "On Status Competition"; Marchand, *Advertising*; Stearns and Stearns, *Anger,* chap. 5.

41. Stearns, *Jealousy,* chap. 4; Stearns and Haggerty, "Role of Fear"; Stearns and Knapp, "Men and Romantic Love."

42. Elaine S. Abelson, *When Ladies Go A-Thieving: Middle Class Shoplifters in the Victorian Department Store* (New York, 1990); Patricia O'Brien, "The Kleptomania Diagnosis: Bourgeois Women and Theft in Late Nineteenth-Century France," in Stearns, *Expanding the Past,* 105–17.

43. Miriam Formanek-Brunell, "Sugar and Spice: The Politics of Doll Play in Nineteenth-Century America," in *Small Worlds: Children and Adolescents in America, 1850–1950,* Elliott West and Paula Petrik, ed. (Lawrence, Kans., 1992), 107–24; Karin Calvert, *Children in the House: The Material Culture of Early Childhood* (Boston, 1992), 117 and passim.

44. Inez McClintock and Marshall McClintock, *Toys in America* (Washington, D.C., 1961), 212; Janet Pagter, *The Fascinating Story of Dolls* (New York, 1941); Max von Boehm, *Dolls and Puppets* (Boston, 1956), 156, 191–92.

45. John Burroughs, "Corrupting the Innocents," *Independent* 61 (December 1906): 1424; "The Ethics of Toys," *Nation* 85 (September 1907): 224–25; see also Angelo Patri, *Child Training* (New York, 1922), 21–22.

46. Ruth Frankel, "Choosing the Right Toys," *Hygeia,* Dec. 1931, 1106; see also Marian Faegre, "Playthings That Help Children Grow," *Ladies Home Journal* 50 (December 1933): 38; Jane Franklin, "A Grandmother Talks about Picking Toys," *American Magazine* 114 (December 1932): 86.

47. Patty Smith Hill and Grace Brown, "Avoid the Gifts That Over-Stimulate," *Delineator* 85 (December 1914): 22–23; Sarah Canstock, "The Significance of Playthings," *Good Housekeeping* 69 (December 1918): 35. Boys were developing emotional attachments to toy soldiers in the same turn-of-the-century period. See Kenneth D. Brown, "Modelling for War? Toy Soldiers in Late Victorian and Edwardian Britain," *Journal of Social History* (Winter 1990): 237–54.

48. Daniel T. Rodgers, "Socializing Middle-Class Children: Institutions, Fables, and Work Values in Nineteenth-Century America," *Journal of Social History* 13 (1980). On big business and white-collar growth, see Alfred Chandler, *The Visible Hand* (Cambridge, Mass., 1974); Daniel Bell, *The Coming of Post-Industrial Society* (New York, 1973), 121–64; Daniel T. Rodgers, *The Work Ethic in Industrial America, 1850–1920* (Chicago, 1978), 88 ff.; Daniel Nelson, *Managers and Workers: Origins of the New Factory System in the United States, 1880–1920* (Madison, Wis., 1975), 37 ff.; Judith A. Merkle, *Management and Ideology: The Legacy of the International Scientific Management Movement* (Berkeley, Calif., 1980); Robert F. Hoxie, *Scientific*

Management and Labor (1915; repr., New York, 1966); Frederick W. Taylor, *Shop Management* (New York, 1911), and *The Principles of Scientific Managment* (New York, 1911); William H. Whyte, Jr., *The Organization Man* (New York, 1956), 140, 276 ff.

49. C. Wright Mills, *White Collar: The Industrial Middle Classes* (New York, 1953); Arlie Russell Hochschild, *The Managed Heart: Commercialization of Human Feeling* (Berkeley, Calif., 1983); Susan Porter Benson, *Counter Cultures: Saleswomen, Managers, and Customers in American Department Stores, 1890–1940* (Urbana, Ill., 1986); Susan van Horn, *Women, Work, and Fertility, 1900–1986* (New York, 1988).

50. Baritz, *Servants of Power.*

51. Hochschild, *Managed Heart;* see esp. de Swaan, "Politics of Agoraphobia."

52. Benson, *Counter Cultures;* Edward Kilduff, *The Private Secretary* (New York, 1915), 50, 57 (see also later editions to 1935); William H. Leffingwell and Edward M. Robinson, *Textbook of Office Management* (New York, 1950), 386 ff; Hugo Münsterberg, *Psychology and Industrial Efficiency* (Boston, 1913), 128, 205; Mary Smith, *Handbook of Industrial Psychology* (New York, 1944); Stanley M. Herman, *The People Specialists* (New York, 1968), 245 ff.

53. Walter Dill Scott, et al., *Personnel Management: Principles, Practice, and Point of View* (New York, 1941); R. C. Borden and Alvin Busse, *How to Win a Sales Argument* (New York, 1926); Laurence Siegel, *Industrial Psychology* (Homewood, Ill., 1969), 347–57; Susan Porter Benson, "The Clerking Sisterhood: Rationalization and the Work Culture of Saleswomen in American Department Stores, 1890–1960," in *Worker's Struggles, Past and Present,* James Green, ed. (Philadelphia, 1983), 107–16; Margery W. Davies, *Woman's Place Is at the Typewriter: Office Work and Office Workers, 1870–1930* (Philadelphia, 1982), 95.

54. Mayo, *Human Problems,* 84.

55. De Swaan, "Politics of Agoraphobia."

56. Hochschild, *Managed Heart;* Annette Garrett, *Counseling Methods for Personnel Workers* (New York, 1945); Baritz, *Servants of Power,* passim; Michael Zuckerman, "Dr. Spock, the Confidence Man," in C. Rosenberg, ed., *The Family in History* (Philadelphia, 1975), 187–93; Daniel Miller and Guy Swanson, *The Changing American Parent* (New York, 1958), 143 and passim.

57. Arthur Jersild, et al., *Joys and Problems of Childrearing* (New York, 1949); Miller and Swanson, *Changing American Parent.*

58. Jay Mechling, "Advice to Historians on Advice to Mothers," *Journal of Social History* 9 (1975): 44–63; Paul J. Woods, et al., "A Mother-Daughter Comparison on Selected Aspects of Child-Rearing in a High Socioeconomic Group," *Child Development* 31 (1960): 121–28; Ruth Staples and J. W. Smith, "Attitudes of Grandmothers and Mothers toward Child-Rearing Practices," *Child Development* 25 (1954): 91–97; John R. Seely, R. Alexander Sim, and Elizabeth W. Loosley, *Crestwood Heights* (Toronto, 1956), 166; Martha S. White, "Social Class, Child Rearing Practices, and Child Behavior," in Neil Smelser and William Smelser, eds., *Personality and Social Systems* (New York, 1963), 286–96; Leone Kell and Jean Aldous, "Trends in Child Care over Three Generations," *Marriage and Family Living* 22 (1960): 176–77; Russell Green and Edgar O'Neil, eds., *Perspectives on Aggression* (New York, 1976), 117.

59. Stearns and Stearns, "Historical Issues in Emotions Research"; Catherine Lutz and G. White, "The Anthropology of Emotions," *Annual Review of Anthropology* 15 (1986): 405–36; Stearns and Haggerty, "Role of Fear."

60. Dorothy Canfield Fisher and Sidonie Gruenberg, *Our Children: A Handbook for Parents* (New York, 1932), 117; Ruth Sapin, "Helping Children to Overcome Fear," *Parents' Magazine* 8 (May 1, 1933): 14–16. On changes in children's knowledge of death, Uhlenberg, "Death and the Family," 243–52.

61. James Walvin, *Victorian Values* (Athens, Ga., 1988); Elisabeth Kubler-Ross, *Death: The Final Stage of Growth* (Englewood Cliffs, N.J., 1979), esp. 5–6, 19–21; Ralph Houlbrooke, ed., *Death, Ritual, and Bereavement* (London, 1989), chaps. 7, 9, 11. John Demos offered some parallel thoughts on increased anxiety about death among middle-aged Americans in *Past, Present, and Personal: The Family and the Life Course in American History* (New York, 1986), 119–20.

62. J. O. Leibowitz, *The History of Coronary Heart Disease* (Berkeley, Calif., 1970), 163–67; Saul J. Kowal, "Emotions and Angina Pectoris: An Historical Review," *American Journal of Cardiology* 5 (1960): 421–27.

63. Stearns and Stearns, *Anger*, chap. 3; Seidman, *Romantic Longings*.

64. B. W. Richardson, "Induced Diseases from the Influence of the Passions," *Popular Science Monthly* 8 (November 1875): 60–65. Fernaud Papillon, "Physiology of the Passions," *Popular Science Monthly* 4 (March 1874): 552–64. On the shift from purely mechanistic concepts of the heart's action to concern about strain and general nervousness—a transition taking shape in the final decades of the nineteenth century—see Robert Kugelmann, *Stress: The Nature and History of Engineered Grief* (Westport, Conn., 1992), 121–36.

65. S. Weir Mitchell, *Wear and Tear; or, Hints for the Overworked* (1887; repr., New York, 1973); Francis G. Gosling, *Before Freud: Neurasthenia and the American Medical Community, 1870–1910* (Urbana, Ill., 1987); Tom Lutz, *American Nervousness, 1903: An Anecdotal History* (Ithaca, N.Y., 1991); Janet Oppenheim, *Shattered Nerves: Doctors, Patients, and Depression in Victorian England* (New York, 1991).

66. On growing concerns about degeneration, see Carole Haber, *Beyond Sixty-Five: The Dilemma of Old Age in America's Past* (Cambridge, Eng., and New York, 1983); "Studies of Blood Pressure," *Scientific American Supplement* 56 (31 October 1903); C. C. Guthrie and F. H. Pike, "Relation of Pressure in the Coronary Vessels to the Activity of the Isolated Heart," *Science* n.s. 24 (13 July 1906): 52–54; "Estimation of Blood-pressure," *Nature* 74 (25 October 1906): 638–40; "Blood Pressure and Mental Conditions," *Scientific American* 97 (12 October 1907): 262; W. R. Tyndale, "Blood Pressure as an Indication of Condition," *Journal of Proceedings and Addresses of the Fifty-First Annual Meeting of the NEA*, 1913, 703–6; James T. Patterson, *The Dread Disease: Cancer and Modern American Culture* (Cambridge, Mass., 1987).

67. Mary A. Harrison, "Children's Sense of Fear," *Arena* 16 (November 1896): 960–69; "A Study of Anger," *Scientific American Supplement* 49 (5 May 1900): 2036 (also published in *Current Literature* 27 [1900]: 47); Frank Hoffman, *Psychology and Common Life* (New York, 1903), 161; "The Ptomaines of Passion," *Current Literature* 42 (May 1907): 569; "Worry," *Living Age* 253 (15 June 1907): 693–95.

68. "A Physician's Indictment of Mental Healing," *Saturday Evening Post*, Nov. 1908, 81. On jealousy as a physical ailment see "Jealousy as a Curable Disease and as an Admirable Attribute," *North American Review* 187 (February 1908): 317–19; see also William S. Sadler, M.D., "Can We Really Stop Worrying?" *Ladies Home Journal* 28 (September 1911): 21–22. Note that this surge of interest oscillated between seeing emotions as a cause of illness and seeing somatic changes as causing emotions that

then caused illness. The distinction probably mattered far less than the warning signals both views now pinned on intense emotions.

69. Fred W. Eastman, "The Physics of the Emotions," *Harper's Magazine* 128 (January 1911): 302; "Grieving," *Independent* 64 (February 1908): 477; "Love as a Disease," *Literary Digest* 48 (April 1914): 818; "The Cult of Joy," *Living Age* 291 (December 1916): 683.

70. Samuel McComb, "Right Thinking and Right Living," *Harper's Bazaar* 47 (February 1919): 58.

71. Ralph Waldo Trine, "A Healthy Mind in a Healthy Body," *Woman's Home Companion* 40 (April 1913): 13; " 'Sobbing Sickness' Appears in War-Devastated Countries," *Literary Digest* 61 (3 May 1919): 66–70; Dr. Abraham Myerson, "The Disease of Worry and the Tonic of Joy," *Ladies Home Journal* 38 (March 1921): 12–13, 82–84; William S. Sadler, M.D., "What You Need to Know about Your Blood Pressure," *American Magazine* 101 (May 1926): 46–47, 212–16.

72. George F. Gorham, M.D. "The Physiological Effect of Faith," *Outlook* 62 (19 August 1899): 888–92, 890; John B. Watson, "The Heart or the Intellect?" *Harper's Monthly Magazine* 156 (February 1928): 345–52, 345, 346; Walter B. Cannon, "What Strong Emotions Do to Us," *Harper's Monthly Magazine* 145 (July 1922): 235–41.

73. Edward Shorter, *From Paralysis to Fatigue: A History of Psychosomatic Illness in the Modern Era* (New York and Toronto, 1992); Jean Delumeau, *La Peur en Occident, XIV–XVIII siècles: Une cité assiégée* (Paris, 1978).

74. Modell, *Into One's Own*; Meyer Friedman and Ray H. Rosenman, *Type A Behavior and Your Heart* (New York, 1981).

75. Anthropologists have shown how prohibitions most emphasized in childrearing crop up also in a society's favored (most feared) disease patterns. John W. M. Whiting and Irwin L. Child, *Child Training and Personality* (New Haven, Conn., 1953). Recent popularized literature on the relationship between emotions and health focuses quite specifically on the heart and vascular system. For the best general statement, see Friedman and Rosenman, *Type A Behavior*, 17–24 and passim; Hochschild, *Managed Heart*, 25, 33, 113; Leonard R. Sayles, *Behavior of Industrial Work Groups* (New York, 1958), 82.

76. Christen Brinkgreve and M. Konze, "Verhältnisse in der niederlandischen Gesellschaft (1938–1977): Analyse und Interpretation der Ratgerber Rubrik einer Illustrier-tin," in P. Gleidmann, ed., *Materielen zu Norbert Elias Zivilisationsheorie* (Frankfurt, 1979), 399–410.

8. The Impact of the New Standards

1. Margaret S. Clark, "Historical Emotionology: From a Social Psychologist's Perspective," in Andrew E. Barnes and Peter N. Stearns, eds., *Social History and Issues in Human Consciousness: Some Interdisciplinary Connections* (New York and London, 1989); Catherine Lutz, *Unnatural Emotions: Everyday Sentiments on a Micronesian Atoll and Their Challenge to Western Theory* (Chicago, 1988); S. Shott, "Emotions and Social Life: A Symbolic Interactional Analysis," *American Journal of Sociology* 84 (1979): 1317–34.

2. Steven L. Gordon, "The Socialization of Children's Emotions: Emotional Culture, Competence, and Exposure," in Carolyn Saarni and Paul Harris, eds., *Children's*

Understanding of Emotion (Cambridge, 1989); D. Stern, *The Interpersonal World of the Infant* (New York, 1985).

3. Peter N. Stearns with Carol Z. Stearns, "Emotionology: Clarifying the Study of the History of Emotional Standards," *American Historical Review* 90 (1985): 813–30; Jay Mechling, "Advice to Historians on Advice to Mothers," *Journal of Social History* 9 (1975).

4. Cas Wouters, "Developments in Behavioral Codes between the Sexes: The Formalization of Informalization in the Netherlands, 1930–85," *Theory, Culture, and Society* 4 (1987): 405–27.

5. Stephanie Shields, "Gender and Emotion," paper presented at the International Society for Research on Emotions, Fifth Annual Meeting, Rutgers University, 27 July 1990; Roland Marchand, *Advertising the American Dream: Making Way for Modernity, 1920–1940* (Berkeley, Calif., 1985); Vincent Vinikas, *Soft Soap, Hard Sell: American Hygiene in an Age of Advertisement* (Ames, Iowa, 1992).

6. On theoretical issues of timing, Peter N. Stearns and Deborah C. Stearns, "Historical Issues in Emotions Research: Causation and Timing," *Sociological Perspectives on Emotion* 2 (1994), forthcoming.

7. Beth L. Bailey, "Scientific Truth . . . and Love: The Marriage Education Movement in the United States," *Journal of Social History* (Summer 1987); Arthur T. Jersild, et al., *Joys and Problems of Childrearing* (New York, 1949); Daniel Miller and Guy Swanson, *The Changing American Parent* (New York, 1958); Gordon Clanton, "Jealousy in American Culture, 1945–1985: Reflections from Popular Literature," in D. Franks and E. D. McCarthy, eds., *The Sociology of Emotions* (Greenwich, Conn., 1989); Lewis Terman, *Psychological Factors in Marital Happiness* (New York, 1938); Margo Horn, *Before It's Too Late: The Child Guidance Movement in the United States, 1922–1945* (Philadelphia, 1989); Jürgen Gerhards, "The Changing Culture of Emotions in Modern Society," *Social Science Information* 28 (1989).

8. Paul J. Woods, et al., "A Mother-Daughter Comparison on Selected Aspects of Child-Rearing in a High Socioeconomic Group," *Child Development* 31 (1960): 121–28; Lee Salk, *Preparing for Parenthood* (New York, 1974); P. E. Sears, "Doll Play Aggression in Normal Young Children: Influence of Sex, Age, Sibling Status, and Fathers' Absence," *Psychological Monographs* 65, no. 323 (1951); Melvin L. Kohn, "Social Class and the Exercise of Parental Authority," in Neil Smelser and William Smelser, eds., *Personality and Social Systems* (New York, 1963), 297–314; Martha S. White, "Social Class, Child Rearing Practices, and Child Behavior," in Smelser and Smelser, eds., *Personality and Social Systems*, 286–96; Leone Kell and Jean Aldous, "Trends in Child Care over Three Generations," *Marriage and Family Living* 22 (1960): 176–77; Russell Green and Edgar O'Neil, eds., *Perspectives on Aggression* (New York, 1976), 117.

9. Christopher Lasch, *Haven in a Heartless World: The Family Besieged* (New York, 1977).

10. Ayala Pines and Eliot Aronson, "Antecedents, Correlations, and Consequences of Sexual Jealousy," *Journal of Personality* 51 (1983); Peter N. Stearns, *Jealousy: The Evolution of an Emotion in American History* (New York and London, 1989); Stearns, *Jealousy*, 112; Shula Sommers, "Adults Evaluating Their Emotions: A Cross-Cultural Perspective," in Carol Zander Malatesta and Carroll E. Izard, eds., *Emotion in Adult Development* (Beverly Hills, Calif., 1984), 324; Peter Salovey and Judith Rodin, "Coping with Envy and Jealousy," *Journal of Social and Clinical Psychology* 7, no. 1 (1988): 15–33.

11. Willard Waller, *The Family* (New York, 1938), 586; Carl R. Rogers, *Becoming Partners* (New York, 1972), 142, 181; Gay Talese, *Thy Neighbor's Wife* (New York, 1981); Carolyn Symonds, "Sexual Mate-Swapping: Violations of Norms and Reconciliation of Guilt," in J. M. Hensher, ed., *Studies in the Sociology of Sex* (New York, 1971), 87–88.

12. E. E. Le Masters, *Modern Courtship and Marriage* (New York, 1957), 132–33; Maureen Daly, *Profile of Youth* (New York, 1949); Ernest A. Smith, *American Youth Culture* (Glencoe, Ill., 1962); Ellen K. Rothman, *Hands and Hearts: A History of Courtship in America* (Cambridge, Mass., 1987); Willard Waller, "The Rating and Dating Complex," *American Sociological Review* 2 (1937): 727–34. See also two important recent histories: Beth L. Bailey, *From Front Porch to Back Seat: Courtship in Twentieth-Century America* (Baltimore, Md., 1988); and especially John Modell, *Into One's Own: From Adolescence to Adulthood in America, 1920–1975* (Berkeley, Calif., 1989).

13. Shula Sommers, "Reported Emotions and Conventions of Emotionality among College Students," *Journal of Personality and Social Psychology* 46 (1984): 214; Grant S. McClellan, ed., *American Youth in a Changing Culture* (New York, 1972). On current jealousy responses, see several essays in Peter Salovey, ed., *The Psychology of Jealousy and Envy* (New York, 1991).

14. Peter N. Stearns and Timothy Haggerty, "The Role of Fear: Transitions in American Emotional Standards for Children, 1850–1950," *American Historical Review* (Feb. 1991).

15. Wouters, "Behavioral Codes"; Agneta Fischer, "Emotion Scripts: Social and Cognitive Facets of Emotion," paper presented at the Symposium Emoties, University of Amsterdam, 11 September 1992.

16. Paul C. Rosenblatt, *Bitter, Bitter Tears: Nineteenth-Century Diarists and Twentieth-Century Grief Theories* (Minneapolis, 1983); Margaret Stroebe, Mary Gergen, Kenneth Gergen, and Wolfgang Stroebe, "Broken Hearts in Broken Bonds," *American Psychologist* 47 (1992); Charles W. Brice, "Paradoxes of Maternal Mourning," *Psychiatry* 54 (1991); E. Lindermann, "The Symptomology and Management of Acute Grief," *American Journal of Psychiatry* 101 (1944): 141–48.

17. Jai Ghorpade and R. J. Lackrits, "Influences behind Neutral Responses in Subordinate Ratings of Supervisors," *Personnel Psychology* 34 (1981): 511–22; P. J. Andersini and M. B. Shapiro, "Women's Attitudes toward Their Jobs," *Personnel Psychology* 31 (1978): 23; Charles W. Walker and Robert H. Guest, *The Man and the Assembly Line* (Cambridge, Mass., 1952), 92 ff., 143; Leonard Goodwin, "Occupational Goals and Satisfaction of the American Work Force," *Personnel Psychology* 22 (1969): 313–25; see also the 1941–1980 vols. of *Analysis of Work Stoppages*, which is published annually by the Bureau of Labor Statistics of the U.S. Department of Labor (Washington, D.C.); and the U.S. Department of Labor, Bureau of Labor Statistics, *Strikes in the United States, 1880–1936* (Washington, D.C., 1937). A full analysis of strike trends would require integration of anger control with more familiar factors such as political climate, unemployment rates, and pay trends; but the probability of an emotional factor is high. See Peter N. Stearns and Carol Z. Stearns, *Anger: The Struggle for Emotional Control in America's History* (Chicago and London, 1986), chap. 5.

18. Charles C. Smith, *The Foreman's Place in Management* (New York, 1946), 119; Studs Terkel, *Working* (New York, 1974), 32, 81, 260, 285 ff., 547, and passim.

19. Dr. James R. Higgins, private interview at North Hills School District, Pittsburgh,

Pennsylvania, 20 October 1983. (Dr. Higgins is a counselor education specialist and director of pupil personnel services at North Hills. Additionally, he has been active in both the national and the state Pupil Personnel Movement since its inception, coauthoring both the original and the 1983 Pennsylvania State Pupil Personnel Guidelines. He is currently president of the Pennsylvania Association of Pupil Personnel Administrators.) See also Robert W. Stroughton, James McKenna, and Richard P. Cook, "Pupil Personnel Services: A Position Statement," mimeograph, Washington, D.C., April 1969; "Pupil Personnel Services in Pennsylvania: A Position Statement," mimeograph, Pittsburgh, Pa., 1983; Victor Lipman, "Mr. Glasser's Gentle Rod," *American Education* 14 (1978): 28–31; Haim Ginnot, "I Am Angry, I Am Appalled, I Am Furious," *Today's Education* 61 (1972): 23; Helen Sobehart, "Toward a History of Anger in the Schools," seminar paper, Carnegie-Mellon University, December 1983.

20. Lillian Breslow Rubin, *Worlds of Pain: Life in the Working-Class Family* (New York, 1976), 76–78, 115–16, and passim; John D. Baldwin, *Marriage without B.S.* (New York, 1979), 143; Judson T. Landis and Mary G. Landis, *Building a Successful Marriage* (New York, 1953), 292 ff.; George H. Gallup, *The Gallup Poll: Public Opinion, 1935–1971* (New York, 1972), 1028.

21. Sommers, "Adults Evaluating Their Emotions"; on the concealment theme more generally, Antoine Prost and Gérard Vincent, eds., *A History of Private Life*, vol. 5, *Riddles of Identity in Modern Times* (Cambridge, Mass., 1991).

22. "Perspective," *Fundamentalist Journal*, May 1988, 12; Philip Greven, *Spare the Child: The Religious Roots of Punishment and the Psychological Impact of Physical Abuse* (New York, 1991).

23. F. J. Roethisberger and William J. Dickson, *Management and the Worker* (Cambridge, Mass., 1941), 349; Terkel, *Working*; Sar A. Levitan and William B. Johnson, *Work Is Here to Stay, Alas* (Salt Lake City, Utah, 1973), 66.

24. Elaine Tyler May, *Homeward Bound: American Families in the Cold War Era* (New York, 1988), 37, 38.

25. Paula Fass, *The Damned and the Beautiful: American Youth in the 1920s* (New York, 1977), 260; August Hollingshead, *Elmtown's Youth* (New York, 1949); for a fuller exploration, see Bailey, *Front Porch to Back Seat*; Terman, *Psychological Factors*, 86, 137, 336; Peter N. Stearns and Mark Knapp, "Men and Romantic Love: Pinpointing a Twentieth-Century Change," *Journal of Social History* 26 (Summer 1993): 769–96.

26. Allan Bloom, "The Death of Eros: Did Romeo and Juliet Have a Relationship?" *New York Times Magazine*, May 23, 1993, 26–27. On Gladys Bell, see John C. Spurlock and Cynthia A. Magistro, " 'Dreams Never to Be Realized': Emotional Culture and the Phenomenology of Emotion," *Journal of Social History* (1994); theirs is a more extensive interpretation. This analysis of changes in love also parallels Barbara Ehrenreich's discussion of the decline of commitment, even to the extent of noting the reassessment of health as a factor generating change. I differ on timing, however, and to an extent on gender-specificity, and I see the shift as part of a larger change in American emotional culture than Ehrenreich tackles. Ehrenreich, *Hearts of Men: American Dreams and the Flight from Commitment* (New York, 1984).

27. Lillian Rubin, *Just Friends: The Role of Friendship in Our Lives* (New York, 1985); George Chauncey, Jr., "Christian Brotherhood or Sexual Perversion? Homosexual Identities and the Construction of Sexual Boundaries in the World War One Era," in Peter N. Stearns, ed., *Expanding the Past: A Reader in Social History* (New York and London, 1988); E. Anthony Rotundo, "Romantic Friendship: Male Intimacy and

Middle-Class Youth in the Northern United States, 1800–1900," *Journal of Social History* 23 (1989).

28. Linda Rosenzweig, *The Anchor of My Life: Middle-Class American Mothers and Daughters, 1880–1920* (New York, 1993).

29. The quotations are from letters dated 23 July 1933 and 5 June 1928, Adele Siegel Rosenfeld Papers, unprocessed collection, Schlesinger Library, Cambridge, Mass. The second letter is also dated "(July 1928)," and the notation concerning the form of address appears in turquoise ink. See also a letter dated 13 July 1930 that illustrates the same casual tone, cited in Rosenzweig, *Anchor of My Life,* chap. 8; Jane Emmet Drake to her mother Helen Pratt Emmet, n.d., 1938, folder 1, box 5, unprocessed collection, Alan Summersby Emmet Papers, Schlesinger Library; 4 March 1945, Adele Mongan Fasick Diary, Schlesinger Library.

30. Nancy Friday, *My Mother, Myself: The Daughter's Search for Identity* (New York, 1977).

31. Joseph Veroff, Elizabeth Douvan, and Richard A. Kulka, *The Inner American: A Self-Portrait from 1957 to 1976* (New York, 1981). Thus parents dropped happiness-with-children ratings by over 60 percent, while comparably increasing nuisance ratings. See R. D. Parke and P. N. Stearns, "Fathers and Child Rearing," in Glen Elder, John Modell, and Ross Parke, eds., *Children in Time and Place* (New York, 1992), 167.

32. Paul Popenoe, *Marriage Is What You Make It* (New York, 1950), 17; Terman, *Psychological Factors*; Robert Lynd and Helen M. Lynd, *Middletown: A Study in Contemporary American Culture* (New York, 1929).

33. On student sensitivity to teacher anger, Fritz Redl, "Aggression in the Classroom," *Today's Education* 58 (September 1969): 30; Levitan and Johnston, *Work Is Here,* 67–68; Theodore V. Purcell, *The Worker Speaks His Mind on Company and Union* (Cambridge, Mass., 1953), 188–230; Walker and Guest, *Man and the Assembly Line,* 99; E. L. Miller, "Job Attitudes of National Union Officials," *Personnel Psychology* 19 (1966): 395–410; A. H. Cochran, "Management Tigers and Pussycats," *Personnel Journal* 50 (1971): 524–26; Thomas Greening, "Sensitivity Training: Cult or Contribution?" *Personnel* 41 (1964): 18–25; C. J. Lilley, "Supervisors Don't Criticize Enough," *Personnel Journal* 31 (1952): 209–12.

34. Burt Scanlan, "Sensitivity Training: Clarification, Issues, Insights," *Personnel Journal* 50 (1970): 549; Chris Argyris, *Interpersonal Competence and Organizational Effectiveness* (Homewood, Ill., 1962), 174 ff.; Stearns and Stearns, *Anger,* 134–38.

35. Amy Vanderbilt, *New Complete Book of Etiquette* (New York, 1954), 127; Anne Shannon Moore, "Golden Sorrow," *Good Housekeeping* 80 (April 1925): 176; Phillipe Ariès, *The Hour of Our Death* (New York, 1981); Elisabeth Kubler-Ross, ed., *Death: The Final Stage of Growth* (New York, 1975).

36. Moore, "Golden Sorrow," 181; Brice, "Maternal Mourning." On therapists' debates over the appropriate approach to grief, see Stroebe, Gergen, Gergen, and Stroebe, "Broken Hearts."

37. Robert N. Bellah, et al., *Habits of the Heart: Individualism and Commitment in American Life* (New York, 1983); P. Shaver, J. Schwartz, D. Kirson, and C. O'Connor, "Emotion Knowledge: Further Exploration of a Prototype Approach," *Journal of Personality and Social Psychology* 52 (1987): 1060–86.

38. Peter N. Stearns, "Girls, Boys, and Emotion: Redefinitions and Historical Change," *Journal of American History* 90 (1993): 36–74; Joseph Pleck and Jack Sawyer, eds., *Men and Masculinity* (Englewood Cliffs, N.J., 1980); David Buss, "Conflict between the Sexes: Strategic Interference in the Evocation of Anger and Upset," *Journal of*

Personality and Social Psychology 56 (1989); Barbara Eichenreich, *The Hearts of Men: American Dreams and the Flight from Commitment* (New York, 1983).

39. Francesca M. Cancian and Steven L. Gordon, "Changing Emotion Norms in Marriage: Love and Anger in U.S. Women's Magazines since 1900," *Gender and Society* 2 (1988); Frances Cancian, *Love in America: Gender and Self-Development* (Cambridge, 1987); Willard Gaylin, *Feelings: Our Vital Signs* (New York, 1988). On emotional contagion, with some evidence of growing aversion to the process, Elaine Hatfield, J. T. Cacioppo, and R. C. Rapson, "Primitive Emotional Contagion," *Review of Personality* (1992): 151–77; Gerhards, "Changing Culture." Patients often seek therapists who will share their emotional experiences; see Hatfield, Cacioppo, and Rapson, "Contagion," 166–67.

40. *Oxford English Dictionary,* 2d ed. (Oxford, 1989); William and Mary Morris, *Dictionary of Contemporary Usage* (New York, 1958), 201. A fuller study of empathy, historically and philosophically, is, happily, being undertaken by the philosopher Viviane Rosenberg. Interestingly, heightened "empathy" was one of the touted results of hallucinogenic drugs widely used by middle-class youth in the 1960s, again suggesting an important but now difficult emotional goal. See John C. Burnham, *Bad Habits: Smoking, Taking Drugs, Gambling, Sexual Misbehavior, and Swearing in American History* (New York, 1992).

41. Carol Z. Stearns, "Sadness," in Jeanette Haviland and Michael Lewis, eds., *Handbook of Emotion* (New York, 1993); N. L. Stein and J. L. Jewett, "A Conceptual Analysis of the Meaning of Negative Emotions: Implications for a Theory of Development," in C. Izard and P. B. Read, eds., *Measuring Emotions in Infants and Children,* vol. 2 (Cambridge, Mass., 1986). The rise in rates of depression, beyond increased diagnosis, has been widely noted but not explained. Probable links to changes in emotional standards deserve more historical-psychological research.

42. Stearns and Stearns, *Anger,* chap. 7. On using closets to "vent hostility," see Popenoe, *Marriage Is What You Make It,* 205. Possibly the later twentieth century will be as noted for people walking into closets as for those coming out.

43. Wendy Wiener, "Setting the Record Straight: An Exploration of the Meaning of Diary Keeping," *Narrative Study of Lives* 1 (1993): 30–58.

44. Sara Keisler and Lee Sproull, "Group Decision Making and Communication Technology," *Organizational Behavior and Human Decision Processes* 52 (1992): 96–123.

45. The confusion between twentieth-century individualism, which undeniably gained ground, and emotional spontaneity, which really did not, needs reemphasis; see Arthur Mitzman, "The Civilizing Offensive: Mentalities, High Culture, and Individual Psyches," *Journal of Social History* 20 (1986): 663–88; Lutz, *Unnatural Emotions.*

46. Stearns and Stearns, *Anger,* chap. 5.

47. Stearns and Haggerty, "Fear."

48. Anthony Platt, *The Child Savers: The Invention of Delinquency* (Chicago, 1969); Joseph Kett, *Rites of Passage: Adolescence in America, 1790 to the Present* (New York, 1977); E. Anthony Rotundo, "Boy Culture: Middle-Class Boyhood in Nineteenth-Century America," in Mark Carnes and Clyde Griffen, eds., *Meanings for Manhood* (Chicago, 1990); David I. MacLeod, *Building Character in the American Boy: The Boy Scouts, YMCA, and Their Forerunners, 1870–1920* (Madison, Wis., 1983).

49. Robert Coles, *Children of Crisis: A Study of Courage and Fear,* 3 vols. (Boston, 1967–71), esp. vol. 3.

50. Ruth Sapin, "Helping Children to Overcome Fear," *Parents' Magazine* 8 (1 May

1933): 40; Brian Melendez, "Honor Code Study," *Harvard University Report,* September 1985.

51. Walter B. Kolesnick, *Educational Psychology* (New York, 1963), 458; Robert Geiser, "What to Do If You Can't Stand That Kid," *Teacher* 91 (1973): 14–16, 19; David Reisman with Nathan Glazer and Reuel Denney, *The Lonely Crowd: A Study of the Changing American Character* (New Haven, Conn., 1973); John R. Ban, "A Lesson Plan Approach for Dealing with School Discipline," *Clearinghouse* 55, no. 8 (April 1982): 345.

52. Stearns, *Jealousy,* chap. 6.

53. Ben B. Lindsay and Wainwright Evans, *The Companionate Marriage* (New York, 1927), 86, 72–73; Arnold Gesell, "Jealousy," *American Journal of Psychology* 17 (1905): 484; Emory S. Bogardus, *Fundamentals of Social Psychology* (New York, 1928), 44; Stearns, *Jealousy,* chap. 5.

54. Francis S. Miller and Helen Laitern, *Personal Problems of the High School Girl* (New York, 1945), 72; Elizabeth B. Hurlock, *Adolescent Development* (New York, 1949); Evelyn Duvall, *Facts of Life and Love for Teenagers* (New York, 1950), 210, 231; Ruth Fedder, *A Girl Grows Up* (New York, 1937), 180; see also Oliver M. Butterfield, *Love Problems of Adolescence* (New York, 1941), 77–89; Ruth Fedder, *You: The Person You Want to Be!* (New York, 1957), 63.

55. Lawrence M. Friedman and Robert V. Percival, "Who Sues for Divorce? From Fault through Fiction to Freedom," *Journal of Legal Studies,* 1981, 80–81.

56. Herbert Jacob, *Silent Revolution: The Transformation of Divorce Law in the United States* (Chicago, 1988), 45; Glenda Riley, *Divorce: An American Tradition* (New York, 1951), 163–64.

57. Jacob, *Silent Revolution.*

58. Austin Sarat, "Alternatives in Dispute Processing: Litigation in a Small Claims Court," *Law and Society Review* (Spring 1976): 342, 344, 346; Laura Nader, ed., *No Access to Law: Alternatives to the American Judicial System* (San Diego, Calif., 1980), xvii; Stanley J. Lieberman, "A No-Lose Proposition," *Newsweek,* 21 Feb. 1984, 14; Sarat, "Dispute Processing," 353.

59. James Reston, *Deadline: A Memoir* (New York, 1991), 270.

60. Modell, *Into One's Own;* Andrew Cherlin, *Marriage, Divorce, Remarriage* (Cambridge, Mass., 1981); Veroff, Douvan, and Kulka, *Inner American.*

61. Stearns, *Jealousy,* chaps. 2, 4. On the relationship between sibling closeness and later male friendship style in the nineteenth century, see Rotundo, "Romantic Friendship."

62. Stearns, *Jealousy,* 161; Stearns, "Girls, Boys, and Emotion." Cancian and Gordon, "Changing Emotion Norms"; Cancian, *Love in America*; Stearns and Knapp, "Men and Romantic Love"; Buss, "Conflict between the Sexes."

63. The need for further study of embarrassment again relates both to historical and to contemporary perspectives. Changing social relations are often productive of new forms of embarrassment, as Goffman has pointed out in suggesting that more democratic contacts on the job created new potential embarrassments by the 1950s. I am more impressed with the new, suppressive use of embarrassment, which gives the emotion a decided new twist, deepening its personal and social impact and the discomfort it causes and linking it to feelings less of status inferiority than of infantilization. Parallel to this, it seems to me, has been an effort to ease more minor, conventional forms of embarrassment by making interview situations less stiff, insisting on less punctilious sexual decorum, and so on. One subordinate theme worth pursuing involves the history of blushing and reactions to it. Blushing, rather charming

in Victorian context when embarrassment had few heavy duties, recedes in notice in our own age, when embarrassment is more central and its invocation more uniform than random individual proclivity to blushing can express. Again, the strong suggestion is that embarrassment itself has an important modern history. But the nature, causes, and uses of embarrassment clearly deserve much more exploration than they have received in any kind of emotions research. See E. Goffman, "Embarrassment and Social Organization," *American Journal of Sociology* 62 (1956).

9. The Need for Outlets

1. Jean L. Briggs, *Never in Anger: Portrait of an Eskimo Family* (Cambridge, Mass., 1970); Edwin I. Megargee and Jack E. Hokanson, eds., *The Dynamics of Aggression: Individual, Group, and International Analyses* (New York, 1970), passim.

2. Cas Wouters, "Social Stratification and Informalization in Global Perspective," *Theory, Culture, and Society* 7 (1990): 69–90; Cas Wouters, "Formalization and Informalization: Changing Tension Balances in Civilizing Processes," *Theory, Culture, and Society* 3, no. 2 (1986): 1–18.

3. The role of emotional standards in diplomacy is not a well-researched area. For a general theory, see the forthcoming book by Thomas Sheff, *Bloody Revenge: Emotions, Nationalism, and War* (Boulder, Colo., 1994); Allan Winkler, *The Atom and American Life* (New York, 1993); Paul Boyer, *By the Bomb's Early Light: American Thought and Culture at the Dawn of the Atomic Age* (New York, 1986).

4. E. L. Miller, "Job Attitudes of National Union Officials," *Personnel Psychology* 19 (1966): 395–410; A. H. Cochran, "Management Tigers and Pussycats," *Personnel Journal* 50 (1971): 524–26; Thomas Greening, "Sensitivity Training: Cult or Contribution?" *Personnel* 41 (1964): 18–25; C. J. Lilley, "Supervisors Don't Criticize Enough," *Personnel Journal* 31 (1952): 209–12.

5. C. Wright Mills, *White Collar: The American Middle Classes* (New York, 1953), 184; William H. Whyte, Jr., *The Organization Man* (New York, 1956), 152.

6. *New York Times,* 25 June 1992; editors of the *New Republic, Bushisms* (New York, 1992).

7. I am greatly indebted to Professor Rom Harré for suggestions in this area.

8. "Synanon House: Where Drug Addicts Go to Salvage Their Lives," *Life* 52 (9 March 1962): 52–65; G. Samuels, "Where Junkies Learn to Hang Tough," *New York Times Magazine,* 9 May 1965; Daniel Casriel, M.D., *So Fair a House: The Story of Synanon* (Englewood Cliffs, N.J., 1963).

9. John H. Scanzoni, *Opportunity and the Family* (New York, 1970), 139; Howard Clinebell and Charlotte Clinebell, *The Intimate Marriage* (New York, 1970), 98; Judson T. Landis and Mary G. Landis, *Building a Successful Marriage* (New York, 1953), 264; *Ladies Home Journal,* April 1970: 145; Janet Sayers, *Sexual Contradictions: Psychology, Psychoanalysis, and Feminism* (London, 1986), 151; Lillian Breslow Rubin, *Worlds of Pain: Life in the Working-Class Family* (New York, 1976), 76–78, 115–16, and passim.

10. Elizabeth Pleck, *Domestic Tyranny: The Making of Social Policy against Family Violence from Colonial Times to the Present* (New York, 1987); Sayers, *Sexual Contradictions,* 126, 151.

11. Gillian Avery, *Childhood's Pattern: A Study of the Heroes and Heroines of Childhood Fiction, 1770–1950* (London, 1975); Kristen Drotner, *English Children and Their*

Magazines, 1751–1945 (New Haven, Conn., 1988); Bernard Wishy, *The Child and the Republic* (Philadelphia, 1968); for an important theory on modern leisure and excitement, see Norbert Elias, *Quest for Excitement: Sport and Leisure in the Civilizing Process* (Oxford and New York, 1986).

12. John C. Burnham, *Bad Habits: Drinking, Smoking, Taking Drugs, Gambling, Sexual Misbehavior, and Swearing in American History* (New York, 1992); Arthur Mitzman, "The Civilizing Offensive: Mentalities, High Culture, and Individual Psyches," in Peter N. Stearns, ed., *Expanding the Past: A Reader in Social History* (New York and London, 1988). Burnham's study, fascinating in its links among various twentieth-century degeneracies (and probably overdoing implied Victorian purity), breaks down somewhat, in my opinion, on the causation issue.

13. The continued limits on leisure in American reality are revealed in the relatively modest gains in leisure time since the 1950s (in contrast to Western Europe). Juanita Kreps, "Lifetime Allocation of Work and Leisure," *Social Security Research Report*, no. 22 (1969).

14. Steven Seidman, *Romantic Longings: Love in America, 1830–1980* (New York, 1991); Kevin White, *The First Sexual Revolution: The Emergence of Male Heterosexuality in Modern America* (New York, 1993).

15. Burnham, *Bad Habits*; Timothy Jay, *Cursing in America: A Psycholinguistic Study of Dirty Language in the Courts, in the Movies, in the Schoolyards, and on the Streets* (Philadelphia, 1992); Cas Wouters, "On Status Competition and Emotion Management," *Journal of Social History* 24 (1991): 699–717.

16. Colin Campbell, *The Romantic Ethic and the Spirit of Modern Consumerism* (London, 1989); Richard W. Fox and Jackson T. Lears, eds., *The Culture of Consumption: Critical Essays in American History, 1860–1960* (New York, 1983).

17. Patricia O'Brien, "The Kleptomania Diagnosis: Bourgeois Women and Theft in Late-Nineteenth-Century France," in Stearns, ed., *Expanding the Past*; Helga Dittmar, *The Social Psychology of Material Posessions: To Have Is to Be* (New York, 1992).

18. Roland Marchand, *Advertising the American Dream: Making Way for Modernity, 1920–1940* (Berkeley, Calif., 1985); Ellen Furlough, "Selling the American Way in Interwar France: *Prix Uniques* and the Salons des Arts Ménagers," *Journal of Social History* (Spring 1993): 491–519.

19. Benjamin Rader, *American Sports: From the Age of Folk Games to the Age of Spectators* (Englewood Cliffs, N.J., 1983).

20. K. C. Constantine, *The Man Who Liked Slow Tomatoes* (New York, 1983), 85–86.

21. Allen Guttmann, *Sports Spectators* (New York, 1986), 149 ff. Professional wrestling also took on vast symbolic function, though not primarily for the middle class. See Bruce Lincoln, *Discourse and the Construction of Society: Comparative Studies of Myth, Ritual, and Classification* (New York, 1989), for a superb analysis.

22. Guttmann, *Spectators*, 149 ff.; Claude S. Fischer, "Change in Leisure Activity, 1890–1940," *Journal of Social History* 27 (1994), forthcoming; Steven Pope, "Negotiating the Folk Highway of American Sport," *Journal of Social History* 27 (1994), forthcoming; W. A. Crasgie and J. R. Hulbert, eds., *A Dictionary of American English* (Chicago, 1942), 2:93a.

23. *Pittsburgh Post Gazette*, 3 Dec. 1990.

24. For a more gender-based analysis, for example, see Elizabeth G. Traube, *Dreaming Identities: Class, Gender, and Generation in 1980s Hollywood Movies* (Boulder, Colo., 1992).

25. Tania Modleska, *Loving with a Vengeance: Mass-Produced Fantasies for Women* (Hamden, Conn., 1982), 82, 86; Sandy Rouma, "Soap Operas and Anger," *Washington Post,* 5 May 1991.

26. Lary May, *Screening Out the Past: The Birth of Mass Culture and the Motion Picture Industry* (New York, 1980).

27. Otto Friedrich, "Up, Up, and Awaaay," *Time,* 14 March 1988, 66; Elizabeth Mogul, "Superman and American Masculinity," unpublished paper, Carnegie-Mellon University, April 1991.

28. Jean Delumeau, *Sin and Fear: The Emergence of a Western Guilt Culture, Thirteenth–Eighteenth Centuries* (New York, 1990); Drotner, *English Children,* argues that youth media gained in importance as youth were increasingly cut off from adults, making emotional signals all the more revealing and, to a degree, formative. Edna Barth, *Witches, Pumpkins, and Grinning Ghosts* (New York, 1981). This point relates to other judgments about the experience of movie audiences: see May, *Screening Out the Past;* and for Europe, Charles Rearick, "Song and Society in Turn-of-the-Century France," *Journal of Social History* 22 (1988): 59–63. The adjustment obviously requires comparison with nineteenth-century recreational experiences.

29. Charles Gillett, *The Sound of the City: The Rise of Rock and Roll* (New York, 1970).

30. "A New Esthetic Called Cheese," *New York Times,* 7 Aug. 1992, B1; Burnham, *Bad Habits.*

31. Wouters, "Formalization and Informalization"; Wouters, "On Status Competition."

32. Max Weber, *The Protestant Ethic and the Spirit of Capitalism* (New York, 1958); Henry Gates, ed., *"Race," Writing, and Difference* (Chicago, 1986); Peter N. Stearns, "Suppressing Unpleasant Emotions: The Development of a Twentieth-Century American Style," in Andrew E. Barnes and Peter N. Stearns, eds., *Social History and Issues in Human Consciousness: Some Interdisciplinary Connections* (New York and London, 1989).

33. Peter N. Stearns, *Jealousy: The Evolution of an Emotion in American History* (New York and London, 1989), chap. 6; Richard H. Smith, Sung Hee Kim, and W. Gerrod Parrott, "Envy and Jealousy: Semantic Problems and Experimental Distinctions," *Personality and Social Psychology Bulletin* 14 (1988): 401–9; for an older view, R. B. Hupka, et al., "Romantic Jealousy and Romantic Envy," *Journal of Cross-Cultural Psychology* 16 (1985): 423–46; and M. Silver and J. Sabini, "The Social Construction of Envy," *Journal for the Theory of Social Behavior* 8 (1978): 313–31; and especially P. M. Spielman, "Envy and Jealousy: An Attempt at Clarification," *Psychoanalytic Quarterly* 40 (1971): 59–82; Christopher Lasch, *Haven in a Heartless World: The Family Beseiged* (New York, 1977).

34. Researchers widely assume that envy has increased, but there has been no real historical study. Helmut Shoeck, *Envy: A Theory of Social Behavior* (New York, 1966), is poor. See J. Sabini and M. Silver "Envy," in Rom Harré, ed., *The Social Construction of Emotion* (Oxford, 1986), 167–83. Peter Salovey, ed., *The Psychology of Jealousy and Envy* (New York, 1991), 23–25.

35. The redefinition of disgust has been vigorously sketched for the nineteenth century as a zesty Victorian emotion with implications for bodily hygiene and social division. See Alain Corbin, *The Foul and the Fragrant: Odor and the French Social Imagination* (Cambridge, Mass., 1986). But the subsequent history of disgust in the twentieth century amid the new emotionology of restraint has yet to be traced; for youth, at least, disgust may have been an outlet.

36. C. P. Snow, *The Two Cultures: And a Second Look* (New York, 1963); Peter N.

Stearns, *Life and Society in the West: The Modern Centuries* (San Diego, 1988), 311–47.

10. Pre-Conclusion

1. Peter N. Stearns and Deborah C. Stearns, "Historical Issues in Emotions Research: Causation and Timing," *Sociological Perspectives on Emotion* 2 (1994), forthcoming; Celia B. Stendler, "Sixty Years of Child Training Practices," *Journal of Pediatrics* 36 (1950).
2. Elisabeth Kubler-Ross, ed., *Death: The Final Stage of Growth* (New York, 1975); Margaret Stroebe, et al., "Broken Hearts in Broken Bonds," *American Psychologist* 47 (1992): 1205–12. For important new work on legal recognition of grief in homicide cases and in monetary damage suits in claims over wrongful death see Mark T. Knapp, "Bereavement and the Law," unpublished paper, Carnegie Mellon University, 1992.
3. Carole Tavris, *Anger: The Misunderstood Emotion* (New York, 1982); "The Sixth Deadly Sin," *New York Times,* 16 March 1983.
4. Robyn Dawes, *House of Cards: Psychotherapy and Professional Opinion without Science* (New York, 1994); James R. Kincaid, *Child-Loving: The Erotic Child and Victorian Culture* (New York, 1993).
5. Gordon Clanton, "Jealousy in American Culture, 1945–1985: Reflections from Popular Literature," in D. Franks and E. D. McCarthy, eds., *The Sociology of Emotions* (Greenwich, Conn., 1989); Peter N. Stearns, *Jealousy: The Evolution of an Emotion in American History* (New York and London, 1989), chap. 7; John Masterson, "Pretty Eyes and Green, My Love," *Psychology Today* 18 (1984).
6. Michael Lamb, ed., *The Role of the Father in Child Development* (New York, 1976); Ross D. Parke and Peter N. Stearns, "Fathers and Child Rearing," in Glen Elder, John Modell, and Ross Parke, eds., *Children in Time and Place* (New York, 1993), 147–64; Jack Nichols, *Men's Liberation: A New Definition of Masculinity* (New York, 1975); Francesca M. Cancian and Steven L. Gordon, "Changing Emotion Norms in Marriage: Love and Anger in U.S. Women's Magazines since 1900," *Gender and Society* 2 (1988); David Buss, "Conflict between the Sexes: Strategic Interference in the Evocation of Anger and Upset," *Journal of Personality and Social Psychology* 56 (1989).
7. Carl F. Kaestle and Helen Damon-Moore, *Literacy in the United States: Readers and Reading since 1890* (New Haven, Conn., 1991); Harvey Levenstein, *Paradox of Plenty: A Social History of Eating in America* (New York, 1993), 179–94.
8. William Waites, *The Modern Christmas in America* (New York, 1993); Karen Judson, "Anger: The Shapes of Wrath," *Better Health and Living,* Feb. 1988, 57–58.
9. Xerox/Carnegie Mellon University, *Basic Quality Training: Prework* (Stamford, Conn., 1992); Richard H. Haswell, "Minimal Marking," *College English* 45 (1983): 601.
10. Cas Wouters, "On Emotion Management and the Integration of Classes and Sexes: A Report of Some Changes in Twentieth-Century Etiquette Books," paper presented at the tenth Anniversary Conference, Theory, Culture, and Society, August 1992; Gordon Clanton and Lynn G. Smith, eds., *Jealousy* (Englewood Cliffs, N.J., 1977); Nena O'Neill and George O'Neill, *Open Marriage: A New Life Style for Couples* (New York, 1972).
11. David Reisman, *The Lonely Crowd: A Study of the Changing American Character*

(New Haven, Conn., 1961); Christopher Lasch, *Culture of Narcissism: American Life in an Age of Diminishing Expectations* (New York, 1979); Charles W. Sykes, *A Nation of Victims: The Decay of the American Character* (New York, 1992); Robert N. Bellah, et al., *Habits of the Heart: Individualism and Commitment in American Life* (New York, 1983); Warren Susman, *Culture as History: The Transformation of American Society in the Twentieth Century* (New York, 1985); Barrington Moore, Jr., *Injustice: The Social Bases of Obedience and Revolt* (New York, 1978).

12. James R. Averill, "Emotion and Anxiety: Sociocultural, Biological, and Psychological Determinants," in Amélie Rorty, ed., *Explaining Emotion* (Berkeley, Calif., 1980), 37–68; Arlie Russell Hochschild and Anne Machung, *The Second Shift: Working Parents and the Revolution at Home* (New York, 1989).

13. Arlie Russell Hochschild, *The Managed Heart: Commercialization of Human Feeling* (Berkeley, Calif., 1983).

14. Lillian Rubin, *Just Friends: The Role of Friendship in Our Lives* (New York, 1985); Edward Shorter, *From Paralysis to Fatigue: A History of Psychosomatic Illness in the Modern Era* (New York, 1992); Carol Z. Stearns, "Sadness," in Jeanette Haviland and Michael Lewis, eds., *Handbook of Emotions* (New York, 1993).

15. Joseph Veroff, Elizabeth Douvan, and Richard A. Kulka, *The Inner American: A Self-Portrait from 1957 to 1976* (New York, 1981).

16. Abram deSwaan, "The Politics of Agoraphobia: On Changes in Emotional and Relational Management," *Theory and Society* 10 (1981).

17. Ruth Benedict, *Patterns of Culture* (New York, 1934), 120–59, discussing the island of Dobo; Edward Schieffelin, "The Cultural Analysis of Depressive Affect: An Example from New Guinea," in Arthur Kleinman and Byron Good, eds., *Culture and Depression: Studies in the Anthropology and Cross-Cultural Psychiatry of Affect and Disorder* (Berkeley, Calif., 1985), 101–3.

11. Conclusion

1. Peter N. Stearns, "History of Emotion: The Issue of Change," in Jeanette Haviland and Michael Lewis, eds., *Handbook of Emotion* (New York, 1993).

2. David Reisman, *The Lonely Crowd: A Study of the Changing American Character* (New Haven, Conn., 1961); Christopher Lasch, *Culture of Narcissism: American Life in an Age of Diminishing Expectations* (New York, 1978).

3. Edward Shorter, *From Paralysis to Fatigue: A History of Psychosomatic Illness in the Modern Era* (New York, 1992); Cas Wouters, "Human Figurations: Essays for Norbert Elias," *Amsterdams Sociologisch Tijdschrift*, 1977, 438, 446; David Buss, "Conflict between the Sexes: Strategic Interference in the Evocation of Anger and Upset," *Journal of Personality and Social Psychology* 56 (1989); on changes in word use, see *Oxford English Dictionary*, 2d ed. (Oxford, 1989); Noah Webster, *American Dictionary of the English Language* (1828; repr., New York, 1970); on emotionally disturbed children, Benjamin Spock, *The Common Sense Book of Baby and Child Care* (New York, 1945), 250; and Ruth Strang, *An Introduction to Child Study* (New York, 1959), 348.

4. Frederick Lewis Allen, *The Big Change: America Transforms Itself, 1900–1950* (New York, 1952); Michael E. Parrish, *Anxious Decades: America in Prosperity and Depression, 1920–1941* (New York, 1992); Elaine Tyler May, *Homeward Bound: American Families in the Cold War Era* (New York, 1988); Stanley Coben, *Rebellion*

against Victorianism: The Impetus for Cultural Change in 1920s America (New York, 1991).

5. Abram de Swaan, "The Politics of Agoraphobia: On Changes in Emotional and Relational Management," *Theory and Society* 10 (1981); Arlie Russell Hochschild and Anne Machung, *The Second Shift: Working Parents and the Revolution at Home* (New York, 1989).

6. Nancy Friday, *Jealousy* (New York, 1985).

7. On fabrication of middle-class standards, Peter Bailey, " 'Will the Real Bill Banks Please Stand Up?' Towards a Role Analysis of Mid-Victorian Working-Class Respectability," in Peter N. Stearns, ed., *Expanding the Past: A Reader in Social History* (New York and London, 1988), 73–90; Susan Porter Benson, *Counter Cultures: Saleswomen, Managers, and Customers in American Department Stores, 1890–1940* (Urbana, Ill., 1986); William Julius Wilson, *The Truly Disadvantaged: The Inner City, the Underclass, and Public Policy* (Chicago, 1987).

8. On previous class clashes over emotional style, Arthur Mitzman, "The Civilizing Offensive: Mentalities, High Culture, and Individual Psyches," in Stearns, ed., *Expanding the Past*, 365–89; Peter Burke, *Popular Culture in Early Modern Europe* (New York, 1978). Gender culture also warrants attention, but this has been incorporated into the foregoing analysis. See Peter N. Stearns, "Girls, Boys, and Emotion: Redefinitions and Social Change," *Journal of American History* 90 (1993): 36–74.

9. Kermit Hall, *The Magic Mirror: Law in American History* (New York, 1989).

10. Jürgen Gerhards, "The Changing Culture of Emotions in Modern Society," *Social Science Information* 28 (1989); Christen Brinkgreve, "On Modern Relationships: The Commandments of the New Freedom," *Netherlands Journal of Sociology* 18 (1982).

11. Peter N. Stearns and Deborah C. Stearns, "Biology and Culture: Toward a New Combination," *Contention* 3 (1993).

12. Mark Rowlands, review of Andrew E. Barnes and Peter N. Stearns, eds., *Social History and Issues in Human Consciousness: Some Interdisciplinary Connections* (New York, 1989) in *Journal of the History of Behavioral Sciences* (1993).

13. Stephanie A. Shields and Beth A. Koster, "Emotional Stereotyping of Parents in Childrearing Manuals, 1915–1980," *Social Psychology Quarterly* 52 (1989); R. D. Parke and P. N. Stearns, "Fathers and Child Rearing," in Glen Elder, John Modell, and Ron Parke, eds., *Children in Time and Place* (New York, 1992).

14. On the "naturalist" approach, Stearns and Stearns, "Biology and Culture"; on the vital-affects research, David N. Stern, *The Interpersonal World of the Infant: A View from Psychoanalysis and Developmental Psychology* (New York, 1985).

15. Peter N. Stearns, "Problems of Historical Causation in Emotions Research," *Amsterdams Sociologisch Tijdschrift* (Jan. 1993).

16. For the argument that the twentieth-century family resembles its preindustrial counterpart, with Victorianism being the oddity, see Peter Willmott and Michael Young, *The Symmetrical Family* (London, 1973).

Index

Printed in the United States
99183LV00003B/124/A